THE MAKING OF A DISCIPLE

OF A DISCIPLE

A Study of Discipleship from the Life of Simon Peter

KENNETH FREDERICK

BJU PRESS

Greenville, SC 29614

Library of Congress Cataloging-in-Publication Data

Frederick, Kenneth.
  The making of a disciple : a study of discipleship from the life of Simon Peter / Kenneth
Frederick.
    p. cm.
  Includes bibliographical references and index.
  ISBN 1-57924-671-0 (pbk.)
   1. Discipling (Christianity) 2. Peter, the Apostle, Saint.

BV4520 .F74 2001
225.9'2--dc21

2001043053

Note: The fact that materials produced by other publishers may be referred to in this volume does
not constitute an endorsement by Bob Jones University Press of the content or theological position
of materials produced by such publishers. The position of Bob Jones University Press, and of the
University itself, is well known. Any references and ancillary materials are listed as an aid to the
reader and in an attempt to maintain the accepted academic standards
of the publishing industry.

Cover and title page image: *The Repentant St. Peter* by Carlo Dolci. From the Bob Jones University
Collection.

The Making of a Disciple: A Study of Discipleship
from the Life of Simon Peter
Kenneth Frederick, Ph.D.

Cover and design by Jeff Gray
Composition by Jennifer Hearing

To my wife Jan,
Who for 44 years
Has shared my labors and my joys
And who shares them still

TABLE OF CONTENTS

FOREWORD

"Peter is one of us!" These words, simple as they may appear, suggest both the paradox and the power of the personality behind Ken Frederick's *The Making of a Disciple*. "On the one hand," continues Dr. Frederick, "the apostle Paul—his dramatic conversion, his expansive missionary endeavors, his vital epistles—often seems beyond our reach in Christian experience. Not so with Peter. The pages of his story reveal him to be so human, so much like us that we feel we understand him more than we do Paul or John, Moses or Abraham."

Peter is one of us, a man among men; and yet, as it turned out, he became much more than just a man among men. He became a key instrument in the founding of the Christian Church. How did this happen? By what means did this ordinary man become a man of God—the man God intended him to be? The story of Simon Peter's pilgrimage from a blustering fisherman to the beloved apostle is an intensely personal story because it is, in fact, *our* story. You and I were the two unnamed disciples who went fishing with Peter (John 21:2-3). We were with him when Christ first called "Follow me, and I will make you fishers of men" (Matt. 4:19); and we were at his side when he sat, with furrowed brow and upraised hand, at the feet of the Master in the school of discipleship.

As Peter was the center of our Lord's attention in his discipleship program, so are we in *The Making of a Disciple*. Dr. Ken Frederick's *The Making of a Disciple* is not just another discipleship manual and it is not just another biography. It combines the best features of both forums. It leads us into a life and thereby teaches us not simply to know but to live.

My friend Ken Frederick is well qualified to lead us in the study of *The Making of a Disciple*. As his subject, Peter, he is "one of us"—in the sense that he knows and loves people. The passion of his life has been that of his Master: to go and make disciples of all nations (Matt. 28:19-20). It is this passion that gave focus to his doctoral studies, to his ministry as a pastor, and to his service as a faculty member in three Christian colleges. This master passion has led him to short-term and extended missionary service in fields ranging from South America to Eastern Europe to the Far East to Great Britain. It is my pleasure to commend to you both the author and his work.

Thurman Wisdom, Dean Emeritus
School of Religion
Bob Jones University

PREFACE

The last words we read from the apostle Peter are these: "But grow in grace and in the knowledge of the Lord Jesus Christ." Grace is what God does to and for us. Knowledge of Christ is the result of our experience with Him. Peter knew both. He certainly experienced the Lord Jesus while the Master was on this earth. But he was also the recipient of the Lord's great grace. I have tried to show these qualities in Peter's development as a disciple and apostle in this study, which I have titled *The Making of a Disciple*.

Simon Peter first came to interest me when almost accidently I came across W. H. Griffith Thomas's work and decided to use it as a text for a short Bible study course in a small Bible college in the 1960s. My subsequent interest in Peter has been in the form of various sermons and expositions of portions of his life from the Gospels as well as studies in his two epistles. Through all these contacts with Peter, I have felt drawn to him as to no other individual in the Old or New Testaments, with the possible exception of King David. When the opportunity came for me to put these years of study and meditation onto the printed page, I felt no hesitancy at all. For some time I have pondered the thought that Simon Peter demonstrates in living reality what the Lord seeks to do in all of us as His disciples. Therefore, the title of this work: *The Making of a Disciple: A Study of Discipleship from the Life of Simon Peter.*

All who place their faith in Jesus Christ as their only Savior are His disciples. Becoming a disciple is only the beginning of God's plan, however. He commands His disciples to move on—to grow in their faith. This process of growth involves discipling of believers toward spiritual maturity, a process that continues through the lifetime of every believer. Therefore, all who are a part of Christ's church—from children to senior adults—are to grow in their spiritual maturity. Confusion comes when we teach that discipleship is only a program and do not take into consideration that it is more a process. The command to "make disciples" refers to leading people to faith in Christ, which is the evangelistic task of His church. "Discipling" is the process of maturing believers in their faith so that they grow in Christlikeness and begin to use their gifts in the body of Christ. Thus "discipling" is for all believers as they continue in their spiritual maturation.

Much has been made of "discipleship" in our churches in recent years. So much so, that it may seem that a book on discipleship is not what should be added to our Christian library shelves. Relating these thoughts on discipleship specifically to Peter, however, provides helpful insights into the Lord's desires toward our spiritual development. By examining Peter's responses (or lack of them) to the Lord's teaching, we can gain for ourselves a better understanding of what we all seek—to know Christ better and to grow in the grace that He provides. To that end this volume goes forth with the fervent prayer that what follows may in some measure exhort and testify that this is the true grace in which we stand (I Pet. 5:12).

ABBREVIATIONS

AMP	Amplified Bible
ASB	American Standard Bible (1901)
EBC	*Expositor's Bible Commentary*
Gk.	Greek
ISBE	*International Standard Bible Encyclopedia*
KJV	Authorized King James Version (1611)
NT	New Testament
OT	Old Testament
UBD	*Unger's Bible Dictionary*
WDT	*Wycliffe Dictionary of Theology*
ZPEB	*Zondervan Pictorial Encyclopedia of the Bible*

$\mathcal{I}$NTRODUCTION

The Lord Jesus Christ commanded His church to evangelize the lost and then to edify the believers. For each of these functions—evangelism and edification—the Scripture employs the concept of discipling; that is, we are told to "make disciples" (evangelism) and we are told to teach these converts (discipleship). In His selection and development of Simon Peter, we observe how the Lord Jesus "discipled" one of His own. Peter's experiences help us to understand more clearly the Lord's purposes in "the making of a disciple."

THE MAKING OF A DISCIPLE

Every one that is perfect shall be as his master (Luke 6:40).

"Few biographies are written of ordinary men," observes Schuyler English, "unless they be autobiographies."[1] The more outstanding or uncommon a person's life, however, the more compelling his story.

Whatever else we might say about the apostle Peter, the record of his life in the Gospels and Book of Acts shows him to be anything but an "ordinary man." He was, of course, a man among men, displaying all the qualities of a tradesman who worked hard and faced the rigorous demands of daily life with manly resolve.[2] The unique character growth Peter displays in response to the Lord's teachings and is set forth so clearly in Scripture provides powerful insight into the "making of a disciple," those contacts and instructions designed by the Lord Jesus to develop the Galilean fisherman into "a servant and an apostle of Jesus Christ" (II Pet. 1:1).

Peter is one of us! On the one hand, the apostle Paul—his dramatic conversion, his expansive missionary endeavors, his vital epistles—often seems beyond our reach in Christian experience. Not so with Peter. The pages of his story reveal him to be so human, so much like us that we feel we understand him more than we do Paul or John, Moses or Abraham. The Gospels and Acts provide many threads with which to weave a fascinating biographical sketch of the apostle Peter. What a striking and compelling story awaits us in the pages of Scripture as we enter upon the life of Peter.

Value in studying Peter's life

Peter merits our studied attention for several reasons. First, Simon Peter's *prominence among the Twelve* is at once apparent, for he is "not the kind of flower that is born to blush unseen!"[3] We are told

---

[1] E. Schuyler English, *The Life and Letters of Saint Peter* (1941), p. viii. "Certainly few such biographies are read," English reminds us.

[2] David Gill expands this aspect of Simon Peter in *Peter the Rock*, which he subtitles *Extraordinary Insights from an Ordinary Man*. Like all "ordinary people," Gill explains, Peter had his particular strengths and weaknesses, but as a result of meeting and then following Jesus, "this ordinary guy became one of the key figures in the history of the world." David W. Gill, *Peter the Rock* (1986), p. 13. These contacts with the Lord and the lessons learned as a disciple are what I find outstanding and uncommon in Peter's life story.

[3] J. Stuart Holden, *The Master and His Men* (1955), p. 29. "Quick, impulsive, generous, impetuous—he was a man who must express his feelings; a man who, if he sees anything, must say so—must suit his actions to his perception. . . . Adjournments

3

more about Peter in the biblical record than any other of the Lord's disciples. Peter appears first in every listing of the Apostles in the NT.[4] Together with James and John, he formed that inner circle of disciples whom the Lord brought into privileged contact with Him for more intimate teaching.[5] On those specific occasions when Peter takes the lead and speaks out in the presence of the disciples, we are left with the distinct impression that the others would have it so.[6] And Peter is the principal figure in the infant church throughout the first twelve chapters of the Book of Acts before Luke shifts his focus to that remarkable personality, the apostle Paul. For his prominence alone Peter deserves our attention.

But Peter also was *participant to unique experiences*. In our own time, astronauts have walked on the moon, but no human has walked on water as Peter did that first century. He also saw the Lord in His glory on the Mount of Transfiguration, experienced the thrilling response of three thousand people to his sermon on Pentecost, raised Dorcas from the dead through the power of Christ, and called for God's immediate judgment on Ananias and Sapphira. He also had the unique experience of hearing the Lord call him both "blessed" for his confession of Christ as Messiah and "Satan" after attempting to hinder the Lord from going to the cross at Jerusalem. Unusual episodes such as these stir our desire to know more about the compelling figure who demonstrated such extraordinary capacities.

Thirdly, Peter demonstrates that it is possible for a believer *to learn from his mistakes*—to accept rebuke from the Lord for past failure, repent, and go forward for God. While human biographers may draw a self-serving veil over the ugly features of their subject, the divine biographer, the Holy Spirit, includes those embarrassing moments in Peter's life.[7] We all remember Peter's denial of the Lord during His

---

were no part of his make-up. . . . Such a man will make mistakes. But he'll make other things, too, that are not mistakes," pp. 29-30.

[4]Matt. 10:2; Mark 3:16; Luke 6:14; Acts 1:13.

[5]Mark 5:37; 9:2; 14:33.

[6]"It was Peter who asked the meaning of a difficult saying (Matt. 15:15; Luke 12:41). It was Peter who asked how often he must forgive (Matt. 18:21), and who inquired what was to be the reward of those who had left all to follow Jesus (Matt. 19:27). It was Peter who asked about the fig tree which had withered away (Mark 11:21), and about the meaning of the things which Jesus had said about the approaching end (Mark 13:3). It was to Peter the Jews came to ask if Jesus paid his taxes (Matt. 17:24). It was Peter who answered when Jesus asked who had touched him in the crowd (Luke 8:45). It was Peter who asked questions of the risen Christ (John 21:20-22)." William Barclay, *The Master's Men* (1959), p. 19.

[7]"Critics have often found fault with the Bible for its frank exposures of human evil," notes Fereday, "but its fearlessness in this particular is one of the many proofs

trial and his failure to follow through with his boast that he would not forsake the Lord.[8] Lovingly the Lord Jesus restores Peter to full fellowship and then commissions him to shepherd His people.[9] But every time we recall Peter's denial, we must also remember that he repented and returned to the Lord.

A study of Peter is warranted also because his life and epistles are *part of the sacred Scriptures,* which, inspired of God, are "profitable for doctrine, for reproof, for correction, for instruction in righteousness" (II Tim. 3:16). We may profit in measure from the study of any of the great personages of the past or present—Christians, such as Martin Luther, Adoniram Judson, or Count Zinzendorf; world leaders, such as Churchill, Gandhi, or Napoleon—but those on the pages of Holy Writ, as shown by the men of old, are there preserved by God Himself for our example and written for our admonition.[10] When we couple Peter's life as recorded in Scripture with his two epistles, also part of the Bible, we have double reason for giving special heed to these portions of the inspired Word of God.

A biblical study of Simon Peter will also serve as a refutation to the false and misleading claims by the Roman Catholic Church regarding Peter and the papacy. Much confusion surrounds the Lord's words to Peter in Matthew 16:17 ff. about the foundation of the church and the keys to the kingdom. Beyond Rome's invalid appropriation of apostolic succession beginning with the apostle Peter, there are popular misconceptions regarding him—that he stands as heaven's gatekeeper and so forth. Though our refutations will not be the major thrust of the book, those doctrinal and ecclesiastical errors involving Peter will be addressed from a biblical perspective.

Finally, a study of Peter's life will provide insights into the Lord's purpose and process of *making a disciple.* Simon, son of Jona, is a dynamic example of how the Lord proceeds, beginning with salvation, to teach and to train His disciples to be like Him.[11] "The disciple is not above his master," said the Lord Jesus, "but every one that is perfect shall be as his master" (Luke 6:40). There is an acknowledged relationship between a pupil and his teacher. The teacher possesses authority to instruct based on his own training and experience. His

---

of its divine origin, and how thankful should we be to have the whole truth laid out before us." W. W. Fereday, *Simon Peter: Apostle and Living Stone* (n.d.), p. 6.

[8]Matt. 26:33, 69-74.

[9]John 21:15-17.

[10]I Cor. 10:11.

[11]See Appendix A for a condensed harmony of the life of Peter in the Gospels and Book of Acts.

position is in that sense "above" the pupil; the pupil is not above the teacher. The pupil submits himself to the instruction and discipline of the teacher. As an apprentice looks to the master craftsman for expert example, so disciples (learners) look to their masters (teachers). The result of the process is that of learners, or disciples, who are "complete," or perfect.

Paul understood God's purpose for believers. He sought to "present every man perfect in Christ Jesus" (Col. 1:28). That is, he wanted each believer complete, or mature. He reminded Timothy that the goal for every believer is "that the man of God may be perfect, throughly furnished unto all good works" (II Tim. 3:17). Here is the one all-inclusive goal of Christian ministry, revealed to us in three phases: saved ("the man of God"), growing in Christlikeness ("may be perfect," i.e., complete), and equipped to serve ("throughly furnished unto all good works").

There is no more comprehensive life story in Scripture that enables us to discern how to "be like Jesus" than that of the humble fisherman from Bethsaida in Galilee. If we take Peter out of the Gospel accounts, stories would lose much of their color and interest. With Peter in, though we have only what Christ said to Peter and what Peter said to Christ and what Peter did, there remains, as MacCartney concludes, "a Gospel that can be preached to the ends of the earth, wherever a human heart beats."[12]

Focus on discipleship

Several years ago a missionary on furlough acknowledged to me, "When I arrived on the mission field, I already knew how to lead people to Christ, but I immediately discovered that I did not know how to disciple them." I took his honest confession as an affirmation of the need for all believers, but especially Christian workers, to become skilled in making disciples.

Disciple making is a biblical injunction. Our Lord's final instructions embodied this need. "And Jesus came and spake unto them, saying, All power is given unto me in heaven and in earth. Go ye therefore, and **teach** all nations, baptizing them in the name of the Father, and of the Son, and of the Holy Ghost: **teaching** them to observe all things whatsoever I have commanded you: and, lo, I am with you alway, even unto the end of the world" (Matt. 28:18-20). We must be careful to distinguish between "teach" in v. 19 and "teaching" in v. 20, since they are two different Greek words. The first is from

---

[12]Clarence Edward MacCartney, *Peter and His Lord: Sermons on the Life of Peter* (1937), pp. 10-11.

matheteuo, which means "to make a disciple." We call this evangelism, because we are bringing the unsaved into vital union with Christ in salvation through the proclamation of the gospel. "Teaching" in v. 20 is from *didasko*, the more traditional word for instruction (notice the root of the word "didactic" in it). This is "discipling" in the more accepted sense today—that of promoting the new convert's growth in Christ. Writing for another generation, John A. Broadus expressed the great need at that time to bring into English the word "disciple" as a verb,[13] citing not only this verse but also two others in which *matheteuo* is found and carries the thought "to disciple," thus "to make disciples."[14] It is now common in our church ministries to refer to "discipling" a new convert, thus teaching disciples. "Discipleship" as used in this book will refer to our efforts to nurture immature believers to maturity in Christ so that they are equipped to serve God effectively, especially in reproducing themselves in other converts.

To disciple a person, therefore, is to establish a student-teacher relationship with another believer, often a new convert. It is to bring him into the authoritative relation that a pupil has with his instructor. In that relationship, the learner assumes the obligation to submit to the teacher's authoritative instruction, accepting what he says as true because he says it. The pupil submits to the teacher's requirements as right simply because he has the authority to make those requirements. The authority of human teachers, of course, has limits. The Christian teacher is not God; but Jesus Christ, the master teacher, has "perfect wisdom and unlimited authority . . . the basis of all true discipleship"[15] and the Christian teacher seeks to emulate his own Master.

Evangelism and edification, that is, making disciples and teaching them the things of Christ, can be described as the process of leading a person to Christ for salvation, guiding him in continued growth toward Christlikeness, and equipping him to render effective service in the will of God. Wilson compares these three phases to a tree: evangelism is the root; growth toward Christlikeness is the plant itself, ever reaching upward; and service is the fruit evidenced.[16] Utilizing these three phases—salvation, growth in maturity, and equipping to serve—Allen Hadidian has developed a definition of discipling that also includes several identifying marks.

---

[13] John A. Broadus, *Commentary on the Gospel of Matthew* (1886), p. 593.

[14] Matthew 13:52, translated "instructed," and Acts 14:21, translated "taught," as here in Matthew 28:19.

[15] Broadus, p. 593.

[16] Valerie Wilson, "What Is Christian Education?" *Baptist Bulletin* 39, no. 6 (December, 1973): pp. 15-16.

	Discipling others is the process by
	which a Christian with a
Example	life worth emulating
Commitment	commits himself
Time	for an extended period of time
Numerical Limitation	to a few individuals who have been
Phase 1	*won to Christ,* the
Direction	purpose being to
Guardianship	aid and guide their
Phase 2	*growth to maturity* and equip them to
Phase 3	*reproduce themselves* in a third spiritual
	generation.[17]

Clearly Hadidian has chosen to limit his discipleship efforts to a "few good men." This leads to the question: Is discipleship for a limited few, or are all believers to be included? The answer is both. There is no question that the Lord Jesus limited His choice to the Twelve from among all those disciples who followed Him at the first. Paul echoed this emphasis in his instructions to Timothy. "And the things that thou hast heard of me among many witnesses, the same commit thou to faithful men, who shall be able to teach others also" (II Tim. 2:2). Obviously, Timothy was to look for "faithful men," implying a selection process. And Timothy himself was a select disciple of Paul. But on the other hand, Timothy was one among "many witnesses" who heard Paul teach. The apostle Paul worked on two levels, it appears—the general population of believers and a more select group, perhaps particularly suited for leadership training.[18]

Paul also understood that growth in Christlikeness or maturity should be sought for all believers. He described his ministry to the Colossians as "warning *every man,* and teaching *every man* in all wisdom; that we may present *every man* perfect in Christ Jesus" (Col.

---

[17]Allen Hadidian, *Discipleship* (1987), p. 29. "As we just discussed," he continues, "the term *discipling others* involves the work of evangelism. But because the content of this material is geared toward working with Christians, when I use the term *discipling* in the remaining chapters, my emphasis will be on phases 2 and 3, that is, on maturity and reproduction." This is the same emphasis I will explore as we study the "making of a disciple," the life of Simon Peter.

[18]Michael J. Wilkins describes five discipleship models in *Following the Master: A Biblical Theology of Discipleship* (1992), pp. 26-34 (italics are mine). (1) *Disciples are learners,* stressing the literal meaning of the word "disciple" ("learner"). (2) *Disciples are committed believers*; there are two levels within the church—ordinary Christians and committed followers. (3) *Disciples are ministers.* Jesus' training of His disciples is an example of how church leaders should be trained today. (4) *Disciples are converts; discipleship comes later;* that is, a disciple is one who has been evangelized and the later process of growth is called discipleship. (5) *Disciples are converts who are in the process of discipleship;* that is, discipleship is not a subsequent step in the Christian life but rather is synonymous with the Christian life,

1:28).[19] Will some believers respond more quickly, demonstrating a greater capacity for spiritual growth, perhaps even consider Christian service? Without a doubt. Does that mean that in our discipling we neglect others who show little or no indication of going on with Christ? Absolutely not. While engaging the committed to deeper and sustained growth in Christ, we must also be alert to the needs of all believers entrusted to our care. This requires discernment, of course. And it requires an allocation of time in appropriate amounts commensurate with our purposes for each individual.

Jesus and the Twelve

From the beginning, men like Peter were the focus and method of our Lord's ministry on earth. "Christ's strategy of ministry centered on His men. He was always with them, encouraging them, rebuking them, and working His ministry in front of them. He was investing in a few men, calling them to be with Him, grounding them in His truths. He invested in those few men so that when He left they could continue the work that He had begun.[20] Men were His method. They became the main focus of His ministry."[21]

Peter will be our pattern in our quest to learn what goes into the making of a disciple. With Peter we will walk the dusty roads with our Lord as He journeys among men. We will touch the fevered brows of those in need of healing and cheer the yearning hearts of the discouraged. We will stand perplexed at the snarling hatred of the Jewish leaders who sought to destroy Christ and His work. But our consolation is that we will also find ourselves in the exquisite companionship of the Son of God as He dwells among us and teaches us to be like Himself. "Christ's hopes about Simon's usefulness finally came true," observes Robertson, adding that there is "thus hope for us all."[22]

Though we shall focus extensively on the major events in Peter's life as a disciple and apostle, we shall also correlate those sections of

---

closely linked to what is sometimes called "lordship salvation." Wilkins provides helpful summaries of the strengths and weaknesses of these five models together with representative writers and their works. My own special interest when drawing implications for discipleship from Peter's development is to expand on the fourth model—disciples are converts. Discipleship, therefore, is the believer's growth in Christlikeness that follows.

[19]Throughout this book all italics in verses are mine.

[20]See Acts 1:1.

[21]Hadidian, p. 11.

[22]A. T. Robertson, *Epochs in the Life of Simon Peter* (1939), p. x. Other books by Robertson include *Epochs in the Life of Jesus, Epochs in the Life of Paul,* and *John the Loyal.*

the Gospels and Acts in which Peter, though not specifically named, must have been party to the events. This necessitates some study and familiarization with a harmony of the Lord's life and ministry as revealed in the Synoptics and the Gospel of John. The apostle John, for example, makes no mention of Peter throughout Christ's early Judean ministry,[23] so we are left only with supposition as to whether Peter and the other early disciples accompanied the Lord on this tour. If they did, it would not have been unusual for them to journey south to Judea since they first met Jesus at the fords of the Jordan when John the Baptist proclaimed Him to be the "Lamb of God."[24] Thus, these men were familiar with the Judean territory, probably also being among those zealous Jews who traveled to Jerusalem for the annual feasts, including Passover. If they had accompanied Jesus into Judea, they would have witnessed His cleansing of the temple, heard Him recount His conversation with Nicodemus, and certainly pondered His success in securing Samaritan believers following His conversation with the Samaritan woman at the well.

The Synoptic writers also record large sections of the Lord's early Galilean ministry to the multitudes, which included the Sermon on the Mount and His parables of the kingdom,[25] without connecting Peter specifically to these occasions. But these extensive sermons and ministries among the people doubtless had a profound effect on Peter in his early associations with the Lord Jesus. Our purpose, wherever Peter is mentioned even in a passing manner, is to correlate Peter's response (or lack of it) to the Lord's strategy in developing him as a disciple. We will strive to point out connections and developments, and like A. B. Bruce, seek to avoid superficiality, realizing that "it is possible to be so brief and sketchy (in the Gospel record) as to miss not only the latent connections of thought, but even the thoughts themselves."[26] While concentrating on the major movements throughout Peter's life as a disciple, we shall also pay attention to those strategies and details that, properly understood, shed as much light on Peter's character as the major epochs in his life. Peter was "a man worth the making and Jesus knew it. He loved Peter from the start and to the end. Peter came to justify Christ's love and patience with him."[27] We shall see "the making of a disciple" as our Lord lovingly and patiently guides His chosen vessel through the necessary lessons of his training.

---

[23]John 2:13–4:42.

[24]John 1:29.

[25]Matt. 5-7, 13.

[26]A. B. Bruce. *The Training of the Twelve,* 3rd ed. (n.d.), p. v.

[27]Robertson, p. 3.

The Making of a Disciple

Peter's development as a disciple must not be divorced from the Lord's purpose to train the Twelve to continue His work after His return to the Father.[28] As there are common elements to all believers' growth, so there were common threads in our Lord's dealings with the Twelve as a group. But throughout His disciple-making process with them, He also dealt with specific, individual needs,[29] and in our study of Peter we will examine such incidents affecting his training. Just as the same elements—the sunshine, showers, seed, soil, skill of the gardener—go into the care and development of various gardens, so it will be in Peter's development among all the other disciples. Their fellowship with Christ will bring out their individual traits of personal temperament. "Strikingly is this so when Peter—in every way the foremost of the group—is considered. For ever in association with the others, he is inevitably in contrast to them all."[30] Obscure and seemingly unrelated events in Peter's life turn out to be most instructive, coming, as they do, from the hand of a sovereign Lord—a reminder to us not to despise "the day of small things" (Zech. 4:10).

Disciple making is purposeful; it focuses on a goal. For Christ, that meant a specific strategy for the continuation of His work on earth.

> Mark it well. Not for a moment did Jesus lose sight of His goal. . . . In fact, at first glance it might even appear that Jesus had no plan . . . [or we] might discover some particular technique, but miss the underlying pattern of it all. This is one of the marvels of His strategy. It is so unassuming and silent that it is unnoticed by the hurried churchman. . . . Nevertheless, when His plan is reflected upon, the basic philosophy is so different from that of the modern church that its implications are nothing less than revolutionary.[31]

---

[28]A most helpful work is *The Master Plan of Evangelism* (1964) by Robert E. Coleman. Calling his work a "strategy of evangelism around which His [Jesus'] life originated while He walked on the earth" (p. 13), Coleman enunciates eight guiding principles that explain the Master's plan of world evangelization.

[29]"Whence shall we buy bread, that these may eat?" the Lord Jesus asked Philip (John 6:5) to provoke a specific response in the disciple. "And this [Jesus] said to prove him: for he himself knew what he would do" (v. 6). Clearly, the Lord worked with various disciples on different levels of development, as shown by His questioning of Philip and later of Peter in the same chapter.

[30]Holden, p. 29.

[31]Coleman, pp. 18-19.

A word of caution

As noted earlier, the Lord Jesus told us that a pupil is not above his teacher, that after the student has been trained, he will be like his teacher.[32] Notice, the Lord does not say the student will *know* as much as his teacher but he will be *like* his teacher. This is an awesome responsibility. Those we disciple will be like us, will follow our Christian lifestyle, as children follow their parents. If this is true, and we have the Lord's word that it is, what would your disciple be like?

There is a constant temptation in discipling others to confuse personal relationships and satisfactions with the Lord's purposes for the disciple. John had no greater joy than to see his spiritual children become adult or mature in their walk with the Lord.[33] Just as parents thrill to the prospect of seeing their children grow up into responsible adulthood, so we should continue to move our disciples toward maturity when they no longer need the constant supervision we provide. We must remember that we are not called to make disciples unto ourselves. As the Corinthian believers were not baptized unto Paul, Peter, or Apollos,[34] but unto Christ, so too our converts must learn that their loyalty is to the Lord Jesus Christ. They are to grow in grace and in the knowledge of Christ.[35]

Discipling requires that a delicate balance be maintained between building a disciple's life and moving that person to Christian maturity—temporary dependence aimed at final independence, or perhaps I should say interdependence. New converts must see in us a growing, victorious Christian. We must purposefully, yet humbly, say with Paul, "Be ye followers of me, even as I also am of Christ" (I Cor. 11:1). But there also comes the time when the disciple must stand for himself.

Peter's own testimony bears witness to his ability to grasp this balance. In his first epistle to the scattered, persecuted believers in Asia Minor, the apostle writes, "exhorting, and testifying that this is the true grace of God wherein ye stand" (I Pet. 5:12). He had learned firsthand of the grace of God in his life. Now he seeks to help others receive that same grace, exhorting them to stand in that grace, sealing it with his own testimony, thus keeping in motion that same process the Lord started in his life those many years earlier on the shores of the Sea of Galilee.

---

[32]Luke 6:40.
[33]III John 4.
[34]I Cor. 1:12-13.
[35]II Pet. 3:18.

MEETING THE MASTER

When Peter meets the Master, he is a already a mature man, married and firmly settled into his fishing trade. His conversion to Christ results in a name change prophetic of his future life and ministry. Following a miraculous catch of fish in which the Lord Jesus shows His supreme wisdom and authority, Peter obeys the Lord's call to leave his fishing enterprise and, following the Master, to become a fisher of the souls of men.

PETER'S CONVERSION

We have found the Messias (John 1:41).

Come, Thou long-expected Jesus,
Born to set Thy people free;
From our fears and sins release us:
Let us find our rest in Thee.
Israel's Strength and Consolation,
Hope of all the earth Thou art;
Dear desire of every nation,
Joy of ev'ry longing heart.

—Charles Wesley

Setting: Bethabara beyond Jordan, fall, A.D. 29[1]
Scripture: John 1:19-51

Peter's life story is a "symphony" of three movements: fisherman, disciple, apostle.[2] His first contact with Christ occurs during John the Baptist's ministry as he preaches and baptizes in "Bethabara[3] beyond Jordan" (John 1:28). As a *fisherman* from Galilee in the north, Simon acknowledges Jesus as the Messiah after his brother urges him to meet the Lord. For at least one year after that initial conversion to Christ the Messiah,[4] Simon attends to Jesus with fluctuating interest, possibly returning south to Judea with Him on festive occasions but also maintaining his fishing enterprise in Galilee. Then after the Lord specifically calls the Twelve to be with Him,[5] Peter is among those who will spend increasingly more time with the Lord, receiving His training as a

---

[1]Dates cited are based on *Chronological Aspects of the Life of Christ* (1977) by Harold W. Hoehner. See also Appendix B for a complete chart from Hoehner. Use of the chronology helps us to understand the time element involved in our Lord's ministry with Peter and the disciples.

[2]Some authors include a fourth phase, that of "writer," since Peter is the author of the two epistles that bear his name; one author adds "martyr."

[3]"House of the ford," on the east bank of the Jordan River. MS evidence supports the reading "Bethany beyond Jordan," differentiating it from the Bethany nearer Jerusalem, home to Lazarus and his sisters, Mary and Martha.

[4]When I speak of Peter's "conversion," I am aware that the Lord's ministry is before the Cross and the Resurrection. I am also aware that the Holy Spirit will not indwell the disciples until Pentecost. Thus, it is more difficult to pinpoint that moment of faith when, to use the language of the Epistles, Peter is "saved," or converted. I have chosen this first time Peter meets Jesus, in response to Andrew's invitation to meet the Messiah, as the logical beginning of Peter's faith in Christ, as faint as that faith may have been at the start. Since discipleship necessarily begins with conversion, I will develop Peter's first contact with the Lord Jesus as analogous to what we would call one's conversion to Christ.

[5]Mark 3:14.

devoted *disciple*. Following this extensive training, Peter the *apostle* takes the lead among the believers after the Lord's ascension. It is Peter who exerts his natural and official leadership qualities early in Acts— replacing the infidel Judas Iscariot, preaching in the power of the Holy Spirit on Pentecost, opening the gospel door to the Gentiles. Fisherman, disciple, apostle—and even writer.[6] We shall witness the drama of Peter's development as the Lord brings him to conformity to His will.

Behold, the Lamb of God

God called John the Baptist to a ministry of preparation for the coming of the Messiah. "There was a man sent from God, whose name was John" (John 1:6). In Malachi, the last book before the "silent years" between the Testaments, the preincarnate Christ proclaimed, "Behold, I will send my messenger, and he shall prepare the way before me" (Mal. 3:1).[7] Isaiah described the one who would prepare the way for the Messiah as "the voice of him that crieth in the wilderness, Prepare ye the way of the Lord, make straight in the desert a highway for our God" (Isa. 40:3). To this great task, God called John.

Luke sets the historical scene:

> Now in the fifteenth year of the reign of Tiberius Caesar, Pontius Pilate being governor of Judaea, and Herod being tetrarch of Galilee, and his brother Philip tetrarch of Ituraea and of the region of Trachonitis, and Lysanias the tetrarch of Abilene, Annas and Caiaphas being the high priests, the word of God came unto John the son of Zacharias in the wilderness. And he came into all the country about Jordan, preaching the baptism of repentance for the remission of sins (Luke 3:1-3).

Matthew records the public's acceptance of the Baptist. "Then went out to him Jerusalem, and all Judaea, and all the region round about Jordan, and were baptized of him in Jordan, confessing their sins" (Matt. 3:5-6).

We do not know how Peter and the other fishermen from Galilee first become attracted to the Baptist's preaching and baptizing. Perhaps it is on one of their trips to Jerusalem to supply fish from the Sea of Galilee to the city's markets that they first hear the rumors of the strange, powerful preacher from beyond Jordan.[8] We are told only that

---

[6]Since Peter was with Jesus when some very important events occurred, his personal testimony to these incidents as recorded in his two Epistles provides special insight and blessing to believers.

[7]See also Matt. 11:10; Mark 1:2; Luke 7:27.

[8]John tells us he had an acquaintance with the high priest in Jerusalem (John 18:15). Some people speculate that this friendship stemmed from a business venture

the religious leaders in Jerusalem become concerne
tion people are giving to John. As public curiosity
sent priests and Levites from Jerusalem to ask him
(John 1:19). Referring to himself simply as a voic
wilderness, John allows no suggestion that he is t
the prophet Elijah. When they ask why he then oc̶c̶u̶p̶
nent role in baptizing those who come to him, John reminds them of
the lowly nature of his baptism when compared to the powerful ministry of the one "whose shoe's latchet I am not worthy to unloose"
(v. 27). John's understanding of his unique place in God's economy
prompted the Lord Jesus on another occasion to commend the Baptist:
"Verily I say unto you, among them that are born of women there hath
not risen a greater than John the Baptist" (Matt. 11:11).

Our Lord's presentation of Himself to John for baptism offers the
wilderness preacher the unique opportunity to proclaim the message
that every Jew could understand: "Behold the Lamb of God, which
taketh away the sin of the world" (John 1:29). All Jews knew of the
Passover lamb, which had been killed on the night of the escape from
Egypt to save the Israelites from the terrible judgment of God.

> Speak ye unto all the congregation of Israel, saying, In the
> tenth day of this month they shall take to them every man a
> lamb, according to the house of their fathers, a lamb for an
> house. . . . Your lamb shall be without blemish . . . and the
> whole assembly of the congregation of Israel shall kill it. . . .
> It is the Lord's passover (Exod. 12:3, 5-6, 11).

Thoughtful Jews should have realized that John proclaimed with
this message that a Savior had come to deliver them from their sins.
Among those who heard the Baptist's preaching were several fishermen from Galilee who had gathered with the crowds east of the
Jordan to hear this rugged preacher of righteousness.

Then one day as these fishermen follow John, they hear a new
message from the rugged prophet[9] who is a "man among men, whose
life was hard and whose speech was tempered with no flattery or

---

in which John supplied fish from the Sea of Galilee, an interesting conjecture, but
one on which Scripture is silent. In some manner, Peter and his friends discovered
John the Baptist's ministry and sought to know more about him.

[9]In his imaginative treatment of Peter's life during the Roman rule, Lloyd
Douglas paints the following portrait of the Baptist as he preached. "He was indeed a
striking figure, tall, lean, lithe, bronzed. His heavy, tousled hair indicated an immense
latent vitality. His massive head was held high above broad, bony shoulders. The
craggy face was bearded, the forehead deep-lined, the dark eyes deep-set. He had the
bearing of a man who had thought much and suffered. The crowd was very still.

erity."[10] Upon seeing Jesus, John proclaims, "Behold the Lamb God!" (John 1:29, 36). Indeed, the prophet Isaiah had proclaimed that Jehovah's suffering servant would be as a Lamb slain for the sins of the world. "All we like sheep have gone astray . . . the Lord hath laid on him the iniquity of us all. . . . He is brought as a lamb to the slaughter" (Isa. 53:6-7).

Two of these fishermen now have the opportunity to meet Christ personally and to hear His words directly. We learn shortly that one of the men is Andrew, Simon Peter's brother (John 1:40). No doubt the unnamed disciple is John, the brother of James and son of Zebedee, because he humbly refers to himself elsewhere in his Gospel as the disciple whom Jesus loved.[11] John gives us little clue to his thoughts and feelings surrounding his initial encounter with Jesus, deeming "the minutest memorials of that time unspeakably precious."[12] For the true believer, no place is more sacred than that place where one first meets the Lord Jesus in saving faith—whether it be the church altar, the automobile, the battlefield, the bedroom, or the crowded city street. Christians must never lose the wonder of it all, the thrill of meeting Jesus for the first time! The details still reverberate in our soul's memory. John the Apostle did not forget, and neither should we.

The Baptist's message strikes a chord with Andrew and his fishing companion. They desire to know more of this promised Redeemer. Anticipating their interest, Jesus extends Himself to the inquiring disciples with His own question, "What seek ye?" (v. 38). Calling Him "Master," the customary address of one who would be their teacher, they ask, "Where dwellest thou?" Not out of a desire simply to know an address, but that they might obtain an audience with Him away from the throng, the men continue their search into the uniqueness of this one heralded by John the Baptist. "Come and see" (v. 39)[13] is the Lord's invitation to all, for He invites us to "taste and see that the

---

Stretching forth his long, brown arms, the prophet began to speak in a tone and mood of quiet entreaty. . . . It was as one speaking from a great distance; from another age; from another world." Lloyd C. Douglas, *The Big Fisherman* (1948), p. 104.

[10] E. Schuyler English, *The Life and Letters of Saint Peter* (1941), p. 33.

[11] John 13:23; 20:2; 21:20.

[12] A. B. Bruce, *The Training of the Twelve* (n.d.), p. 2.

[13] This begins the first phase of a four-phase disciple-development plan by Jesus as described by Bill Hull. The phases are built on four key statements, each of which inaugurates a new phase of training. (1) *"Come and see"*: In this formative stage, Jesus extends an invitation for people introduced to Him and His work. (2) *"Come and follow me"*: This is the developmental stage in which Jesus trains and establishes mature believers. He shows them how and does it with them. (3) *"Come and be with me"*: By adding correction to the developmental stage, Jesus challenges those who

Lord is good: blessed is the man that trusteth in him" (Ps. 34:8). Peter himself writes much later, "If so be ye have tasted that the Lord is gracious" (I Pet. 2:3). "They came and saw where he dwelt, and abode with him that day: for it was about the tenth hour."[14]

> Master, where abidest Thou?
>   Lamb of God, 'tis Thee we seek;
> For the wants which press us now
>   Other aid is all too weak.
> Canst Thou take our sins away?
>   May we find repose in Thee?
> From the gracious lips today,
>   As of old, breathes, "Come and see."[15]
>
> —Author Unknown

What was it like for Andrew and John to sit at the feet of Jesus for the rest of the day to hear the master teacher expound the OT Scriptures that spoke of His messiahship? No doubt they responded as those two discouraged disciples on the road to Emmaus, who also spent a portion of that first resurrection day with the Lord Jesus. "Did not our heart burn within us," they told the others, "while he talked with us by the way, and while he opened to us the scriptures?" (Luke 24:32). We do not know the content of that teaching, but the Lord's word did not return to Him void. The effect is profound. The two disciples will never be the same now that they have met the Messiah, the Son of God.

The long-expected Messiah

Simon's conversion to Christ is as simple as it is profound, for indeed what is salvation other than simply placing our faith in Jesus Christ? We come to accept Him for who He is and what He will do for us. As we address ourselves to the study of the simple story of Peter's encounter with Christ, we sense "the same feeling with which men make pilgrimages to sacred places; for indeed the ground is

---

have leadership skills to be with Him. Out of this come the Twelve, those receiving special position and authority. (4) *"Remain in me"*: In the final phase, Christ expects the disciples to reproduce. He deploys them into the world to obey His command and make disciples. Bill Hull, *The Disciple Making Church* (1990), pp. 22-24.

[14]Jewish reckoning of time began at 6:00 A.M. while the Roman day started earlier at midnight. Thus, when John says it was "about the tenth hour," we are not certain which time frame he uses. If John is using the Jewish reference, then it was 4:00 in the afternoon. If he refers to Roman time, however, it was 10:00 A.M., providing almost an entire day for Andrew and John to visit with Jesus. (John's other references to the time of day are John 4:6 and 19:14.)

[15]"Rabbi, Where Dwellest Thou?—Come and See," *Rhyme and Reason*, ed. by Bob Jones (1981), p. 36.

holy."[16] We learn for the first time that Andrew is brother to Simon Peter and that the two brothers live in Bethsaida, a seaside fishing village near the Sea of Galilee (John 1:44).[17] As a new follower of Christ, Andrew's first concern is for his own family.[18] Taking responsibility to share the message of his newfound Messiah, Andrew urges his brother Simon to investigate for himself. "We have found the Messias, which is, being interpreted, the Christ" (v. 41). Several times in the Gospels we see Andrew bringing people to Christ. In addition to his own brother, Andrew brought the little boy with his lunch to Jesus (John 6:8-9). It was Andrew, along with Philip, who introduced the Greeks to Jesus when they came seeking Him (John 12:20-22). What a great tribute to pay to anyone—that he is the one who introduced me to Jesus Christ! As God gives us opportunity to point people to Christ, others will say that of us too.

The Jews who knew OT prophecies were among those, such as Simeon and Anna, who waited "for the consolation of Israel" (Luke 2:25) and "looked for redemption in Jerusalem" (v. 38). We could include men such as Andrew, John, Simon, and the others mentioned in this narrative. Their immediate response to Jesus as the Messiah shows that their hearts were prepared to receive Him when He came and with that reception came a new allegiance to the Christ. The culmination of centuries of praying and longing has come to pass! The Messiah is here!

---

[16]Bruce, p. 3

[17]Bethsaida is mentioned in the NT more often than any other city except Jerusalem and Capernaum. Three different sites have been proposed as ancient Bethsaida. It is generally agreed that it was somewhere near the northern end of the Sea of Galilee, but which side of the Jordan's mouth it was on is problematic. Two cities have been considered the most likely location. El-'Araj is right on the lake and near the Jordan's mouth. It has a harbor and thus meets most of the specifications. It is, however, very small. *ZPEB,* vol. 1 (1976), p. 542. North of el-'Arja about two miles and connected by what was a fine road is another site bearing the simple name of et-Tell ("the mound"), the site originally proposed in 1838 by Edward Robinson as Bethsaida. This tell is near the Jordan and has evidence of being a larger city complete with wall, aqueduct, and fine buildings. Perhaps the fishing settlement first occupied the shore position and was later located to a more advantageous site to the north by Herod. This identification would solve more of the questions presented in the Gospel accounts as well as those of the ancient secular historians. The recent archaeological excavations at et-Tell have yielded sufficient evidence to conclude that this is probably the site of Peter's hometown. One house uncovered has been named the "Fisherman's House" because it contained lead net weights, anchors, needles, and fishhooks. Though the site is one and a half miles from the Galilean shore, the dig has confirmed that this site once was right on the water. "Bethsaida Rediscovered" by Rami Arav, Richard A. Freund, and John F. Shroder, Jr., *Biblical Archeology Review,* January-February, 2000, pp. 44 ff.

[18]"It seems very clear from the record that Simon was not present at the baptism of Jesus of Nazareth," English, p. 37.

Come, Thou long expected Jesus
Born to set Thy people free.[19]

But what sort of "freedom" did these Jewish men expect? Certainly not a Savior from sin so much as a deliverer who would release the Jewish nation from bondage and lead it, as Moses led the people from Egypt and through the wilderness back to the borders of Canaan, "back to a time of peace and prosperity."[20] Peter and the other men have a long road of teaching ahead of them before they will learn to accept the spiritual nature of the Lord's kingdom and not think exclusively of the political overthrow of the Roman tyrants who rule their land. "My kingdom is not of this world," Jesus would tell Pilate. "If my kingdom were of this world, then would my servants fight, that I should not be delivered to the Jews: but now is my kingdom not from hence" (John 18:36). Their concept of Christ's kingdom and their participation in it will become a thorn in their side, a concept to be debated and fought over, before they realize that His kingdom will be built, not through man's methods, but through demonstration of the power of God.

Simon Johnson

Calling him by his own name, Simon,[21] Jesus begins the conversation that will lead to Simon's conversion. What do we know of this one who stands in the presence of the Christ? Simon is, first of all, a *Galilean*. While growing up in Bethsaida in Galilee (John 1:44; 12:21), Simon and Andrew no doubt learned the fishing trade from their father Jona.[22] As youths, Jona's sons probably formed friendships with the sons of Zebedee, James and John, and when they were ready to go into the fishing business for themselves, the two sets of brothers entered into a fishing partnership.[23] As a Jewish lad in the "Galilee of the Gentiles" (Matt. 4:15), Simon nonetheless received some measure of religious training, probably brought up among those who waited "for the consolation of Israel" (John 1:41; Luke 2:25, 38). As a Galilean,[24] Peter no doubt took on those traits that marked their celebrated character, for the Galileans had a reputation for independence and vitality, for

---

[19]Charles Wesley, "Come, Thou Long-Expected Jesus," *Great Hymns of the Faith* (1968), p. 84.

[20]English, pp. 26-27.

[21]From the Heb. Simeon, "hearing," a common Jewish name in the New Testament.

[22]Simon was the son of Jona (Matt. 16:17), but his mother is not mentioned in Scripture.

[23]Luke 5:10.

[24]In his novel, Douglas describes the Galileans over whom Herod Antipas would

bluntness and simplicity.[25] They spoke a peculiar dialect, a pronunciation deemed harsh among the more refined. It stayed with Peter all his life, betraying him in Pilate's judgment hall[26] and on the Day of Pentecost.[27]

Simon is also a *family man*. That Simon was a married man is certain from the Gospel record and the Epistles. Not long after Jesus begins His extended Galilean ministry, He heals Simon's mother-in-law.[28] From the apostle Paul's language in I Corinthians 9:5, it would appear that Peter took his wife with him on missionary trips. It appears that Simon settled in Capernaum in a house that was large enough to give residence to his family, including Andrew, his wife's mother, and also to Christ, who seems to have lived with him.[29]

Simon's words and actions also mark him as a *man among men*. It is with Simon's unvarnished character that we are most familiar. What words describe this "rock-the-boat fisherman"?[30] "Impulsive," "uninhibited," "outspoken" leap out at us. We need think only of his impul-

---

rule in his tetrarchy: "He knew very little about the Galileans, except what everybody knew; that they were a stolid, inoffensive, pious people, who minded their own small business, and had no ambitions to make their country known abroad. They grew their own grain, wine, flax, and wool. They fished in the Lake Gennesaret. Their men were adept at fashioning articles of household furniture, sometimes showing themselves to be excellent craftsmen. Their women wove serviceable fabrics for domestic uses. Their lives were self-contained and, in consequence, narrowly circumscribed. They almost never traveled beyond their own communities, except on the occasion of the annual 'Passover' when considerable numbers of them made a pilgrimage to Jerusalem where a week was spent in the performance of religious rites. Customarily they took along some of the products of their lathes and looms, which they offered for sale at the bazaars. They wore no distinctive costume, but were readily identified in the city by their accent and colloquialisms. They were self-conscious and shy in the presence of urbane strangers, aware that they were considered outlanders," p. 36.

[25]Hoehner is more cautious in drawing conclusions about the Galilean temperament. "The temperament of the Galileans has often been characterized as having a frequent tendency to 'flare up' in the manner of the typical Galilean, Peter . . . (but) it is seen that there is no real basis for such claims. Their love of the Law is demonstrated by their strict adherence to its precepts and they were not steeped in the traditions of men as were the Judeans. Many times they have been looked down upon by the Judeans because of their religious convictions and because of their peculiar accent, but especially in Jesus' time there appears little foundation for the accusations. All in all it has been seen that these people in Antipas' territories were an honourable people. It has been said that the Galileans thought more of their honour while the Judeans thought more of their money. What higher compliment can be paid to any people?" Harold W. Hoehner, *Herod Antipas* (1972), p. 56-58.

[26]Mark 14:70.
[27]Acts 2:7.
[28]Mark 1:30-31.
[29]Mark 1:29, 36; 2:1.
[30]Frank G. Carver, *Peter the Rock-Man* (1973), p. 7.

sive call to Jesus to join the Master in His walk on the lake. Or his uninhibited promise never to forsake the Lord. Or his outspoken request to erect three tents on the mount to bask in the glory of the transfiguration experience. Yet as we view these imperfections, we must marvel at the Lord's capacity to take such a raw and unfinished figure and mold him into a trophy of divine grace, as He seeks to make of us all. "Peter is so human, so like ourselves in his downsitings and uprisings, so compassed with infirmity, that we are encouraged to hope that perhaps the Great Potter may be able to make something even of our common clay."[31]

The Rock

Immediately upon meeting Simon, the Lord gives him a new name. "Thou art Simon the son of Jona: thou shalt be called Cephas, which is by interpretation, A stone" (John 1:42). In today's English, we would call him "Simon Johnson," or Simon, the son of Jona. "*Cephas*," the new name the Lord gives to him, is the Aramaic word for "rock," which in Greek is *petros* and is transliterated in English to "Peter." Thus, Cephas is not simply a name; it is a common noun meaning "rock," the effect being that the Lord now calls Peter "Rock-man,"[32] a name to live up to! "It's not difficult to imagine the quiet laughs and sly winks of the others when they heard of it. The idea of Simon being called Rock! It was really too funny. Or is it? Well, the entire story of Peter is that of a man trying to live up to the Master's expectation—and promise . . . 'Thou shalt be Peter.' "[33] So with prophetic insight, the Lord announces to His new convert his destiny. "Through fellowship with Christ, and by virtue of His atoning sacrifice and the power of His indwelling Spirit the impetuous and bombastic fisherman of Galilee was to develop into a rock of faith and testimony, an apostle of the Lord Jesus Christ."[34] No doubt the Lord Jesus is informing Simon Peter that now that he has met the Master,

---

[31]F. B. Meyer, *Peter: Fisherman, Disciple, Apostle* (1950), p. 5.

[32]More than most studies of the life of Peter, Gill's work reflects the current evangelical style of seeking relevance, often sacrificing reverence in the process. Gill is aware of this, however, as shown in his explanation of Peter's name change. "This name helps us grasp how people in the first century would react to being introduced to him. It is only out of respect for tradition, and a wish not to appear flippant, that I will continue to call him Peter instead of the more accurate Simon 'the Rock' Johnson." David W. Gill, *Peter the Rock* (1986), p. 14. He does continue a style throughout the book, however, that reflects a contemporary appeal, though the ideas he presents are substantive, deserving of consideration.

[33]J. Stuart Holden, *The Master and His Men* (1955), p. 31-32.

[34]English, p. 40.

he will be changed from weakness to strength, from what he is to what the Lord wants him to be. No longer will Simon be what he once was. Instability will give way to firmness. Peter has a long course to follow on the path to discipleship, but he has taken the first step. He has met the Christ, the Messiah, and he is now a follower of the Lamb.

In rapid succession other potential disciples meet Christ at this time, including Philip (vv. 43-44) and Nathanael (vv. 45-51). Philip's urgent words show his faith in the OT promises concerning the Messiah. "We have found him, of whom Moses . . . and the prophets, did write, Jesus of Nazareth, the son of Joseph" (v. 45). Though Nathanael expresses commonly held misgivings about a messiah from Nazareth (v. 46),[35] Jesus overwhelms him with His knowledge of his past (v. 48). In devout expression of belief, Nathanael proclaims, "Rabbi, thou art the Son of God; thou art the King of Israel" (v. 49).

Though he will return to his fishing profession and continue there for at least another year, Simon is a changed man with a new name. "And thou shalt be called by a new name, which the mouth of the Lord shall name" (Isa. 62:2). Peter, the stone, will be given with all overcomers, "a white stone, and in the stone a new name written, which no man knoweth saving he that receiveth it" (Rev. 2:17). He has met the Messiah and has placed his faith in Him—the first, life-changing step to becoming a disciple of the Lord. Peter is not perfect when he meets the Lord—he still possesses his old nature.[36] But God takes him as he is—a "bewildering mixture of weakness and strength,

---

[35]"Can any good thing come out of Nazareth?" asks Nathanael, reflecting the condescending attitude held by those in Judea toward the Galileans. "The contempt in which Galilee was held by the Judeans was due to no inferiority of the northern area either in its history or its resources and beauty. Rather, the disdain which Judea felt for Galilee was the result of her pride of Jerusalem, the center of Israelitish worship of God, and her disapproval of the constant contact with the Gentiles that the Jews of Galilee had to maintain by reason of her geography" (English, pp. 18-19).

[36]M. R. DeHaan draws a parallel between the Lord's use of both names "Simon" and "Cephas" (Peter) and the believer's two natures after conversion. "These two names suggest to us two births, the natural and the spiritual. By his first birth he was Simon; by his second birth he became Peter. When he became Peter he did not cease to be Simon, however" (p. 19). DeHaan shows through Peter's life the conflict between the two natures of the believer—sinner and saint, the old man and the new man. Though he draws more distinctions from our Lord's use of these two names than Scripture may warrant, he presents a necessary biblical truth that new converts need to know, namely, that after conversion, believers continue to face battles between the flesh and the spirit (Gal. 5:17; Rom. 7:18). "Simon does not become Peter, but God creates a brand new nature, a new man by the new birth, and places it alongside the old, so that he is not only Simon, but also Peter, and, therefore, 'Simon Peter.'" *Simon Peter: Sinner and Saint* (1954), p. 19.

stardust and mud"[37] to make out of him what he should be as a disciple of the Lord. "You are . . . you shall be," Jesus says to all. What we are is important, but what we are becoming is far more important. Our Lord here gives to Peter not only a glimpse of possibility but also a pledge of help in obtaining those possibilities. For from the Gospels, we learn that Peter[38] was boastful (Luke 22:33), self-confident (Mark 14:29), impulsive (Matt. 14:28), impatient (John 18:10), greedy (Matt. 19:27), and a swearer and liar (Mark 14:71).[39] Yet the Lord eventually tempers these very human traits with His gracious spirit so that at the end of His discipleship process Peter shows those Christlike qualities that mark those who have been in the presence of Jesus.

Nothing will ever be the same now with Peter. He has met the Lord Jesus. So it is with all who come to Him in faith and repentance. Peter's experience is that of every child of God. "When once we have seen the risen Christ, our Saviour, in that moment life should take on new meaning."[40]

Implications for Discipleship

1. *Discipleship begins with conversion.* I must begin with the obvious—that to be a disciple of the Lord Jesus Christ, one must first be converted. I have taken Peter's first meeting with Jesus as the point of his change of life and direction, his conversion. Peter has a long course to follow on the path to discipleship, but he has taken the first step. He has met the Christ, the Messiah, and he is now a follower of the

---

[37]Clovis G. Chappell, *Sermons on Simon Peter* (1959), p. 14.

[38]"Today the proper noun 'Peter' is also a verb. As to the reason for this even Webster is not sure. But I have an idea that Simon's new name is now forced to do double duty because its wearer made so many failures. He petered out so many times." Chappell, p. 17.

[39]Tim LaHaye uses Peter as his biblical illustration of one of the four basic temperaments, citing the weaknesses and strengths of his "sanguine" personality. "The four temperament classification is not categorically taught in the Bible," explains LaHaye, "but our four biographical studies of Bible personalities will show temperamental strengths and weaknesses. The Bible shows that power over weakness is possible only when one receives Jesus Christ personally as Lord and Savior and yields one's self completely to his Spirit. . . . As you study [the theory of temperaments], pause to thank God that you have access to a source of power that can change your life and make you the kind of person both you and God want you to be," Tim LaHaye, *Transformed Temperaments* (1971), p. 18. LaHaye's concepts can be helpful to believers, but my point is that Peter's transformation to a "Rock-man" was brought about by the Lord and the power of the Holy Spirit working in his life. We should be grateful that we have such a bountiful record on Peter's life transformation in Scripture to encourage us that God can do the same for us.

[40]English, p. 40.

Lamb. As the Lord changed Peter's name, conversion for the sinner involves a name change. Before conversion we are "children of disobedience" (Eph. 2:2) and "children of wrath" (Eph. 2:3). But conversion brings us into God's family; we become His children and are no longer under Satan's sway. "But as many as received him, to them gave he power to become the sons of God, even to them that believe on his name" (John 1:12).

2. *As witnesses for Christ, we are but a part of God's great work.* Several factors contributed to Peter's conversion to Christ. First, the preaching of John the Baptist provided a focus on Christ and His mission in the world. Second, a sense of oppression generated unrest in the hearts of the people. Third, after he found the Messiah, Andrew wasted no time telling the good news to his brother so that Peter could also come to Christ. In fulfilling our commission to "make disciples" of all nations, we must include these factors in our teaching, preaching, and witnessing. Unsaved people need the preaching of the Word of God that addresses the unrest they know dwells within their souls. And they need the gentle touch of a consecrated believer who says, "Let me introduce you to Jesus. Let me tell you about who He is and what He came to do."

3. *Every new convert needs to attain assurance of salvation.* Salvation hangs upon Christ's work for us and our assurance rests upon God's Word to us. We are saved because we trust Christ for who He is and what He claims to be—the Son of God with power to save us from our sins. We have assurance of salvation because we accept the Bible record. I have often used the following three statements to summarize assurance for new believers: (1) *"It is finished"* (John 19:30). The finished work of Christ on the cross is sufficient for our salvation. Nothing we do can make salvation more complete. We are complete in Christ (Col. 2:10). (2) *"It is written"* (Matt. 4:4). God said it; I believe it; that settles it. God has told us in His Word that to have Christ is to possess life (I John 5:12). (3) *"It is I"* (Luke 24:39). The

indwelling presence of Christ produces a Christlike spirit and life (Gal. 2:20).

4. Be prepared to offer specific guidance to the convert.[41] When a new Christian is introduced to me, I want him to be able to answer this basic question: "On what Bible verse do you base your salvation?" I find often that new converts struggle with this most basic step. Disciplers must provide new converts with assurance from the Word of God concerning their conversion to Christ. It is important for new Christians to understand that their salvation rests in the finished work of Christ, not any works they have done. New converts should be asked to read and mark key passages in their Bibles such as the following references. Then they should be directed to commit them to memory.

Words of Assurance

I John 5:11-13—*God has promised eternal life to those who receive His Son, Jesus Christ.*

"And this is the record, that God hath given to us eternal life, and this life is in his Son. He that hath the Son hath life; and he that hath not the Son of God hath not life. These things have I written unto you that believe on the name of the Son of God; that ye may know that ye have eternal life, and that ye may believe on the name of the Son of God."

Eph. 2:8-9—*We do not work for salvation; it is the free gift from God that must be received.*

"For by grace are ye saved through faith; and that not of yourselves: it is the gift of God: not of works, lest any man should boast."

II Tim. 1:12—*God will keep us.*

"For the which cause I also suffer these things: nevertheless I am not ashamed: for I know whom I have believed, and am persuaded that he is able to keep that which I have committed unto him against that day."

---

[41]See Appendix C for specific follow-up materials to assist new converts in assurance of salvation and other first steps as a Christian.

John 6:37—*If you come to Jesus, He will not turn you away.*

"All that the Father giveth me shall come to me; and him that cometh to me I will in no wise cast out."

Rom. 10:13—*God has promised to save all who call on Him for salvation.*

"For whosoever shall call upon the name of the Lord shall be saved."

Phil. 1:6—*What God has started, He will finish.*

"Being confident of this very thing, that he which hath begun a good work in you will perform it until the day of Jesus Christ."

Rev. 3:20—*If you open your heart's door, Jesus will come in.*

"Behold, I stand at the door, and knock: if any man hear my voice, and open the door, I will come in to him, and will sup with him, and he with me."

Ps. 119:89—*God's Word is settled.*

"For ever, O Lord, thy word is settled in heaven."

John 1:12—*Through faith we become members of God's family.*

"But as many as received him, to them gave he power to become the sons of God, even to them that believe on his name."

FOLLOWING THE MASTER

Following His call to Peter to be a fisher of men, the Lord Jesus engages in an intensive preaching and healing ministry throughout Galilee, making Capernaum His headquarters. His purpose is to allow Peter to observe His actions, just as an apprentice is first introduced to a trade by observing the master craftsman. Specific teaching to Peter will come in due course. For now Peter is simply called to follow Christ, to fellowship and associate with Him, but most importantly, to observe Him.

CALL TO SERVICE

From henceforth thou shalt catch men (Luke 5:10).

> *In simple trust, like theirs who heard,*
> *Beside the Syrian sea,*
> *The gracious calling of the Lord,*
> *Let us, like them, without a word,*
> *Rise up and follow Thee.*

> —*John Greenleaf Whittier*

Setting: Lake Gennesaret in Galilee, spring, A.D. 31
Scripture: Luke 5:1-11; also Matt. 4:18-22; Mark 1:14-20

Following conversion and entrance into discipleship come early lessons from the Master, including His words and actions as well as impressions gained by observation. Though the scriptural curtain drops completely on Peter after his conversion at the fords of the Jordan and we have no record of his whereabouts for one full year,[1] there are, nevertheless, impressions and lessons from the Lord Jesus designed to develop the faith of these few disciples. John records, for example, a specific miracle from this time span—Christ's turning the water to wine at the wedding in Cana.[2] This "beginning of miracles," as John describes it, further manifests Christ's glory so that "his disciples believed in him." Their initial faith, including Peter's, however undeveloped it may have been this early in the Lord's ministry, is not a disappointing faith. The miracle at Cana gives Peter an added sense of Christ's uniqueness, to be sure, and provides him with needed encouragement to continue following his new Master.

Jesus then goes up to Jerusalem for the Passover,[3] where He cleanses the temple, again profoundly affecting those disciples who accompany Him to Judea (is Peter among them?). The Lord Jesus

---

[1]Mark passes completely over this first year (Mark 1:13-14), announcing John the Baptist's imprisonment immediately after finishing his account of Christ's temptation. But during the Lord's early Judean ministry, the apostle John notes that "John [the Baptist] was not yet cast in prison" (John 3:24). Since Mark's Gospel bears considerable Petrine influence, could it be inferred from Mark's omission of Christ's early Judean ministry that Peter did not in fact accompany Jesus to the Passover at Jerusalem? For external and internal evidences to support the view that Mark was dependent on Peter for his materials, see Henry C. Thiessen, *Introduction to the New Testament* (1949), pp. 142-44.

[2]John 2:1-11.

[3]John 2:13. Christ's three-year public ministry spanned four springs, thus encompassing four Passovers. Since it appears that Christ traveled to Caesarea Philippi with

again makes an impression on those disciples who are with Him from Galilee, for when noting the energy displayed by Christ as He disposes of the moneychangers in the temple, John tells us that the disciples remembered later the OT words "The zeal of thine house hath eaten me up."[4] Impressions about the Lord—His wisdom, power, and authority—continue to unfold to the disciples.

While Jesus is in Jerusalem for the Passover, Nicodemus, who is also impressed with Christ's ministry, requests his interview with the Lord, "Rabbi, we know that thou art a teacher come from God: for no man can do these miracles that thou doest, except God be with him" (John 3:2). Nicodemus's commendation offers Christ the opportunity to speak directly of His mission from the Father. Though it is still three years hence, the Lord Jesus knows that His "hour" will come when He will be lifted up to die on the cross. Trusting Nicodemus to reflect on his knowledge of the OT Scriptures, Jesus proclaims, "And as Moses lifted up the serpent in the wilderness, even so must the Son of man be lifted up: that whosoever believeth in him should not perish, but have eternal life" (vv. 14-15). In addition to His cleansing of the temple and His conversation with Nicodemus, the Lord Jesus also takes time while in Judea during this Passover season to baptize other disciples (v. 22). Though no mention is made of it in Scripture, perhaps it is reasonable to suppose that Peter also, at some early point in his association with Jesus, showed his allegiance to Christ by submitting to His baptism, as did these followers in Judea.

Turning northward again, Christ "must needs go through Samaria" (John 4:4) to minister to the solitary woman at the well, and at the conclusion of His two days of ministry there, "many more believed because of his own word" (v. 41). John seems intent on showing us that the Lord Jesus is gathering about Himself followers who will accompany Him to learn from Him. Whether Peter or James or any of

---

His disciples during the next to last Passover, He could have attended three of these Passovers, including this one mentioned in John 2:13, possibly one in 5:1 (Hoehner holds that 5:1 is the Feast of Tabernacles, p. 59), and His final one in 11:55, when He was crucified. Hoehner presents a condensed outline of Christ's ministry from before the first Passover to the Passover of A.D.. 33, when Christ was crucified. Harold W. Hoehner, *Chronological Aspects of the Life of Christ* (1977), pp. 60-63.

[4]John 2:17, a quotation from Psalm 69:9. Regarding the exchange of currency, the Orthodox Jew was forbidden to cast into the temple treasury any money bearing the image of any king or the resemblance of any man or beast. Jews from outside Palestine, when they came to Jerusalem, found it necessary to change their coinage into accepted shekels and also to purchase animals for sacrifice. Our Lord gave public protest to this use of the outer court of the temple as a place for the purchase of beasts and bargaining for exchange rates of money.

the other early disciples from Galilee have any significant association with Him as yet is not stated.

So what can we say of Peter during this interim of one year? Having returned from that first meeting with Christ at the Jordan River, Peter most certainly resumes his fishing enterprise,[5] for that is where we next find him—beside the lake of Gennesaret. He may have accompanied Jesus from Galilee to Jerusalem for Passover; he may have been among those baptized; he probably was among those few early disciples who witnessed the Lord's first miracle. Beyond those brief suppositions, we have no further word. Of this we can be fairly certain, however: Having met the Christ, Peter has a vague consciousness of the Master's exalted dignity, that he is in the presence of someone who is like none else he has ever met. Christ has won Peter's heart, and there is nothing now to hinder forming a yet closer tie between Himself and His chosen follower.

At the fords of the Jordan, when Peter first met the Lord, Jesus sowed the seed of His Word in Peter's heart. Having done that, the Lord left it to germinate until the proper time when He would return to find it ready to bear the ripe fruits of a growing faith.[6] Robertson uses an analogy to a sculpture: While some statues are cast in a mold and made in an instant, others are chipped and carved little by little, then shaped and polished. The latter process demands more time and patience, but this is exactly the process that the great master-sculptor will lovingly follow over the months ahead in developing Peter.[7] We have no reason to think that Peter and the other disciples have given up their fishing business in Bethsaida and Capernaum. There is no relapse or loss of faith or of interest on the part of these early believers. They have expressed their faith in Jesus and hold Him as the Messiah, but they have not given up their regular vocations.

A sermon from a boat

A careful reading of the Synoptic accounts shows the Lord Jesus ministering alone in Cana and Nazareth in Galilee, eventually moving to Capernaum by the spring of A.D. 31, His ministry taking Him to

---

[5]"On the whole we must regard the four earliest-called of Christ's disciples, as being of the class which still subsists in all the maritime countries of the earth, and which always bears the name of 'fisherman.' Everywhere they are known as hard-working toilers, exposed to much suffering; ill-remunerated, and generally poor." *The Life and Writings of St. Peter* (1872) by the anonymous author of *Essays on the Church*, p. 28.

[6]Richard C. Trench, *Notes on the Miracles of Our Lord* (1953), p. 138.

[7]A. T. Robertson, *Epochs in the Life of Simon Peter* (1939), pp. 19-20.

the region around Lake Gennesaret.[8] As we will see by later events, it is likely that Jesus took up residence with Peter in Bethsaida, which was adjacent to Capernaum, just as He abode with Mary, Martha, and Lazarus at Bethany when ministering in Judea. Of the Synoptic accounts[9] of our Lord's call to Peter and his fisherman friends along the shores of the Sea of Galilee, Luke's is the most complete. It also furnishes us with the next extended look at Peter's development as a disciple.[10]

> And it came to pass, that, as the people pressed upon him to hear the word of God,[11] he stood by the lake of Gennesaret, And saw two ships standing by the lake: but the fishermen were gone out of them, and were washing their nets. And he entered into one of the ships, which was Simon's, and prayed him that he would thrust out a little from the land. And he sat down, and taught the people out of the ship (Luke 5:1-3).

The scene before us is this: The several men—Simon Peter and his brother, Andrew, together with the sons of Zebedee, James and John—have been out on the lake all night, with the result that they have torn their nets but caught no fish. When morning comes, they

---

[8]Also called the Sea of Galilee (Matt. 4:18). This lake in northern Palestine provided livelihood for many fishermen from the surrounding villages, such as Capernaum and Bethsaida, Peter's hometown. The name "Gennesaret" is derived from the Hebrew word signifying "harp," called so from its harplike shape. One wonders if the sudden storms for which Gennesaret, or the Sea of Galilee, is infamous are not violent discords on this beautiful "harp."

[9]Matt. 4:18-22; Mark 1:16-20; Luke 5:1-11.

[10]Matthew and Mark record briefly the external result of the Lord's call to the men to follow Him. Luke, on the other hand, explains in detail the internal workings that took place in Peter's soul. All three accounts refer to the same incident, and any alleged discrepancies are nothing more than would ordinarily occur in a narration by three different persons of an event that lasted some hours, which included Jesus' teaching from the boat, the miraculous catch of fish, and Peter's response to it. G. Campbell Morgan insists, however, that the events in Matthew and Mark are different from Luke's, but he surmises that the Lord had called these men earlier—the Matthew and Mark narratives—but not long after they left Him to return home to their fishing business. Thus, Christ had to call them once more, and this would be the event recorded in Luke. G. Campbell Morgan, *The Gospel According to Luke* (1931), p. 72. That the men returned to their fishing after the events at the fords of the Jordan there can be no doubt. It is not necessary to separate the calls as Morgan has done, but if indeed there were two separate callings, this also supports my contention that Jesus proceeded with gradual steps in calling these men to Himself.

[11]Bible teaching and preaching are foundational to the ministry of the local church. People's deepest needs are satisfied only through the Word of God. Spiritually robust churches are those in which the people come to hear the Word of God, not to applaud the popular entertainment performances so pervasive throughout many churches today.

head for shore, Peter and Andrew taking one final cast into the shallow waters near the shore (Mark 1:16) while James and John clean their nets of the rubbish accumulated after a night of fishing, a regular morning's work for the fishermen (v. 19). This downtime allows the Lord to speak to the people without distraction.

As was typical in the Lord's early public ministry, the people crowd to Him, though toward the end of His ministry, when He speaks more earnestly about the cost of discipleship and His suffering at Jerusalem, the crowds leave Him. For now, however, the people flock to Him for His words. To be free from the press of the crowd following Him, Jesus borrows Peter's fishing boat for a pulpit and preaches to those gathered on the beach, the shoreline and gently sloping hills surrounding the lake providing a natural amphitheater. There are no accidents with the Lord. He knows which of the two available boats belongs to Peter. And since He has business to attend to later with Peter, the Lord chooses this particular vessel, making Himself "at home in Simon's boat, clearly implying previous acquaintance and fellowship."[12] Jesus might have borrowed someone else's boat, but He asks help from Peter,[13] no doubt to bring him into closer contact, to have him attend to His words. We may be certain that God's Spirit has also been working in the heart of this Galilean fisherman to heighten his faith in his newfound Lord.

Go out into the deep

His message to the people concluded, Christ turns to the disciple for whom He clearly intends further development. "Now when he had left speaking, he said unto Simon, Launch out into the deep, and let down your nets for a draught" (Luke 5:4). Though the Lord commands Peter to drop his nets to catch fish, the Lord has His own plans "to take the fisherman in his net."[14]

One can almost see the look of amazement, perhaps even some amusement, in Peter's face—"always a mirror, never a mask"[15]— when he hears Jesus' words to launch out again into the lake to seek a

---

[12]Robertson, p. 22.

[13]"Peter loaned Jesus his boat and his house; another loaned him the foal of an ass; another the Upper Chamber; another, a soldier, loaned him his sponge at the Cross; Simon the Cyrenian loaned him his shoulder with which to carry the Cross; Joseph of Arimathea loaned him his grave; and the women loaned him their spices. There is always something—time, money, sacrifice, prayer, hope—that we can loan to Christ. When we see him in the Day of Judgment, may each one of us be able to recognize him as the One to whom we loaned something." Clarence Edward MacCartney, *Peter and His Lord* (1937), pp. 13-14.

[14]Trench, p. 139.

[15]MacCartney, p. 14.

catch of fish. Disappointed at their failure from the previous night and
now hungry too, "Simon answering said unto him, Master,[16] we have
toiled all the night, and have taken nothing" (v. 5). Peter's hesitation is
understandable. The one giving the order is but a carpenter, certainly
possessing no fisherman's experience or abilities, as does Peter. "He
might be an excellent wood-worker," Peter might mutter to himself,
"but He knows nothing about fishing. That's my specialty." Then again,
Peter's thoughts might have drifted back to the previous night of futility—all toil and no results. And now to go through the toil all over
again, tired as he is, with the nets hung up to dry and the sun continuing to rise? To go out to the deep,[17] not the shallows where he can more
easily net some fish?

But something about this man and His presence causes Peter to lay
aside his misgivings. "Nevertheless [in spite of my own better judgment and apprehensions] at thy word [because You have commanded
it] I will let down the net" (v. 5).[18] One year earlier, Peter might have
totally resisted, but the intervening months have given him certain impressions of the Master and have conditioned him with a willingness
to obey the Lord's request. Trench takes this more optimistic view of
Peter's response, as though the fisherman would say to the Lord, "We
have accomplished nothing during the night, and had quite lost hope
of accomplishing anything; but now, when Thou biddest, we are sure
our labour will not any longer be in vain."[19]

With a wide sweep of the net out in the deep, Peter and those with
him bring in a miraculous catch of fish, so much so that their net
begins to break and their partners in a second boat, coming to their
assistance, fill both boats with the catch. What an impressive catch it
is, even for these seasoned Galilean fishermen! Again we see the
insight the previous year's interim provides Peter. Before his yearlong
acquaintance with Christ, Peter might have looked on this miracle as
demonstrating that Jesus the carpenter would make the perfect fishing
partner! But beginning with that first session with Christ, Peter has

---

[16]*Epistata*, "overseer," not *rabbi*, "teacher," a title for Christ that Luke never uses
in his Gospel. Peter acknowledges Jesus as "Master," not in the sense of teacher but
out of a recognition of His authority. See also Luke 17:13.

[17]"If we could only learn the lesson of going in deeper right where we are, and
when we have apparently done all that seems possible or when we have failed to do
anything at all. . . . [Simon had] the pessimistic mood so common in ministers and all
Christian workers who feel sure that they can do wonders somewhere else instead of
going deeper where they are." Robertson, p. 24.

[18]"That is all the church has, the Christian minister, the Christian worker as the
authority, and for the hope, of our labors—the Word of Jesus," MacCartney, p. 14.

[19]Trench, p. 140.

begun to experience spiritual insights, and he is able now to see events with an eye to the eternal. He is learning that the spiritual is better than the worldly and carnal, that God calls for loyalty and commitment to a cause greater than ourselves.

Leave me alone

Peter cannot believe the catch of fish. He is "astonished, and all that were with him, at the draught of the fishes which they had taken" (Luke 5:9). What does Peter say after this great catch? "Lord, You *are* a fisherman after all! How did you learn it? I know what we should do. We will make You a partner in our business. We will call it 'The Fisher Brothers *and* Jesus Enterprise.'" No, he says nothing of the kind. Rather, falling prostrate at Jesus' feet, he blurts out impulsively, "Depart from me; for I am a sinful man,[20] O Lord" (v. 8). Knowledge of one's own innate sinfulness is requisite in the Lord's disciple. Isaiah pronounced woe on himself as he saw himself sinful and unholy in the presence of a holy God. Now in Christ's presence, Peter also sees himself a great sinner—the first step in genuine Christian experience and service. Wolston notes that when "the work of conviction of sin in [young converts] has been deep, and the sense of deliverance correspondingly great; then immediate devotedness to the Lord is usually apparent."[21] What Christ means to us depends wholly on our sense of need as a sinful child of Adam. What use we are to Him depends on our admission that we are nothing and that He is everything.

Observing Peter's reaction to the miracle, we must conclude that Peter responds exactly as the Lord desires and anticipates. His intention is to increase Peter's consciousness of his sense of sin before taking him on any further steps of discipleship. Peter's confession shows this deepening conviction "altogether of an intenser kind than he had at the meeting at Bethabara, that he was in the presence of no mere prophet or teacher, but of the great Lord of creation."[22] In his confession of sin, Peter opens a window into his inner soul where we observe that strange mixture of "good and evil, of grace and nature, which so frequently reappears in his character in the subsequent history."[23] What do we see in Peter? Already we discern a reverential awe of the Lord in the presence of His power. We see also a tender conscience that is

---

[20]MacDuff comments: "The Greek word for 'man' implies a deep consciousness of his personal unworthiness and sin. It is *aner hamartolos* not *anthropos*." J. R. MacDuff, *The Footsteps of St. Peter: Being the Life and Times of the Apostle* (1887), p. 69.

[21]W. T. P. Wolston, *Simon Peter: His Life and Letters* (1926), p. 10.

[22]MacDuff, p. 69.

[23]A. B. Bruce, *The Training of the Twelve* (n.d.), p. 15.

quick to call unbelief for what it is—sin. And we see a self-humiliation that is genuine. Though Peter has a long path to tread as a disciple in the making, the Lord will not leave him unattended.

Catch men alive

When God speaks to us, He does so in language we can understand. At their first meeting, Jesus gave Simon a new name, Cephas, or "Rock." The Lord will expect Peter to live up to that prophetic designation. Now Jesus applies a second metaphor to him, "fisher of men" (Mark 1:17), though we must concur with Robertson that "there seems to us at this juncture little foundation for either figure of speech as a just portrayal of Simon."[24] A new epoch is about to begin in Peter's life, however, and the Lord speaks once again in unmistakable language. Issuing a call into His service, the Lord explains by His analogy with fishing that these humble men, who certainly understood the fishing enterprise, will from this moment forward be called to "catch men" (Luke 5:10). The Lord's expression is quite strong, for He uses a verb that means "to catch alive."[25] Peter will be a *catcher of men alive*[26]—to catch men for life eternal, instead of catching fish for death. It is though Jesus says that when they catch fish, the fish die; but when they catch men alive, when they "exchange the humility of their earthly for the dignity of their heavenly calling,"[27] souls will truly live. What an encouragement to every worker for Christ, that people caught in our spiritual nets of the gospel of grace will live and not die—though such spiritual work is always more difficult than the physical effort needed to fish with ordinary nets.

Forsaking all to follow Jesus

"And when they had brought their ships to land, they forsook all, and followed him" (v. 11). Mark, drawing perhaps on one of those observations related to him by Peter, notes that Peter and Andrew "straightway . . . forsook their nets" (Mark 1:18) to follow Christ, while James and John "left their father Zebedee in the ship with the hired servants, and went after him" (v. 20).[28]

---

[24]Robertson, p. 30.

[25]Gk., *zogreo.*

[26]Robertson also notes: "Jesus makes a prophecy about Simon: 'Thou shalt catch men,' using a periphrastic future which implies permanent occupation" (p. 28).

[27]Trench, p. 137.

[28]Robertson quotes Easton: "Older commentators sometimes puzzled over the fate of the fish caught in the miraculous draught." Robertson continues: "Surely that

Call to Service

In this second step toward discipleship—the Lord's specific call to Peter to serve Him—the Lord Jesus comes to Peter while he is engaged in his ordinary work of fishing, uses Peter's boat for His preaching, and speaks of the work of fishing to illustrate and prepare Peter for his higher service. So God speaks to us in our ordinary tasks of life, using our daily duties to lead us to a higher plane of service. What a dignity this places on everyday life! Many Christians are under the impression that they would find it much easier to be a committed Christian under exceptional circumstances, and perhaps that is true. But to glorify God in daily life by faithfulness and obedience, that is the real test of loyalty for the believer. Not every experience in the Christian life is a mountaintop event, for "God is ever coming to us in simple and ordinary ways,"[29] and we must develop our eye of faith to see His hand in such events.

These humble fishermen left *all*, though it may have been but a few boats and ragged nets.[30] The value of what they left is not what is important. What is important is their willing spirit of renunciation, not the intrinsic value of what they forsook to follow the Master. "These Apostles might have left little when they left their *possessions,* but they left much when . . . they left their *desires.*"[31]

Peter will not travel alone, however, in his venture with Christ. On this pivotal occasion, Jesus calls not only Peter but also his brother, Andrew, together with Zebedee's sons, James and John. The Lord is gathering to Himself men who will learn from Him and to whom He will entrust the spread of the gospel. Three of these four—Peter, James, and John—will, from this moment, be indelibly linked in our minds with Christ as an inner circle. In due course we shall see them with

---

is a side issue after the turn given to the miracle by Jesus. At any rate Zebedee was quite able to dispose of the fish in the market" (p. 31).

[29]W. H. Griffith Thomas, *The Apostle Peter* (1956) p. 10.

[30]After dealing with Peter's statement that he had "left all," Bob Jones Jr. vividly describes Peter's possible reasoning that he had left his fisherman's hut for the open spaces, his nets and the thrill of the catch for feeding the throng with fish from the Savior's hands. Dr. Jones continues: "With sweet insistence the Savior might have said, 'And what else did you leave, Peter?' 'Oh, yes, Lord, I left Nancy.' It may not have been 'Nancy.' It may have been Rachel, or Rebecca, or Mary, or Elizabeth, but the fisherman's boat must have had a name. I can fancy how he left it beached on the sand, keel up. He had been called to be a fisher of men; and they are caught in busy market place, in town, and countryside. The waters of Galilee waited in vain for the boat." Dr. Bob Jones Jr., *All Fulness Dwells* (1942), p. 51, from the sermon "What Shall We Have?" I remember hearing Dr. Jones preach this message on one occasion, and he paused dramatically after the name Elizabeth before revealing to us that Peter was speaking of his boat, not some feminine love.

[31]Trench, p. 150.

the Lord in the death room at the raising of Jairus's daughter, on the mountain as witnesses of the Lord's splendor, and in the garden accompanying the Lord in His dire agony. From the day that these disciples met the Lord, "their hopes for Israel and for themselves were set in Him. But it had not occurred to them that their lives were to be part and parcel of His earthly program."[32] But that is what Jesus seeks of these men as disciples. To accomplish this, the Lord will bring them even closer to Himself, as we will see later, to that of apostle. What Peter and his brethren have demonstrated throughout this teaching and miracle by the Lord is a willingness to obey Him implicitly. We become Christians through faith in God's Word and in God's Son as our Savior from sin. But we become useful Christians, fulfilling God's purpose in our life, by unquestioning obedience to the Word and to the will of God.[33] From Peter we learn that there must be repentance, just as he acknowledges his sinful heart. And there is also faith, as he shows by addressing Jesus as Lord—faith and repentance. But there is also obedience. He forsakes all to follow Jesus.[34] Salvation costs nothing, for it is the free gift of God. Discipleship, on the other hand, costs a great deal in laying aside our own desires and obeying God's will and purpose that He lays down for us.

Implications for Discipleship

1. *Discipleship is not simply a program; it is following Christ and becoming like Him.* Discipleship is life. To grow as a disciple is to grow as a Christian. That life begins in relationship to the Master and moves into all areas of life. After his conversion to Christ at the Jordan, Peter returned to his home in Galilee while the Lord engaged in His early ministry without the aid of any disciples. Through His miracles He manifested His glory and others came to place their trust in Him. Christ's early ministry reinforced in Peter a sense of uniqueness for Christ, so that when the Lord, on

---

[32]E. Schuyler English, *The Life and Letters of Saint Peter* (1941), p. 43.

[33]English, p. 50.

[34]Bruce moves beyond their leaving of any material possessions to that of family relationships: "The four, the twelve, forsook *all* and followed their Master. Did the 'all' in any case include wife and children? It did in at least one instance—that of Peter; for the Gospels tell how Peter's mother-in-law was healed of a fever by the miraculous power of Christ. From a passage in Paul's first epistle to the Corinthian church, it appears that Peter was not the only one among the apostles who was married. From the same passage we further learn, that forsaking of wives for Christ's sake *did not mean literal desertion* [emphasis Bruce]. Peter the apostle led his wife about with him, and Peter the disciple may sometimes have done the same. The likeli-

this occasion of the miracle of the fish, called him to His service, Peter left all to follow Christ. We may also be certain that the Holy Spirit was at work in Peter's heart to heighten faith in his newfound Lord. The Gospels present "following Christ" in several ways. Sometimes the word is used simply in a physical sense, as, for example, people "followed" Jesus from one point to another.[35] "Following Jesus" is also a technical expression for going after Him as His disciple. The disciple is the one who has counted the cost, has made a commitment of faith, and has then "followed" Jesus. "Following Jesus meant togetherness with him and service to him while traveling on the Way, but that following was manifested in either a physical or figurative sense, depending upon the ministry to which Jesus called his followers."[36]

2. *Discipleship is progressive.* Few converts are thrust into service as quickly and as boldly as the apostle Paul in Acts 9. The more normal pattern is that which we observe in Peter's relationship to the Lord Jesus. Peter is first converted to Christ, returns to his fishing enterprise for a time, and then is called into the Lord's service through the miracle of the catch of fish. In the same manner, the sinner repents and places his faith in Christ for salvation. Then, through biblical input from other more mature believers, the new Christian is brought face to face with the authority of Christ. As the claims of Christ are laid before him, he learns to follow Christ implicitly as he follows the example of these believers.

3. *The new convert is a mixture of faith and doubt.* Except in those rare instances when dealing with an unusually mature

---

hood is that the married disciples, like married soldiers, took their wives with them or left them at home, as circumstances might require or admit. Women, even married women, did sometimes follow Jesus; and the wife of Simon, or of any other married disciple, may occasionally have been among the number. At an advanced period in the history we find the *mother* of James and John in Christ's company far from home; and where mothers were, wives, if they wished, might also be. The infant church, in its original nomadic or itinerant state, seems to have been a motley band of pilgrims, in which all sorts of people as to sex, social position, and moral character were united, the bond of union being ardent attachment to the person of Jesus," pp. 17-18.

[35]Luke 22:54.

[36]Michael J. Wilkins, *Following the Master* (1992), p. 125.

convert, the Christian leader should observe the same procedure in discipling converts. Once assurance of salvation is established, disciplers must act in the role of authority figures for the convert—helping him to see the need for all spiritual exercises that promote growth. To the extent that the disciple is willing to follow the teaching of Scripture, he will grow in his understanding of God's purpose for his life, remembering that discipleship is not an end in itself; it is a journey, a life.

4. *We should disciple converts in accordance to their experience.* God speaks a language that not only captures our attention but also is understandable. Christ used an incident—the catch of fish—that Peter could understand and relate to. Christ called a fisherman to be a fisher of souls. But He also used a star to call the magi from the East and water to bring the Samaritan woman to salvation. This should cause us to be careful in our dealing with new converts to use explanations and illustrations that make sense to them. We must not become so overly familiar with our own biblical jargon that we fail to connect with them. And might it also be said that the Lord will deal with them with language and analogies they understand best? May He not call a doctor to heal sick souls? A fireman to rescue the perishing? A nurse to comfort the afflicted? A teacher to instruct others in righteousness? May God use us to bring others to Himself and be the instruments through whom He calls others to further service.

EARLY LESSONS

All men seek for thee (Mark 1:37).

Master, speak! Thy servant heareth,
Waiting for Thy gracious Word;
Longing for Thy voice that cheereth,
Master, let it now be heard.
I am listening, Lord, for Thee;
What hast Thou to say to me?

—*Frances R. Havergal*

Setting: Capernaum in Galilee, spring, A.D. 31
Scripture: Mark 1:21-39; also Matt. 4:23-25; 8:14-17; Luke 4:31-44

For the first year and a half of the Lord's public ministry, Peter has had only two significant contacts with the Master as recorded in the Gospels. First, Peter responded in faith to Christ as the Messiah. The Synoptics say nothing about this meeting at the fords of the Jordan, John alone recording Peter's conversion to Christ and his subsequent name change. Second, Peter was among those fishermen who, hearing the Lord's call to be fishers of men, progressed from ordinary disciple to a special ministry—he was to be a catcher of men. Between these two events our Lord conducted His early Judean ministry in the south. Again, only John recorded those events.[1]

We resume the story of Peter immediately following that second contact with the Lord on the shores of Lake Gennesaret. During the subsequent preaching, teaching, and healing ministry by Christ in Galilee, Peter gains, through personal contact and quiet observation, deeper insight about his Master—knowledge Peter will gain by association with Christ before He explains its significance. This companionship with the Master will be necessary training for Peter leading to the Lord's choosing the Twelve. Though our present study examines only those few passages in which Peter is specifically named, we must remember that the Lord's influence on Peter and the others now begins to be more frequent. To see Peter's growth in loyal adherence to Jesus, we will note some of the instances in which his name is not mentioned, but we must call special attention to those that single him out sharply. It is quite probable that Peter is "the moving spirit at times when the disciples acted together. At any rate he acquiesced in what was said

---

[1]John 2-4.

43

and done."[2] Through their constant fellowship with Him, Peter and the other followers will be brought to new heights of admiration and affection for this one who "came into Galilee, preaching the gospel of the kingdom of God, and saying, The time is fulfilled, and the kingdom of God is at hand: repent ye, and believe the gospel" (Mark 1:14-15).

As His custom was

Fired in their imaginations by the gracious words and powerful healings from Christ, citizens from the garrisons and fishing villages throughout Galilee grow increasingly curious about this carpenter-teacher from Nazareth. Jesus began His teaching, preaching, and healing work, not in Capernaum, where we now find Him, but in His hometown of Nazareth. Immediately following Satan's temptations, Jesus "returned in the power of the Spirit into Galilee: and there went out a fame of him through all the region round about. And he taught in their synagogues, being glorified of all. And he came to Nazareth, where he had been brought up" (Luke 4:14-16*a*). Luke's use of the word "returned" (v. 14) perhaps is a reference to the Lord's previous (though unrecorded) visits to Galilee during the first year, but since Luke also says He returned to "where he had been brought up," we should no doubt think of this as an intimation to His own early years in Nazareth as a youth.

There appears to be a progression in Luke's mind as he uses three different Greek words, all translated "fame," to describe the growing interest of the people in the Lord' ministry. The first occurrence of "fame" (v. 14) is from the Greek word *pheme*, the basis for our English word "fame." *Pheme* properly means "fame or report." The second occurrence of "fame" (v. 37) is a translation of *echos*, "a sound, noise, report," while the third (5:15) is *logos*, "a word, what someone has said, a saying." The stages of the Lord's increasing popularity are thus marked. First, a report of Jesus' fame begins to spread everywhere. He is becoming famous. In a little time the rumor or report becomes a noisy roar, the whole countryside being affected by it. At last His fame becomes intelligent, a *logos*, a word, a distinct message.[3] May we not assume that Peter must have experienced this same forward movement of thought concerning Jesus that Luke describes? Traveling with the Lord throughout the region, Peter would have witnessed the unfolding evidence of the uniqueness of the Christ of God.

---

[2]A. T. Robertson, *Epochs in the Life of Simon Peter* (1939), p. 35.
[3]G. Campbell Morgan, *The Gospel According to Luke* (1931), p. 63.

Luke also presents Christ's initial announcement of His ministry in Nazareth prior to His transfer of His center of interest to Capernaum. "And he taught in their synagogues, being glorified of all. And he came to Nazareth, where he had been brought up: and, as his custom was, he went into the synagogue on the sabbath day, and stood up for to read" (Luke 4:15-16). Going to the town where He had lived as a boy, where He had been brought up as a youth, He goes to the little synagogue to which He had gone so often—"as His custom was." He is about to begin His great messianic ministry, yet He goes to the place they all knew Him as the carpenter. "What emotions must have filled His heart as He remembered the earliest times, when with faltering footsteps He had gone as a Child, and listened to the reading of the law."[4]

Since the readings of the OT proceeded according to a standard schedule, Christ that particular Sabbath takes the occasion of the reading of the Isaiah passage to proclaim His mission. "The Spirit of the Lord is upon me, because he hath anointed me to preach the gospel to the poor; he hath sent me to heal the brokenhearted, to preach deliverance to the captives, and recovering of sight to the blind, to set at liberty them that are bruised, to preach the acceptable year of the Lord" (vv. 18-19, from Isa. 61:1-2). The effect is electric as Jesus, with all eyes riveted on Him, proclaims, "This day is this scripture fulfilled in your ears" (v. 21). He then proceeds to chide the people for failing to appropriate the spiritual advantages that had been offered them through His presence among them. Filled with anger, the worshipers draw Jesus forcibly out of the synagogue, rush Him down the street and through the city gates, and force Him to the crest of a hill, where they intend to kill Him. "But he passing through the midst of them went his way" (v. 30). It is following this rejection that Jesus "came down to Capernaum, a city of Galilee, and taught them on the sabbath days" (v. 31). The Lord's evident authority inherent in His "gracious words" (v. 22) continue to impress the people who hear Him speak in the synagogue. What a refreshing contrast with what they are used to hearing from the religious leaders of the day! They cannot help but compare His authoritative words and divine presence with that of the impassive scribes, who, though given to the work of the Scriptures, trusted only the words of men—the tradition of the elders—for their authority.

What new teaching is this?

It is on the first Sabbath after his call to be a catcher of men that we find Peter accompanying the Master into the synagogue in

---

[4]Morgan, p. 65.

Capernaum. The service is interrupted by the lunatic cries of a man possessed of an "unclean spirit" (Mark 1:23), a man stricken in mind and body by the devilish enemy, a man in need of moral and physical cleansing. Sensing the divine presence of Jesus, "the Holy One of God" (v. 24), the evil spirit screams his fear of impending doom, but to no avail. Jesus rebukes the demon, commanding him not only to be quiet but also to leave the poor, afflicted man. After an intense struggle, "when the unclean spirit had torn him, and cried with a loud voice, he came out of him" (v. 26).

The stir over Jesus of Nazareth has begun. Soon the rumors will turn into a full-throated roar as His fame spreads. "What new thing is this?" neighbor whispers to neighbor. "What new teaching is this?" friends question as they repeat the rumors and the unfolding saga surrounding the carpenter from Nazareth. And most intriguing of all: "Even those from the spirit world obey Him," they marvel. "And immediately his fame [*akoe*, "the thing heard, report"] spread abroad throughout all the region round about Galilee" (v. 28). News such as this had not stirred the populace since Peter was a lad, when Judas of Galilee[5] had led his celebrated but unsuccessful escapades against the Roman bandits! Perhaps one greater than Judas is among them![6]

Tell it to Jesus

With the service in the synagogue concluded, Jesus makes His way through the streets of Capernaum on His way toward Simon Peter's humble fisher's dwelling,[7] the disciples near at hand discussing the synagogue miracle. Their conversation leads to a discussion of a

[5]See Acts 5:37. Bruce connects Simon the Zealot (Simon Zelotes, Luke 6:15) with the famous rebellion in Galilee some twenty years before Christ began His ministry, when Judea and Samaria were brought under the direct government of Rome and the census of the population was taken with a view to subsequent taxation. "How singular a phenomenon is this ex-zealot among the disciples of Jesus! No two men could differ more widely in their spirit, ends, and means, than Judas of Galilee and Jesus of Nazareth. . . . One had recourse to the carnal weapons of war, the sword and the dagger; the other relied solely on the gentle but omnipotent force of truth." A. B. Bruce, *The Training of the Twelve* (n.d.), pp. 34-35.

[6]Frank G. Slaughter begins his biblical novel on Peter, *Upon This Rock* (1963), with an imaginary encounter by the thirteen-year-old Simon with Judas of Galilee. Simon's father Jonas has taken the lad to Jerusalem, where Simon's imagination is stirred when he hears the rebel's call to action against the Romans. Later, when Simon is back in Galilee, his hopes aroused by Judas of Galilee are crushed when the rebel is defeated and crucified by the Romans in a battle at Sepphoris.

[7]John already revealed that Peter's home was in Bethsaida on the northern shore of the Sea of Galilee (1:44). Most probably Bethsaida was closely situated to Capernaum since Mark associates the Lord's ministry in the synagogue at Capernaum with that of His healing of Peter's mother-in-law in his home. It may be that although the old family residence of Jona was still in Bethsaida, Peter resided in the home of

need much closer to them all. Simon's mother-in-law lay sick of a "great fever," as Luke, the doctor, calls it.[8] We can imagine their musings. "What do you think? If the Master can drive out an evil spirit, can't He help this sick woman? Can a fever be harder to drive out than an evil spirit?" Immediately ("Anon"),[9] says Mark, they tell Jesus about her, begging Him to help her.[10]

Entering the doorway to Peter's house (Mark calls it the house of Simon and Andrew), which He must have done many times before as Peter's guest-in-residence, the Lord goes directly to the bedside of the stricken woman. In answer to the disciples' question—Can a fever be harder to drive out than an evil spirit?—He rebukes the fever. Then taking her by the hand, He lifts her up, and "immediately her fever left her" (v. 31). As evidence of the thoroughness of the Lord's miraculous touch, she hastens to serve them, perhaps hastening to perform one of those love chores that mothers-in-law cherish for their own family. Was it simply by chance that the Lord Jesus went to Simon's house that day? Or did the Lord know of Peter's special need? After all, Peter has given up all to follow Jesus and having abandoned his fishing trade to do so quite possibly placed a heavier burden on his wife, who might now be anxious as to how the family will manage. But the Lord comes into her house, takes her mother by the hand, and heals her with a word. Could it be that in that act she saw the wisdom of her husband's decision to follow the Master? I do not know. But before Peter left again, it is quite possible, following the healing of her own mother, that she assured him: "You follow Him fully, Simon. I see how well you are on the right track. He has the heart and the power to care for us in all things."[11]

---

his mother-in-law in Capernaum. In the vicinity of the ruins of the second century synagogue at Capernaum, archaeologists have unearthed the remnants of a modest home (under a Roman Catholic church, of course), which some have thought to be where Peter lived with his wife and mother-in-law. Various Christian inscriptions have been found at the site, indicating that later believers found reason to gather there, perhaps because of its link to Peter.

[8]Luke 4:38.

[9]Since Mark presents Jesus as the faithful servant of God, he stresses a servant's immediate obedience through his extensive use of the Greek word *euthus*, which is found forty times in his Gospel, fully one-fourth of the occurrences being found in this first chapter. The KJV employs several synonyms for *euthus*: "immediately" (17 times, as in 1:12, 28; etc.); "forthwith" (3 times, as in 1:29, etc.); "straightway" (19 times, as in 1:10, 18, etc.) and "anon" (1:30). Most of the uses relate to Christ's ministry as a particularly appropriate action of an obedient servant.

[10]"besought," Luke 4:38.

[11]W. T. P. Wolston, *Simon Peter* (1926), p. 19.

Two gracious healing events in one Sabbath—that of the lunatic and that of Peter's mother-in-law—profoundly affect the people. They begin to wonder if they, too, might not benefit from this healer of human sufferings. The stir continues all that day[12] until, as evening approaches, people from all over the city flood to the doorway of Peter's house, seeking entrance to the miracle-working carpenter from Nazareth. "It is not difficult to imagine the effect of this wonderful sunset experience on Simon as he stood in his own doorway and saw the might of the Master with men."[13]

We cannot pass from this incident involving Peter's mother-in-law without an additional observation. That Peter was a married man is obvious from Scripture, as this healing of Peter's mother-in-law shows and which all the Synoptics recount. The apostle Paul affirms Peter's marital status when, writing to the Corinthians, Paul claims the right to a wife, though he chose not to exercise that right.[14] The Roman Catholic Church holds Peter to be their first pope and the vicar of Christ, yet demands celibacy of their priests and of the pope, all of which is obviously insupportable. Paul's qualification that a bishop be the husband of one wife,[15] as well as his prohibition of celibacy, particularly as practiced by the false teachers of the day,[16] refute Rome's claim for celibacy. Peter was a married man. To hold as is sometimes argued that Peter divorced his wife the moment he took upon himself the priest's orders only furthers the unbiblical pose that surrounds the entire fallacious Roman system.

Everyone's looking for You

What a day Peter has experienced! The events flash repeatedly before his mind as he attempts to get some sleep, a needed respite from the flush of excitement packed into the day of healing in the synagogue and at his house. Finally, deep in slumber, he does not hear Jesus rise "a great while before day" (v. 35) to go to a "solitary place" far from the throng to strengthen Himself through prayer to the Father. If, as I am led to believe, Jesus had spent much time already in Peter's home, it would not have been unusual for Peter to find his Lord's sleeping mat untouched. He had seen it often before. Knowing the Lord's spiri-

---

[12]The Jewish day ran from 6:00 P.M. of one day to 6 P.M. of the next, on the ground, no doubt, that darkness preceded light in the Creation, and Moses spoke of "the evening and the morning" (Gen. 1:5) as one day.

[13]Robertson, p. 37.

[14]I Cor. 9:5.

[15]I Tim. 3:2.

[16]I Tim. 4:3.

tual exercises, Peter hurries to the scene of Jesus' early morning vigils. "And Simon[17] and they that were with him followed after him" (v. 36).[18] Rushing to the Lord's side, his sandals soaked with the dew of the morning, Peter impulsively blurts, "All men seek for thee" (v. 37). The roar surrounding Jesus grows louder; His fame increases.

"Everybody is looking for You," Peter tells the Lord, perhaps offering this as an excuse for interrupting the Lord's vigil with the Father. But what is Peter really saying? How are we to understand the sentiments flowing from Peter's mind? Can we not say that he has been tremendously impressed with the Lord's power over the unseen demonic world? Should we not believe that Peter has already rehearsed in his mind the gracious and authoritative words with which the Lord has captured the imaginations of the crowds? What could be more re- warding than the fulfillment of every Jew's ambition—to be free from Roman taxation and tyranny, to see peace restored to their own land? And Peter would be an integral part of that glorious endeavor! Here is the proof: "All men seek for thee!" If not with actual words, certainly with heart sentiment—"If there was ever any doubt, Lord, look at how popular You are among the people!"—Peter informs Jesus of His ob- vious popularity with the people. "Lord, You are absolutely the most famous figure in town and we—these brothers and I who have hurried out here to tell You—are proud to be part of Your great movement!"

Interrupted from His devotions, but not disturbed, the Lord re- sponds—with actions more than words, though words were spoken. "The acts of Him, who is the Word, are, and are intended to be, them- selves also words for us."[19] The time for explanations is not yet come. Further observation of the Master is needed. "Let us go into the next towns, that I may preach there also; *for therefore came I forth*" (v. 38). The Lord had demonstrated His power and dignity and glory to the people of Capernaum the previous day. Now in the chill dawn of the early morning, to those perturbed disciples He says in effect: "I am not going back to Capernaum, though all men seek Me, because there are others waiting for Me. I must go and preach to them, because for that purpose came I forth." Whether they understand Him perfectly or

---

[17]"Clearly [Peter] was already a leader among them. Leaders will always come to the front. Our Lord's popularity manifestly impressed His disciples, and His reply, so deliberately avoiding popularity, must have surprised them." W. H. Griffith Thomas, *The Apostle Peter* (1956), p. 13.

[18]"The declaration made by the evangelist is really very striking; it means that they pursued Him, they hunted Him down." G. Campbell Morgan, *The Gospel According to Mark* (1927), p. 39.

[19]Richard C. Trench, *Notes on the Miracles of Our Lord* (1953), p. 152.

not,[20] the seriousness of His response shows that Jesus related all that He did—His teaching, His travels, His miracles—"to the eternal Purpose, to the Divine programme, to the Divine mission. 'To this end came I forth.' "[21]

Peter and the other disciples saw only the Lord's growing popularity among the people. He has healed the sick, cast out demons, restored sight, brought hope to the desperate. This could be but the foretaste of something far grander, Peter seems to be thinking, something far greater than he has ever contemplated for himself and the others. But the Lord Jesus quickly corrects His new disciple by reminding Peter, in so many words, that He has come to do the Father's will, not simply gather to Himself people's acclaim. His ministry is to preach the gospel of the kingdom, and others too must hear that saving message. They are in the next towns and the towns beyond those. "Let us be about the Father's business," He urges.

Christ will not be swayed by fickle crowds. He is on a mission from the Father and He continues to preach in the synagogues "throughout all Galilee, and cast out devils" (v. 39). It is difficult to imagine how much our Lord accomplished during these early years of His ministry, only a portion of which the Gospel writers use for their purposes. We must agree with John that "there are also many other things which Jesus did, the which, if they should be written every one, I suppose that even the world itself could not contain the books that should be written" (John 21:25). Matthew completes the picture:

> And Jesus went about all Galilee, teaching in their synagogues, and preaching the gospel of the kingdom, and healing all manner of sickness and all manner of disease among the people. And his fame went throughout all Syria: and they brought unto him all sick people that were taken with divers diseases and torments, and those which were possessed with devils, and those which were lunatick, and those that had the palsy; and he healed them. And there followed him great multitudes of people from Galilee, and from Decapolis, and from Jerusalem, and from Judaea, and from beyond Jordan (Matt. 4:23-25).

Peter's lessons in discipleship have taken a serious turn. Occasional sessions with Christ are put aside for what will now be continuous as-

---

[20]"One thing is certain and it is that these early disciples did not understand Jesus as they came to do after his resurrection and ascension," (Robertson, p. 36).

[21]Morgan, *The Gospel According to Mark,* p. 43.

sociation and fellowship. Simon's knowledge of Christ will increase markedly as he continues to follow the Master.

Implications for Discipleship

1. *The dispensational aspect of Jesus' dealings with His disciples must be recognized.* Jesus began His ministry in Galilee preaching the good news of "the kingdom of God." "The time is fulfilled," He proclaimed, "and the kingdom of God is at hand: repent ye, and believe the gospel" (Mark 1:14-15). Whatever else our Lord's followers understood about His mission on earth, the kingdom element lay near the surface, ready to emerge when aroused. Even after His Resurrection, the disciples ask yet again: "Lord, wilt thou at this time restore again the kingdom to Israel?" (Acts 1:6). Thus, His ministry with His disciples included their need to understand His earthly mission and their role in that mission as well as the further need of preparation for future ministry in the church.

During His earthly ministry, the Lord's "disciples" fell into three general groups. First, there were the curiosity seekers who followed Him for food and healing, concerns that included incipient hope for an earthly kingdom. A second group of followers "believed" in Him, accepting for the most part His teachings and mission but needing further development that would come through adherence to the Lord's teaching. The third[22] and smallest of the three consisted of those who not only believed on Him but, additionally, took the Lord's demands for discipleship seriously, counted the cost, and committed themselves exclusively to Christ.

Taking these together—the dispensational aspect of the Lord's public ministry and the varied companies whom the Gospel writers depict as Christ's disciples—we are forced to admit that the term "discipleship" as practiced by the Lord Jesus would encompass a broader concept than we would normally apply to Christian work today. We associate "discipleship" almost exclusively with teaching and training a new convert so that he grows in maturity in Christ. Is there also a place in our discipleship principles and practices for

---

[22]Pentecost identifies these three groups as the "curious," the "concerned," and the "committed." J. Dwight Pentecost, *Design for Discipleship* (1971), pp. 14-17.

employing the broader sense of discipleship? That of providing opportunities for the curious to learn more about
Christ as they see the power of God working in our own
lives and service? That of showing by our actions as well as
our words our own Christlike spirit?

2. *In discipling others, actions come first; specific teaching
   follows later.* There are basically two approaches that may
   be used when teaching a disciple.[23] The first is the formal
   approach: the teacher sits down with the disciple and
   teaches him biblical principles. In the second informal
   method, the teacher uses the everyday circumstances of life
   to impart spiritual principles. This was Christ's primary
   method of teaching. Because His disciples were always
   with Him wherever He went, He was able to use the situations He encountered as occasions in which to instruct His
   disciples. The Lord's specific instruction often came after
   the disciples had opportunity to observe the Lord's actions.
   That seems to be the Lord's procedure with Peter at this
   time—one of action and service, preferring that Peter witness firsthand His power and presence with instruction to
   come later. As the apprentice is first introduced to the trade
   by observing the actions of the master craftsman, Peter is
   to observe the Master at work as He relieves the physical
   and spiritual sufferings of the people. Specific teaching to
   explain these powerful acts will follow in due time.

Griffith Thomas cites four impressions that these incidents
must have produced in Peter: (1) *The need of help.* Surrounded by so much sorrow and suffering, true disciples
need open eyes and longing hearts to provide blessing to
others. (2) *The value of earnestness.* How deeply must Peter
have been struck with our Lord's strenuous life! (Mark
1:39-45). (3) *The duty of work.* Those whom God chose in
the Bible—Abraham, Moses, David, Daniel, Paul—would
have had an easier life, no doubt, if they had not been called
to special work, but "choice" men work hard. (4) *The deepening of trust.* This is the profoundest impression made on
Peter as he now lives in the presence of Christ, growing in
trust at every step. Trust comes by the direct revelation of

---

[23] Allen Hadidian, *Discipleship* (1987), p. 84.

Christ to the soul as we study His Word and abide in Him. In proportion to our fellowship will be our faith and then our faithfulness (Rom. 10:17).[24]

3. *Don't short-circuit the development of new converts.* This gradual process by which the Lord brought His disciples into contact with Himself and provided experiences to strengthen and reward their initial trust in Him is an aspect of discipleship procedure in our churches that needs careful attention. If we adopt a "one size fits all" approach to discipleship, we run the risk of impeding development by ignoring the need in believers for gradual growth in knowledge and understanding. After conversion, challenge them to invest their lives in a more permanent arrangement, but then give them some time and space. Hull suggests that after calling your disciples to ministry, give them time to make their decision. Review with them the commitment, and then give them several days to think it over. But also give your disciples an initial taste for ministry. Without choking them on too much too soon, expose your disciples gradually to the nature of Christian ministry, both the bitter and the sweet. Assign limited tasks for them to do, giving them a taste and a hunger for more.[25]

4. *Discipleship training is simply nurturing the new convert toward maturity.* Though we speak of "discipleship" with relation to NT believers, the word "disciple" is not found in the NT beyond the Gospels and the Book of Acts. The Epistles speak rather of growth in Christlikeness, maturity, attaining the full stature of Christ, and so forth. So in a NT setting, our "discipleship" ministry is that of promoting growth in one who is born again and toward whom we have a fiduciary responsibility to nurture in the Christian faith. After an individual is converted to Christ, the slow process of providing correct biblical instruction and experiences that promote growth must be planned—the goal being Christlikeness, the achieving of that next step needed for maturity. The example and power of Christ in His ministry with His disciples, particularly Peter, give us important principles in achieving success in this endeavor.

[24]Thomas, pp. 15-16.
[25]Bill Hull, *Jesus Christ Disciple Maker* (1984), pp. 60-62.

THE TWELVE

He . . . calleth unto him whom he would (Mark 3:13).

Jesus calls us; by Thy mercies
Savior, may we hear Thy call,
Give our hearts to Thy obedience,
Serve and love Thee best of all.

—Mrs. Cecil F. Alexander

Setting: The hill country in Galilee near the lake, summer, A.D. 31
Scripture: Mark 3:13-19; also Matt. 10:1-42; Luke 9:1-6

The selection by Jesus of the Twelve from among the group of disciples gathering around Him marks an important step in His ministry. Prior to this time, the Lord Jesus labors single-handedly, confining His ministry to a limited area around Capernaum in the north and, on festival occasions, Jerusalem in the south. His teaching and preaching is also limited to the gospel of the kingdom, though glimpses of the cross peer through His words at times. After He chooses the Twelve, His teaching takes on a deeper and more elaborate nature and His activities become broader and much more inclusive.[1] Several events during the Lord's second year of ministry precede His choice of the Twelve, incidents that further foment the uproar accompanying His preaching, healing, and teaching. Though the Gospel writers mention Peter specifically in only a few scattered episodes during this stretch, he and the other fledgling disciples must have found in their yearlong association with Christ abundant support on which to build their faith following their initial commitment to Him.

It is about this time that Christ heals the leper, who, not able to contain his joy and enthusiasm, begins "to publish it much, and to blaze abroad the matter" so that Jesus refrains from public appearance in the city, "but was without in the desert places: and they came to him from every quarter" (Mark 1:45). He also heals the palsied man brought by four friends to the crowded house, where the friends tear up the roof to get him to Jesus.[2] The stir continues. "We never saw it on this fashion" (Mark 2:12), respond the throng.

The Lord also finds Levi (also called Matthew) sitting at the receipt of custom and calls him to follow Him.[3] Luke informs us that

---

[1]A. B. Bruce, *The Training of the Twelve* (n.d.), p. 29.
[2]Mark 2:1-12.
[3]Matt. 9:9; Mark 2:13-14.

Matthew "made him a great feast in his own house" (Luke 5:29) to which "there was a great company of publicans[4] and of others that sat down with them." Matthew says they were "publicans and sinners," certainly not approved companions for an upcoming leader, such as Jesus of Nazareth. The reaction is predictable. The Pharisees demand to know why the disciples' Master eats with publicans and sinners.[5] Interceding on their behalf, for they are still learning more of this one who has called them to follow Him, Jesus explains: "I am not come to call the righteous," He says, "but sinners to repentance" (Matt. 9:13). With both words and actions, the Lord continues to cause a stir, the reports surrounding Him intensifying, while the disciples, including Peter, witness it all.

It is at this time, too, that He teaches that "the sabbath was made for man, and not man for the sabbath."[6] It is, therefore, inevitable that the Pharisees, now increasingly bitter toward Christ, would take the occasion of Christ's healing of the man with the withered hand on the Sabbath as reason enough to consult with the Herodians[7] "how they might destroy him" (Mark 3:6). Once again, the disciples have their own religious ideas pricked anew by the Lord's expanded teaching about the most elemental of Jewish observances—their holy day, the Sabbath.

---

[4]The publicans were "tax gatherers" (Gk. *telonai*), cruel and dishonest men (see John the Baptist's words to them in Luke 3:13), often enriching themselves through their position of influence. Being considered traitors, they were despised by their own people. Hoehner explains: "In the Ptolemaic era taxes were farmed out to the publicani. These people were leased a particular district for which they had made the highest bid, and whatever was collected in excess of their bid was to their gain. The publicani were usually quite wealthy. . . . The so-called 'publicans' in the New Testament were mere tax collectors having no connection with the wealthy publicani of the Roman Republic. The latter farmed the taxes of an entire province and were nearly always foreigners. The publicans, on the other hand, were Jews . . . collecting one form of tax in a town or small district. From the example of Levi it would seem that each had his own tax office where he collected his particular tax." Harold W. Hoehner, *Herod Antipas* (1972), pp. 77-78.

[5]Matt. 9:11.

[6]Mark 2:23-28.

[7]Among the Jews, the Herodians were a party "keenly opposed to Jesus (Matt. 22:16; Mark 3:6; 12:13) but of which no explicit information is given by any of the evangelists. The party was, probably, formed under Herod the Great, and appears to have had for its principle that it was right to pay homage to a sovereign who might be able to bring the friendship of Rome and other advantages, but who had personally no title to reign by law and by religion. On this question they differed from the Pharisees (Matt. 22:16-17), although they coalesced with them in disguised opposition, or in open union against Jesus, in whom they saw a common enemy. The Herodians were obviously something more than a political party, something less than a religious sect." *UBD* (1960), p. 479.

The Twelve

Jesus does not allow the conspiracy to destroy Him to succeed. He knows His "hour" has not come,[8] so He withdraws Himself to the shores of the lake once more, taking His disciples with Him, far away from the hate-filled Pharisees. Even there at the shore, a great multitude of people—from Galilee, from Judea, from Jerusalem, from Idumea, from beyond Jordan, from Tyre and Sidon—follow Him.[9] People continue to come to Jesus and His reputation grows stronger as He gathers more and more followers from every district of the country.

Jesus ordains twelve

"And it came to pass *in those days*, that he went out into a mountain to pray, and continued all night in prayer to God" (Luke 6:12). "In those days," says Luke. What days? "Those days" when the multitudes, growing increasingly enamored of Jesus, seek healing from Him, but also "those days" of spiraling hostility from the religious elite, particularly the Pharisees. "The hostility to our Lord on the part of the rulers was becoming more and more manifest, and more and more bitter. It is equally true that His fame was spreading, that it had become a report, and in measure an understanding."[10]

Prior to His choosing of the Twelve, Jesus spends the night on the mountain in prayer to the Father. A close study of the Gospel of Luke reveals insights into the Lord's prayer life not found in either Matthew or Mark. It is Luke who informs us that Jesus prayed at His baptism (3:21) while the heaven opened and the Holy Spirit descended on Him. The Lord often withdrew Himself from the crowds to go to a quiet place of prayer (5:16). It was during His season of prayer on the mount that He was transfigured before His inner circle of disciples (9:29). His agonizing in prayer in the garden brought solace to His soul before the cross (22:41, 44). And He prayed specifically for Peter in anticipation of the disciple's failure (22:32). Now as He anticipates the selection of the Twelve, Jesus "went out into a mountain to pray, and continued all night in prayer to God" (Luke 6:12).[11]

This is a pivotal scene. The time has come for the Lord to move from a solitary ministry to one of equipping His followers to assume His work after He is gone from them. Much still lies ahead in the

---

[8]John 7:30; 8:20; 13:1.

[9]Mark 3:7-8.

[10]G. Campbell Morgan, *The Gospel According to Luke* (1931), p. 85.

[11]"I would like to read that in churches where they are going to elect deacons and officers. Ballots and elections, and so often candidating for votes, even for bishops! Before Christ chose the first twelve, He spent a whole night alone in the mountain, and in prayer." Morgan, p. 86.

Lord's preparation for these men, but the selection must be made, so He "calleth unto him whom he would: and they came unto him" (Mark 3:13). "Calleth unto Him" is from *proskaleo*. "The middle voice shows that our Lord in calling these individuals did it in His own interest. They were to be for Himself. . . . He did not allow any to offer themselves. He did the choosing."[12] It is our Lord's sovereign choice whom He will have as His Twelve. His will settles all. "Neither popular election nor ambitious desire on the part of His servants had anything to do with the matter."[13]

Why twelve?

The time has come for the Lord to limit His followers, who have grown so numerous, to a few close companions. His success in gaining disciples has been phenomenal, so much as to make His movements from one place to another too difficult an ordeal to all concerned. This would certainly be true throughout the latter stage of His ministry when He begins His steady movement toward the cross at Jerusalem. It is simply impossible for all to "follow" Him in the literal sense. That a small core of committed men should be with Him at all times as companions to His wanderings, ministering to His daily needs, is now a logical regard.

> These twelve, however, as we know, were to be something more than travelling companions or menial servants of the Lord Jesus Christ. They were to be, in the mean time, students of Christian doctrine, and occasional fellow-laborers in the work of the kingdom, and eventually Christ's chosen trained agents for propagating the faith after He Himself had left the earth.[14]

Our Lord's choice of the Twelve demonstrates His desire to further His ministry through men, not just static programs. Coleman calls this the Lord's principle of "selection."[15] Men were His method—men willing to learn. But the principle of selection also means that the Lord will concentrate on a few to keep the group small enough to be able to work effectively with them. "This does not mean that Jesus' decision to have twelve apostles excluded others from following Him, for as we know, many more were numbered among His associates,

---

[12]Kenneth S. Wuest, *Mark in the Greek New Testament* (1957), p. 70.

[13]W. W. Fereday, *Simon Peter* (n.d.), pp. 19-20.

[14]Bruce, p. 30.

[15]Robert E. Coleman, *The Master Plan of Evangelism* (1964), p. 21.

and some of these became very effective workers in the Church. . . . Nevertheless, we must acknowledge that there was a rapidly diminishing priority given to those outside the twelve."[16]

So the Lord begins the process of naming the Twelve. One by one they are called, perhaps beginning with Simon. Peter learns a blessed lesson that day on the mountain, namely, "The Lord wants me to be with Him; He wants my company."[17] Christ chooses twelve men as His apostles, the listing of whom appears four times in the NT.[18] Though the lists vary internally due to name variations, several features stand out. Peter is always named first;[19] Judas Iscariot is always last. Of the twelve, eleven are from Galilee; only Judas Iscariot[20] is from Judea. At least two pairs of brothers are included—Peter and Andrew together with James and John. James the son of Alphaeus and Judas "brother[21] of James" (Luke 6:16) may also be a pair. Furthermore, we note that within the listings, there are three groups of four men each. The groups are always headed by the same men: Peter, Philip, and James the son of Alphaeus, though the order within the groups varies with the different accounts. Even within the three groups, it appears that the first, headed by Peter, is chosen for even more personal fellowship and training since Peter, with James and John, will comprise that inner circle around the Lord.

Why twelve? Bruce suggests an important symbolic reason. The number twelve "expressed in figures what Jesus claimed to be, and what He had come to do, and thus furnished a support to the faith and a stimulus to the devotion of His followers. It significantly hinted that Jesus was the divine Messianic King of Israel, come to set up the

---

[16]Coleman, pp. 24-25. "Other things being equal," Coleman observes, "the more concentrated the size of the group being taught, the greater the opportunity for effective instruction," pp. 26-27.

[17]W. T. P. Wolston, *Simon Peter* (1926), p. 22. "Have you learned yet, dear reader," Wolston asks, "that the Lord loves your companionship, and desires to have your affection?"

[18]Matt. 10:2-4; Mark 3:16-19; Luke 6:14-16; Acts 1:13.

[19]No doubt Matthew intends to convey the idea that Peter was "first among equals," not simply that he is naming Peter first, which Expositor's Bible says would be "a trifling comment" (*EBC* vol. 8, 1984). Matthew's suggestion supports the notion of Peter's prominence among the others.

[20]Gk. *Iskariotes*, "inhabitant of Kerioth," south of Hebron on the southern border of the tribe of Judah (Josh. 15:25).

[21]Or "*son*"? With the absence of an actual Greek word in the text, the King James translators have assumed that the phrase *Ioudon Iakobou* ("Jude, of James") should be "Judas *brother* of James," the translators indicating supplied words with italics. Others assume the relationship is that of "*son*" rather than brother. The silence of the text leaves us only to assume the actual relationship.

kingdom."[22] This symbolism is later reinforced by the Lord's own words when He speaks of His apostles sitting on twelve thrones and judging the twelve tribes of Israel.[23]

Though these twelve are the first of our Lord's choice ones, their glory certainly is not of this world—a "very insignificant company indeed."[24] Yet our Lord's choosing is consistent with God's ways.

> For ye see your calling, brethren, how that not many wise men after the flesh, not many mighty, not many noble, are called: but God hath chosen the foolish things of the world to confound the wise; and God hath chosen the weak things of the world to confound the things which are mighty; and base things of the world, and things which are despised, hath God chosen, yea, and things which are not, to bring to nought things that are: that no flesh should glory in his presence (I Cor. 1:26-29).

Think of someone starting a movement today, especially a movement with a worldwide vision. The first thing necessary is a list of influential people, the more influential the better—statesmen, politicians, economists, society leaders, professors, popular entertainment figures—"anyone, in fact, who will lend distinction and draw a crowd."[25] But Christ's kingdom is "not of this world" (John 18:36), and His new apostles are called for their spiritual capacities, not any personal influence they wield among their peers.

To be with Jesus

Mark says that Jesus "ordained"[26] twelve, that is, "made" them into a group; He constituted them as a body. The Twelve, including Peter, will become His constant companions until His mission on earth is completed. The Lord's purpose for selecting the Twelve is threefold (Mark 3:14-15): (1) "That they should be with him"; (2) "and that he might send them forth to preach"; (3) "to have power to heal sicknesses, and to cast out devils." As His apostles, they receive assurance of the Lord's *presence*, His call to *preach,* and His *power* to heal sickness and to cast out demons.[27]

---

[22]Bruce, p. 32.

[23]Matt. 19:28.

[24]Bruce, p. 37.

[25]J. Stuart Holden, *The Master and His Men* (1955), p. 11.

[26]Or "made," from *poieo.*

[27]Mark 3:14-15.

The Lord Jesus, first of all, purposes that the Twelve should be with Him on a more permanent basis: "That they should be with him." Our Lord assures His newly appointed apostles of His continued presence and companionship—a necessary feature of their relationship with the Master if they are to continue to learn from Him. Coleman calls this the "association" principle, that Christ stayed with them: "Having called his men, Jesus made it a practice to be with them. This was the essence of His training program—just letting His disciples follow Him."[28] From the beginning, when Andrew and John first approached Jesus after John the Baptist proclaimed Him to be the Lamb of God, the Lord offered this invitation: "Come and see" (John 1:39). Nothing more was said, but in the quiet of Christ's abode, they were free to spend the hours communing further with this one introduced to them by the Baptist. Later, along the seaside, Jesus again advanced the invitation to "come ye after me" (Mark 1:17) to which the Lord adds, "and I will make you to become fishers of men." Matthew, too, had responded to the invitation "follow me" (Matt. 9:9). Constant association of the learners with the Master is crucial to their growth in understanding His heartbeat.

We must not pass over this call to fellowship and companionship too hastily to get to the second aspect of His purpose, their call to preach. The invitation to "be with Him" is as important to Peter and the others as the later commissions to preach and heal. That is, fellowship and service must be kept in their proper balance and we dare not stress the one without the other. Fellowship without service, of course, tends only to mysticism and perhaps even fanaticism. But "service without fellowship is sheer presumption, futile mechanism. Together they are as soul and body."[29] It is to our shame and is a tragedy to modern Christianity that service has been separated from fellowship with Christ in so many aspects of our Christian life and witness. We risk the Lord's condemnation of our lack of godliness and failure to achieve power.

The Lord calls us to serve, but our first need is to know Him intimately so that our hearts may beat as one and our minds be akin to His will. Martha had to learn that lesson. Bothered by her sister's failure to be constantly busy about household chores, Jesus reprimanded her by showing that Mary, by attention to Jesus and His word, had chosen "that good part" (Luke 10:42). Nothing substitutes for communion with the Lord and feeding on His Word. Meals will always

---

[28]Coleman, p. 38.
[29]Holden, p. 13.

need to be prepared and dishes washed, but time spent with Christ "shall not be taken away" (v. 42). Our first need is not what we *do* as apostles but what we *are*. Much later Peter will write to believers to "grow in grace, and in the knowledge of our Lord and Saviour Jesus Christ" (II Pet. 3:18). What we are as growing followers of Christ is as important as any service He calls us to do.

To cement their association and promote companionship, Jesus will take Peter and the other apostles "with Him"[30] on various preaching tours: to Tyre and Sidon to the northwest of Galilee,[31] to the borders of Decapolis[32] and parts of Dalmanutha to the southeast,[33] and to the villages of Caesarea Philippi to the northeast.[34] These journeys, as we shall see, are partly because of the opposition of the Pharisees and the hostility of Herod but primarily because Jesus knows the need to get alone with His disciples. Later He will spend several months with them in Perea east of the Jordan.[35] As opposition increases there, Jesus moves to other sections of the country where He may retain His close fellowship with His apostles free from disruptions.[36] When the time comes for Him to go to Jerusalem for those final days, He will take "the twelve disciples apart" from the rest and make His way slowly to the city.[37] And during that final week of passion, He will barely let the apostles out of His sight. Even when He prays in the Garden of Gethsemane, they will be only a stone's throw away.[38] As the end draws near, Jesus will cherish every moment with His men. What companionship! Doubtless this explains why the Gospel writers devote so much attention to the Lord's last days leading up to the Crucifixion.

---

[30]"There is a deeper meaning than that of physical proximity in the words 'with Him.' It suggests spiritual sympathy, the acquisition of His outlook, aims, and impulses, for which the fact of living and journeying together gave opportunity. These men must become learners before they can teach. They must become convinced themselves before they can be convincing. They must know the reality of the Truth with which they are to be entrusted, of which they are to be the voices. They must become, in recognizable degree, like Him, if they are winsomely to proclaim Him. Their mere declaration of the Gospel—however accurate—apart from personal demonstration, can only be powerless. . . . There is no other way to Christ-likeness but Christ." Holden, pp. 13-14.

[31]Mark 7:24; Matt. 15:21.

[32]Mark 7:31.

[33]Mark 8:10.

[34]Mark 8:27.

[35]Luke 13:22–19:28; John 10:40–11:54; Matt. 19:1–20:34; Mark 10:1-52.

[36]John 11:54.

[37]Matt. 20:17; Mark 10:32.

[38]Luke 22:41.

Fully half of all that they record about Jesus happens in the last months of His life and most of this in the last week.[39]

Thus began Christ's extended ministry with the Twelve. "The time which Jesus invested in these few disciples was so much more by comparison to that given to others that it can only be regarded as a deliberate strategy. He actually spent more time with His disciples than with everybody else in the world put together. He ate with them, slept with them, and talked with them for the most part of His entire active ministry."[40] Yet we must not forget that even when Jesus ministered to the multitudes, the disciples were present to witness it. Peter in particular would receive special attention as preparation for his future work for the Lord.

To preach

Peter's training is not an end in itself. Christ brings His apostles to Himself "that he might send them forth to preach" (Mark 3:14). To accomplish this, the Lord constitutes them a body; He names them; He calls them "apostles."[41]

> Such was the event of the morning after the night of prayer; and there began everything of true organization, everything of true ecclesiastical value, in the history of the Church. There began the arrangements for the mighty service to be rendered to the Lord of the Church. He communed with God; He called all His disciples; He chose twelve; He named them apostles; and presently He sent them forth.[42]

What did they "preach"? In delaying his account of the naming of the Twelve until the Lord actually sends them out to preach the gospel of the kingdom, Matthew writes, "These twelve Jesus sent forth, and commanded them, saying, Go not into the way of the Gentiles, and into any city of the Samaritans enter ye not: but go rather to the lost sheep of the house of Israel. And as ye go, preach, saying, The kingdom of heaven is at hand" (Matt. 10:5-7). "The kingdom of heaven is at hand." This was the basis for repentance preached by John the Baptist[43] and Jesus Himself at the start of His ministry.[44] The Twelve are to pick

---

[39]Coleman, p. 42.

[40]Coleman, pp. 42-43.

[41]"Send forth" is from *apostello*, "to send forth." An apostle is one sent forth from another to serve as his official representative. The Twelve were now the Lord's official representatives with the delegated authority assigned to them by the Lord.

[42]Morgan, p. 89.

[43]Matt. 3:3.

[44]Matt. 4:17.

up the strain. They are to preach this "good news" only to the Jews—
not to the Gentiles, nor even the Samaritans.

Jesus has already intimated in His early conversation with
Nicodemus that His ultimate mission is to die on the cross.[45] And He
presented Himself as the Messiah to the Samaritan woman.[46] But the
Lord also speaks explicitly that His ministry would in its fulness
reach beyond Israel to all nations. Quoting Isaiah 42:1-4, Jesus had
said earlier, "Behold my servant, whom I have chosen; my beloved, in
whom my soul is well pleased: I will put my spirit upon him, and he
shall shew judgment to the Gentiles. . . . And in his name shall the
Gentiles trust" (Matt. 12:18, 21).[47]

So why only to the Jews? The answer is twofold. There is a *dispensational* aspect to the Lord's early ministry in and through His
apostles. The "kingdom of the heavens," promised of old by God,
was that kingdom over which David's seed was to rule.[48] It is now
"at hand." All had been accomplished that was necessary before the
bringing in of the kingdom. The King is now present among His
people and ready to establish the kingdom. God in His foreknowledge
knew that Israel would reject their King and His kingdom; nevertheless,
here the King offers Himself and theirs is the choice—to accept or
reject Him. But the "at hand" kingdom was set aside, waiting the "day
of the Lord" when that kingdom will be established and the Son of
David will sit on the throne.

There is also a *developmental* aspect to this command to preach, a
natural progression of ministry that should begin with the Jews since
the apostles, as Jews, would have natural inclinations to separate from
the Gentiles and the Samaritans.[49] If the Samaritans and Gentiles had

---

[45]John 3:1-16.

[46]John 4:25-26.

[47]Matthew 12 is critical because it contains one of the Lord's prohibitions
against further preaching to the Jews (v. 16), His explanation of the sin of blasphemy
against the Holy Spirit (v. 31), the Jews' refusal to receive Him despite the light given
to them (vv. 41-42), and the parable of the man with an unclean spirit whose end is
seven times worse (v. 45) than those who seek to do the Father's will (v. 50). There
follows chapter 13 in which the Lord then moves from "the kingdom of heaven" to
"the mysteries of the kingdom of heaven" in which, speaking to His disciples, He explains, "it is given unto you to know the mysteries of the kingdom of heaven, but to
them it is not given. . . . Therefore speak I to them in parables: because they seeing
see not; and hearing they hear not, neither do they understand. And in them is fulfilled
the prophecy of Esaias, which saith, By hearing ye shall hear, and shall not understand;
and seeing ye shall see, and shall not perceive . . . and should be converted, and I
should heal them" (vv. 11-15).

[48]I Sam. 7:7-16.

[49]Thinking ahead to Peter's preaching of the gospel to Cornelius, we marvel how

received unreservedly Jesus' message, it might have inhibited the Jews from following Christ. When the Holy Spirit first came on believers at Pentecost, they preached to those Jews and Jewish proselytes in Jerusalem at the time. And the believers were to be witnesses to Christ beginning at Jerusalem, among their own people, and gradually spread the message to Judea, Samaria, and to the entire known world. The Lord knows where He will take His apostles in their training, but He must start where they are and deal with their present needs and circumstances.

And to have power

"And to have power[50] to heal sicknesses, and to cast out devils" (Mark 3:15). Later when the Lord actually sends the Twelve on their preaching tour, Mark informs us that Jesus "called unto him the twelve, and began to send them forth by two and two; and gave them power over unclean spirits. . . . And they went out, and preached that men should repent. And they cast out many devils, and anointed with oil many that were sick,[51] and healed them" (Mark 6:7, 12-13). Their power to heal and to cast out demons authenticated their message, as the Lord's powerful miracles did for His ministry.

The apostles' authority to cast out demons and to heal was a derived authority, coming from the Master Himself, who has all power. Believers stand in that same relation to the Lord today for, when commissioning His people to evangelize the world, He states that "all power [exousia] is given unto me in heaven and in earth" (Matt. 28:18). We follow in the train of those disciples authorized and commissioned by the Lord. "For the Son of man is as a man taking a far journey, who left his house, and gave authority [exousia] to his servants, and to every man his work, and commanded the porter to watch. Watch ye therefore: for ye know not when the master of the house cometh" (Mark 13:34-35).

The Lord has not finished His instructions to His disciples. Though He has now constituted the Twelve, there are other lessons to learn to accompany their own service. During this interim of several months, the Lord delivers His Sermon on the Mount[52] and the parables of the

---

God dealt with Peter's prejudices toward Gentiles so that He could summon Peter to Cornelius's house.

[50]Gk. *exousia*, "authority."

[51]They were not commanded to heal all the sick they met. Matthew says, "heal the sick" (10:9), but the Greek has no article. "Heal sick" is the idea. "Probably they restricted their miracles, as Jesus Himself usually did, to those who showed desire and faith." John A. Broadus, *Commentary on the Gospel of Matthew* (1886), p. 220.

[52]Matt. 5-7.

mysteries of the kingdom.[53] Though Peter's name does not appear in
these accounts, we may be certain he is present, gaining the insights
that he will later confess concerning His Lord. Peter—fisherman, disciple, and apostle. As we continue our study of Peter, we shall examine
those few occasions on which Peter inserts himself into the narrative
and learn our necessary lessons on how the Lord deals with him.

Implications for Discipleship

1. *Effective discipleship focuses on a limited number.* The
   Lord called Peter and others to be His close companions,
   His apostles. He then worked unceasingly with them to
   prepare them for what lay ahead of them. Pastors should
   single out those responsible men who lead in the assembly
   and provide the training that will enable them to reproduce.
   Anyone who is willing to follow Christ, given the proper
   training, can become a strong disciple capable of developing others. "The first duty of a pastor as well as the first
   concern of an evangelist is to see to it that a foundation is
   laid in the beginning upon which can be built an effective
   and continuing evangelistic ministry to the multitudes. This
   will require more concentration of time and talents upon
   fewer men in the church while not neglecting the passion
   for the world."[54]

2. *It is as important to ground the new convert as it is to win
   him to the Lord.* This is not to minimize the value of a soul.
   It is an effort to implement the Lord's twofold commission
   to teach and ground converts as well as win them.[55] The
   Lord's strategy was amazingly simple. All He did to teach
   these apostles His way was to draw them close to Himself.
   He was His own school and curriculum. Knowledge was
   communicated in the living personality of one who walked
   among them. "Personal appointment to be in constant association with Him was as much a part of their ordination
   commission as the authority to evangelize."[56]

---

[53]Matt. 13.
[54]Coleman, pp. 33-34.
[55]Matt. 28:19-20.
[56]Coleman, p. 40.

3. Discipleship takes time. The Lord had little time of His own, and what time He had alone He spent in communion with the Father. The disciples were His spiritual children, and the only way for a father to raise his children correctly is to spend time with them.

"You can lead a soul to Christ in from 20 minutes to a couple of hours. But it takes from 20 weeks to a couple of years to get him on the road to maturity, victorious over the sins and the recurring problems that come along. He must learn how to make right decisions. He must be warned of the various 'isms' that are likely to reach out with their octopus arms and pull him in and sidetrack him."[57]

4. Discipling includes a personal guardianship of the convert. Hadidian speaks of guardianship as an essential element in the discipling relationship. The discipler oversees the spiritual walk of the convert, consistent with the admonition to believers to "obey them that have the rule over you, and submit yourselves: for they *watch for your souls*, as they that must give account" (Heb. 13:17). "Being a guardian is having the attitude that God has entrusted to your care a person, and for that reason you are that person's spiritual guardian. In a sense, it is the assuming of a parent-child relationship with a new believer. . . . Guardianship means giving parental care to your 'child' until he is able to stand on his own."[58] Christ was the master guardian, always alert to the needs of His disciples and willing to take the steps necessary to protect them from harm and error.

---

[57]Dawson Trotman, *Born to Reproduce* (n.d.), p. 36. "Daws" Trotman, founder of the Navigators, died on June 18, 1956, rescuing another person from drowning. He lost his life saving someone else. His commitment to Scripture memorization and follow-up of converts charted the course for the Navigators in its early years. "Soulwinners are not soulwinners because of what they know," he would say, " but because of Whom they know and how well they know Him and how much they long for others to know Him," p. 38.

[58]Allen Hadidian, *Discipleship* (1987), p. 24.

LEARNING FROM THE MASTER

Growth is critical for a disciple. Though Peter still battles his old character traits, he possesses one outstanding quality—a willingness to obey the Master. As an apostle in regular communion with the Lord, Peter will hear profound truths from the Lord, such as His Sermon on the Mount and His exposition of the kingdom parables. These marvelous lessons will enable Peter to grow in knowledge. But he will also grow in faith, as he demonstrates by walking on the lake. And he will grow in conviction when, after many superficial followers refuse Jesus' hard message and abandon Him, Peter affirms the Lord's deity. These three areas of growth—knowledge, faith, conviction—are necessary for every believer who seeks to follow Christ.

GROWING IN KNOWLEDGE

Have ye understood all these things?" (Matt. 13:51).

> *We may not climb the heavenly steeps*
> *To bring the Lord Christ down:*
> *In vain we search the lowest deeps,*
> *For Him no depths can drown.*
>
> *But warm, sweet, tender even yet*
> *A present help is He;*
> *And faith has still its Olivet,*
> *And love its Galilee.*
>
> *—John Greenleaf Whittier*

Setting: Throughout Galilee, summer, A.D. 31
Scripture: Mark 5:22-43

When Christ chose Peter and the others as His apostles, He did so that "they should be with him, and that he might send them forth to preach, and to have power to heal sicknesses, and to cast out devils" (Mark 3:14-15). To fulfill that first objective—companionship—the Lord keeps the Twelve at His side constantly as He enters into an extended preaching and healing ministry throughout Galilee. Class will always be in session with the Master Teacher. The disciples' own ministry of preaching and healing will come soon enough. In fact, this personal appointment to constant fellowship with the Lord Jesus is as much a part of their ordination commission as their authority to preach. "Indeed," notes Coleman, "it was for the moment even more important, for it was the necessary preparation for the other."[1]

During His second year of ministry as He moves about in Galilee, Jesus preaches two major messages centering on the kingdom—His Sermon on the Mount[2] and His parables of the mysteries of the kingdom.[3] It is at this time also that Herod throws John the Baptist into prison for his outspoken criticism of Herod's wretchedly immoral life.[4] From his dismal confinement, the Baptist sends two of his disciples to

---

[1]Robert E. Coleman, *The Master Plan of Evangelism* (1964), p. 40.
[2]Matt. 5:1–8:1; Luke 6:20-49.
[3]Matt. 13:1-52.
[4]Josephus relates that the Baptist was confined to a dungeon in the castle of Machaerus ("the black fortress"), built by Hyrcanus, one of the Asmonaean princes, on the northeast shore of the Dead Sea (*Antiquities,* xviii, 5, 2).

ask of Jesus, "Art thou he that should come, or do we look for another?" (Matt. 11:3). Christ reminds them of what He has already done to authenticate His mission. "Go and show John again those things which ye do hear and see: the blind receive their sight, and the lame walk, the lepers are cleansed, and the deaf hear, the dead are raised up, and the poor have the gospel preached to them. And blessed is he, whosoever shall not be offended in me" (vv. 4-6).

There is no need for the Baptist to stumble ("be offended") at the Lord's ministry, different as it is in outward manifestation from John's. Using the Baptist's lapse to affirm the forerunner's mission and also to correlate His ministry with that of John's, Christ shows that the people rejected the messages of both the Baptist and Himself, receiving, therefore, judgment from the hand of God. Those cities so blessed with the divine presence of the eternal Son of God—Chorazin, Bethsaida, and Capernaum—would receive the worst judgment of all (vv. 20-24). Those who would come to Him, however, would find "rest [for their] souls" (vv. 28-30). The nation of Israel would reject Him, but He would welcome all who come to Him for deliverance of soul and body. Peter may have winced as he heard the Lord's condemnation of his own hometown, but the apostle knows in his heart that he has found that rest in his own soul.

Do you understand?

Clearly, the Lord expects that after their extended time of association with Him, the Twelve have grown in their understanding. "Have ye understood all these things?" (Matt. 13:51) the Master asks at the end of His parables of the mysteries of the kingdom. We could apply this question to the entire year of teaching, preaching, and healing the apostles witnessed following their appointment. What did Peter and the others see and hear during this interval that comprised the Lord's "lesson plans" for the Twelve?

First, it is during this time that Christ, while presenting the kingdom as promised to David in the OT,[5] preached His Sermon on the Mount. In a sense, this sermon is a "constitution" of the Lord's coming kingdom, showing the type of government that will characterize His reign when He establishes it on the earth. The sermon contains no reference to the cross, the new birth, or justification by faith. This ser-

---

[5]II Sam. 7:12-17. In what we call the Davidic Covenant, God promised not only to place David's family on the throne but also to establish it forever so that it would not be overcome. That the covenant refers to Christ as its fulfillment is shown by Heb. 1:5, in which God spoke the opening words of II Sam. 7:14 to the Lord Jesus. In Luke 1:31-33 the angel refers to this passage and declares that Jesus is the promised seed of David, who is to sit forever on David's throne.

mon is not the gospel; the "good news" we proclaim to the unsaved is Christ's death, burial, and resurrection as atonement for our sins.[6] We preach the good news that the Son of God was lifted up on the cross, where He paid the penalty for our sins.[7] The gospel message is "repentance toward God, and faith toward our Lord Jesus Christ" (Acts 20:21). However, the ethical content of the Sermon on the Mount is binding on any age. Christians, who are heirs of Christ's kingdom, will find in His proclamations principles by which God's people should live for Him.

Second, as the Jews display deliberate unwillingness to embrace Jesus or to believe His message, the Lord takes up *teaching the disciples through parables*. Mark, after citing several of the Lord's parables, concluding with the parable of the mustard seed, writes: "And with many such parables spake he the word unto them, as they were able to hear it. But without a parable spake he not unto them: and when they were alone, he expounded all things to his disciples" (Mark 4:33-34). The Lord did this to help His disciples increase their understanding through a more subtle confrontation with the truth. It is His gracious way of stimulating their thinking and awakening their spiritual perceptions. While the crowd at large is not ready for the direct revelation of the truth, Jesus can through parables continue to speak to His men and then to provide further explanations when they are alone.[8] In introducing the parables of the kingdom, Jesus refers to Israel's judicial blindness, which formed the focus of God's message to His people. God tells the prophet that he is to preach but the people will not understand him. They have closed their eyes and ears to God's truth; their heart is grown hard. Though Isaiah delivers his message, the people will not turn back to God.[9]

The Gospel writers, thirdly, intersperse *various healing incidents* with these two discourses, including the healing of the centurion's servant at Capernaum,[10] the raising of the widow's son in Nain,[11] and the healing of the demoniac,[12] following which the Pharisees accuse Jesus of exorcising demons through the power of Satan. As He crosses the Sea of Galilee on His way to Gadara, He shows His power over nature

---

[6]I Cor. 15:1-4.
[7]John 3:14-17.
[8]*EBC* vol. 8 (1984), p. 654.
[9]Matt. 13:14-15, quoting Isa. 6:9-10.
[10]Matt. 8:5-13.
[11]Luke 7:11-17.
[12]Matt. 12:22-23.

by calming the storm on the lake.[13] All these miracles, in addition to the specific teaching of the Sermon on the Mount and the parables of the mysteries of the kingdom, aid the Twelve in understanding the unique authority of Christ. Such knowledge is essential for deepening their faith. So when, at the end of the year's ministry, Jesus asks, "Have ye understood all these things?" they quickly respond, "Yea, Lord." But the Lord tempers their hasty reply. "Therefore every scribe which is instructed unto the kingdom of heaven," He says, "is like unto a man that is an householder, which bringeth forth out of his treasure things *new and old*" (Matt. 13:52). "Instructed unto the kingdom of heaven" means "*discipled* unto the kingdom of heaven." It is in this verse, together with Matt. 28:19, that Broadus says we greatly need the verb "*to disciple.*"[14]

As the Master Teacher, the Lord Jesus understands that students learn new lessons through association with what they already know. Disciples learn the new in terms of the old. In the Sermon on the Mount, the Lord employed the formula: "Ye have heard that it was said by them of old time . . . but I say unto you" (Matt. 5:21-22, etc.), explaining the principles of His kingdom through what they already know from the old economy. When employing parables to teach the multitudes, the Lord spoke of familiar objects—a sower and seed, fish and a net, a priceless pearl—but with new meaning to the disciples who had ears and hearts to apprehend the truth hidden within the story. Old objects were endowed with new parabolic meaning. And His healings were not simply awesome wonders; they brought about deliverance from bodily infirmities, of course, but even more importantly, deliverance of the sin-stricken soul.

Two specific incidents, each containing references to Peter, show us how Peter is growing in his understanding. They are the Lord's healing of the woman with the blood disease and the raising of Jairus's daughter to life.[15] Peter becomes more aware than ever that he is in the presence of one whose knowledge is full and deep, and whose "touch"

---

[13]Matt. 8:18, 23-27.

[14]Also Matt. 27:57 and Acts 14:2. Broadus also cites the need for a verb "to shepherd" for Matt. 2:16, John 21:16, etc. "The Jewish Scribes gloried in teaching only old things, but the Christian Scribe learned such new lessons as these parables have just been giving, and so could fling out ("bringeth forth") things new and old." John A. Broadus, *Commentary on the Gospel of Matthew* (1886), p. 308.

[15]Referring to the healing of the woman with an issue of blood, Trench comments: "In all three reports which we have of this miracle, it is mixed up with that other of the raising of Jairus's daughter, and cuts that narrative in two. Such overflowing grace is in Him, the Prince of life, that as He is hastening to accomplish one work of grace and power, He accomplishes another, as by the way." Richard C. Trench, *Notes on the Miracles of Our Lord* (1953), p. 204.

is far reaching. He is on the way to answering more convincingly the Lord's query, "Do you understand the meaning of all that you have seen me do and say?"

Help me

Of the two incidents bearing directly on Peter, the first shows the Lord's *touch of concern*. "And, behold, there cometh one of the rulers of the synagogue, Jairus by name; and when he saw him, he fell at his feet, and besought him greatly, saying, My little daughter lieth at the point of death: I pray thee, come and lay thy hands on her, that she may be healed; and she shall live. And Jesus went with him; and much people followed him, and thronged him" (Mark 5:22-24). Jairus pleads with the Master to come and touch his daughter so that she will be healed. Matthew says the daughter is "even now dead" (Matt. 9:18), anticipating what will actually be true when Jesus reaches the house.[16] Jairus is identified as one of those rulers of the synagogue (Gk. *archisunagogos*) charged with oversight of the order of worship and the care of the synagogue in general. The synagogue, in all likelihood, is that in Capernaum,[17] where Jesus now is located following His return to the west side of the Sea of Galilee after healing the demoniacs in Gadara.

Here is a Jewish leader who has considerable influence on the people. In faith he simply requests that the Lord come and touch his only child, a twelve-year-old daughter, who is dying or perhaps already dead—that touch of concern that in his thinking would have special efficacy coming from this worker of wonders. "And Jesus arose, and followed him, and so did his disciples" (Mark 5:19), with perhaps Peter nudging his way toward the front, eager to see the Master extend His compassion to the troubled father.

If I can just touch His clothes

All three Synoptics interrupt the narrative of the trek to the house of Jairus[18] with the account of another also seeking healing of her own:

---

[16]Broadus, p. 204.

[17]Archaeologists have unearthed ruins of a gorgeous white limestone synagogue, built around 200 A.D., on the site where almost certainly Jesus ministered.

[18]Fereday sees in this woman and the twelve-year-old girl an illustration of the two sides of the gospel—the human and the divine. The young girl was dead. All help must therefore come to her from God, for man is powerless in the presence of death. The woman, on the other hand, played her own part. She came to Jesus, and, in faith, put in her plea for blessing. In like manner, men are "dead in trespasses and sins" (Eph. 2:1) and need the quickening power of God. And yet men have their responsibility to "come" to the Savior in response to His call of love. "We may find it difficult to reconcile these two aspects of divine truth, but both are assuredly found in the Word of God." W. W. Fereday, *Simon Peter* (n.d.), p. 25.

"And a certain woman, which had an issue of blood twelve years, and had suffered many things of many physicians, and had spent all that she had, and was nothing bettered, but rather grew worse" (Mark 5:25-26). The unnamed woman[19] suffers a chronic bleeding from the womb, which has persisted twelve years, rendering her permanently unclean,[20] excluded from the synagogue worship and separated from her friends. Luke the physician says that though she had spent all her living on physicians, none of them could heal her.[21] Having heard of others being healed with Jesus' touch, she concludes, "If I may but touch his clothes, I shall be whole" (v. 28). She is determined to "touch" Jesus with no mere slight brush of her hand but seeks to grasp or clutch His garment, for that is the meaning of "touch." Approaching Jesus unnoticed from the rear, for the people thronged about Him as He made His way to Jairus's house, she firmly grasps "the hem of his garment," the fringe, or tassel,[22] of blue, which the Jewish men wore as reminders to obey God's commands.[23] These were the "borders of their garments" (Matt. 23:5), which the hypocritical Pharisees enlarged to show their self-righteous superiority. To the stricken woman, however, she sees represented in the blue tassels of the Lord's garment heaven's truly perfect one.

Her grasp is the *touch of faith* as she is moved in part by a sense of the Lord's unique power, perhaps not able to fully explain it to herself. All she knows is that others have come to Jesus of Nazareth and He has healed them. She will seek the same for herself. "And straightway the fountain of her blood was dried up; and she felt in her body that she was healed of that plague" (Mark 5:29). The bleeding stops and immediately she feels a soundness in her body that assures her that she has been healed.

> *The healing of His seamless dress*
> *Is by our beds of pain;*
> *We touch Him in life's throng and press*
> *And we are whole again.*[24]
>
> —*John Greenleaf Whittier*

---

[19]Broadus cites Eusebius ("Hist." VII. 17) who says that tradition gives this woman the name Veronica. Broadus, p. 206

[20]Lev. 15:25-33.

[21]Luke 8:43.

[22]Gk. *kraspedon*. "If we think of the outer garment as merely an oblong cloth thrown around the person like a large shawl—as it undoubtedly was in many cases—then 'tassel' is the more natural idea; and in that case, '*the* tassel' would be simply the one nearest to her." Broadus, p. 205.

[23]Num. 15:37-41.

[24]John Greenleaf Whittier, "Our Master," *Sourcebook of Poetry* (1968), p. 134.

Who touched me?

Not only has something happened to the needy woman, but Jesus too senses that something has happened to Him. Healing energy has gone out of Him for someone's benefit. Although He knows who it is, He asks, "Who touched me?" (v. 31). No one comes forward to respond. Moreover, to Peter and the disciples, it seems like an absurd and useless question, particularly as they press their way through the crowd to get to Jairus's house. "Master, the multitude throng thee and press thee, and sayest thou, Who touched me?" (Luke 8:45). For the Lord to pause and ask questions at a critical time as this, when a little girl lies dying or even dead, must have caused the disciples deep consternation. The real emergency lies on a bed yet some distance away, not among the noisy, pushing crowd.

But the Lord knows that the woman, in addition to the touch of healing, needs the *touch of salvation*. To allow her to slink away unnoticed and unforgiven would be tragic. "He looked round about" (Mark 5:32). Wuest notes that the verb is imperfect in tense, speaking of continuous action, and middle in voice, speaking of action done in one's own interest. That is, Jesus kept on looking around for the woman, and He was doing it for Himself, regardless of what the disciples had said. "His scrutinizing gaze was His answer to the protest of the disciples."[25] The disciples, including Peter, are surprised at the sensitivity of Jesus to contact with the crowd. All of them deny anything untoward against the Lord Jesus and Peter, speaking for the group, as much as tells the Lord that His is a foolish question for everybody is pushing and shoving one another. But Jesus knows the difference between the jostling of a crowd and the tender touch of a woman in need. And the disciples are unaware of the tremendous emotional and physical drain on the Lord that accompanied His ministry to the people—something every pastor, teacher, missionary, and Christian worker have experienced in seeking to meet the spiritual needs of the flock. "And Jesus said, Somebody hath touched me: for I perceive that virtue[26] is gone out of me" (Luke 8:46).

> *I seem to touch Thy garment's hem*
> *In all these wondrous works of Thine;*
> *And straightway from Thy heart, through them,*
> *Flows healing virtue into mine.*[27]
>
> —*W. M. L. Jay*

---

[25]Kenneth S. Wuest, *Mark in the Greek New Testament* (1957), p. 112.

[26]Gk., *dunamis*, "force, power, strength."

[27]W. M. L. Jay, "His Garment's Hem," *Rhyme & Reason* (1981), p. 125.

The woman responds to Jesus' searching eyes. She realizes what has happened to her, and, though trembling with fear, she comes forward, prostrates herself before Jesus, and "declared unto him before all the people for what cause she had touched him, and how she was healed immediately" (Luke 8:47). Mark relates she "told him all the truth" (5:33).

"And he said unto her, Daughter, thy faith hath made thee whole;[28] go in peace, and be whole of thy plague" (Mark 5:34). This is the only occasion in the Gospels when Jesus addresses a woman as "daughter," not as a man to a woman, but more as a father to a child. Perhaps Jesus means by this that her faith is not just in Him, but in the one whom He came to reveal—the Father. In that one word—"daughter"—Christ "drove the clouds away and showed her the blue sky with the golden sunshine all about her. By one word the shackles of her pain and impotence fell from her, and she stood in all the light and liberty of conscious relationship with God."[29] But before He can say "Daughter," He has to bring her from secret discipleship into the place of confessed discipleship. She must be made to know that it is her faith in God that brought about her healing. "The woman, much alarmed at the publicity, owns up; and Jesus graciously reassures her, confirming her cure and telling her that it is her *faith* that has enabled her to receive it. Her faith was trust in Jesus; but it meant, ultimately, a trust in God, no doubt."[30] The Lord's benediction, "Go in peace," is not simply "Go with a blessing." It is "Go *into* peace"; that is, enter into the peace that will henceforth mark your life and eternity.

The interruption having been completely handled with compassion, the Lord Jesus continues toward the house of Jairus with His disciples, the crowd more rowdy than ever.

He takes her by the hand

No sooner ("while He yet spake")[31] has Jesus finished His words of comfort and deliverance to the woman, "there came from the ruler

---

[28]"The perfect tense vividly represents the healing as standing complete," Broadus, p. 205.

[29]G. Campbell Morgan, *The Gospel According to Matthew* (1929), p. 97.

[30]C. F. D. Moule, *The Gospel According to Mark* (1969), p. 45.

[31]This is one of the many touches Mark provides throughout his Gospel that leads us to conclude that he is narrating the scene as told to him by Peter, an eyewitness. We can imagine Peter's enthusiasm and amazement as he would retell this incident over and over in Mark's hearing: "You should have been there to see the woman's face light up with delight at the Lord's words of deliverance. And then, Jesus had no sooner finished talking with her than messengers came from Jairus, telling the Master not to bother to come; the girl was dead."

of the synagogue's house certain which said, Thy daughter is dead: why troublest thou the Master any further?" (Mark 5:35). Their candid message is simply this: "Since death is final, why trouble Jesus any further?" Ignoring their news, Jesus reassures the father, "Be not afraid, only believe" (v. 36).

Permitting none except Peter, James, and John to follow any farther, Jesus advances toward the ruler of the synagogue to enter into his house. The mourners are already at work, causing a "tumult" with their loud choral lamentations coupled with the clapping of hands in rhythm.[32] "Why make ye this ado, and weep?" He chides. "The damsel is not dead, but sleepeth" (v. 39). Since the girl's death is not final, Jesus speaks of it as "sleep," showing that He intends to bring her back to life. But the mourners misunderstand Him and they "laughed him to scorn" (v. 40). Putting all of them out of the house, for He does not want the noisy crowd present when He performs the wonderful miracle, He takes the father and mother, together with Peter, James, and John, and enters the room where the young girl is lying.[33] Standing by the side of the bed, Jesus takes the young girl's hand, and, speaking gently, calls to her "*Talitha cumi*," an Aramaic expression that only Mark preserves and then translates for us: "Damsel ["little girl"], I say unto thee, arise" (v. 41). As evidence of the Lord's *touch of life,* the young girl gets up and walks around, possibly going first to her mother, then to her father, and finally to the Lord who has brought her back to life.[34]

The Lord gives two commands. "And he charged them straitly that no man should know it" (v. 43). No one is to know about the miracle who does not need to know. News of this miraculous gift of life would leak out soon enough. Latent within the Lord's command, however, may be also a touch of judgment on the people for their hardness of heart, a judicial blindness being exacted on the crass followers who have no capacity to receive the Lord's true mission. The second command is as instructive as it is tender. He commands that they should give the girl something to eat. Perhaps before her death, while she

---

[32] The "minstrels" of Matt. 9:23 are flute players or pipers. Persons of wealth might afford to hire such musicians, so perhaps Jairus, as a man of some influence, was a man of some material means.

[33] These two miracles that are so intertwined in the Gospel narratives contain yet another feature—the woman suffered her blood hemorrhage twelve years, also the age of the little girl.

[34] Jesus restored three people to life—the little girl here on a bed; the young man at Nain carried on his bier; and Lazarus, who had lain four days in his grave. W. H. Griffith Thomas sees in these three miracles a progression: Here a little girl had just died; the widow's young son at Nain (Luke 7:12) was being taken out for burial;

was still in that delicate balance between life and death, the young girl had complained to her mother, "I'm not hungry; I just don't feel like eating." Now that she is alive again, the true Bread of Life commands that she be given nourishment. How like our Lord!

These two miracles provide insights into the Lord's power over sickness, sorrow, and even death. Peter is gaining an understanding of the Lord's sympathy with people's intimate needs. He is learning of the Lord's humility, as He avoids the fleeting popularity of the fickle crowd and the false enthusiasm of the uncommitted. He is learning to appreciate the Lord's sensitivity to the smallest particular, even that of a woman's desperate touch out from the middle of a faceless mob.

These two incidents, tied together as they are in their narratives (and even in their use of the number twelve), reveal a special quality of the Lord Jesus—His extraordinary sensitivity to the needs of others while all others—even the disciples—miserably fail in this regard. Morgan catches the gist of this when he says we need a "new language" to do justice to that beautiful word "sensitive" when applying it to the Lord Jesus. In Him sensitiveness was "responsiveness, quick, immediate, full, generous, magnificent."[35]

We also have in these narratives a wonderful revelation of how Jesus understood people. That is why He tarried to talk to the woman and help her. He understood her need of an additional touch. "Daughter!" He called her. But perhaps the most beautiful moment of understanding in all the narrative is His last touch. He lifts the dead child by His hand. She arises to life at the music of His voice. Then He commands that they should give her something to eat. "With a touch gentle enough for a little maiden's dimpled hand, and with a voice musical enough to bring the sweet spirit back from the far-off place, He did not forget that she wanted something to eat. Oh, the understandingness of Jesus!"[36]

Peter—fisherman, disciple, apostle designate. He has much to learn. But what has he learned already? He has learned that the throng

---

while Lazarus, a mature man, had been in the grave four days (John 11:17). *Outline Studies in the Gospel of Matthew* (1961), p. 134. Trench also notes these three miracles and refers to the present miracle of the young girl: "Wherein life's flame, like some newly-extinguished taper, was still more easily re-kindled, when thus brought into contact with Him Who is the fountain-flame of all life. Immeasurably more stupendous than all of these, will be the wonder of that hour, when all the dead of old, who will have lain, some of them for many thousand years, in the dust of death, shall be summoned forth and shall leave their graves at the same quickening voice (John 5:28-29)." Trench, p. 203. Nothing is too great for the power of Christ.

[35]G. Campbell Morgan, *The Gospel According to Mark* (1927), p. 129.

[36]Morgan, p. 130.

may press upon him and his Lord, yet no one really "touch" Him, whereas the slightest brush of faith will secure a full and satisfying blessing. He has seen Jesus heal his mother-in-law. Now he sees how faith must be exercised if blessing is to come. And he learns in Jairus's experience that Jesus is the one who overpowers the power of death, that death cannot be in His presence.[37] To all of which the Lord will continue to hold Peter accountable. "Have ye understood all these things?" (Matt. 13:51) the Master inquires, not for His information but to cause Simon Peter to ponder the purpose and meaning of the experiences flowing from the Lord's hand and heart as He continues in "the making of a disciple."

Implications for Discipleship

1. *Effective discipling includes clearly defined goals and a plan to achieve those goals.* Jesus' calling of His men to a relationship with Him was a calling to a goal and a task.[38] He called them to follow Him, to be with Him, to learn of Him, to preach for Him. When a discipler meets with his disciples, he needs to have his goals in mind and not be content just to see what happens. Goals provide direction for the sessions and checkpoints for later evaluation. Hadidian suggests these initial questions to help a discipler formulate his goals. "How do I bring a young Christian to the point of maturity? What are the goals I should have for his life, and how do I get him there?"[39]

2. *Teaching is more than telling; learning is more than listening.* The Lord taught with words, but He also spoke with actions. And He expected His disciples, His pupils, to understand what He taught. To that end He challenged them to go beyond mere listening to seek to comprehend the deeper sense of what He was teaching. Our converts need information, but simply relying on study notes from a workbook is not sufficient. New disciples need opportunity to interact with us so that they can demonstrate that they understand the truth. The four Gospels record more than a hundred questions that Jesus asked. Through His use of questions, Jesus

---

[37]W. T. P. Wolston, *Simon Peter* (1926), pp. 25-26.

[38]Allen Hadidian, *Discipleship* (1987), p. 25.

[39]Hadidian, p. 26. In formulating these goals, Hadidian notes, "the discipler will want to impart content, knowledge, and skills to the young Christian. That impartation requires planned, personal, and consistently held meetings with the convert."

was constantly "stimulating thought, guiding learning, and challenging pupils to accept the new teaching because they saw the rightness for themselves."[40] Don't assume that because the disciple has heard a truth once, he need never hear it again. Peter gave us these words in his second epistle. "Wherefore I will not be negligent to put you always in remembrance of these things, though ye know them, and be established in the present truth" (II Pet. 1:12). He wanted to stir up his readers "by putting [them] in remembrance" (v. 13). It is through repetition that our disciples learn.

3. *To whom much is given, much is required.* As His ministry unfolded, the Lord Jesus spent less and less time with the multitudes while giving more time to His disciples. The parables of the mysteries of the kingdom are a case in point. Jesus spoke in parables so that His disciples, who had willing hearts and eager minds, would be further instructed but the multitudes left ignorant, for they had rejected the light they were given. That meant, of course, that the disciples were under greater obligation, but the Lord assured them that as they received and acted on His teaching, He would provide greater insight. The more God teaches us from His Word, the greater we are accountable to Him to be doers of the Word and not just hearers.

4. *Knowledge is critical to the growing disciple.* The disciples did not understand quickly all that Jesus sought to teach them. Their ability to grasp the deeper truths of the Lord's ministry was hindered by their own frailty. But Jesus patiently endured these frailties because, in spite of their failures, they were willing to obey Him. To obey is to learn. Our capacity to receive revelation will grow provided we continue to practice the truth we understand.

---

[40]Clifford A. Wilson, *Jesus the Master Teacher* (1974), pp. 129-30.

GROWING IN FAITH

Lord, bid me come unto thee on the water (Matt. 14:28).

Knowledge alone life's problems cannot meet;
We learn to live while sitting at Thy feet.

—Bob Jones

Setting: Around Galilee and the lake, spring, A.D. 32
Scripture: Matt. 13:53–14:36

Jesus has just finished His extensive teaching through parables the "mysteries" of the kingdom of heaven, including the parable of the sower, the parable of the wheat and tares, and the parable of the mustard seed, deliberately obscuring their meaning to the unbelieving masses while enlightening His disciples.[1] Knowledge imparted by the Master is indispensable for producing a discerning and informed disciple. At the conclusion of the teaching, the Lord quizzes them. "Have ye understood all these things?" (Matt. 13:51). They answer with a quick and confident "Yes," but the Lord knows that they are but sophomores in His training school, for knowledge alone is insufficient. They must continue to sit at His feet to "know Him," not just to receive instruction from Him. This includes Peter, who shortly will experience a momentous event forever attached to his impetuous nature. But before that singular experience and others that follow involving Peter, we must note several serious developments in the Lord's ministry in Galilee.

This is the last period of the Lord's far-reaching Galilean ministry. His public ministry does not close for good, for after Peter's confession at Caesarea Philippi—still to come—the Lord will continue to minister publicly. But concentrating even more on His disciples, He will shift the focus to the meaning and extent of His death on the cross at Jerusalem. For now, through a series of withdrawals[2] or retreats, Christ will spend increased time with the Twelve, away from the crowds and

---

[1]Matt. 13:3-53; Mark 4:1-32; Luke 8:4-15.

[2]Hoehner lists the following "withdrawals" and wanderings by Jesus after Herod Antipas hears of Him: (1) to the eastern shore of the Sea of Galilee (Mark 6:3-32; Matt. 14:3); (2) to Bethsaida and Gennesaret (Mark 6:45, 53; Matt. 14:22, 34); (3) to Tyre (Mark 7:24; Matt. 15:21); (4) to Sidon, the Sea of Galilee, and the Decapolis (Mark 7:31; Matt. 15:21, 29); (5) to Dalmanutha (Mark 8:10) or Magadan (Matt. 15:39); (6) to Bethsaida (Mark 8:22); (7) to Caesarea Philippi (Mark 8:27; Matt. 16:13); (8) to the Mount of Transfiguration (Mark 9:2; Matt. 17:1); (9) through Galilee to Capernaum (Mark 9:30, 33; Matt. 17:22); (10) to Judea and Transjordan (Mark 10:1; Matt. 19:1-2). Harold W. Hoehner, *Herod Antipas* (1972), p. 200. Hoehner fully explains these ten withdrawals in his Appendix IX, pp. 317-30.

alone with His men. Two significant personal experiences by Jesus—rejection by His own townsmen in Nazareth and the assassination of John the Baptist—precipitate the first of His withdrawals.

Isn't this the carpenter's son?

Following His lengthy teaching through parables, the Lord Jesus returns to His hometown of Nazareth.[3] Arriving at the scene of His boyhood and early manhood, He is immediately accosted by those who oppose His teaching in the synagogue, adding to the opposition that Matthew has already described in chapters 12 and 13. They have heard of His fame, and the fact that it has reached the attention of Herod the tetrarch[4] indicates the extent of the uproar. "Whence hath this man this wisdom, and these mighty works?" they challenge (Matt. 13:54). How can a local son, one whom they know so well—and His family too—deserve all this notoriety? "Is not this the carpenter's son?[5] is not his mother called Mary? and his brethren,[6] James, and Joses, and Simon, and Judas? And his sisters, are they not all with us?" (vv. 55-56). They cannot believe that such a man so well known to them is the acclaimed miracle worker and preacher, though they do not dispute the genuine-

---

[3]Luke records a similar visit by Jesus to Nazareth at the beginning of His ministry (4:16-20). This is much later, after a prolonged preaching and healing tour throughout Galilee and near the close of the Lord's public ministry there.

[4]Matt. 14:1. "The last place in which any man becomes famous is the royal palace. Everybody knows the rumour before it reaches the king." G. Campbell Morgan, *The Gospel According to Matthew* (1929), p. 182.

[5]Mark says simply "the carpenter" (6:3). Both Matthew and Mark are correct, for it was quite expected that a son would follow his father's occupation, which Jesus evidently continued after Joseph's death. The word "carpenter" (*tektone*) denotes an artificer, a craftsman in wood. *EBC* vol. 8, quotes Justin Martyr (*Dialogue* 88.8, c. A.D. 150) as saying that Jesus was a maker of plows and yokes (p. 335). Also, the *EBC* notes that the definite article ("*the* carpenter's son") suggests there was only one carpenter in town. The people in Nazareth would remember Jesus as "the carpenter" or "that carpenter's boy." "Jesus' labor as carpenter accentuates the wonder of His incarnation. He became fully man. His example makes all productive labor honorable, and in His case it no doubt contributed to the support of the family. His familiar role in the community was an added occasion of offense to those who heard Him teaching in the synagogue." *ZPEB* vol. 1, p. 757. It has become fashionable in some evangelical circles to find special attachment to "the Carpenter" as a term of affection toward Jesus, since it so closely associated with His humanness. Care must be exercised, however, that believers do not become too irreverent when referring to the Son of God. Familiarity does breed a certain lack of respect, which we should not allow to replace the dignity the Lord deserves as the incarnate Son of God.

[6]We know from John 7:5 that as late as six months before Christ's crucifixion, His brothers did not believe in Him. And from His request to the apostle John at the cross that he care for His mother, Mary, we infer they were still not in sympathy with Him. But the Lord's appearance to James after the Resurrection (I Cor. 15:7) ended all doubts. James and the other brothers became believers (Acts 1:14).

ness of His miracles.[7] "And they were offended in him" (v. 57). They found obstacles to belief in all of this commotion about Jesus of Nazareth. They stumble over the fact that He is all too familiar to them.[8] They stumble at His authoritative yet gracious words. They stumble at His gentle spirit. They stumble at His lack of formal training, demanding to know how He could be so wise. "But Jesus said unto them, A prophet is not without honour, save in his own country, and in his own house. And he did not many mighty works there because of their unbelief" (vv. 57-58). Throughout the Lord's ministry, we notice that He does not perform healing or other miracles on those who do not believe. We need not suppose that Jesus refused to heal anyone who came to Him. Those who came to him showed the reality of their faith in His power. But as illustrated by these hometown folk, Jesus did not heal them because they refused to come to Him for aid.

Off with his head!

Beginning with 4:12, Matthew appears to have arranged his record of the Lord's ministry less out of a need to present a certain order of events than to prove, through a selection of topics, that Jesus is the Messiah. He does so to show the true nature of Christ's messianic kingdom. Beginning with chapter 14, Matthew follows more closely the time sequence of events, with but few alterations. This last year of the Lord's public ministry reflects an increasing polarization to the Lord. Opposition sharpens as Jesus moves forward with His ministry. At times He will reveal Himself further to His disciples. They will perceive some truth and entirely reject other truth. But they become more important to Jesus as the opposition from the Jewish leaders increases. And in the distance, faint but discernible, rises the shadow of the cross.

Matthew informs us of an earlier event—Herod's assassination of the Baptist—that causes the king to think that Jesus is John back from his grave. A guilty conscience, playing disaster with Antipas's mind, causes him to suppose that any alarming incident is directly related to

---

[7]Their questions about Jesus' wisdom and miracles demonstrate the falsity of those apocryphal stories of fanciful miracles supposedly ascribed to Jesus' childhood. It was out of the question, as far as these townspeople are concerned, that such a young artisan from a rough town, with no special breeding or education, could accomplish such remarkable feats. *EBC* vol. 8, p. 336.

[8]Broadus notes: "They think of him as he used to be, and are slow to believe that he has become superior to themselves. Somewhat similar is the difficulty parents often have in believing that their children are grown and can do mature work—they keep remembering them as children." John A. Broadus, *Commentary on the Gospel of Matthew* (1886), p. 313.

his own sinful conduct. "At that time Herod the tetrarch[9] heard of the fame of Jesus, and said unto his servants, This is John the Baptist; he is risen from the dead; and therefore mighty works do shew forth themselves in him" (Matt. 14:1-2). This particular Herod, son of Herod the Great,[10] is distinguished from the numerous other Herods by the name Antipas,[11] shortened from Antipater. As tetrarch of Galilee, Antipas has now ruled about thirty-two years, being the civil ruler of Galilee from the time of Jesus' return from Egypt with Joseph and Mary to His present public ministry. Antipas lives at Tiberias on the southwest shore of the Sea of Galilee, sometimes called the Sea of Tiberias.[12] Though we have no scriptural record of Jesus ever visiting or preaching in Tiberias, word of His fame reaches the palace. The recent preaching tour of the Twelve (Matt. 10) no doubt contributed greatly to the stir made by Jesus throughout the region, though it appears that this is the first time Antipas has paid any attention to Jesus' ministry.[13]

Matthew and Mark both interject into their narratives their descriptions of the events surrounding Herod's assassination of the Baptist.[14] Introductory to that, they also describe John's imprisonment, which occurred at least one year earlier—this for the Baptist's condemnation of the king's[15] immoral marriage to Herodias, his brother's wife. Mark characteristically provides vivid details—that Herodias would have killed the Baptist long before, that Antipas had a remarkable affection for the Baptist and kept him safely tucked away, that he took opportu-

[9]"Tetrarch" means the ruler of a fourth part of a region, the title given to Herod Antipas, ruler of Galilee and Perea (Matt. 14:1; Luke 3:19; 9:7; Acts 13:1). Eventually the literal sense of the word faded out and it came to be used of a petty prince, lower in rank and authority than a king. *ZPEB* vol. 5 (1976), p. 683. Unger cites Josephus as concluding that the tetrarchies of Antipas and Philip (Luke 3:1), sons of Herod the Great, were regarded as constituting in actuality a fourth part each of their father's kingdom. *UBD*, p. 1086.

[10]One way to remember the Herods of the NT is this: Herod the Great murdered the infants, Herod Antipas beheaded John the Baptist, and Herod Agrippa killed James and imprisoned Peter. The Agrippa Paul faced (Acts 25:13) was Herod Agrippa II, son of the king who killed James. With the death of Herod Agrippa II, the line of the Herods ceased.

[11]Antipas plays a major role in Lloyd Douglas's *The Big Fisherman*, a historical novel on the life of Simon Peter. Douglas shows acquaintance with historical circumstances of first century life and politics in Galilee, Judea, Idumea and Arabia, perhaps obtaining his insights from the writings of Josephus and other early secular historians.

[12]John 6:1; 21:1.

[13]Jesus has ministered in Galilee over two years, "but it was in accordance with the luxurious and rather slothful character of the Tetrarch, that he should be thus ignorant (of Jesus' activity)." Broadus, p. 315.

[14]Matt. 14:3-12; Mark 6:16-29.

[15]Technically, Herod Antipas was not a "king," though the title was probably used popularly out of courtesy to the tetrarch (Matt. 14:9; Mark 6:14). Additionally,

nity to speak with the Baptist. Urged by Herodias to murder John, whose only crime was speaking the truth,[16] Antipas would have proceeded with the dark deed. Fearing uncontrollable rebellion from the people, however, he delayed any action. Herodias found the "convenient day"[17] she sought when on a special occasion for the king, Herodias's daughter[18] obtained from Antipas the promise of John's head on a platter. So died John the Baptist, the last of the OT prophets.

"And his disciples came, and took up the body, and buried it" (Matt. 14:12). There are some who still consider themselves John's disciples.[19] The Baptist's murder must have been a great shock to them. They come to give the Baptist, the "first Christian martyr,"[20] a proper burial. They then "went and told Jesus." Besides being the first religious teacher and baptizer of many of Jesus' own disciples, John was the Lord's cousin. "When Jesus heard of it, he departed thence by ship into a desert place apart" (v. 13). The connection is with Herod Antipas's sudden opposition to the Lord Jesus, not reaction to the Baptist's murder, as Matthew has just informed us. Knowing the rising opposition and perhaps also sensing that His disciples need some rest and quiet, and to seek solace for Himself too, the Lord directs them across the northern portion of the Sea of Galilee to some less populous site[21] further removed from Antipas. Not that Jesus feared Herod. On a later occasion, the Pharisees warn Jesus to escape for His life because Herod wants to kill Him. Jesus replies, "Go ye, and tell that fox, Behold, I cast out devils, and I do cures to day and to morrow, and the third day I shall be perfected. Nevertheless I must walk to day, and to morrow, and the day following: for it cannot be that a prophet perish out of Jerusalem" (Luke 13:32-33). Jesus is saying, "Herod

---

Rome's custom to call all eastern rulers by the popular title of "king" may have contributed to its use.

[16]"You cannot murder truth, though you may silence the voice that utters it," Morgan, p. 187.

[17]Mark 6:21.

[18]Salome, Herodias's daughter by her first husband, Herod Philip. Josephus, *Antiquities*, xviii, 5, 4.

[19]Years later in Acts, we still find some people identified as disciples of John. Apollos, "knowing only the baptism of John" (Acts 18:25), needed further instruction from Aquila and Priscilla. Later Paul found people at Ephesus who knew only the baptism of John, to whom the apostle preached Christ and baptized them in the name of the Lord Jesus Christ (Acts 19:1-6).

[20]Only in "one sense," explains Broadus, hastening to add that this honor is usually assigned to Stephen, p. 321.

[21]Only Luke identifies the retreat site as "Bethsaida" (9:10), but this is not Peter's hometown. There may have been several Bethsaidas ("fishertons") around the Sea of Galilee, this one also on the northeast side of the lake but outside Herod's territory.

cannot kill me. I still have work to do." But Jesus "withdraws" from Herod, abandoning him to his fear, his terror, his condemning conscience. Herod will not see Jesus at all until Pontius Pilate sends the Lord to him just hours before His crucifixion, and even then, Jesus has no word for Herod.[22]

Give them something to eat

The "ubiquitous crowd"[23] does not give up that easily. "And when the people had heard thereof, they followed him on foot out of the cities" (Matt. 14:13). John gives us the time of year when this takes place—"And the passover, a feast of the Jews, was nigh" (John 6:4). It was April, fully one year before Christ would observe His final Passover in Jerusalem before His crucifixion. Quintin Hogg notes that because it is Passover time, this may account for the large crowd that eventually assembles that day. Men, women, and children have been passing by for days in caravans and, as they journey, they must have heard of the murder of John the Baptist and of the raising of Jairus's daughter. They would have seen, too, the crowds that streamed out from Capernaum and around the northern end of the Sea of Galilee to follow Jesus so as to hear what He has to say. While the Lord is "communing with His disciples under the shade of the oak and walnut tree, there came the hum of many voices, from the slope between them and the shore, until at last a crowd had assembled, 'five thousand men, besides women and children,' probably not far short of ten thousand in all, expectant of what the great Rabbi might teach them."[24]

"And Jesus went forth, and saw a great multitude, and was moved with compassion toward them, and he healed their sick" (Matt. 14:14). Such are the people coming to Him that the Lord, instead of turning in disgust or weariness from them, has "compassion toward them." We must not think that when Christ worked some miracle of healing it required but His voice and nothing more. The story of Christ's ministry indicates that there was a strong effort, followed by a feeling of exhaustion, after He put forth healing power. We saw a hint of this when

---

[22]Morgan notes with pathos that one brief encounter between Antipas and Jesus during the Lord's trial. "(Herod) had long wanted to see Him, and he had been intensely curious about Him; and it is an awful fact that he and Pilate were made friends over the death of Jesus. Herod never heard a single accent of the voice of Jesus. Though he cross-questioned Him, gathered his soldiers about Him, laughed at Him, mocked Him, made sport of Him, and put Him to shame, through the whole process Christ never opened His mouth. There are men for whom Christ has no word," Morgan, p. 187.

[23]Morgan, p. 188.

[24]Quintin Hogg, *The Story of Peter* (1900), pp. 63-64.

He said of the healing of the woman with the hemorrhage that "virtue,"[25] or strength, had gone out of Him. Clearly the animosity aroused in Herod Antipas, coupled with the beheading of John the Baptist, brings about a need for solace and solitude for the Lord Jesus. But as He gathers with His disciples for these moments of solitude, the needs of the multitudes bring Him into action once more. "He healed their sick."

The scene that is about to unfold must have made an indelible impression on Peter. While Jesus has been talking, the sun sinks behind the hills on the western side of the lake. "Send the multitude away" suggest some of the disciples. "The villages around here are small and some of them quite a distance away. The hungry crowd needs somewhere to buy food." It is then the Lord Jesus offers His never-to-be forgotten command: "They need not depart; give ye them to eat" (v. 16). It was earlier in the afternoon that Jesus had put the question to Philip—"Whence shall we buy bread, that these may eat?" (John 6:5), leaving the matter for him and the others to ponder. All Philip can come up with is an estimate of what it would take for even a frugal snack for the people. "Philip answered him, Two hundred pennyworth of bread is not sufficient for them, that every one of them may take a little" (v. 7). So when it comes time for action, the Lord shows them that His power to meet the need far exceeds anything within themselves. Indeed, John notes that Jesus asked this question of Philip "to prove him." The best the disciples can do is to ferret out a lad with five small, flat loaves of bread into which he would stuff portions of the two fish he also brought with him. The scene before us is well known, being the only miracle by the Lord Jesus recorded in all four Gospels. Clothed in their multicolored robes, the great crowd sits down in companies on the "green" grass,[26] another special touch by Mark made possible by Peter's eyewitness account of the happenings. ("Oh, John Mark, you should have seen how fresh and green, yet golden in the setting sun, the grass gleamed that brisk spring afternoon!")

Through "the wideness of God's mercy," they all eat, consuming as much as they want, much to Philip's consternation, perhaps, since he had tried in vain to figure out how to provide just "a little" for each. "Open thy mouth wide, and I will fill it" (Ps. 81:10), God promises. The twelve baskets of remaining food amply demonstrate God's desire to do "exceeding abundantly above all that we ask or think" (Eph. 3:20). John records the crowd's reaction to the miraculous meal. "Then those

---

[25]Gk., *dunamis.*
[26]Mark 6:39.

men, when they had seen the miracle that Jesus did, said, This is of a truth that prophet that should come into the world" (John 6:14).

Walking on the water

No sooner does the meal end than Jesus "constrained his disciples" to get into a boat to return to the western shore while He dismisses the crowd. Perhaps Peter's sailor eyes spotted an ugly look to the darkening sky, causing him to hesitate casting off for the short sail across the lake; but the Lord compels them for, as John informs us, "When Jesus therefore perceived that [the multitude] would come and take him by force, to make him a king, he departed again into a mountain himself alone" (John 6:15). The same crowd that said "This is the promised prophet" would force Jesus to become head of a kingdom of their own making— after all, Jesus could provide the ultimate welfare program! The Lord Jesus would have none of it, refusing both motive and method. Indeed, He would have hard words for these superficial followers in Capernaum the very next day. And knowing His disciples would be sorely tempted to side with the multitude, He constrains them to leave by boat.

Jesus is alone "on the land," Mark notes (6:47), in prayer to the Father; but the disciples are not "alone," for He "saw them toiling in rowing" (v. 48). A violent head wind has started playing on the "harp" Genessaret, rendering the sail useless, so the little company of men resort to rowing to get to the western shore. They have but five or six miles for their trip; yet after several hours of hard labor at the oars, they have made little progress, finding themselves "in the midst of the sea" (Matt. 14:24). "Even to those who had followed the sea from their youth, the situation was so fraught with peril that they saw little chance of escape except by going with the wind back to the shore they had just left. But this would be to disobey their Lord. Therefore they continued to fight with frantic futility."[27] Battling with outward dangers, the disciples also face inner foes that are equally threatening. Had not Jesus commanded them to cross the lake? Did He not know that He has called them to an impossible task, one for which they have insufficient strength? Why does He not come and change the impossible into the possible? Such questions fill their minds, tormenting them all with a sense of frustration and defeat as they battle the raging windstorm.

A little before the dawn of the morning, through a slight break in the dark clouds, the moon offers a dim gaze at a form approaching the boat. The frightened disciples, not knowing the shape, are startled at the seeming apparition and cry out, thinking, perhaps, it is some visi-

---

[27]Clovis G. Chappell, *Sermons on Simon Peter* (1959), p. 20.

tor from the shadowy unseen world coming to warn them of their doom. Perhaps it is even one of those evil spirits from the hills of Gadara, they think, not long ago cast into the herd of swine that plunged to their death in that very lake. The disciples never think the vision may be Christ, a shame to their clouded minds. For help indeed is present, but they know it not.

"It is I; be not afraid" (v. 27), speaks the Master. Now they all recognize His comforting voice. The change in Peter is as astounding as it is instant. "Master," he cries, "if it's You,[28] call to me to come to You across the water." In reply Peter hears the simple invitation, "Come!" "And when Peter was come down out of the ship, he walked on the water, to go to Jesus" (v. 29). Peter the fisherman, who knows and respects the dangers of the lake, nevertheless finds in this supernatural act of Jesus—the Master walking on the water—an experience into which he would have no fear to enter! "Just invite me to come to You and I will come." What a step of faith!

In the hieroglyphics of Egypt, the emblem of impossibility was two human feet resting on the water. In this one impetuous stroke, Peter reaches the impossible. Yet that is exactly what the Lord Jesus promised. "The things which are impossible with men are possible with God" (Luke 18:27). A sudden and severe gust of wind strikes the waves as Peter is on the water, and seeing the turmoil, Peter grows afraid and begins to sink into the sea right beside Jesus.[29] Finding the elements beneath him unstable, he cries to the Lord to deliver him. "Lord, save me" (Matt. 14:30). It is then the Lord completes His lesson on faith for His impulsive disciple. "O thou of little faith, wherefore didst thou doubt?" (v. 31). The Lord does not rebuke Peter for "no faith." It is as though the Lord Jesus asks, "Why did you surrender your faith?" Jesus questions Peter, not to show him how he came to his doubt but to assert the sheer folly of that doubt. "Faith in God is always and forever completely sane."[30] The Lord honored Peter's walk on the water as long as he did not doubt. The "boisterous" waves took him away from the Lord and into difficulty. Only then could the disciple be made to see that faith's eye must be totally fixed on the Savior. We look away from all that will distract and look to Jesus,

---

[28]Peter's expression implies that he takes for granted that it is the Lord. Peter does not question the Lord's identity; he is saying "*Since* it is You, bid me come."

[29]"What a parable is this for preachers and politicians who get their courage from the wind of popular favor." A. T. Robertson, *Epochs in the Life of Simon Peter* (1933), p. 59.

[30]Chappell, p. 25.

who is the leader and source of our faith (giving the first incentive for our belief) and is also its finisher (bringing it to maturity and perfection).[31]

Only Matthew records Peter's walk on the water and the Lord's rescue of His rash disciple. Peter's personal struggle was only part of the wild tempest scene. The others were themselves in total fear for their own lives, which they held to be in imminent danger. The contrary wind, the heaving waves, the startling apparition, the general confusion brought about by the darkness completely engaged their own thoughts for self-preservation. They had no time to pause to take in Peter's hasty actions: "Look, men, Peter's walking on the water!" But there it is—Peter's leap from the boat to the water, however weak and halting in faith, nevertheless obtained a blessing.

"And when they were come into the ship, the wind ceased. Then they that were in the ship came and worshipped him, saying, Of a truth thou art the Son of God" (vv. 32-33). Here is the first time the phrase "thou art the Son of God" appears in Matthew. We must look at this as an important step upward in their understanding of Jesus and not read into it any postresurrection understandings on the part of the disciples. They are still learners, acquiring, step by step, deeper and fuller appreciation of Christ.[32] After His earlier calming of the tempest, the disciples could say only, "What manner of man is this, that even the winds and the sea obey him!" (Matt. 8:27). Now they elevate Him to "the Son of God," seeing in the title some messianic meanings, though mixed with superficial understanding. Mark infers this when he chides them: "They were sore amazed in themselves beyond measure, and wondered. For they considered not the miracle of the loaves: for their heart was hardened" (6:51-52).

There is a difference here between this picture of Peter with his "little faith" and the rejecters' "unbelief" back in Nazareth. In the case of the people of Nazareth, we see men who thought they knew all about Him and refused to accept the things that astonished them.

---

[31]Heb. 12:2 (Amp.)

[32]Robertson comments on the disciples worshiping Jesus as "the Son of God" following His rescue of Peter from the waves and refuting Plummer's assertion that the disciples "perhaps even yet are not sure that he is the Messiah," (on Matt., p. 210). "Andrew and Simon took him as Messiah at the first in Bethany beyond Jordan. The Baptist called him the Son of God. Nathanael called him the Son of God. The Samaritans termed him the Savior of the world (John 4:42). Jesus claimed to be Messiah in the synagogue in Nazareth (Luke 4:21). Simon had fallen at Jesus' feet in adoration after the miraculous draught of fishes (Luke 5:8). Jesus openly claimed to be the Son of man (Mark 2:10; Matt. 9:6; Luke 5:24). In Jerusalem they heard Jesus claim equality with God (John 5:18). The message to the despondent Baptist claimed Messiahship in fact (Matt. 11:2-6; Luke 7:18-22). . . . To be sure the apostles had not

Because of their critical attitude, He could do nothing for them. But Jesus rescues these bewildered disciples, stills the lake, hushes the wind, and makes His power manifest to them.[33]

Knowledge alone does not fit a disciple for his life and service; that fitness comes from the Lord Jesus, the "Wisdom of God," which is ours only through sitting at His feet to learn of Him. Then the challenge is to step out in faith—to trust and obey the voice of our Lord. Peter has a surer grasp of this growing component of a disciple's life. He is stronger in faith as he has seen his faith rewarded and also challenged to greater heights.

Implications for Discipleship

1. *Disciples need to be challenged to greater faith.* Though the Lord rebuked Peter for his "little faith," yet that little faith allowed Peter to do something extraordinary—until the circumstances got to him and he began to sink below the waves. But he responded to the Lord's challenge to come to Him.

> When a person is asked to trust God in a new area of life, you might say that all his spiritual faculties are energized. For example, his prayer life is rekindled. Trust in God usually brings with it bended knees. When a person is challenged to greater faith, his sense of need for God is heightened. He is also motivated to live a holy life. When he has to trust God, he is motivated to make sure that his life is blameless. There is a seriousness in dealing with sin when he is challenged to greater faith.[34]

2. *Disciples possess a special attachment to their first spiritual teacher.* The disciples of John the Baptist showed great respect for their wilderness preacher of righteousness. Even

---

yet come to understand that Jesus is a spiritual, not a political, Messiah. But the facts in all the Gospels call for the acceptance of him as the Messiah with their understanding of the term long before this incident in the boat. Humbly and with awed reverence they here worship Jesus as the Son of God, according to Matthew, please observe, not in John's Gospel." Robertson, p. 60.

[33]Morgan, p. 190.

[34]Allen Hadidian, *Discipleship* (1987), p. 126. Hadidian gives several principles to follow to stretch the disciple's faith: Give him responsibility and then increase it when he responds well to it. Have him read books that show how faithful men trusted God. Have him read about the godly men of the Bible. Hand out personal challenges that you have written, pp. 127-28.

at his death, they desired to honor him with a proper burial. New converts have a special place in their hearts for their spiritual fathers, the ones who introduce them to the Lord Jesus Christ. Christian leaders should realize that they are being watched and followed by their spiritual children. Therefore, their words and deeds should always conform to the standard of righteousness that honors Christ. Though they do not win people to themselves but to the Lord, nevertheless, they are the earthly representatives of the Lord to converts. "Nothing is a substitute for a godly life. When you are gone, the disciple will never forget the qualities he saw lived out in your life."[35]

3. *Spend time alone with your disciple.* The discipler must spend time with his disciple if he is to be successful in making a disciple. We have already seen in our study of the life of Peter that the Lord chose the Twelve that they might be with Him. As the opposition intensified toward the Lord Jesus and because the uncommitted crowd wanted to make Him their earthly King, He retreated with His disciples to a lonely place to spend time alone with them. How much time should a discipler spend with his disciple? As much as possible, though if time is limited, effort should be made to maximize the time available. Limited face-to-face time can be supplemented through phone calls or e-mail. Hadidian suggests some practical things to do together:

> Eat out together.
> Exercise together.
> Shop together.
> Go to church together.
> Travel together.
> Pray together.
> Witness together.
> Go to sporting events together.
> Do homework together.[36]

---

[35]Hadidian, p. 92.

[36]Hadidian, pp. 99-100. There is value to spending time with your disciple. (1) He will see you in different situations. (2) Unity will develop. (3) He will learn your ways and follow your walk. (4) The informal nature of these occasions enables the disciple to be more open with you and honest about his victories or problems, pp. 100-101

GROWING IN CONVICTION

To whom shall we go? thou hast the words of eternal life (John 6:68).

> *Thou art the bread of life, O Lord, to me,*
> *Thy holy Word the truth that saveth me;*
> *Give me to eat and live with Thee above;*
> *Teach me to love Thy truth, for Thou art love.*

—*Mary Ann Lathbury*

Setting: Capernaum, Tyre and Sidon, Decapolis, Magdala; summer, A.D. 32
Scripture: John 6:22-71; Matt. 15:1-29

What a notable day and night we have just witnessed in the life of Peter and his Master. After John the Baptist's murder and Herod Antipas's reaction to Christ's growing popularity throughout Galilee, Christ took Peter and the other disciples quietly apart to the eastern side of the Sea of Galilee, to the slopes of a hill near what is now known as Golan. The crowd of neighbors from Capernaum, joined by the pilgrims bound for the Passover at Jerusalem, followed Christ to the Golan, where He preached to them. There followed the miraculous feeding of the five thousand and the still further miraculous act of Peter walking on the water during the night storm on the lake. The disciples, having recovered sufficiently from the terrible storm, received the Lord Jesus into their boat, expressing their growing conviction of His uniqueness. "Of a truth thou art the Son of God" (Matt. 14:33). They find themselves suddenly at their destination on the western shore with Peter rehearsing in his own mind the strange intermingling of fear and faith he had just experienced at the Master's invitation.

At the synagogue again

Now on the morning after these events, the multitudes return also across the lake in borrowed boats to Capernaum. "When the people therefore saw that Jesus was not there, neither his disciples, they also took shipping, and came to Capernaum, seeking for Jesus" (John 6:24). Crowding into the synagogue,[1] where Jesus is teaching, they demand of Him when it was He came there, setting the tone for their confrontational exchanges about to ensue with Jesus. To this idle and gaping crowd, delighted at getting plenty to eat without working,

---

[1]John 6:59.

95

Jesus addresses His great discourse on the "Bread of Life." His message essentially is this: As the OT manna in the wilderness had come from God in heaven, so He has come from the Father to be the Bread of Life for all who would believe in Him.

Christ's powerful presentation of Himself as the Bread of Life leads to a crucial test for the disciples—not only the Twelve led by Peter, but more directly these superficial disciples following Him only for what they can get from Him. Some such sifting is now needed, for the crowd's shallow fascination with Christ's miracles continues unabated.

> And when they were come out of the ship, straightway they knew him, and ran through that whole region round about, and began to carry about in beds those that were sick, where they heard he was. And whithersoever he entered, into villages, or cities, or country, they laid the sick in the streets, and besought him that they might touch if it were but the border of his garment: and as many as touched him were made whole (Mark 6:54-56).

The events just witnessed—the feeding of the five thousand, the walking on the water—occur at the end of our Lord's second year of public ministry. During this past year, Peter has responded to the Lord's call to service, has been consecrated as one of the Twelve, and has accompanied the Lord on His preaching and healing tour. It was a year in which we also have observed Peter learning from the Master—growing in knowledge of His ways, growing in faith in His power, and soon to grow in expressing his convictions about the person and ministry of the Lord Jesus. From this point forward during the last year of the Lord's ministry, we will note how He prepares, in mind and heart, Peter and His other disciples for that supreme Passover still one full year away. For now, the Lord must deal with the growing obsession among the masses that they should compel Jesus to become their king.

"When did you get here?" someone in the crowd shouts to Jesus at the synagogue in Capernaum, perhaps expecting the Lord to describe some miraculous transport by angelic hosts. The Lord does not answer the question. They ask Him *when He* came there, but He tells them *why they* came there.[2] The Lord sounds a note clearer than ever about the nature of His kingdom. He knows they long for an earthly king, a second David or Judas "the Hammer" Maccabee, or certainly another

---

[2]G. Campbell Morgan, *The Gospel According to John* (n.d.), p. 105.

Moses, who could again bring down food from heaven or water from a rock. Christ has to show them that His kingdom is founded not on physical force but essentially as a spiritual one. He offers emancipation, not from Rome or the Herods but from sin and Satan. He provides food, but it is food for the soul not the body. "Jesus answered them and said, Verily, verily, I say unto you, Ye seek me, not because ye saw the miracles, but because ye did eat of the loaves, and were filled. Labour not for the meat which perisheth, but for that meat which endureth unto everlasting life, which the Son of man shall give unto you: for him hath God the Father sealed" (John 6:26-27).

Referring no doubt to the events of the previous day, Christ compares Himself to the bread from heaven, as much as to say that He is among them to give them something better than He had given them the day before. Much earlier in His ministry, Jesus had made the same offer to the Samaritan woman at the well, when He spoke of water instead of bread. "Jesus answered and said unto her, Whosoever drinketh of this water shall thirst again: but whosoever drinketh of the water that I shall give him shall never thirst; but the water that I shall give him shall be in him a well of water springing up into everlasting life"—(4:13-14). Different circumstance; same message. He gave them "food which perishes"; it left them hungry a few short hours later. He would offer them spiritual food that would endure—"to everlasting life," repeating His claim that He is the Son of God, that He is authorized by the Father and sealed by Him.

I am the bread of life[3]

The discussion that follows grows out of the claim the Lord makes: "I am the bread of life." That claim brings strong reactions from the people, raising significant controversy. This discourse on "the bread of life"[4] is more a colloquy between Jesus and the unbelieving crowd than a sermon from Him. Picture this exchange:

Crowd: "Since You have just said we should work the works of God, tell us what God demands and we will do it."

---

[3]"Before Abraham was, I AM" proclaimed Christ (John 8:58). Jesus Christ is the great "I AM." Here He proclaims, "I am the bread of life." Later John records Jesus as saying, "I am the light of the world" (8:12), "I am the door" (10:9), "I am the good shepherd" (10:11), and "I am the resurrection and the life" (11:25). He also states, "I am the way, the truth, and the life," (14:6) and, "I am the true vine" (15:1). What a varied and complete ministry the Lord Jesus has to His people! Whatever we need, He provides.

[4]John 6:28-65.

Jesus: "I'll tell you; believe on Me as the divine one sent from God."

Crowd: "You show us a sign and we will believe. Maybe like Moses—he gave our forefathers heavenly food."

Jesus: "God gave them that food, not Moses. And by the way, even the food Moses gave the people was in reality the same bread of which I speak. Food means life and I give life to the world."

Crowd: "Well, then, give us that bread."

Jesus: "First, let Me tell you something more about that bread of life. Those who come to Me will never hunger—or thirst, for that matter. If you come to Me, I will not turn you out, though through your continual refusal to believe Me, you will not come to Me. Why? I have the promise from the Father that none of those who come to Me will be lost. They have everlasting life and the Father will raise them up at the last day."

Crowd: "Wait a minute! How can You say You came down from heaven? We know who You are. We know all about Your family.[5] They are from around here, certainly not from heaven."

Jesus: "It is important to know that no one can come to Me except the Father draw him to Me. The prophet Isaiah confirms this, saying that the people shall be 'taught of God.'[6] I tell you the truth—I am from the Father in heaven; and because I am from the Father, only I can tell you of Him. Believe on Me and you will have everlasting life because I am the living bread. And one thing more—that bread that I offer is My *flesh*. I will give My life for the life of the world."

Crowd (murmuring among themselves): "How can He give us His flesh to eat?"

---

[5]Morgan: "We see at once that their difficulty was created by their incomplete knowledge of Him. There is a sense in which it can be understood. The mystery of His Person had not been revealed, nor could be. As He moved amongst them, He was to them a Man, and nothing more. They thought they knew all about Him. They thought they knew His father and His mother. Seeing that they thought they had perfect knowledge, the problem of course presented itself at once as to how He could say that He had come from heaven," p. 114.

[6]A quotation from Isa. 54:13. "Mark the significance. You cannot come to Me, said Jesus, except you are drawn; but that is no excuse for your ignorance, because God is drawing you; 'They shall all be taught of God.' Then what follows is full of significance; 'Everyone that hath heard from the Father, and hath learned, cometh unto Me.' Mark the two things: the drawing of God, and learning by man, which means that on his part there must be response. So, in language full of mystic value,

Jesus: "If you expect to receive this everlasting life, you must eat My flesh and drink My blood.[7] Then you will dwell in Me and I will dwell in you. Compare that with your ancestors who ate the food from Moses. They are dead. You eat this bread I offer and you will live forever."

Crowd: "What You have just said is offensive[8] to us and difficult to receive."

Jesus: "Are you tripping over what I have just told you? What if you saw Me return to My Father in heaven? Would you then believe in Me? No, you would not believe Me because you refuse to receive what I say to you. My words are spiritual; they bring life to those who believe and receive them. But I know that there are some of you—even from the very beginning of My ministry—who have refused to believe in Me."

Through the vivid illustration of eating His flesh and drinking His blood, the Lord seeks to raise these would-be disciples out of their materialistic thinking into the sphere of spiritual truth. But the exchange proves too objectionable for the frustrated hangers-on whose passions toward Christ remain on the elemental level. "Who is He to speak of Himself as the 'Bread of heaven'?" they question. They come to Him seeking a leader who will break from off their necks the Roman yoke, but He speaks mystic truths they cannot comprehend. In their hearts they have no craving for His spiritual food. So while He speaks to them, murmurs of dissent are heard. First a few individuals, then several, finally section by section the audience breaks away. Among those who turn their back on Him are not only the Pharisee and the Sadducee and the Herodian but many who had joined themselves to Him with the fair desire to become His disciples.[9]

He told these people that the real reason for their blindness was found in the fact that they were not learning, were not responsive to the Divine drawing; and until they were, there could be no apprehension, 'Except a man be born anew, he cannot see the Kingdom of God.' " Morgan, pp. 115-16.

[7]This is not a reference to the Lord's Supper, which is only the symbol, the shadow. The substance is the Lord's death by which He obtained for us eternal life. "The Lord Jesus was seeking to show the people by the simple illustration of eating, what it is to take Him as Saviour. Food and drink become part of us and sustain our lives, and so our Lord, dwelling in us, sustains our spiritual lives. It was the Passover time, when the people were thinking especially of killing a lamb and eating its flesh, and of the time when they had sprinkled the blood of the lamb on their doors that the firstborn might not die. The Lord Jesus, the Lamb of God (John 1:29), knew that they could understand His references." *Pilgrim Bible* (1952), p. 1389.

[8]"This is an hard [*skleros*, "harsh, objectionable"] saying" (John 6:60).

[9]Quintin Hogg, *The Story of Peter* (1900), p. 78.

John reports: "From that time many of his disciples went back, and walked no more with him" (John 6:66). The testing and sifting of the "disciples" greatly decreases their number, for the Lord's hard test breaks the spell toward Jesus by the Galilean crowd, whose hero He was but the day before. Now after they learn that He is in no sense a political messiah and that He has no more loaves and fishes for them, but that He Himself claims to be a kind of heavenly manna that they must eat, many of the nominal disciples in disgust desert Him and leave the synagogue. "Henceforth there is no more wild enthusiasm in Galilee for Jesus. By degrees the crowded synagogue was emptied."[10] These faithless ones fall from the ranks of disciples, for from the time that they discover that following Christ is not "a rose-strewn pathway to power and prominence, they desert the Lord."[11]

You have the words of eternal life

We see from John's record that many who followed Christ as disciples, even from the early days of His ministry, were interested only in what the Lord could do for them in a physical sense. Peter, standing with Christ and the other apostles at the door of the synagogue, witnesses their defection. Not far from them stretch the broad waters of the now quiet lake. Southward towards Tiberias, eastward towards the lake, northward towards the foothills of Lebanon, crowds of people stream away from the synagogue to their various destinations. All have this in common—they have turned their backs upon Christ. Just that morning Christ was their popular hero; evening finds Him a rejected teacher. In the morning they were ready to take Him by force and make Him king; in the evening He is left alone with a small knot of followers, among whom is Simon the fisherman. "Alas! that so hopeful a morning should have had so hopeless an ending. Alas! too, that amongst that crowd, breaking from Him and rejecting His counsels, were many whom He had fed and healed and sought to comfort at the expense of His own rest and quiet."[12]

They show no interest in Him as the one who reveals the Father or who provides everlasting life. John names them as disciples because they surrounded Jesus to hear Him teach, but when the Lord shows the fatal flaw of their impure motives—physical food only, not eternal life—they forsake Him. Jesus knows who believe on Him,[13] and to

---

[10]A. T. Robertson, *Epochs in the Life of Simon Peter* (1933), p. 62.

[11]Bob Jones, *All Fulness Dwells* (1942), p. 127.

[12]Hogg, pp. 78-79.

[13]John 6:64.

those possessing true faith, the Lord seeks to deepen and enlarge their faith. The Lord forestalls any defection among the Twelve with a terse question: "Will ye also go away?" (v. 67).[14] He asks this not to gain information, of course, but to put them also to the test. The superficial are gone. No more will they walk with Jesus. "So much the worse for them. It is a poor thing to turn away from Christ in a day of difficulty."[15]

Standing near the Lord Jesus, Peter, disappointed and perhaps somewhat indignant over the interchange between Christ and the crowd and their sudden defection, nevertheless rises to the challenge. Speaking as representative of the Twelve, he responds: "Lord, to whom shall we go? thou hast the words of eternal life" (v. 68). Peter has caught something of the meaning of the Lord's words to the crowd, for Jesus had said that the words He spoke to them are living and spiritual. We must remember—the Lord Jesus has not yet died, nor does Peter believe He will die. Yet Peter's heart is deeply attached to Jesus. When He was in the storm, Peter's only desire was to go to Him, to be near Him. And when Peter did not quite make it, the Lord went to him to save him. Now Peter expresses his desire to remain with the Lord and his confession echoes the testimony of every true believer: "Lord, to whom shall we go?[16] thou hast the words of eternal life."

> And to whom shall *we* go if not to Christ? He hath still the words of life. To whom shall we go but to Christ, who answers every need, who is the inexhaustible supply? Who else can grant and what other welcomes? Where shall we turn but toward the sound of His voice and the sight of His face, where hasten but toward His outstretched hands and welcoming smile, where bring our need but to His fulness, where speed but to the embrace of His love? To whom shall we go but to Him who, ascended in the beauty of His Resurrection to the glory on high, sends back to all the sons on earth the invitation, "Whosoever will, let him come!"[17]

"And we believe and are sure that thou art that Christ, the Son of the living God" (v. 69). Peter is growing in his convictions for he says,

---

[14]The question in Greek anticipates a *negative* answer: "You will not go away, will you?"

[15]W. T. P. Wolston, *Simon Peter* (1926), p. 44.

[16]The title to a sermon by Bob Jones Jr., in which he beautifully develops the thought "To whom shall we go if not to Christ" to receive salvation, and victory, and strength, and wisdom, and confidence, and comfort, and peace, and above all joy. *All Fulness Dwells*, pp. 129-35.

[17]Jones, p. 136.

"You *have*" . . . and "You *are*." That is, "You *have* the power to do what You claim to do because You *are* the eternal Son of God." Peter's newly expressed conviction says, in effect, "We found no rest for our souls till we heard you speak; it was your message about the ever-present Kingdom of Heaven, the open gate to the Father's home. . . . You alone have satisfied our souls, how can we turn from your teaching to the husks that the swine do eat?"[18] Peter has come to the fixed conviction that Jesus is indeed the anointed one, the Christ, the Son of the living God.[19] "We believe and are sure," says Peter. It is a glorious confession of Christ as the Holy One, consecrated to God to fulfill His messianic task—"belonging to God, and appointed by God."[20]

Jesus knows, however, that this confession is not the conviction of all the Twelve. "Have not I chosen you twelve, and one of you is a devil?" (v. 70). The exception was, of course, Judas Iscariot (v. 71). How dissimilar the two—Simon Peter and Judas Iscariot. "In contrast with Simon Peter, who denied Jesus, it can be said that Judas acted by choice, Peter by impulse. Whereas Judas regarded Jesus as a means of attaining his ambition, Peter thought of Jesus as a friend. Judas was motivated by selfishness; Peter by fear."[21] The Lord's words must be seen as one more attempt on His part to warn Judas of the terrible actions he will take later. In mercy the Lord tells Judas He knows all about him and by inference says, "If you want to change, to repent, there is still time." But to his everlasting destruction, Judas pays no attention to this loving warning. He continues in his deceit and finally is used of Satan to betray the Lord.

Tell us the parable

Peter has grown in knowledge, in faith, and now in conviction. But there is yet more to learn. A semiofficial delegation of religious inquisitors arrives from Jerusalem to question Jesus about the conduct of His disciples. "Then came to Jesus scribes and Pharisees, which were of Jerusalem, saying, Why do thy disciples transgress the tradition of the elders? for they wash not their hands when they eat bread" (Matt. 15:1-2). Their question concerned not the sanitary handling of food but their perception that the Lord's disciples paid no attention to the fastidious regulations imposed on ceremonial cleanliness. Jesus subdues these Pharisees and teachers of the law by showing how they

---

[18]Hogg, p. 80.

[19]Or "the Holy One of God." ASB (1901); see Mark 1:24.

[20]William Hendriksen, *Exposition of the Gospel According to John* (1970), p. 248.

[21]*EBC* vol. 9 (1981), p. 80.

have displaced true religion of the heart with mere outward ceremony and form (vv. 4-9). Jesus then calls the multitude to Himself, bidding them to hear and understand what He has to say about the matter. "Not that which goeth into the mouth defileth a man," Jesus explains, "but that which cometh out of the mouth, this defileth a man" (v. 11).

Not only do the disciples fail to understand the parable but they also express concern that the Pharisees and scribes were offended with His words. To which Jesus indicates that though the Pharisees and the scribes had the scrolls and interpreted them in the synagogues, they truly did not understood them. On the contrary, they were blind, failing to comprehend the Scriptures they claimed to follow and leading others astray as well.

Once more we observe Peter in his role as spokesman for the Twelve. "Then answered Peter and said unto him, Declare unto us this parable" (v. 15). Or, "Lord, we don't understand what You have said about defilement coming out of the mouth, not into the mouth. Will You explain this more?"

> And Jesus said, Are ye also yet without understanding? Do not ye yet understand, that whatsoever entereth in at the mouth goeth into the belly, and is cast out into the draught? But those things which proceed out of the mouth come forth from the heart; and they defile the man. For out of the heart proceed evil thoughts, murders, adulteries, fornications, thefts, false witness, blasphemies: These are the things which defile a man: but to eat with unwashen hands defileth not a man (vv. 15-20).

With an earthy illustration, Jesus reminds them that food taken into the body through the mouth goes into the stomach, only to be excreted (v. 17), a process that has no effect on a person's spiritual purity. But because the heart is essentially evil, all action springing from that evil heart has a profound effect on a person's spiritual state. What defiles a person is what he is in his heart, not what he has done in ceremonial cleansing of the hands.

Another withdrawal

Jesus "withdraws" again[22] to a region outside the control of Herod Antipas,[23] this time to Tyre and Sidon, cities about thirty and fifty

---

[22]The first of the Lord's "withdrawals" was to the desert place east of the Sea of Galilee, where He fed the five thousand. I discussed the Lord's withdrawals or retreats in chapter 7. See also Harold W. Hoehner, *Herod Antipas* (1972), p. 200.

[23]Hoehner describes the extent of Antipas's tetrarchy. "The area of Galilee was

miles to the northwest on the Mediterranean coast, into Gentile country. Jesus had healed Gentiles before[24] but always on Jewish territory.[25]

> And, behold, a woman of Canaan came out of the same coasts, and cried unto him, saying, Have mercy on me, O Lord, thou son of David; my daughter is grievously vexed with a devil. But he answered her not a word.[26] And his disciples came and besought him, saying, Send her away; for she crieth after us. But he answered and said, I am not sent but unto the lost sheep of the house of Israel. Then came she and worshipped him, saying, Lord, help me. But he answered and said, It is not meet to take the children's bread, and to cast it to dogs. And she said, Truth, Lord: yet the dogs eat of the crumbs which fall from their masters' table. Then Jesus answered and said unto her, O woman, great is thy faith: be it unto thee even as thou wilt. And her daughter was made whole from that very hour (vv. 22-28).

Christ's reluctance to respond to the request of the Canaanite woman turned not just on the fact that she was a Gentile, or that this was Gentile territory, but on her appeal to Him as the Son of David and on His being conscious of the purpose of His earthly ministry to the Jews. Because of her faith, making appeal to His mercy, she receives the "crumbs" of which she spoke. Through His honoring this

---

about 750 square miles and of Perea about 850 square miles, in all 1,600 square miles. Each area was divided into five toparchic districts. Although the territories were not joined physically, it is reasonable to suppose that there was freedom of movement between them," p. 51.

[24]Matt. 4:24-25; 8:5-13.

[25]"In the Jewish literature Galilee and Perea were considered Jewish territories along with Judea. Although there was no geographical connection between Galilee and Perea, one can see the wisdom of rule by the same tetrarch." Hoehner, p. 56.

[26]English proposes that Jesus paid no attention at first to the woman of Canaan, not because He lacked compassion but rather *because of* His compassion. Noting that Canaan was the enemy of Israel, the woman appealed to Him as the Son of David, the King of Israel. When the rightful King of Israel sits upon the throne of David, "in that day there shall be no more Canaanite in the house of the Lord of hosts" (Zech. 14:21). "As the Son of David His only action with her must have been judgment. So, in His mercy and grace, when the disciples asked Him to send her away, He said (so that she could hear, we may be sure): 'I am not sent but unto the *lost* sheep of the house of Israel.'" E. Schuyler English, *Studies in the Gospel According to Matthew* (1941), p. 109. English emphasizes the significance of the word "lost" so that the woman understood that if He considered the house of Israel lost and in need of a Savior, how much more would she, a Canaanite, need salvation. Sensing her worthlessness, she cries to the Lord for help. "The grace that kept Him from answering the first time . . . was grace that led Him to meet her need the second time," p. 110. Marvelous grace of Jesus!

Gentile woman's faith, it appears that Jesus wanted His disciples (and the woman as well) to recognize that His life and ministry had been circumscribed by His offer of the kingdom to the Jews. The thought is like that of John 4:22, in which the Lord, speaking to the Samaritan woman, said, "Salvation is of the Jews." Recognizing that the woman grasps His reason for withholding His grace, He honors the faith of this uncovenanted Canaanite and heals her daughter. "The faith that simply seeks mercy is honored."[27]

Jesus continues His movements in territory north and east of Galilee, again just outside Herod's rule. "Nigh unto the sea of Galilee" (Matt. 15:29) is on the eastern side of the lake, Gentile Decapolis, in the region where He previously healed the demoniac of Gadara. This may account for the fact that here "great multitudes came unto him, having with them those that were lame, blind, dumb, maimed, and many others, and cast them down at Jesus' feet; and he healed them: insomuch that the multitude wondered, when they saw the dumb to speak, the maimed to be whole, the lame to walk, and the blind to see: and they glorified the God of Israel" (vv. 30-31). There follows a second mass feeding, this time of four thousand (vv. 32-39) and following the miracle, Jesus sends the multitude away and crosses the lake by ship to come to the region of Magdala.[28]

These have been dizzying days for Peter. He has traveled with the Lord Jesus, heard Him speak words of healing and comfort, witnessed deeds of mercy and kindness. He has seen Jesus refrain from creating antagonism toward the local authorities, especially Herod Antipas, deliberately withdrawing from Herod's territory to provide time for the tumultuous crowds to simmer down in their fervency to make Him their king. The impressions on Peter have been varied and deep. But now it is time to be held accountable. Peter will have to be tested by the Lord to determine the disciple's progress. How the Lord accomplishes that we will yet see, as He withdraws once more to a lonely place to put His disciples to a serious test of their growth.

---

[27]*EBC* vol. 8, p. 356.

[28]A small town on the western shore of the Sea of Galilee, between Capernaum and Tiberias, mentioned only here in Scripture. Mark 8:10 calls the place Dalmanutha. It was the birthplace of Mary Magdalene. *UBD*, p. 678. Speaking of Magdala and the fishing industry around the lake, Hoehner writes: "Countless fishing boats dotted the Sea of Galilee, which in turn was surrounded with villages inhabited by fishermen. For this reason the most important town in the area bore the Hebrew name Magdala or Magdal Nunia 'fish tower.' In Greek it was called 'Tarichaeae' from the word *tarichos* used of salt or pickled fish which were sold all over Palestine. According to Josephus it had a population of 40,000 and a fishing fleet of 230 (or 330) boats," pp. 67-68.

Implications for Discipleship

1. *Christ demands total commitment.* Modern American
   Christianity has developed a mindset that allows a person
   to "commit" himself to Christ as Savior but continue to live
   a lifestyle wholly identified with the world. A professional
   athlete may express faith in Christ, yet continue to use foul
   language, drink beer, and engage in immoral activities in
   the cities where he plays his athletic contests. His concept
   of Christianity is that Christ would follow him and condone
   his worldly lifestyle. Scriptures demand that the true believer come out from among the evil ones and be separate
   (II Cor. 6:14-18).

2. *Use concepts people understand.* Jesus used common objects to explain deep spiritual concepts. His use of food
   with these superficial followers, or water with the
   Samaritan woman, or a baby's birth with Nicodemus,
   shows His desire to speak in such a way that people would
   understand clearly what He taught. Often people in need
   provide believers with important contact points to deal with
   spiritual needs. It is important to take advantage of these
   leads and show them how Scripture relates to their problems.
   When you do, you often are able to talk with them in terms
   they understand and are willing to accept.

3. *Be alert to decisions for Christ from impure motives.* The
   "disciples" who left Jesus were interested only in advancing their own agenda and in making Him their king. When
   Christ preached His hard message on eating His flesh and
   drinking His blood, that is, the need to appropriate Him as
   their life, they walked away, proving their superficial involvement as a would-be disciple. "They went out from us,
   but they were not of us; for if they had been of us, they
   would no doubt have continued with us: but they went out,
   that they might be made manifest that they were not all of
   us" (I John 2:19). People often make false professions for
   Christ out of a desire for relief from a tragic personal situation or a disastrous financial predicament. That such decisions are sometimes made from impure motives should
   embolden us to be certain that those who turn to Christ are
   genuine converts.

TESTING BY THE MASTER

After a year of close companionship, daily observation, and profound teaching, it comes time for the Lord to examine His followers. The daily influence of the Master on Peter is now to be revealed through the Lord's penetrating questions. Following Peter's confession of Christ, the Lord reveals His anticipated death on the Cross in Jerusalem, to which Peter strenuously objects. Taking Peter, James, and John to the Mount of Transfiguration, the Lord shows forth the glories of His coming kingdom.

PETER'S GREAT CONFESSION

Thou art the Christ, the Son of the living God (Matt. 16:16).

> *Crowns and thrones may perish,*
> *Kingdoms rise and wane;*
> *But the Church of Jesus*
> *Constant will remain;*
> *Gates of hell can never*
> *'Gainst that Church prevail;*
> *We have Christ's own promise,*
> *Which can never fail.*
>
> —*Sabine Baring-Gould*

Setting: Caesarea Philippi, summer A.D. 32
Scripture: Matt. 16:1-28

As every student knows, tests follow the teacher's instruction. It is to be the same with the Lord's "learners," His disciples. What transpires between the Lord and His apostle, the rock, marks a turning point in Peter's history and a landmark in his experience when, at Caesarea Philippi, he confesses that Jesus is the Christ, the Son of the living God. The impact this event has had on subsequent church history demands that we examine carefully Peter's confession and our Lord's commendation.

The Lord Jesus has deliberately, it seems, avoided any direct agitation of Herod Antipas now that the tetrarch has been alerted to Jesus' ascendancy in Galilee.[1] Though the crowds clamor for Christ to be their king, the Lord eases their misdirected fervency by withdrawing from them, first to the lonely place east of the Sea of Galilee, where He feeds the five thousand, then northwest to Tyre and Sidon on the Mediterranean coast, where He brings deliverance to the Syro-Phoenician's daughter. Following a circuitous route eastward and southward to Decapolis, the Lord again feeds a crowd of four thousand, returning briefly to Galilee by crossing the lake to Magdala.

The Pharisees and Sadducees confront Jesus again, this time in an attempt to trick Him by asking for a "sign from heaven" (Matt. 16:1). The Lord chides them for their ability to discern weather signs while failing to see and heed the "sign" they already possess, the Scriptures. The prophet Jonah, for example, has already spoken (v. 4), but through

---

[1]Matt. 14:1.

109

their false teachings and impious influence,[2] these religious elite voided Scripture's effect. "Take heed and beware of the leaven[3] of the Pharisees and the Sadducees" (v. 6), Jesus warns the Twelve.

The disciples show that they still do not understand completely the Lord's intent for them, for they assume His warning is issued "because we have taken no bread." Perhaps they have rightly perceived the Lord's disappointment with the crowd, that their only interest in Him is His ability to feed them. Do the disciples still harbor some of the same unfounded hope in their hearts? Does He touch a painful nerve in them with this warning? Is it because they have made no provision for themselves, assuming that their potential "king" will care for them, as He did the five thousand and the four thousand? No, it is not that at all—as much as that may have been harboring in the disciples' thinking. The Lord has something more fundamental for them to learn. "Beware . . . of the doctrine ["teaching"] of the Pharisees and of the Sadducees" (v. 12), He explains.

Secreting the Twelve north out of Galilee and away from the rule of Antipas, the Lord heads in the direction of Mount Hermon, to Caesarea Philippi.[4] This is the Lord's last and most important withdrawal from Galilee and before His final journey south,[5] a journey northward that includes not only Peter's confession of Jesus as

---

[2]"How slowly have men been able to see the worth of moral values in a world of ceremonies and rules and customs!" A. T. Robertson, *Epochs in the Life of Simon Peter* (1939), p. 66.

[3]Mark adds, "and of the leaven of Herod" (8:15). "Mark 8:15 has long presented a difficulty. If *zume* means 'influence,' then Jesus' warning would have been twofold. On the one hand he would be warning them against the influence of the Pharisees who were thinking in terms of a political Messiah who would deliver them from the Roman oppressor, a view which fits within the Pharisaic concept of the Torah and the tradition of the elders. On the other hand, he was warning them against the influence of the Herod(ians)/Sadducees' interest in maintaining a political *status quo*. It is, then, entirely legitimate for Jesus to have mentioned both the Pharisees and Herod(ians)/Sadducees in one breath. This he did without implying that the two were in any way agreed except on the policy of opposing Jesus, as seen in Mark 3:6. Matthew's replacement of Herod by the Sadducees does not alter the meaning. The warning was to beware a wrong concept of an external Messianic kingdom brought about by force." Harold W. Hoehner, *Herod Antipas* (1972), p. 213.

[4]At the foot of Mount Hermon, Caesarea Philippi was first a Canaanite sanctuary for the worship of Baal, perhaps Baal-Hermon (Judg. 3:3; I Chron. 5:23). The Greeks called the place *Paneas* because of its cavern, which reminded them of similar places dedicated to the worship of the god Pan. In 20 B.C. Herod the Great received the whole district from Augustus and dedicated a temple to the emperor. Herod Philip enlarged it and called it Caesarea Philippi to distinguish it from his father's Caesarea on the Mediterranean coast. This place marked the northern limit of Christ's travels in the Holy Land. *UBD*, pp. 160-61.

[5]Matt. 19:1.

Messiah but also the Lord's glorious transfiguration. The Lord is firm in His plan to equip His Twelve in mind and spirit for what lies ahead of them, with Peter at the head of the class. "We shall see Jesus using repetition and variety and practicing patience with these men and even then often unable to lift them out of Pharisaic cobwebs of external ceremonialism and political literalism. Peter by his very volative impulsiveness is the looking-glass by which we can read the attitude of the rest."[6]

Who am I?

After arriving at their northern destination,[7] the Lord Jesus asks the Twelve, "Whom do men say that I the Son of man am?" (v. 13). People do not know what to think of this carpenter-prophet from Nazareth as several opinions now circulate about Him. Had Jesus asked this question of His disciples only a few weeks earlier, they would have told Him that some people looked on Him as a possible king. Now the answer is more complex, for even the coarse and obnoxious Herod Antipas looks on Jesus as a fresh incarnation of John the Baptist. Others see Him as the return of one of the OT prophets who spoke for God, such as Elijah or Jeremiah. Of course, the Lord knows what the multitudes are saying about Him, but He questions the disciples, not to obtain current information but, as He so often did, to make use of a question to draw out a response from these chosen men who follow Him, His disciples.[8] The multitudes at large are perfectly willing to grant that He is a great man, a prophet of some kind, a man of God, but they refuse to believe the truth about Him. They will not believe that He is the Messiah-God. It has always been true that sinful man is "prepared to accept the strangest doctrines and to decline the true revelation of God."[9]

Up to this time, the Lord has refrained from any premature disclosure of Himself, except through veiled references to "mine hour" or "my Father's business" or calling Himself "the Son of man."[10] He has allowed His own character and influence, aided by their receptivity to the Father's insights, to make their own silent but deep impression on them. His second question, however, provides the opportunity for

---

[6]Robertson, p. 48.

[7]Luke notes that Christ was "alone praying" (9:18).

[8]E. Schuyler English, *The Life and Letters of Saint Peter* (1941), p. 59.

[9]Robertson, pp. 60-61.

[10]Some people may wonder about our Lord's designation of Himself as "the Son of man," failing to see that in this title He asserts His deity as well as His humanity. He is "the Son . . . of man." That is, He is the Son (of God) by man.

1. "Whom do *you* say that I am?" (v. 15). Christ's earliest word
was *"Follow* me," which implied trust and obedience. Now He
asks, "hat do you *think* of Me?" Personal conviction is thus shown to
be as necessary as faith. "Ideas and convictions about Christ are the
natural and necessary outcome of contact with and confidence in Him.
'Love with all thy *mind*' (Luke 10:27) is an integral part of our relation
to God."[11] It has been two years since He first chose Peter and the others as apostles. By this time they should know their own minds about
their Master, a matter they had settled long ago when they made their
choice to follow Jesus as the Messiah of Jewish prophecy and hope.
Six months earlier Jesus was the popular hero of Galilee, and they
hoped by force to make Him the national king and throw off the hated
Roman yoke. But now He is in virtual hiding from His enemies and
has been so for months. Jesus is not questioning how accurately Peter
understands His messiahship. He is now concerned to see how Peter
and the apostles have reacted toward His fuller revelation of Himself,
especially in light of the recent defections by the superficial masses.[12]

Even without being told, we should be able to guess who responds
to the Lord's inquiry—who but the impetuous, the vigorous, Simon
Peter. The "ye" in the Lord's question is plural and emphatic, so, at
least in part, Peter responds as spokesman for the Twelve as well as for
himself. "Thou art the Christ, the Son of the living God" (Matt. 16:16),
Peter affirms. Earlier Peter had confessed of Jesus, "We believe and are
sure that thou art that Christ, the Son of the living God" (John 6:69).[13]
With this most recent question, Jesus wants to test their present attitude
toward Him after all their experiences with Him.[14] We have become accustomed to calling Jesus the Son of God, but for the disciples at
Caesarea Philippi, this insight came slowly after months of companionship and instruction. And the Lord's concern is pertinent and the question crucial because of the cross, which, the Lord Jesus will shortly
reveal to them, is only a little over six months away.

Blessed art thou, Simon Bar-jona

This encounter brought about by the Lord's questioning is pivotal,
both for Christ and for Peter. Peter's confession and the magnificent
blessing it brings from the Lord's lips marks a crucial turning point in

[11]W. H. Griffith Thomas, *The Apostle Peter* (1956), pp. 22-23.

[12]Robertson, p. 70.

[13]Or "the Holy One of God" (R.V.). Griffith Thomas notes Peter's progress of
conviction about the Lord Jesus: (1) His Character, "Holy One"; (2) His Office, "The
Christ"; (3) His Authority, "Son . . . God," Thomas, p. 23.

[14]Robertson, p. 71.

His ministry. All before it leads to it, and all that follows in some sense takes its color from it,[15] though Christ's words to Peter have proved "one of the most fertile sources of dispute in Christendom."[16] Here is the Lord's commendation to His apostle: "Blessed art thou, Simon Bar-jona: for flesh and blood hath not revealed it unto thee, but my Father which is in heaven" (Matt. 16:17).

Jesus emphatically declares that Peter's confession is not the result of human instruction but a revelation from God Himself. Over the past months, Peter has learned much about his Lord as he has accompanied Him up and down dusty roads, lodged with Him in dingy towns, and shared nights with Him on the nearby hills. To this knowledge gained by personal fellowship has now come revelation from the heavenly Father. God has taken hold of this uncultured, unlettered Galilean fisherman and has taught him truth—that the blessed one he loves and follows is the Son of the living God. No university can impart this knowledge. No book can provide the revelation that the Father in heaven gives to His own. No human teaching can impart to the soul what God brings to the believing disciple's heart. The secret of the Lord is still with those who reverence and fear Him.

Upon this rock

The Lord continues: "And I say also unto thee, That thou art Peter, and upon this rock I will build my church; and the gates of hell shall not prevail against it. And I will give unto thee the keys of the kingdom of heaven: and whatsoever thou shalt bind on earth shall be bound in heaven: and whatsoever thou shalt loose on earth shall be loosed in heaven" (vv. 18-19). We must first note that in the original text, we have a play on the Greek word for rock in this verse. Though the Lord Jesus probably spoke this commendation in Aramaic, using the word *cephas*, nevertheless, the inspired text we have before us is in Greek and in that text we find these words: "You are *petros*, and upon this *petra* I will build My church." Remember that at their first meeting, Jesus changed Simon's name to Peter—*cephas* in Aramaic, *petros* (from which we get Peter) in Greek. Since there is a definite change in gender in these words, from masculine to feminine, we are compelled to look further into the Lord's meaning for this particular pronouncement. *Petros* has been defined as a movable stone, a piece of rock, while *petra* is seen as essential rock or bedrock. Here is what the Lord Jesus is saying: "You are '*petros*' (a movable stone, a piece

---

[15]Broadus quoting H. J. Coleridge. John A. Broadus, *Commentary on the Gospel of Matthew* (1886), p. 357.

[16]Quintin Hogg, *The Story of Peter* (1900), p. 94.

of rock), and upon this '*petra*' (the bedrock) I will build My *ecclesia* (a called-out people, an assembly); and the gates of *hades* (the grave) shall not prevail against (overthrow) it."

With the "you" expressly in the Greek text, the personal pronoun is emphatic. "*You* are Peter." His repeating the name with emphasis shows its importance. The Lord's intent in speaking this way to Peter seems to be this: "I told you what you would be when we first met. I named you My rock-man. And as My 'man of strength' I have led you on and on to this point. Now we are here at Caesarea Philippi and when I asked you, 'Do you know Me, Simon?' you confessed 'You are the Christ, the Son of the living God.' And I have heard your words and you are blessed, for through My speech and life you have come to the light. Now you are Petros, rock."[17]

Unfortunately, the Lord's few words here have engendered centuries of controversy over the role Jesus assigns Peter in His church. An established principle in biblical interpretation holds that the proper interpretation of any phrase, verse, or passage should be its most obvious meaning, unless that natural interpretation comes into hopeless conflict with the unambiguous teaching of other passages of Scripture. Therefore, it would seem most natural to take Jesus' words to refer to Peter. "You are Peter, and on *you* I will build My church." No other explanation would be even attempted, notes Broadus,[18] but for the fact that the Catholic Church has so abused this interpretation that we instinctively turn away from it.[19] And it suffers from the problem of how to properly understand the Lord's play on *petros* and *petra*.

Rather than see in these words Christ's naming of Peter as the rock, others (perhaps in reaction to the dominant Roman Catholic view) hold that the Lord referred not to Peter himself but to the apostle's confession. "On this rock—your confession of My messiahship, My deity—I will build My church." Thus Morgan:

---

[17]G. Campbell Morgan, *The Gospel According to Matthew* (1929), p. 211.

[18]Broadus, p. 355.

[19]Broadus lists what the Romanists must show in order to establish their claims: (1) They must show that Peter *alone* was to be the founder of Christianity, but specific declarations of Scripture (Eph. 2:20) and its history in Acts and the Epistles oppose this notion (Acts 15; Gal. 2; etc.). (2) They must also show that Peter was vice regent of God and the *sovereign* of all Christians, but no Scripture testifies to this and the whole tone of the NT is against it. (3) They must show that this supposed authority of Peter was *transmissible*, again with no NT evidence. (4) Also they must show that Peter *lived and died at Rome*, which, Broadus notes, is probably true but not certain. (5) Finally, they must show that Peter's supposed transmissible authority was *actually transmitted* to the leading official of the church at Rome. Of this there is no evidence, and it is against the general history of the earliest churches, the tradition itself coming later. Broadus, pp. 356-57.

It is not on Peter that the Church is built. Jesus does not trifle with figures of speech. He took up their old Hebrew illustration—rock, always the symbol of Deity—and said, Upon God Himself I will build my Church . . . on Jehovah God, manifest in time by His Son, administering the affairs of the world through that Son as Messiah. Peter had found the foundation, had touched Jehovah, and by touching Him had become *petros.*[20]

Sensing some element of truth from both of these positions, some hold that Jesus meant both Peter (as representative of all the apostles) *and* his confession of Christ's deity. "The rock on which the Church was to be built was a man confessing, not the man apart from his confession as Romanists insist, nor the confession apart from the man as Protestants urge."[21] This third alternative seems to fit the story we have of Peter when we view his life and witness after the Lord's resurrection. Here at Caesarea Philippi, six months before the Lord's crucifixion, Peter is the first to offer this formal confession of the Lord's deity and sonship, and his prominence continues through the earliest years of the church, as we shall see in the Book of Acts. Peter's life and ministry is a wonderful corollary on his confession. The man cannot be separated from his confession. The foundation of Christ's church is a man confessing, but also progressing in his witness to Christ.

Nothing in our Lord's commendation to Peter should be taken as an offer of sovereignty in the church to him.[22] Peter receives no instruction to minister alone or unilaterally. Later events in Acts confirm this truth. Along with John, Peter is sent by the other apostles to confirm the converts in Samaria.[23] He is held accountable for his actions regarding the conversion of Cornelius by the church at Jerusalem.[24] On a separate occasion, the apostle Paul rebukes him.[25] "He is, in short, *primus inter pares* ('first among equals'); and on the foundation of such men (Eph. 2:20), Jesus built his church."[26] That is precisely why

---

[20]Morgan.

[21]Dr. T. M. Lindsay. Quoted by W. H. Griffith Thomas, *Outline Studies in the Gospel of Matthew* (1961), p. 248.

[22]If the reader would allow me to indulge myself for just one moment. Often when dealing with this passage in class, I tell my students that I would like to give them the shortest poem on the pope. "Was Peter the first pope? Nope."

[23]Acts 8:14.

[24]Acts 11:1-18.

[25]Gal. 2:11-14.

[26]*EBC* vol. 8, pp. 368-69.

Jesus, toward the close of His earthly ministry, will spend so much time with them. But by His commendation to Peter the rock, the Lord clearly intends that the apostle assume leadership in the early church, leadership that will mark Peter as distinctly foundational.[27] Peter's confession of the Lord in this passage is not static or isolated. After the Holy Spirit comes to indwell him and the entire church at Pentecost, we will see that Peter continues to build on this confession, showing that he understood completely the glorious person and work of the Lord Jesus Christ.

The word "church"[28] is found only here and in Matthew 18:17 in the Gospels. The word signified to the Greeks the calling out of citizens to an assembly (from *ekkaleo*, "to call out"). The concept can be compared today to the national guard or other military personnel being "called out" from their homes or places of business for deployment. In the NT the word is applied directly to an actual congregation or assembly of Christians.[29] But in the fullest sense of the word, the church is the entire company of those, from Pentecost to the end of the age, called out by God and possessing true faith in Christ. "All real Christians are conceived of as an ideal congregation or assembly, and this is here described as a house or temple, built upon Peter (and the other apostles) as in Eph. 2:19-22, a temple 'built upon the foundation of the apostles and prophets.'"[30] The Lord places the building of His church in the future—"I will build"—therefore not begun at this time, but rather with the coming of the Holy Spirit to indwell believers at Pentecost. Through the Holy Spirit, God continues to call out a people for His name.[31]

---

[27]In his attempt at "a contribution to the science of history," that is, a historical study of Peter, Oscar Cullman, in his extended analysis of Matt. 16:17-19 speaks out against the Roman Catholic claims of apostolic succession. "In so far as Peter is the rock, he is such in the temporal sense of laying the foundation as an apostle. . . . If we wish to derive further from the saying that after Peter also there must be in the Church a universal leadership that administers the keys, the power to bind and loose, this cannot take place in the sense of a limitation to the future occupants of one episcopal see. This principle of succession cannot be justified either from Scripture or from the history of the ancient Church. In reality the leadership of the Church at large is not to be determined by succession in the sense of a link with one episcopal see." Oscar Cullman, *Peter: Disciple—Apostle—Martyr* (1953), pp. 237-38. What Cullman is arguing for is a church broader than any one organization, including the Roman Catholic Church, thus displaying his ecumenical bias. He writes in his foreword: "For I hold that in addition to the ecumenical achievements of recent decades it is precisely the simple discussion between Roman Catholic and Protestant theologians that is one of the encouraging events in the church history of our times" (pp. 11-12).

[28]Gk., *ekklesia*.

[29]Rom. 16:5; Col. 4:15; Philem. 2; Rev. 2:1.

[30]Broadus, p. 358-59.

[31]Acts 15:14.

The keys of the kingdom

"And I will give unto thee the keys of the kingdom of heaven: and whatsoever thou shalt bind on earth shall be bound in heaven: and whatsoever thou shalt loose on earth shall be loosed in heaven" (Matt. 16:19). From childhood we can remember, no doubt, seeing cartoons of a man with a white beard and flowing robe, standing before the gates of heaven with a great ring of keys in his hand. This is Saint Peter! Verse 19 has brought about the false idea in some people of some special power assigned to Peter to open or shut the entrance to heaven. Such is not the case, let it be said at the start, for the same authority committed to Peter, representing all the disciples, in this verse is promised once more to all of them in Matthew 18:18.

Keys in Scripture often signify power and authority,[32] however, and in His declaration to Peter, the Lord Jesus asserts that Peter, using this authority, will have his actions of binding or loosing (forbidding or allowing) sanctioned by divine authority in heaven.[33] This includes forgiving or retaining sins, which was promised later to the apostles and others after the Resurrection.[34] In Matthew 18:18 the same promise of binding and loosing is clearly made regarding discipline of members of the body of Christ. The disciples are promised that their actions on earth in the matter of discipline among believers in Christ will be counted as correct in heaven. From the abuses of these passages has arisen the Roman Catholic doctrine of priestly absolution, which is totally without foundation. Ministers may teach the conditions of forgiveness, but they have no power of discerning a person's spiritual condition, as did Peter when he confronted Ananias and Sapphira in Acts 5. Peter assumed that authority in the Book of Acts when, using one of those keys, he opened the door of salvation to the Jews. He used another key when he went down to the house of Cornelius and preached salvation to the Gentiles assembled there.

The Lord then issues what would appear to be a strange command: "Then charged he his disciples that they should tell no man that he was Jesus the Christ" (Matt. 16:20). Jesus has presented Himself as the Messiah and is rejected by His people. His disciples, however, continue with Him, but they must grow in their understanding of Him and His mission. Any preaching or testimony from them, before their views are corrected and refined, will do more harm than good. "Jesus charges His disciples to tell no one about his true character for this

---

[32]*UBD*, p. 629.
[33]Broadus, p. 361.
[34]John 20:23.

was bound to be interpreted by the public in the 'rebel' sense."[35] Added to this purpose is that of His judicial judgment on the people of Israel. Because of their continual rejection of Him and His offered kingdom, Jesus pronounces the same judgment on them as Isaiah was commissioned by God to proclaim centuries earlier. Light given, if that light is rejected, becomes light withdrawn.

Get behind Me, Satan!

Mark the change in character of the Lord's ministry among the people. This is a critical moment. "From that time forth began Jesus to show unto his disciples, how that he must go unto Jerusalem, and suffer many things of the elders and chief priests and scribes, and be killed, and be raised again the third day" (v. 21). Not only does the Lord forbid His disciples to preach that He is the Messiah, He also announces plainly that He is going to die. How shattering this must be to their hopes and dreams of prominence in His kingdom-to-be. Peter does not understand the Lord's announcement, though the Lord speaks not only of His death but also His resurrection, and begins to rebuke Him, saying, "Be it far from thee, Lord: this shall not be unto thee" (v. 22). "What You have just announced cannot possibly be in Your plans! How can You, who opened blind eyes and deaf ears, who stilled the storm, who even raised the dead—how can You speak of death?"

What a volume of instruction is in the Lord's immediate answer as He turns and says to Peter, "Get thee behind me, Satan: thou art an offence unto me: for thou savourest not the things that be of God, but those that be of men" (v. 23). Only a moment before it had been "Blessed art thou, Simon Bar-jona." And now, favored disciple as he is, he is "Satan" because behind Peter's words is the temptation of the Devil himself. As he often attempts to do, the enemy uses the servant of God to do his devilish work. Reminiscent of his original temptation to Jesus in the wilderness, Satan once again seeks to thwart His mission by offering a crown without the cross, glory without the suffering. But the Lord Jesus refuses to fall in with Satan's scheme, even though it is spoken through the lips of His trusted disciple Peter. Jesus further warns them: "If any man will come after me, let him deny himself, and take up his cross, and follow me. For whosoever will save his life shall lose it: and whosoever will lose his life for my sake shall find it" (vv. 24-25). The disciple "is not greater than his Lord." If Jesus must bear a cross and die, His disciples must prepare for the same. His desire is that we identify with Him; it is our joy to do so.

---

[35]Hoehner, p. 209.

Implications for Discipleship

1. *Disciples must be tested periodically.* The Lord Jesus understood that after a period of instruction, His disciples needed to demonstrate that they were absorbing the lessons He gave them. Peter shows with his confession of the Lord that he has benefited from companionship with Him. When it came time for questioning, Peter had the answer the Lord Jesus expected of him. The use of questions in teaching, while not designed to impart knowledge, nevertheless gives the student opportunity to demonstrate that he understands the lessons that have been taught. Questions are valuable because they enable the student to see the truth for himself.

2. *Do not be satisfied with partial development.* When He was with His disciples, the Lord Jesus helped them to understand His reasons for previous actions, such as His warning them about the "leaven" of the Pharisees and Sadducees, by which He meant their false teachings. But the spiritually dull disciples, still thinking only of food, missed the point of His teaching, so He asked them to remember what had taken place when He fed the five thousand and the four thousand. They recounted the twelve baskets of food left over from the first miracle and the seven that remained after the second one. With this evidence of Jesus' power, there could be no doubt about His ability to feed them if He chose to do so. "Then understood they how that He bade them not beware of the leaven of bread, but of the doctrine ["teaching"] of the Pharisees and Sadducees" (Matt. 16:12).

   Coleman calls this the principle of supervision—Jesus kept check on them.[36] Jesus kept after His disciples constantly, giving them increasing attention as His ministry took Him closer to the cross. He would not allow them to rest in success or in failure. No matter what they did, there was always more to do and to learn. Here was on-the-job training at its best. "Their encounter with life situations enabled Jesus to pinpoint His teaching upon specific needs and to spell it out in the concrete terms of practical experience. One always appreciates an education more after he has had the opportunity to apply what he knows."[37] The important thing to note

---

[36]Robert E. Coleman, *The Master Plan of Evangelism* (1964), p. 94.
[37]Coleman, p. 99.

about Jesus' supervisory work is that He kept the disciples moving toward the goal He had set for them. His plan of teaching was designed to bring out the best that was in them. Disciples must be brought to maturity. It is crucial that they receive personal supervision and guidance until such a time they are mature enough to carry on alone. Peter demonstrates his maturity as he takes the lead of the Twelve in the Book of Acts, proclaiming the gospel and exercising church discipline—as the Lord promised when He spoke of giving to the apostle the keys to the kingdom of heaven.

3. *Growth in discipleship and maturity demands accountability.* Hull defines accountability as helping people keep their commitments to God, stressing the principle that accountability is a catalyst to obedience.[38] To obey Christ, the church needs accountability, for He told us to teach others all He has commanded us. We cannot make disciples without accountability, which Hadidian defines as "being held responsible for one's actions."[39] Accountability means that the discipler has the right to question his disciple's behavior to see if he has done what he said he would do. Notice how the Lord Jesus included accountability in His development program for His disciples. Most often we see them together as a group—the Twelve or the seventy sent out two by two. Seldom do we find them alone. Disciples need other disciples. They also need to be tested periodically. "Growth in our developing walk with the Lord Jesus will be, in part, proportional to our accountability to others."[40] We need to develop a habit of transparency to one another, to allow some other believer to become an appropriate helper in our saying no to temptations, to keep ourselves honest in our walk with the Lord. Accountability will take many forms—a pastor with a fellow pastor, a wife and husband, two students, close colleagues, neighbors, friends—all of them real people who desire to live godly and separated lives to the glory of Christ.

---

[38]Bill Hull, *The Disciple Making Church* (1990), p. 211.
[39]Allen Hadidian, *Discipleship* (1987), p. 118.
[40]Michael J. Wilkins, *Following the Master* (1992), p. 143.

ON THE MOUNT WITH THE LORD

Eyewitnesses of his majesty (II Pet. 1:16).

I have walked alone with Jesus
In a fellowship divine;
Nevermore can earth allure me,
I am His and He is mine.

On the mountain I have seen Him,
Christ my Comforter and Friend;
And the glory of that vision
Will be with me to the end.

—Oswald J. Smith

Setting: On the Mount of Transfiguration in northern Galilee, A.D. 32
Scripture: Matt. 16:28–17:21; also Mark 9:2-13; Luke 9:28-36

Matthew 16 marks a turning point in the Lord's earthly labors, now in their third year. Only now, following His announcement of the building of His church, has Christ revealed to the Twelve His impending rejection and death to be accomplished at Jerusalem, to be followed by His glorious resurrection. Peter has accompanied his Master to Caesarea Philippi, the "Syrian Tivoli,"[1] and it was near some visible outcropping of rock on Mount Hermon that the Lord, after Peter's great confession, found His simile of the rock on which He would build His church. He had come to His own and they rejected Him. No longer will He preach, "Repent: for the kingdom of heaven is at hand." The proffered kingdom of the Son of David will be set aside for the present to make way for the gospel of the suffering Servant of Jehovah—His death, burial, and resurrection. "From that time forth began Jesus to show unto his disciples, how that he must go unto Jerusalem, and suffer many things of the elders and chief priests and scribes, and be killed, and be raised again the third day" (Matt. 16:21).

The one whom Peter loved and honored to be subjected to an ignominious death—it shall not be! All this was foreign and unacceptable to Simon Peter. Peter's selfish restraint of his Lord, the ugly sentiment reminiscent of the Evil One's own subtle and unholy temptation in the wilderness, met stern rebuke from the Master, who further described for the Twelve His exacting terms of true discipleship.

---

[1]Quintin Hogg, *The Story of Peter* (1900), p. 102.

Christ then startles them: "Verily I say unto you, There be some standing here, which shall not taste of death, till they see the Son of man coming in his kingdom" (v. 28). There can be no doubt that the key to the proper understanding of this perplexing verse is to be found in the verses that immediately follow in Matthew 17:1-6. "Many have read this last verse of chapter sixteen," notes English,

> and have closed the book, wondering as to the meaning of it. It has been said that His coming refers to the destruction of Jerusalem; that may be so, in part.[2] It is said that in the preaching of the Gospel and the power of the resurrection life His claims were substantiated; there is truth in that belief. But the clearest and truest interpretation is surely found in the first five verses of chapter seventeen.[3]

The disciples ponder the meaning too: "Christ says He will suffer and die at Jerusalem, yet He continues to speak of His 'coming kingdom'? And some of us will be favored as being privy to the sight of the Son of man coming in His kingdom? The kingdom is set aside for the cross, yet that same glorious kingdom to be witnessed by a select few? How can this be and what does it all mean?"

Up the mountain with Peter, James, and John

During the last two and a half years of companionship with Christ, there arose, no doubt, within Peter's mind a gradual sense that he would figure significantly in a future messianic kingdom, sharing in its attendant glory. Peter had even echoed the Tempter's manner and method when he passionately strove with Jesus, reasoning that He

---

[2]Broadus holds this view, explaining: "The most reasonable explanation, especially when we compare ch. 24, is to understand a reference to the destruction of Jerusalem. This providentially lifted the Messianic reign to a new stage. It put an end to the sacrifices and the whole temple ritual, and thus taught the Jewish Christians that these need be no longer observed, and to a great extent stopped the mouths of the Judaizers who gave Paul so much trouble. The withdrawal of Christians from Jerusalem before its destruction occasioned an alienation between them and the Jewish people at large. In general, the destruction of Jerusalem made Christianity stand out as no longer even in appearance a mere phase or mode of Judaism, but an independent and universal religion." John A. Broadus, *Commentary on the Gospel of Matthew* (1886), p. 368. What Broadus says is relevant as it relates to the state of Judaism and Christianity following the destruction of Jerusalem in A.D. 70. But the primary application seems to me to be the obvious connection Christ sought to make between His statement of 16:28 and His microcosm of the future kingdom displayed for the inner circle to see on the Mount of Transfiguration. Christ said some of His disciples would see "the Son of man coming in His kingdom."

[3]E. Schuyler English, *Studies in the Gospel According to Matthew* (1935), p. 117.

could have all that He sought, this without the suffering and death: that He could gain the crown without the cross.[4] It becomes necessary, therefore, for the Lord Jesus to take His inner circle of three—Peter, James, and John—to a sanctuary on the mount[5] that they might witness a revelation filled with kingdom significance. "And after six days[6] Jesus taketh Peter, James, and John his brother, and bringeth them up into an high mountain apart, and was transfigured[7] before them: and his face did shine as the sun, and his raiment was white as the light" (Matt. 17:1-2).

With the evening shadows now falling over Caesarea Philippi, four men climb the higher ridges of Mount Hermon, looking back from time to time to view the ever-widening scene below them that showed their lakeside homes in the distance. And then Christ, as He was so often prone to do, seems to have gone on to one side of the narrow pathway to pray. Peter and his two friends, wrapping their heads in their stripped abbas, and wearied out with their afternoon climb, lie down to sleep.[8] How long the trio sleeps, we are not told. They are startled out of their sleep to find the figure of the lowly carpenter of Nazareth shining in the midnight hour.

---

[4]First the suffering, then the glory, the Cross before the crown, is a dominant theme in Peter's First Epistle, which we shall examine in more detail later when discussing his writings.

[5]The mount on which the Lord was transfigured is simply called "an high mountain apart" (Matt. 17:1). Mount Tabor has been named traditionally as the site of the Transfiguration, but since the Lord and His disciples were already at Caesarea Philippi, it is more probable that the mount was somewhere in the region of Mount Hermon. Also, there is evidence that a fortified town named Iturburion occupied Mount Tabor during the time of Christ, making it unlikely as the site for the Transfiguration. *UBD*, p. 1067. Mount Tabor would have been the last place where Christ would have found the solitude He desired.

[6]Though Mark also says after six days (9:2), Luke says, "about an eight days after" (9:28). Mark and Matthew give the intervening days only while Luke includes the days on each end of the period.

[7]From Gk. *metamorphoo* ("transform," or "change in form"). The English word "metamorphosis" is a transliteration of the Greek word. The word suggests "a change of inmost nature that may be outwardly visible." *EBC* vol. 8, p. 385. For this brief moment, Christ made outwardly visible His inward glory. It is in this manner that believers are to be "transformed" (same word, Rom. 12:2; also "changed" in II Cor. 3:18), that is, to allow the outside world to see our inner glory made possible by the indwelling Christ. What we are on the inside should show on the outside. In a counterfeit tactic of Satan and his host, they also are "transformed" (II Cor. 11:14), but here a different word is translated "transformed," *metaskematidzo*, meaning "to change the figure of, to assume the appearance of anyone." Satan and his demons display outward righteousness and light, but inwardly they are wholly evil. What they are on the outside is *not* their essential inner nature.

[8]Hogg, pp. 105-7.

Transfigured

So brilliant is the Lord's glorious transformation that His face and clothing far outshine anything the disciples have ever seen. Relating perhaps Peter's own description of the scene, Mark tells us that no fuller[9] could have bleached the Lord's clothes as white as they shone.[10] By His side and talking to Him appear Moses,[11] the great lawgiver and hero of the Exodus, and Elijah, the fiery prophet and preacher of righteousness to Israel. Why Moses and Elijah? Fereday's explanation of their appearance reflects the common notion: "These are representative characters, speaking to us of the entire company of the glorified saints, many of whom will experience resurrection at the Lord's return, others being changed in a moment, and caught up to meet Him in the air" (I Thess. 4:16-17).[12]

More importantly, what occupies the minds and hearts of these ancient holy men as they commune with the transfigured Lord? Luke informs us that their earnest interest centers on Christ's "decease"[13] (9:31) at Jerusalem. That which repulsed Peter and had so startled the others—His "exodus" from this life to bring us to eternal life—was the only topic on the lips of heaven's saints. This is a strong lesson for Peter. What he saw to be shameful and vile, so far from his own conceptions of Christ, is indeed the conversation of heaven's occupants. His would be an "exodus" from bondage into liberty, "an open door set before suffering humanity which none could shut."[14] They speak for Christ's benefit, no doubt, that He might be supported in view of the sufferings and death to which His mind now focused. Moses of that lesser exodus is talking with Christ of that greater deliverance

---

[9]*Gk., gnapheus*, from *knaptoo*, "to tease cloth, a cloth dresser."

[10]Mark 9:3-4. Luke says Christ's facial features were "altered" and His garments were "white and glistering" (9:29).

[11]"Any question as to whether Moses appeared in a resurrection body lies beyond our knowledge and is idle." John A. Broadus, *Commentary on the Gospel of Matthew* (1886), p. 371. Thomas observes that only now, at the Transfiguration, was Moses' prayer to enter Canaan granted (see Exod. 33:17-23; Deut. 34:1-4) and his request to see God's glory fully answered (cf. "his face," Matt. 17:2, with "Thou canst not see my face," Exod. 33:20; also II Cor. 4:6.) W. H. Griffith Thomas, *Outline Studies in the Gospel of Matthew* (1961), p. 257.

[12]W. W. Fereday, *Simon Peter* (n.d.), p. 52.

[13]*Gk., exodus*. From this point in time in northern Palestine until He finally arrives in Jerusalem at the beginning of His passion week, the cross will occupy the Lord's mind. The space devoted in the Gospels to the last week of Christ's life as compared to the preceding three years of ministry illustrates how the Gospel writers also came to see Christ's suffering and death as paramount and central to their presentation of Christ.

[14]Hogg, p. 108.

from sin. "For Moses, the representative of the law, and the representative of the prophets, Elijah, witnessed to Him who had fulfilled both the law and the prophets. Their work was finished. The stars which had illumined the old night were lost in the blaze of this risen Sun."[15]

One short week earlier,[16] Jesus had promised that there were some of the disciples who would not taste of death until they should see Him coming in His kingdom. Then for an entire week they remained in the northern regions, the Lord continuing with them and allowing them to ponder the significance of His promise. Could it still be possible that in their lifetime Christ would finally set up His promised messianic kingdom? And some of them would be privileged to partake in it! There is great prophetic significance in the Lord's promise. His kingdom has not yet been established and the Twelve are now long dead. How could the Lord's promise, therefore, be fulfilled to these men? Through His marvelous transfiguration, the Lord shows in microcosm all the elements of His glorious kingdom. Peter, James, and John are privileged to witness it on the mount. In this picture of divine glory, we, like these three disciples, are enabled to see that the cross was not the end but only the means toward the end; for that was to be the glorious consummation of everything our Lord had come to perform.[17]

Observe from this transfiguration scene five foreshadowings of His kingdom, when the Lord comes in power to reign on earth: (1) The *Lord Jesus* appears in the body of His glory. He will be the King of kings and Lord of lords. (2) Moses, who died in faith, typifies all those whom Christ will bring with Him (Jude 14; Rev. 19:11-16) who also have *died in faith*. (3) Elijah ("Elias," Matt. 17:3), who was caught up into heaven in a whirlwind (II Kings 2:11), is there typifying all those whom Christ will bring with Him who never died because they will have been *raptured* (I Thess. 4:13-17). (4) Peter, James, and John, present at this scene, represent the *remnant* of Israel who shall see Him coming in power (Rev. 1:7). (5) The multitude at the foot of the mountain (Matt. 17:14) typify the *nations on the earth* when the kingdom is established.

In later years, Peter would write:

For we have not followed cunningly devised fables, when we made known unto you the power and coming of our Lord Jesus Christ, but were *eyewitnesses of his majesty*. For he received

---

[15] J. R. MacDuff, *The Footsteps of St. Peter* (1887), p. 157.
[16] Matt. 16:28.
[17] Thomas, p. 258.

from God the Father honour and glory, when there came such a voice to him from the excellent glory, This is my beloved Son, in whom I am well pleased. And this voice which came from heaven we heard, when we were with him in the holy mount (II Pet. 1:16-18).

For centuries the OT prophets had spoken of the coming of the Lord Jesus Christ in power and glory. Peter is saying, "We were eye-witnesses of the Lord's promise of His power and glory. We heard the voice from heaven giving approval to the one chosen of the Father." Surely this is what the Lord Jesus meant—that these three, including Peter—would not die until they should see this preview of the Son of man coming in His kingdom.[18]

Let's build three tents!

In the midst of this shining transfiguration, Peter does not shine at all, for once again he thrusts himself forward into the scene. While heaven's messengers converse with Jesus, Peter interrupts: "Lord, it is good for us to be here: if thou wilt, let us make here three taberna-cles; one for thee, and one for Moses, and one for Elias" (Matt. 17:4). He was hoping, no doubt, to prolong the experience. Mark adds, again possibly from Peter's recollection, that Peter did not know what to say, for they were all afraid.[19] How we are always drawn to Peter! He is the one, not knowing what to say, but sensing that something—any-thing to relieve the tension—must be uttered. "All of Peter's faults," Whyte observes, "lay in the heat of his heart. He was too-hot hearted, too impulsive, too enthusiastic. His hot heart was always in his mouth, and he spoke it all out many a time when he should have held his peace."[20] So he blurts, "Lord, it's good to be here. Let's build three tents for Moses, for Elijah, and for You, right here on the mountain-top!" Can we blame Peter that such a Shekinah glory vision would cause him to forget everything else except his own rapture? Can we not enter into his desires to remain on the mountaintop, there with the Lord, and never to move again! He does not know, of course, of the lunatic child at the foot of the mountain, or of the father's anguish at his son's predicament, or of the other disciples' impotence. Peter will learn he must sacrifice the glory of the mountain for the healing required at the bottom of the hill.

---

[18]English, pp. 117-18.

[19]Mark 9:6.

[20]Alexander Whyte, *Bible Characters* 4th se. (n.d.), p. 51.

In his failure to understand the import of the unfolding drama, Peter relegates the Lord to the human level of the ancients. But in a rebuke directed to Peter once again, this time for equating Him with the others—Moses, of the Law; Elijah, of the Prophets—the Father Himself speaks from the overshadowing cloud. "This is my beloved Son, in whom I am well pleased; hear ye him" (v. 5). He who is the fulfillment of the Law and the Prophets is now the one to be heard, the final and full revelation of the Father in heaven. God emphatically says, "Hear Him." There is only one voice to listen to now and that is the voice of His beloved Son. "And when the disciples heard it, they fell on their face, and were sore afraid. And Jesus came and touched them, and said, Arise, and be not afraid. And when they had lifted up their eyes, they saw no man, save Jesus only" (vv. 6-8). Why should the trio be afraid? The Father's answer to their wonder and fear, to focus on His beloved Son, is the Father's answer to Peter's remonstrance to the cross: Jesus only. "You shall not be crucified," Peter boldly asserted to His Lord and Master. "You shall win the crown without the cross." The Father's answer is to show Peter two of the honored of Israel—Moses and Elijah—whose only concern is to talk of that shame as a second exodus and of Christ's cross as the coming glory of the world. And then to hide all else but Christ. To see Him alone in His glory. Moses may go and Elijah may go too, but if we have Jesus, we have everything our heart may desire. "We will reach the full measure of our Christian growth when we see Him, and Him alone."[21]

Powerless disciples

"And as they came down from the mountain, Jesus charged them, saying, Tell the vision to no man, until the Son of man be risen again from the dead" (v. 9). Earlier Jesus had asked His disciples not to reveal that He is the Christ. Here the Lord Jesus forbids them to reveal anything of the mountain vision. The time has not yet arrived for the full revelation of the Messiah's glory as they saw it on the Mount of Transfiguration. This is another manifestation of the Lord's deliberate action to pronounce judicial blindness on those who had heard the gospel of the kingdom and had rejected it. On a later occasion, the Lord will once again speak of the Jews' rejection of the light: "Yet a little while is the light with you. Walk while ye have the light, lest darkness come upon you, . . . While ye have light, believe in the light, that ye may be the children of light" (John 12:35-36). He has done

---

[21]English, p. 119.

many miracles in their presence, yet they refuse to believe on Him. Therefore, the judicial blindness prophesied by Isaiah would be fulfilled: "Lord, who hath believed our report? . . . Therefore they could not believe, because that Esaias said again, He hath blinded their eyes, and hardened their heart; that they should not see with their eyes, nor understand with their heart, and be converted, and I should heal them" (vv. 38-40).

The Lord's injunction to remain silent about the mountain experience prompts a question from the disciples. "Why then say the scribes that Elias must first come?" (Matt. 17:10). They had seen Elijah with their own eyes on the mount, but only for a moment, and then the cloud hid him from their view. Peter and the others know from the OT prophets that Elijah should be the forerunner of the Messiah.[22] Well, he has finally come, but why so secret and so brief an appearance? Why did Elijah not accompany them down the mountain? Where is he? Jesus responds, confirming the teaching that Elijah was indeed to come and "restore all things," that is, Jewish restoration to divine favor and national glory.[23] "But I say unto you, That Elias is come already, and they knew him not, but have done unto him whatsoever they listed. Likewise shall also the Son of man suffer of them" (v. 12). Christ explains that the prophecy had been fulfilled in the appearance of the Baptist.[24] But, just as the Jewish people did not know the Baptist in his character as the forerunner of the Messiah, and allowed him to die, so the Son of man would also suffer at their hands. Matthew comments: "Then the disciples understood that he spake unto them of John the Baptist."[25]

The contrast between mountain and valley experiences here are solemn and striking. Coming down from the site of the transfiguration, the four find that Satan has been busy at work during the Lord's ab-

---

[22]Mal. 3:1; 4:5-6.

[23]In his sermon in Acts 3, Peter says that Christ will not return in glory until all the promises *that the prophets have made*, by the command of God, about Israel's being *restored*, have come to pass, including the return of Israel to their land (Deut. 30:1-5).

[24]See also Matt. 11:13-14.

[25]There seems to be no doubt that the prophecy in Malachi, like many other OT passages, has a twofold interpretation—the secondary and symbolic meaning referred to John the Baptist at Christ's first coming; and then the primary fulfillment would be in Elijah's appearing literally before Christ's second coming. There is no contradiction with the Baptist's words in John 1:21, where he rightly denied being the *literal* Elijah, while the Lord here teaches that the Baptist was *symbolically* the Elijah of prophecy. "This entire section, suggesting Scripture to be fulfilled in a wider sense than appears on the surface, shows how often God's Word is found to be much deeper and fuller in meaning than its mere words seem to imply; and it is therefore wise to follow the disciples' example and ask Divine guidance in its interpretation." Thomas, p. 259.

sence. "And when they were come to the multitude, there came to him a certain man, kneeling down to him, and saying, Lord, have mercy on my son: for he is lunatick, and sore vexed: for ofttimes he falleth into the fire, and oft into the water. And I brought him to thy disciples, and they could not cure him" (vv. 14-16).[26] During Christ's absence, the nine disciples who remained at the foot of the mountain were surrounded by a crowd, probably mocking them because they could not heal an epileptic boy. Jesus' rebuke brings immediate cure to the lad (v. 18), but the disciples express great concern. "Why could not we cast him out?" (v. 19). Once more the Lord reminds them of the power of prayer, that this kind of spiritual deliverance is empowered only through "prayer and fasting" (v. 21), and calls His powerless disciples "faithless" and a "perverse generation." Prayer is communion with God, claiming His promises. Fasting is self-denial, the death of the flesh. "Prayer is that by which we *attach* ourselves to God and things of the spiritual world; fasting is that by which we *detach* ourselves from things of time and sense, whether it be from food or pleasure, or lawful ambition and ordinary occupation."[27] Only by unbroken fellowship with the Master and a life entirely yielded to Him may God's promises of the impossible becoming possible be ours.

Implications for Discipleship

1. *Avoid favoritism while providing special training for a select few.* There are times when a Christian makes a conscious decision to include a small, select number in special discipleship training. It was thus with the Lord and His inner circle of Peter, James, and John. Why did He take just the three of them on this occasion? Perhaps because they were the most fit and advanced in their apprehension of spiritual matters. The other nine certainly displayed a lack of faith and power at the foot of the mountain when the man brought his epileptic son to them for healing. Christian leaders must be careful not to show undue favoritism in selecting disciples for special assignment, but such selection can be made properly,

---

[26]English sees great dispensational teaching in this incident that follows Christ's transfiguration. "This experience is typical of the Lord's return in glory. Satan has been very active during the Lord's bodily absence. When He returns then, He will find multitudes waiting for Him, but He will find many possessed of Satan's handiwork. The remnant, typified by the disciples, will be preaching the Gospel of the Kingdom, with power to heal, but they will be helpless because of unbelief. Only the Lord Himself can cast out the devil from this world, and upon His coming again He shall do so." English, pp. 120-21.

[27]Thomas, p. 260.

causing little or no resentment. Coleman writes again on this principle of selectivity:

> Within the select apostolic group, Peter, James and John seemed to enjoy a more special relationship to the Master than did the other nine. . . . So noticeable is the preference given to these three that had it not been for the incarnation of selflessness in the Person of Christ, it could well have precipitated feelings of resentment on the part of the other apostles. The fact that there is no record of the disciples complaining about the pre-eminence of the three, is proof that where preference is shown in the right spirit and for the right reason offence need not rise.[28]

The apostle Paul instructed Timothy to find and teach "faithful men,"[29] indicative of the need for selectivity when it comes to certain types of training, especially leadership training.

2. *This transformation of the Lord reminds us that believers are also to be changed into His image.* Our basic, all-consuming goal for converts is to bring them into conformity to the image of Christ,[30] to see them "transformed." Thomas correlates the ministry of the Trinity with the word "transformed" in the NT. (1) Believers are to be transformed by the renewal of their minds (Rom. 12:2), or our right relation to the will of the Father. (2) Believers are to be transformed by the sight of divine glory (II Cor. 3:18), or our relation to the Holy Spirit. (3) Believers are transformed through prayer (Luke 9:28-29). This, of course, is in relation to the Son of God, for we are told by Luke that it was "as he prayed" that our Lord's "countenance was altered" or made different.[31]

3. *Spiritual work demands spiritual resources.* The disciples left at the foot of the mountain found themselves powerless

---

[28]Robert E. Coleman, *The Master Plan of Evangelism* (1964), p. 26.
[29]II Tim. 2:2.
[30]II Cor. 3:18.
[31]Thomas, p. 261.

to heal the afflicted child. Jesus proclaimed that the situation demanded "prayer and fasting" to bring about relief. Fervent, persistent prayer, accompanied by fasting, that is, disregard for creature comforts or other distractions, brings to the believer spiritual power, constant blessing, and abiding fellowship with God.

> It is not too much to say that today, face to face with huge needs and complexities of modern life, there are many demons the Christian Church has failed to cast out, and this failure, too, is unwarranted when provision for success has been made, is so simple, and has been utilized so often in past years by God's faithful servants.[32]

---

[32]Thomas, p. 260.

FURTHER TRAINING FROM THE MASTER

Jesus has revealed to His disciples His impending death at the hands of the religious elite at Jerusalem, supplementing this sad announcement with the manifestation of His glory on the Mount of Transfiguration. In the interim before His crucifixion, Jesus teaches Peter and the others further lessons on humility, forgiveness, and judgment, showing them that true discipleship has its own reward.

LESSONS ON HUMILITY
AND FORGIVENESS

What thinkest thou, Simon? (Matt. 17:25).

> *Teach me Thy will, O Lord,*
> *Teach me Thy way;*
> *Teach me to know Thy word,*
> *Teach me to pray.*
> *Whate'er seems best to Thee,*
> *That be my earnest plea;*
> *So that Thou drawest me*
> *Closer each day.*
>
> *—Katherine A. Grimes*

Setting: Galilee, late summer or early autumn, A.D. 32
Scripture: Matt. 17:24–18:35

By His glorious transfiguration on the mount, the Lord answered Peter's confusion about His messianic kingdom. Though Christ will suffer at the hands of His enemies at Jerusalem and be killed, His future kingdom surely will be established. His resurrection will guarantee it. Christ has already taught them the principle—first the suffering, then the glory. Refusing Peter's rash desire to set up camp on the mountaintop, the Lord descends to further work and training in the valley. He has brought to them new insights of His kingdom; now they return to the "routine of daily living"[1] in the valley below.

The time is late summer or early fall, a full six months before the Lord's final Passover in Jerusalem. Setting His face southward from Caesarea Philippi, where He has been with His disciples for His final "withdrawal," Christ returns to Galilee. His discipleship training from this point to the climax of His sacrifice on the cross will contain two strands: He will fortify His followers against personal disappointment about the cross, and He will continue to develop in them the qualities they will need as witnesses for Him after His ascension. To that end, after repeating to His disciples the seriousness of His mission at Jerusalem, He introduces "training in temper"[2] as Bruce puts it, that is, necessary lessons on humility and forgiveness—qualities the Lord shows are indispensable for kingdom greatness. For a second time, the Lord announces the anticipated crisis in Jerusalem. "And while

---

[1]W. H. Griffith Thomas, *The Apostle Peter* (1956), p. 39.
[2]A. B. Bruce, *The Training of the Twelve* (n.d.), p. 199.

they abode in Galilee, Jesus said unto them, The Son of man shall be betrayed into the hands of men: and they shall kill him, and the third day he shall be raised again. And they were exceeding sorry" (Matt. 17:22-23). One more winter, followed by the spring of the new year, and then the Shepherd will be smitten, the sheep will scatter, and He who at one time would have been acclaimed king will be finally rejected and put to death.

The Lord's forewarnings of the impending crisis slide from Peter's consciousness, his ears still dull to the Lord's sure promise that He will rise again. Though he is beginning to absorb the impact of Jesus' announced death, Peter still has no clue of His glorious resurrection. With sorrow eclipsing his heart, his attitude, as always, mirrors that of all the other disciples. Their conception of the Messiah has from the beginning been so completely different from the Lord's revelations that they utterly fail to grasp the true nature of the kingdom despite the Lord's repeated teachings. So as they follow Jesus toward Capernaum in Galilee, they argue among themselves as to who will be the greatest among them in any future kingdom. Even if they believed the Lord's prediction that dangerously bleak times, perhaps even disaster, lay ahead of them at Jerusalem, they must have harbored thoughts that surely all those dark days must be only temporary until Christ the King ushers in His kingdom! And when it comes, the advantage will be all theirs as those most intimate with Christ, each vying with the others to occupy the most exalted seats!

The tax man cometh

The last time we saw Peter at Capernaum, he stood with the Lord Jesus at the door of the synagogue and watched the crowds slowly desert Christ. His enigmatic message on the bread of life had winnowed the crowd to the faithful few. As the Twelve make their way toward Peter's house,[3] no crowds surround Jesus. Their enthusiasm for Him is gone, content as they are now to offer only hostile taunts and sneers. "The ebb-tide was running fast now, a terrible ebb-tide indeed, to end in a sea of blood."[4] He may have been a revered prophet at one time, even a hero, but He is now a rejected outcast.

Before the travel-weary band of disciples reaches Peter's house, tax gatherers for the temple draw Peter aside, abruptly ending the disciples' arguments over kingdom prominence. "Doesn't your Master

---

[3]The Scriptures say simply "the house" (Matt. 17:25; Mark 9:33), but since they were in Capernaum, we may reasonably conclude that it was Peter's house, Jesus' quarters when residing in the city.

[4]Quintin Hogg, *The Story of Peter* (1900), p. 115-16.

pay tribute?" they want to know. Now that they have become aware of Christ's increasingly conspicuous teaching and healing work, the tax gatherers may have been uncertain about how to approach Him with their concern. So they allow the Lord Jesus to continue past them, not challenging Him on the matter, and seek out Peter, whom they draw aside from the others. They put the question, not at all an insignificant one, to Peter directly, for it is "full of the profoundest teaching,"[5] allowing as it does the Lord to complete the making of His disciple, Peter the rock.

> *And lessons hard, well mastered, will make plain*
> *The faithful Teacher planning all the way.*[6]
>
> *—Unknown*

The Lord clearly has in mind special instruction for His foundation apostle, teaching Peter a lesson that all disciples must learn: in ourselves we lack the essential kingdom quality of humility and possess as sons of Adam a powerfully jealous spirit of revenge that must yield to His control. The Lord Jesus, who humbly submitted to the Father's will, is about to teach His own disciple to be of the same mind.

This may seem an odd moment for a lesson on humility from the Master. What does the paying of the temple tax have to do with humility? The Lord is about to demonstrate its necessity to Peter. This temple tax[7] was levied on every male Jew between the ages of twenty and fifty to support the temple and its services. The tax was Jewish, not Roman; religious, not civil. It had nothing to do with "tribute to Caesar" nor any other civil authority. It was "a theocratic payment, due to the temple and the temple's God."[8] Beginning in the time of Moses when he numbered the men who came out of Egypt, every male over twenty years old was directed to give a small sum for the support of the tabernacle. Rich and poor gave the same amount—a half shekel—as "a ransom for his soul unto the Lord."[9] Their offering reminded them that they owed their lives to God because He had ransomed them out of Egypt. Much later in Israel's history, when King Josiah repaired the temple, he appealed for special contributions on the basis of this tax "according to the commandment of Moses the servant of the Lord" (II Chron. 24:6). After the Captivity, Nehemiah

---

[5]Richard C. Trench, *Notes on the Miracles of Our Lord* (1953), p. 404.

[6]Anonymous, "In Everything," *Rhyme & Reason* (1981), p. 171.

[7]"double drachma," Gk. *didrachon.*

[8]Trench, p. 404.

[9]Exod. 30:11-16.

made it voluntary.[10] By the time of Christ, the shekel levy was required by custom, if not by law. No devout Jew would dismiss this obligation to the temple as unimportant.

What motivated the tax gatherers to ask Peter if the Lord paid the temple tax? Though no reason is given by the inquirers, implicit in their concern could be guarded criticism of the Lord because of His popularity as a teacher. The normal time for paying the annual tax was in the spring,[11] but it is now late summer or early autumn. Jesus has been long gone from Capernaum, and because of His absence, the tax men may have supposed that He is now delinquent in His obligation, though the Jewish rabbis were known to claim such exemption as teachers.[12] Did Jesus make the same claim? Perhaps the growing hostility toward Christ among the Jewish leaders motivated the tax gatherers to try to discredit Him in any way they could. Or it may even be that if He indeed has paid the assessment, they seek to entangle Him in His words. If, for example, Jesus admits that He paid the temple tax, how could He also claim to be "greater than the temple" (Matt. 12:6)?

Whatever their motivation—guarded concern or outright belligerence—they speak directly to Peter, whom they must have had reason to think would in some measure hold Jesus accountable for doing the right thing. Asking Peter would in their minds, I suppose, be the closest thing to asking the Lord Himself. In his hasty "Yes," Peter shows his natural zeal for the Lord's honor. His motive is good; his own grasp of the entire situation, especially from the Lord's perception, is shaky. "Of course He pays the temple tax," Peter asserts and to his way of thinking nothing more needs to be said. Peter cannot conceive of the Lord being any less loyal to the temple or any less honorable than the others. The street scene affords, nevertheless, a teachable moment for Peter by the Lord. "And when he was come into the house, Jesus prevented[13] him, saying, What thinkest thou, Simon? of whom do the kings of the earth take custom[14] or tribute?[15] of their own children, or of strangers? Peter saith unto him, Of strangers. Jesus saith unto him, Then are the children free" (Matt. 17:25-26).

The Lord approaches Peter directly to ask him about his encounter with the tax men, challenging him to ponder the meaning of the inci-

---

[10]Neh. 10:32-33.

[11]John A. Broadus, *Commentary on the Gospel of Matthew* (1886), p. 379.

[12]Thomas, p. 40.

[13]"anticipated him, saying. . . ." Broadus, p. 379.

[14]Or "toll," Gk. *telos*, a general word for tax.

[15]Gk. *kensos*, properly an "enrollment," a registration for the purpose of taxation.

dent through an analogy of kings, taxes, and the royal family. "What do you think about this, Peter? From whom do kings receive taxes— their own royal family? Or from all the other subjects in their kingdom?"[16] Peter knows, of course, that no child of a king pays tax or tribute to his royal father. "Then the children are free from taxes, aren't they, Peter?" concludes the Lord. We can marvel at the depth of meaning in the Lord's analogy, for throughout this exchange the Lord underscores His exalted position as a royal Son. For Peter to give the temple tax, since it is given to God, is in reality giving the tax *to Christ,* who is in the Father. The taxes, or contributions, therefore, are not to be received *from Christ,* since they are in the final analysis all offered to Him. Therefore, as the royal Son, Christ should not be expected to pay the tax. But "lest we should offend them," Jesus explains, Peter is to pay the obligation for himself and for the Lord.

The lesson put to Peter is this: The Lord Jesus will not put a needless stumbling block before His detractors, nor will He give them any occasion for rejecting His claims. The people would seize on an attitude such as that and demand that since He refused to perform a recognized duty of every Israelite, He cannot possibly be the Messiah.[17] By demonstrating that His own humility prevents Him from taking offense either at the accusers' question or Peter's hasty answer, the Lord refuses to allow His good to be evil spoken of.[18] "Our Lord's disposition to forego a privilege to which He was justly entitled, rather than that men should have an excuse for misapprehending him . . . stands before us all as a part of the example of Christ."[19] His conduct toward the tax gatherers provides a concrete example of Christlike humility, a quality that Peter can now see for himself and emulate.

A strange command follows: "Go thou to the sea, and cast an hook, and take up the fish that first cometh up; and when thou hast opened his mouth, thou shalt find a piece of money: that take, and give unto them for me and thee" (v. 27). In submitting to the temple tax, the Lord places Himself under the same obligation as Peter—"for me and thee," He instructs. The original purpose of this offering under Moses was that of a substitution, gratitude for redemption from

---

[16]"Children . . . strangers" is not a reference to the Jews as "sons" and the Gentiles as "strangers." Peter shows that he understood the Lord's analogy between royal princes and those outside the royal family. There is, nonetheless, in the Lord's pronouncement His claim of a unique relation to the Father as compared to the other Jews. He is God's Son; they are God's subjects.

[17]Broadus, p. 380.

[18]Rom. 14:16.

[19]Broadus, p. 380, adding also the example of Paul in I Cor. 9.

Egypt. With His commendation to Peter to pay the tax, the Lord affirms that original purpose of substitution. The miracle about to unfold through Peter's lone fishing venture is not to satisfy a personal need of the Lord, for Jesus never performed a miracle solely for His personal benefit. The obligation was to the temple and the God of the temple. To obtain the money through these extraordinary means will serve to fortify His claims as the Messiah.[20]

We are left to our imaginations. Peter goes to the nearby lake, so well known to him as the scene of his dragnet fishing exploits, casts in his hook, and in the mouth of the first fish that grabs it, finds, according to the Lord's word, the money[21] needed. Christ does not merely know of the fish and the money. In the "mysterious potency of his will which ran through all nature,"[22] Christ drew the fish to that spot, at that moment, and ordained that it should swallow Peter's hook. Peter retrieves the coin for the intended purpose. There is no reason to say that Christ created the coin for this occasion. Though He restored sight to the blind and strength to the crippled, Christ did not create new eyes or legs. He multiplied the bread and fish in the wilderness, but He made no new bread. At Cana He changed water to wine, not wine of nothing. He created no new Lazarus when He brought the dead man forth from his grave. In His miracles, Christ brought together that which already existed, never passing over into the region of "absolute creation."[23]

We must stand amazed at this simple but profound gesture of humility from the Lord Jesus. The King brings Himself to the place of submission that He might not cause others to stumble. He places Himself in fellowship with Peter, saying, "Peter, you must pay the shekel, but I will pay it with you. You must take this place of submission; I will take it side by side with you."[24] In the common problems of life—tax time—the Lord is with His disciple, just as He was with him in the glory on the mount, where He manifested His kingliness. The relevance of this episode to Peter's training becomes clear as the narrative further unfolds. Jesus has just been declared God's unique Son by the voice out of the cloud (v. 5). His glory is veiled, however,

---

[20]Broadus, p. 380.

[21]Gk. *stater*, "a certain coin." Unger suggests that the coin in this instance was a silver *tetradrachm*, of the same weight as the Hebrew shekel. *UBD*, p. 726. Where the AV has "a piece of money," the RV and the ASB thus render *stater* as "shekel."

[22]Trench, p. 417.

[23]Trench, p. 418. He does not speculate how the coin found its way into the fish's mouth, but does, however, quote Herodotus, Eisenmenger, and Augustine, who relate various traditions about lost items being found in fish.

[24]G. Campbell Morgan, *The Gospel According to Matthew* (1929), p. 227.

as He moves toward betrayal and death, thus establishing a pattern of humility for His followers. Like so many of Jesus' actions at this turning point in His ministry, the full significance of His words and deeds would not be grasped by Peter until after the Resurrection.[25]

Kingdom greatness

Mark, in his Gospel, reminds us of the earlier argument among the disciples about their place in Christ's kingdom. In the light of the Lord's recent revelations about the cross, their conduct is sad and perplexing. After they all enter the house, the Lord approaches them: "What was it that ye disputed among yourselves by the way?" (Mark 9:33). What indeed had they talked about? Christ had only recently confided to them the affliction and anguish that awaited Him at Jerusalem. But when they slipped aside to commune among themselves, they did not seek to lighten the Lord's obvious burden of heart or to share His coming sorrow but only to squabble over their own personal stake in Messiah's kingdom. How slow of heart to learn their lessons! Christ has just taught them about the cross. He has used the temple tax and its attendant miracle as a powerful object lesson on humble submission, but they persist in arguing over kingdom prominence.[26] It is perhaps while Peter is gone to find the shekel that the disciples approach Jesus and in some effort to redeem themselves, ask, "Who is the greatest in the kingdom of heaven?" (Matt. 18:1).

The Lord's answer takes the form of another object lesson. "And Jesus called a little child unto him, and set him in the midst of them, and said, Verily I say unto you, Except ye be converted, and become as little children, ye shall not enter into the kingdom of heaven. Whosoever therefore shall humble himself as this little child, the same is greatest in the kingdom of heaven" (vv. 2-4). Since they were probably in Peter's house, the child could have been Peter's child.[27]

---

[25]*EBC* vol. 8, p. 395.

[26]In parallel accounts, Luke simply speaks of Jesus "perceiving the thought of their heart" (Luke 9:47). Mark provides the insight that even while they approached the house, they had "disputed among themselves" about who should be greatest (Mark 9:33-34) and when Jesus asked them about it, they remained silent. Matthew records for us the question from the disciples. The Synoptics are not in conflict, but rather complementary here. Broadus combines the thoughts: "It is not difficult to suppose that (the disciples) came intending to ask him the question, but hesitated; that perceiving their thought (Luke) he inquired, and they were at first silent (Mark), but at length spoke (Matt.)," p. 381.

[27]A late tradition holds that this child was Ignatius, bishop of Antioch, who was martyred about A.D. 115, but we know no authority for this fanciful conjecture.

Through their misplaced enthusiasm and dreaming, they were disputing who should be the highest official in Christ's coming kingdom. The Lord reminds them that they should see, first of all, that they make certain their own entrance into that kingdom. Humility, a natural and prominent characteristic of a child, is the supreme quality for kingdom greatness, a quality the disciples have just shown that they still lack. They must turn from their worldly ambitions and carnal jealousies and become childlike. "Humility is thus presented as the principal thing in a child to be imitated by Messiah's subjects."[28]

The child is held up as an ideal, not of innocence, or purity, or faith, but of "humility and unconcern for social status."[29] Jesus speaks of humility of mind, not childishness of thought. With such humility comes childlike trust. The kingdom is not gained through any personal merit nor by violent force. It is to the "little children" that God reveals His truth.[30] There follows the Lord's magnificent and moving sermon on the worth of the child.[31] Leaving it to their own hearts to answer the question raised, Jesus takes this little child in His arms and "from that innocent text"[32] preaches to them His child-sermon story of true greatness.

A million to one

Following His sublime proclamation on the worth of a child and the inevitable plight of one who would offend such a child, the Lord elaborates on the need for humility and forgiveness.[33] Having cautioned the disciples against offending the little ones, Jesus proceeds to tell them how they are to deal with "the brother" (v. 15) who offends, that is, when they themselves are offended by someone. In such situations, pride and a vindictive spirit often manifest themselves for they go together. Those filled with personal ambition are often quick to take

---

[28]Broadus, p. 382.

[29]*EBC* vol. 8, p. 397.

[30]Matt. 11:25.

[31]Matt. 18:3-14. In this remarkable paragraph, the Lord shows His estimation of a child's worth and why we should seek children's salvation and spiritual well-being. (1) Children can be converted, v. 3. (2) Humility, the essential quality for kingdom greatness, is already the possession of the child, v. 4. (3) To receive a little child in Christ's name is to receive Him, v. 5. (4) Little children can believe in Him, v. 6. (5) To cause a child to stumble merits severe punishment, vv. 6-9. (6) Children are not to be despised, for they are the subjects of heavenly concern, v. 10. (7) We should seek the child as the shepherd seeks the one lost sheep, vv. 11-14. (8) It is not God's will that any child should perish, v. 14.

[32]Hogg, p. 117.

[33]Matt. 18:15-20.

offense and slow to forgive.[34] So the Lord weaves the fabric of humility and forgiveness. Anticipating the formation of the church, the Lord Jesus bestows to these future leaders what He has already granted previously to Peter—the power to bind and loose, that is, to exercise leadership and discipline with the assembly of God's people. Their actions on earth will have heaven's approval. He then gives a most encouraging promise of His own spiritual presence to those who assemble in His name and seek the heavenly Father through prevailing prayer, themselves agreeing together in the objects of their desires.

All the while the Lord explains the nature of the future role of the apostles in His grand scheme of things. Those words—"thy brother"—must have lingered in Peter's thoughts, perhaps calling forth some long-forgotten grievance against another brother or friend. No sooner does the Lord end His brief discourse than Peter, seeking guidance no doubt in the practical application of the Lord's counsel concerning a "brother," asks, "Lord, how oft shall my brother sin against me, and I forgive him? till seven times?" (v. 21). Once more Peter confronts Jesus with a question. Nowhere do we see Peter's simplicity more clearly than in his questions to the Master. On an earlier occasion, Peter had asked, "Lord, speakest thou this parable unto us, or even to all?" (Luke 12:41). Later he will ask, after reminding the Lord that the disciples, unlike the rich young ruler, have forsaken all to follow Him, "What shall we have therefore?" (Matt. 19:27). "Tell us, when shall these things be? and what shall be the sign when all these things shall be fulfilled?" (Mark 13:4) Peter will ask, together with James, John, and Andrew, during the final week of the Lord's ministry before the cross. On other occasions, Peter interacts with the Lord, not with specific questions, but with obvious concern for enlightenment or help. All these add to the tapestry of his life that we weave in the making of the disciple.

Having returned from his fishing errand, Peter shows he has been paying attention to the Lord's words. He is earnest now in applying the Lord's prescription toward one who has erred against him, and he even offers to forgive the offender up to seven times! Jewish rabbis taught the people to bear injury three times and then to regard their duty to forgive as done. Thinking that seven is much more magnanimous than the Lord would ever expect from him, Peter stretches out his forgiveness "like a child standing on tiptoe to make himself as tall as his father, or climbing to the top of a hillock to get near the skies."[35]

---

[34]Thomas, p. 43.
[35]Bruce, p. 217.

But the Lord's standard is not three or seven but unlimited forgiveness. "Until seventy times seven,"[36] replies the Lord, not simply multiplying Peter's suggestion, but removing all practical limits to the repetitions of forgiveness that Peter may have contemplated as sufficient. As Peter was forgiven far more than he would ever forgive others, our forgiveness is to flow out from us continually as a reflection of God's mercy and grace toward us. To reinforce the lesson, Christ relates another story and in doing so opens Peter's eyes to a portrait of God's forgiveness as it really is. "Therefore is the kingdom of heaven likened unto a certain king, which would take account of his servants"[37] (Matt. 18:23). In reckoning with his servants, the king must deal with two very different attitudes toward forgiveness. One servant owed an enormous amount of money—ten thousand talents[38]—with no means to repay, but he begs the king's forgiveness, which is granted (vv. 24-27). That same servant, who has now been forgiven, immediately takes hold of a fellow servant and demands repayment for the paltry sum of one hundred pence.[39] What the second servant owes is not insignificant, but when compared to the ten thousand talents owed by the first servant, it is a million to one! The contrast is startling and the attitude of the forgiven servant is appalling.

Neither servant had the means to pay his debt. Each man begged for more time so that he could pay the entire sum. But the first servant did not need to repay the debt, for his master forgave him. This forgiven servant, promptly forgetting the mercy he had just been shown, demands payment in full from his fellow servant or he will extract from him the utmost that the letter of the law demands. The one who has been forgiven so much shows himself to be heartlessly cruel when faced with the same need for compassion and forgiveness toward a fellow man.

Now the other servants hear of the mistreatment, report the servant's ingratitude to the master, who lashes out at him. "O thou wicked servant, I forgave thee all that debt, because thou desiredst me: shouldest not thou also have had compassion on thy fellowservant,

---

[36]490 times, or possibly seventy-seven times.

[37]Gk. *douloi*, "slaves." The designation could include high-ranking civil servants, thus the astronomical indebtedness incurred by the first servant is entirely conceivable. We have no need to rationalize that the Lord speaks in hyperbole, though the sums are quite extreme amounts.

[38]Whether in gold or silver, this is a staggering amount of money. Estimates range from twelve to twenty million dollars to one billion dollars.

[39]Various estimates place the current value of one hundred pence anywhere from about $1.50 to perhaps $17. We could paraphrase it to mean "a few dollars."

even as I had pity on thee?" (vv. 32-33). The master initially had compassion on the servant and forgave the huge debt. But now the master is "wroth, and delivered him to the tormentors, till he should pay all that was due him" (v. 34).

In the Lord's story-answer to his question, Peter got all he bargained for and more in a lesson on forgiveness. The Lord concludes by applying a powerful motive for forgiveness. "So likewise shall my heavenly Father do also unto you, if ye from your hearts forgive not every one his brother their trespasses" (v. 35). A true servant of God will take warning and forgive.[40] Those who are forgiven must forgive, lest they show themselves incapable of receiving forgiveness. We may stretch out our forgiveness toward others as wide and compassionate as we dare to make it, even as Peter thought himself to be gracious, and our forgiveness will still be narrower than the wideness of God's forgiveness to the believing sinner.

Implications for Discipleship

1. *Take advantage of "teachable moments."* Teachers learn to recognize those special times when students show they are specially ready for instruction. Their questions are windows to their minds. The Lord saw in the temple tax and Peter's question about forgiveness the opportunity to teach him and the other disciples about humility and forgiveness. Disciplers are gratified when they receive questions from those whom they are discipling, but disciplers must also be aware of incidents and problems in a Christian's life that call for biblical instruction.

2. *Provide the initiative in introducing topics for study.* The Lord knew that the jealous and vengeful disciples needed instruction in humility and forgiveness. Your insight into the state of your disciple's spiritual growth should enable you to devise specific lessons to meet his needs. Follow-up booklets and discipleship manuals are helpful for resource materials, but each disciple must be evaluated individually so that you can provide the special instruction he needs.

3. *Reinforce character qualities.* You will not be able to anticipate every situation your disciple will face. But you can provide character training that will enable him to apply

---

[40]Broadus, p. 393.

what he learns to new situations. The Lord knew that humility and forgiveness were character qualities essential for
kingdom greatness. Learn to identify those several qualities
that are essential for strong believers—humility, compassion, love, obedience, fruitfulness—and work them into
your discipleship sessions. "A disciple must have integrity
and emotional stability *inside* in order to successfully labor
outside in the harvest field. If a disciple does not manifest
substantial character, then be very careful about what kind
of responsibility you entrust to him."[41]

4. *Ask questions.* The four Gospels record more than one
   hundred questions asked by Christ.[42] "What do you think,
   Peter?" asked the Lord, challenging His disciple to engage
   his mind in the matter at hand. The Lord asked various
   questions depending on His purposes. For example, we
   have already seen that He used questions *to stimulate interest and establish a point of contact.* He asked the disciples,
   "Who do people say that the Son of man is?" Some questions helped His learners *to clarify their thinking,* as happened with Peter in the present account. Some questions
   helped pupils *to apply the truth.* For instance, "Which of
   these three do you think proved to be a neighbor to the man
   who fell into the robbers' hands?" One question by the
   Lord helped *to establish a relationship with Him,* as we
   saw with the woman who touched Him for healing. Later
   we will see that Jesus used questions *to examine* Peter.
   "Simon, son of John, do you love Me?" Questions lay at
   the heart of the Lord's teaching methods.

---

[41]Bill Hull, *Jesus Christ Disciple Maker* (1984), p. 176.

[42]For further discussion of the Lord's use of questions, see "Christ the Master
Teacher," by Valerie A. Wilson in *Introduction to Biblical Christian Education*
(1981), Werner C. Graendorf, pp. 58-59.

A LESSON ON TRUE DISCIPLESHIP

"We have forsaken all, and followed thee;
what shall we have therefore?" (Matt. 19:27).

To talk with God,
No breath is lost—
Talk on!

To walk with God,
No strength is lost—
Walk on!

To wait on God,
No time is lost—
Wait on!

—Author Unknown

Setting: Galilee, Judea, and Perea, fall, A.D. 32 and spring, A.D. 33
Scripture: Matt. 19:16–20:16; Luke 12:41-48; John 7–10

The last time we saw Simon Peter he was at Capernaum, where the Lord had returned after a series of withdrawals, the last to the north where Christ showed forth His glory on Mount Hermon. We noticed the striking difference between the cold neglect toward Christ at Capernaum and the enthusiasm that but a few months earlier would have taken Him by force and made Him a king. We now come to a portion of the life and ministry of Christ that occupies a large section of the Gospels but contains only two brief references to Peter. The two episodes are extremely instructive to us as we continue to examine how Christ developed Peter, but they are cast in the larger framework of Christ leaving Galilee for the last time and moving steadily toward Jerusalem and the cross.

We have just seen the Lord take Peter aside to teach him that humility and forgiveness must characterize His followers. But there is still much more to learn. Christ will use the interruption by the rich young ruler to show that absolute allegiance to Him is also essential for salvation and kingdom greatness. Peter seizes on this word from the Lord to remind Him that he and the others have been absolutely loyal to Him; they have forsaken all for His cause. "What are we going to get out of it?" Peter selfishly inquires, once again betraying the unspoken thoughts of them all. True discipleship, Peter will learn, has its own reward.

Journeying to Jerusalem

But we must first trace the Lord's extensive movements prior to His encounter with the rich young man. Matthew describes the Lord's movements after He teaches Peter about forgiveness. "And it came to pass, that when Jesus had finished these sayings, he departed from Galilee, and came into the coasts of Judaea beyond Jordan; and great multitudes followed him; and he healed them there" (Matt. 19:1-2). Behind these two verses lies a complex problem in synoptic harmony.[1] Although Matthew parallels Mark from Matthew 14 to the end, Luke adds a long "central section" (9:51–18:14) to his account of the Lord's ministry. This is Luke's "travel narrative" of Jesus, containing much material not found in Matthew or Mark. Luke too portrays the Lord as leaving Galilee and heading for Jerusalem, as do Matthew and Mark, but in several segments.[2]

Of the entire spring and summer of A.D. 32, when the Lord withdrew from Galilee, winding up His series of retreats at Caesarea Philippi and Mount Hermon before returning to Capernaum, John simply says, "After these things Jesus walked[3] in Galilee: for he

---

[1]Since I am concerned primarily with understanding and applying Christ's work of developing Peter as a disciple and apostle, these questions of chronology, deserving of careful study in forming a harmony of Christ's life and ministry, nevertheless do not affect our observations about Peter, except to provide for us a sense of time and location.

[2]All three Synoptic Gospels indicate that Jesus went up to Jerusalem (Matt. 19:1; Mark 10:1; Luke 9:51). Luke adds two more journeys to Jerusalem (13:22; 17:11). John also identifies three (7:2; 11:7; 11:55). The first of these three journeys to Jerusalem (Luke 9:51–13:21; John 7:10–10:42) begins shortly after Jesus made His secret journey for the Feast of Tabernacles (John 7:2, 10), after which He presumably returned to Galilee. From Galilee He started to make a journey to Jerusalem (Luke 9:51; John 10:22-39) to eventually attend the Feast of Dedication. The ministry between Galilee and Jerusalem was in Samaria (Luke 9:52-56), where He sent out the seventy (Luke 10:1-24) probably into the regions of Samaria and Perea. After their return, Jesus had an extensive ministry (Luke 10:25–13:21) before arriving in Jerusalem for the Feast of Dedication. This marks the end of the first of these final three journeys to Jerusalem.

After the feast Jesus went to Perea ("beyond Jordan," John 10:40-42). In preparing to return to Jerusalem, He had an extensive ministry of miracles and parables probably all in Perea (Luke 13:22–17:10). He finally went to Bethany near Jerusalem to raise Lazarus from the dead (John 11:1-54, esp. vv. 7, 17-18). This marks the close of the second of the final three journeys.

The third journey to Jerusalem is the final one. After raising Lazarus, Jesus went to Ephraim (John 11:54), and from there He possibly continued north to the borders of Samaria and Galilee (cf. Luke 17:11, where Samaria is mentioned before Galilee). From there Jesus made His final journey to Jerusalem as given in Luke 17:11–19:28 and paralleled in Matt. 19:1–21:1 and Mark 10:1-52. In His final journey, His ministry of miracles and parables was probably accomplished primarily in Perea and Judea. Harold W. Hoehner, *Chronological Aspects of the Life of Christ* (1977), pp. 62-63.

[3]"walked about."

would not walk in Jewry,[4] because the Jews sought to kill him" (John 7:1). John's last recorded event is the feeding of the five thousand and the Lord's enigmatic message on eating His flesh and drinking His blood.[5] We learn that John picks up the narrative because the Lord leaves Galilee to attend a feast in Jerusalem.[6]

It is now autumn,[7] the time when "the olives were being shaken from the trees, and the grapes were being trodden out in the wine-presses."[8] Harvest festival time has arrived in the land, portrayed in the joyous Feast of Tabernacles at Jerusalem. Allowing His friends and His own family members to go on ahead to Jerusalem to keep the feast, the Lord Jesus tarries in Galilee. Then subsequently, accompanied by Peter and the other disciples, Jesus journeys south, "not openly, but as it were in secret" (v. 10). He appears suddenly in the temple, and as He teaches the people once more, many go to His side, holding Him to be the "Prophet"[9] promised of old. But others have lingering doubts. They question whether the Messiah would indeed come out of Galilee, which they knew was Christ's home. "So there was a division among the people because of him" (v. 43). It is during these tension-driven days of ministry in Jerusalem that Jesus declares His great prophecy about the Holy Spirit, consoles the woman taken in adultery, and proclaims Himself the Light of the world.[10] But the people, stirred in their anger toward Jesus, take up heavy stones to cast at Him. He escapes from their midst and once more, in the company of His apostles, makes His way back to Galilee for a few weeks, where, we would suppose, He found His way to Peter's house in Capernaum.

A homeless wanderer

No sooner does Jesus arrive back in Galilee than the Pharisees, aware doubtless that Christ has been forced to flee for His life at Jerusalem, come to Him with the professedly friendly suggestion that He should leave Galilee also, seeing that Herod Antipas wishes to mistreat Him as he had mistreated John the Baptist. The people whom He healed and taught and fed turn on Him, just as at Jerusalem. We can imagine Christ with a sigh turning southward once again, taking

[4]I.e., Judea.
[5]John 6:1-65.
[6]John 7:1-10.
[7]September 10-17, A.D. 32, Hoehner, p. 143.
[8]Quintin Hogg, *The Story of Peter* (1900), p. 127.
[9]Deut. 18:15.
[10]John 7-10.

leave of His well-beloved Galilee, and crying, "Woe unto thee, Chorazin; woe unto thee, Bethsaida," and to Capernaum, His own city, a yet deeper woe. Determined to go to Jerusalem, Jesus ministers in Samaria. Knowing how quickly the shades are gathering over Him, and how, in another three or four months, the tragedy of Calvary will have been added to the guilt of Jerusalem, Christ calls some seventy disciples who still adhere to Him and sends them forth two by two, as He had done the Twelve the year previously. They will learn to do without Him and have some valuable practice in the mission work on which in such a very short time the progress of the church will have to depend.

The full ebb tide is running now, and Jesus meets with even less acceptance in Samaria than He has just experienced in Galilee and Jerusalem. When Jesus tarries in Samaria on the way to Jerusalem again, the Samaritans raise their heel at this rejected Jew and refuse to allow Him to enter into their cities. Then flames the indignation of the sons of Zebedee, and they cry to their Master to call down fire from heaven, as Elijah had done, to consume His enemies. But the mission of Christ is to save, and not to destroy; so, turning still farther eastward, He seeks to go to Jerusalem by the only route left open to Him—that lying between the provinces of Samaria and Perea. It appears likely enough that it is at this time that He teaches His apostles to "count the cost" of cleaving to Him. When a would-be disciple seeks to follow the homeless wanderer, He explains: "Foxes have holes, and birds of the air have nests; but the Son of man hath not where to lay his head" (Luke 9:58). The Lord pictures anyone who starts out with Him and then turns away as a ploughman who puts his hand to the plough but looks back. Such a disciple is not fit for the kingdom of God (v. 62). This is not true for His apostles. Though they have attached themselves to what the world might well consider a lost cause, no heart seems to have failed, and no foot to have turned back.

A wonderful journey this, containing never-to-be-forgotten teaching, for during these few short weeks Christ speaks of the rich man and Lazarus, of the Good Samaritan, of the lost coin, the lost sheep, and the lost son. On one occasion, Jesus tells His disciples that it is the Father's good pleasure to give them the kingdom,[11] but they must also be prepared to receive it. The Lord's parable of the servants[12] reminds the disciples of the value of waiting patiently for the master's return. "Blessed are those servants," Jesus says, "whom the lord when he

[11]Luke 12:32.
[12]Luke 12:36-40.

cometh shall find watching" (12:37). And He warns the disciples, "You must be ready too, for when you do not expect Him, the Son of man will come." This prompts Peter—one of the two episodes involving him in this large expanse of Scripture—to utter, "Lord, speakest thou this parable unto us, or even to all?" (v. 41). As He does on several occasions, the Lord answers a question with one of His own. "Who then is that faithful and wise steward, whom his lord shall make ruler over his household, to give them their portion of meat in due season?" (v. 42). Although the Lord elsewhere exhorts everyone to "watch,"[13] in this parable the Lord appears to be speaking directly to the apostles about their responsibility. Servants have a duty to be faithful to their master, awaiting his command.[14] Those in leadership, as these apostles and Peter soon will be, must be willing to follow the Lord's bidding.

Still ever southward, with His face toward Jerusalem, Jesus continues on His way, until we find Him at Bethany, in the house of Martha and Mary. Here takes place the lovely incident of Mary, sitting at the feet of Jesus, and Martha, showing her love by serving Him, distressed, no doubt, by the danger that surrounded her friend and the traces of sorrow in His face. At Bethany, apparently, Jesus headquarters temporarily, walking into Jerusalem for the Feast of Dedication,[15] since Jerusalem is no safe place for Him. The people will not accept Him as a revelation of a life higher than themselves and of truth greater than any that their forefathers had known.

Where should the homeless wanderer find rest? Not in Bethany, that was too near Jerusalem, and so going eastward again He passes over Jordan to that other Bethany, where John had baptized Him when He had returned after His forty days' temptation in the wilderness. There in Perea, by the waters of that Jordan, which came down from His beloved Galilee, Christ will spend the greater part of the last three months of His life. This period must have been spent in comparative retirement, though a few came down from Jerusalem to question Him and to test His orthodoxy, particularly concerning His view about divorce. Among those who come is a ruler, a man to whom one's heart naturally goes out, as did the Master's. He seeks to know "what good thing shall I do that I may have eternal life?" Jesus gives a strange but penetrating answer.

---

[13]Mark 13:37.

[14]"Jesus not only taught the certainty of his return at an unexpected moment but also implied, through various instructions to his disciples, that the community of believers would continue for an unspecified time serving the Lord till his return in the indefinite future." *EBC* vol. 8, p. 967.

[15]John 10:22.

Good or God?

"And, behold, one came and said unto him, Good Master, what good thing shall I do, that I may have eternal life?" (Matt. 19:16). We come face to face with a morally good man, one who called forth the compassion of the Lord Jesus, who, looking on him "loved him" (Mark 10:21). Matthew tells us he was a young man, Luke that he was a ruler, perhaps a leader of a local synagogue but probably not of the Jerusalem Sanhedrin. Mark tells us that he "ran" to Jesus, perhaps catching a glimpse of Christ as he left the house where He had just blessed the children. With all his advantages as a rich (Luke 18:22-23), young (v. 21), "ruler" (v. 18), he is conscious of something lacking that the Lord Jesus might supply. Eager not to miss the Lord's instruction, the young ruler hastens to overtake Jesus and, kneeling reverently, addresses Him, "Good Master."[16] The young man has done many things. Therefore, he asks, "What else should I do? What further good thing must I do to obtain eternal life?" The man is "sincerely and deeply desirous of gaining [eternal life], as he has shown by his conduct heretofore, and shows now by his eagerness to learn from the Galilean teacher who is passing by."[17] Perhaps he is also quite superficial, thinking that some "good thing" is sufficient to meet his need. His purpose may be good, but his plan of attaining eternal life is faulty.

To call Jesus "good" prompts this rejoinder from the Lord. Looking down on the prostrate young man, He inquires: "Why callest thou me good? there is none good but one, that is, God" (Matt. 19:17). "What is your reason for associating goodness with Me?" Jesus is saying, "when strictly speaking, only God is good?" We have become accustomed to referring to another person as a "good man," that is, one who epitomizes goodness or godliness. Jesus seizes on that notion. If the young man is not to recognize Him as God, how could He then be a "good" man, since Christ claimed deity for Himself? Only God is perfectly good and "lessons of goodness are not lessons of mere human ethical wisdom, but of divine instruction."[18] People are prone to think that mere human instruction in morals and religion is sufficient, but they forget that the highest spiritual wisdom must come from Him alone who is perfect wisdom and perfect goodness. Thus, our Lord is saying that He is not a mere human source of goodness and wisdom; His instruction is divine, of which He is "the way, the truth, and the life."

---

[16]"Teacher," from *didaskolos*.

[17]John A. Broadus, *Commentary on the Gospel of Matthew* (1886), p. 405. Contrast this attitude with the lawyer of Luke 10:25, who quibbled, Broadus notes.

[18]Broadus, p. 405.

A Lesson on True Discipleship

To believers today, the Lord's next instruction is at odds with our understanding that it is not by any works of our own that we obtain eternal life. That work is accomplished only through the meritorious working of our Savior. Yet to this one who asks about "eternal life," Jesus meets him on his own ground and says, "Keep the commandments." English calls this "an interesting bit of dispensational teaching,"[19] for indeed we recall that when a similar question would be asked of Paul and Silas by the Philippian jailer, they answer, "Believe on the Lord Jesus Christ, and thou shalt be saved" (Acts 16:31). Indeed that continues to be our message of the hope for eternal life to all. But the young man comes to Jesus still living in the age of the law. Men were responsible to keep the law of God perfectly, though, of course, all failed to do so. Jesus does not order him to do something new or brilliant. Instead He takes him back to the old and familiar, perhaps even trite.[20]

The law was given to show man his sinfulness. Like a giant mirror let down from heaven, the law reveals sin but can do nothing to make one clean. When asked which laws He meant, the Lord Jesus quotes those commands from the Decalogue that dealt with man's responsibility to his neighbor. "Do not murder." "Do not commit adultery." "Do not steal." "Do not lie." "Honor your father and mother." He then summarizes these social obligations with "love your neighbor as yourself." The Lord does not even touch those commandments that deal with the deeper and more fundamental relation to God. He shows the young man that he cannot possibly claim any favor with God when he has not fulfilled the commands regarding responsible conduct toward a fellow man. Of course, the young man claims, "I have kept all these from when I was young. What do I lack?" With divine perception, the Lord strikes at the heart of the problem. "Go sell what you have, give to the poor, and come follow me." Nothing but a total revolution of his life would bring the young man his desired goal, but he cannot bring himself to this commitment. "He had great riches," says the evangelist. It would be also appropriate to say that great riches had him. His reliance on his material worth kept him from seeing in Christ the answer to his quest. Forsaking the Lord's loving help, the young man leaves in painful disappointment, never obtaining his hoped-for eternal life. "His eager longing and hope gave way to gloom—he *could* not give up his

---

[19]E. Schuyler English, *Studies in the Gospel According to Matthew* (1935), p. 137.

[20]This was Naaman's attitude in II Kings 5:11-12.

great possessions."[21] He came running; he departs slowly, distressed and dejected, unwilling to make wholehearted surrender that is the secret of eternal life, here and hereafter.

The principle involved is that of supreme devotion to Christ. That is the lesson of true discipleship. Giving all of one's material possessions and wealth to others is not the path to heaven. But to follow the Lord supremely, one must be willing to rid himself of all that hinders. It is this principle that the Lord embraces and that must be underscored for Peter and the disciples. "The test is different for different people," observes Broadus. "Some find it harder to renounce hopes of worldly honor and fame for Christ's sake . . . and for others the hard trial is to abandon certain gratifications of the various appetites."[22] But the Lord knows the pull of one's pride and stature that constructs a barrier to God too high to scale. "A rich man shall hardly enter into the kingdom of heaven" (Matt. 19:23), Jesus cautions. Whether the metaphor of the camel and the needle's eye is literal or figurative,[23] the meaning is clear as to the difficulty of entrance into the kingdom for one such as the rich young ruler. Wealth, in the Jewish economy, was a sign of God's favor, but now Jesus declares that to enter the messianic kingdom, it is a huge impediment. The disciples are "exceedingly amazed" and ask, "Who then can be saved?" (v. 25). Only divine omnipotence can save anyone, and that includes rich men. "With men this is impossible; but with God all things are possible" (v. 26).

What's in it for us?

"Then answered Peter and said unto him, Behold, we have forsaken all, and followed thee; what shall we have therefore?" (v. 27). Enter Simon Peter once again! Speaking for himself and his companions,[24] Peter finds in the rich young man's refusal to follow the Lord rays of hope for their own reward. "Lord, that rich young man may not have been willing to forsake all to follow You, but we have! What will we get for this loyalty?" Peter sounds somewhat mercenary perhaps, but even if that were his motivation, the Lord Jesus does not receive it

---

[21]Broadus, p. 407.

[22]Broadus.

[23]The "needle" is in all probability a common sewing or embroidering needle. The Lord's expression does seem to teach in a figurative way the impossibility of entering the kingdom of God except through the power of God. However, some see in the metaphor a reference to a gate at Jerusalem, a small gate called "the needle's eye" within a larger gate. To enter the smaller gate, the camel had to be unburdened and forced to his knees. Broadus gives an extensive survey of the various ways the metaphor has been explained. Broadus, pp. 408-9.

[24]"We" is expressed in the Greek and is thus emphasized.

that way. Peter and the others certainly had made genuine sacrifices to follow Christ, and their prospects, in view of what lay ahead in Jerusalem, were dismal. But Jesus promises great rewards to the Twelve[25] and then extends His promise to all who leave anything for His sake.

> Verily I say unto you, That ye which have followed me, in the regeneration[26] when the Son of man shall sit in the throne of his glory, ye also shall sit upon twelve thrones, judging the twelve tribes of Israel. And every one that hath forsaken houses, or brethren, or sisters, or father, or mother, or wife, or children, or lands, for my name's sake, shall receive an hundredfold, and shall inherit everlasting life (vv. 28-29).

Jesus speaks of earthly rewards first—houses, lands, family—multiplied a hundred times over and then of the spiritual blessing of inheriting everlasting life. The expressions of a hundred wives, husbands, and so forth are clearly not to be taken literally because that would be promising a hundred *mothers!* The testimony of God's people, especially those involved in Christian service around the world, verifies the Lord's promise of rewards. Certainly there is blessing to be gained in this life by owning land and houses, in marrying and having children. Even unsaved people can experience these temporal satisfactions. But the satisfaction of following Christ implicitly and doing His will brings the satisfactions those material blessings offer multiplied a hundred times over and more. It is a joy to own a home. It is a joy a hundred times over to fellowship with God's people in their places of abode—whether a shack or a palace. God's people understand this because they have experienced it over and over again.

That's not fair!

Directly after Peter's boast and question, "Behold, we have forsaken all, and followed thee; what shall we have therefore?" our Lord continues to speak of the rewards that He will give His followers. The Lord will remind Peter and the others that such rewards are a matter of divine sovereignty not determined by any order of precedence. "For the kingdom of heaven is like unto a man that is a householder" (20:1).

---

[25]The Twelve will have an exalted position of dignity and honor at the consummation of the messianic kingdom when in the new order of things ("the regeneration") they will judge, or rule over, the twelve tribes of Israel (Matt. 19:28).

[26]The word "regeneration" (Gk. *paliggenesia*) is found only twice in the NT. Here it clearly means a new physical state, when creation shall be renewed and the Son of man reigns on earth. The other occurrence is in Titus 3:5, where the meaning is that of a new spiritual state.

Peter may have surmised that he would receive the greater and more impressive reward since he was among the first to be called by the Lord Jesus. But our Lord gives Peter and his fellow disciples illustration of His warning about the last being first and first last.[27]

The parable depicts justice and grace on the part of the householder, for laborers in each time slot agree to work and are content to receive either specific wages ("a penny," Gk. *denarion*) or "whatsoever is right" (vv. 4, 7). So with this parable,[28] the Lord shows that God will reward as He sees best. Many who enter His service late will receive greater reward than others who entered earlier. This would be true, not only of the Twelve but as a general principle applied to all of God's people. Christ's servants will be rewarded not on the basis of time spent in His service, or the actual results of that service, but according to God's own judgment and sovereign good pleasure. "One simple truth is taught here; a man's reward shall be, not according to length of his service, nor according to the notoriety of his service, but under the will of God according to his faithfulness to the opportunity afforded him."[29] "Is it not lawful for Me to do what I will with Mine own? *So* the first shall be last, and the last shall be first."

Implications for Discipleship

1. *Some refuse commitment to discipleship.* It is sadly true that some who profess interest in Christ, perhaps even making a superficial commitment to Him, are at the last revealed for what they are. They are more concerned about themselves and their possessions than absolute loyalty to Christ. It is not what we give up that converts the soul, but if a person is unwilling to leave off that which keeps him from trusting Christ exclusively, then there is no hope for eternal life. Griffith Thomas sees in the Lord's earlier words on childhood four characteristics of true discipleship: dependence, humility, love, and obedience. In the story of the rich young ruler, he notes these four characteristics unfulfilled. The young man, instead of showing childlike dependence, shows independence, desiring to go his own way. Instead of humility, self-sufficiency, setting his own standards. Selfishness instead of love, giving no thought to others. And disobedience, owning no master but

---

[27]Since this text is repeated in Matt. 20:16, we see that the Lord intended for the parable of the laborers in the vineyard (20:1-15) to illustrate this principle.

[28]Matt. 20:1-16.

[29]English, p. 140.

himself. "The striking contrasts brought together in this passage should enable us all to see clearly the dangers of failing to put Christ first in life."[30] Is Christ the Lord of your life? Christ must be first, and then everything else will fall into its proper place.

2. *A true disciple is willing to shift the spiritual center of gravity in his life.* Earlier the Lord spoke of self-denial and cross bearing. "Then said Jesus unto his disciples, If any man will come after me, let him deny himself, and take up his cross, and follow me" (Matt. 16:24). What did Jesus mean by these demands? Certainly Jesus did not mean the denying of ourselves some luxury or denying the needs of self. Rather, He was focusing on the importance of re-nouncing self as the center of one's life and actions. That was the rich young ruler's dilemma. He sought to follow Christ but also to maintain the center of his life in riches. Self-denial is the decision to give over to God our bodies, our careers, our time, and, yes, our money. It is the "sustained willingness to say no to oneself in order to say yes to God."[31]

3. *Only God can save.* Our best efforts to make disciples are only on the human scale. If a person is to be converted, it must be the sovereign work of God. We see in the story of the rich young ruler that good, upright, morally strong people who seek eternal life, if they fail to yield themselves unequivocally to Christ, face the danger of separating from God forever. Coupled with this is the necessity to work with the Holy Spirit in dealing with lost souls. Any Christian who has pleaded with a lost sinner to come to God senses his own inability to bring about conviction and conversion; that is the work of God the Holy Spirit. Our task is to present clearly and lovingly the gospel of the grace of God.

4. *To follow Jesus is to think like Jesus, act like Jesus, and invest like Jesus.*[32] God grants us a life to spend, not to

---

[30]W. H. Griffith Thomas, *Outline Studies in the Gospel of Matthew* (1961), p. 284.

[31]Bill Hull, *Jesus Christ Disciple Maker* (1984), p. 170.

[32]Hull, p. 172.

save. To invest like Jesus means that we act wisely in the expenditure of our lives. "For whosoever will save his life shall lose it: and whosoever will lose his life for my sake shall find it" (Matt. 16:25). Only in losing ourselves in Christ do we find ourselves in this life. This is the harder way, but it is also the higher way. Jesus asks us to invest our lives in Him, for although salvation itself costs nothing, discipleship will cost us everything.

5. *Rewards are God's prerogative.* Peter had to face this matter of rewards. He claims to have left all for the Lord; now he seeks to know what is in it for him. Jesus tells Peter—and all who would follow Him—that faithful service will receive its own reward. These rewards, however, are not determined by fact or amount of service but by motive and spirit. Jesus says, "Lose yourself in Me and you will find everything you could ever need—in this life and in the life eternal." Griffith Thomas notes that it is useful to compare Christ's three parables dealing with rewards: (1) according to quantity of work when ability is equal (Matt. 25:14-20); (2) according to ability when it varies (Luke 19:12-27); (3) according to motive and thoroughness of worker (Matt. 20:1-16).[33]

---

[33]Thomas, *The Apostle Peter* (1956), p. 48.

LESSONS ON JUDGMENT

Behold, the fig tree which thou cursedst is withered away (Mark 11:21).

Nothing but leaves for the Master,
Oh, how His loving heart grieves,
When instead of the fruit He is seeking,
We offer Him nothing but leaves.

—Mrs. H. S. Lehman

Setting: Bethany and Jerusalem, Passion Week, A.D. 33
Scripture: Mark 11:1-26; also John 11, 12

Cursing and destruction are not the usual methods of the Lord Jesus. But both of these elements come into prominence in the story about to unfold. We must recognize them as integral to the lessons the Lord has for His people, especially Peter. "When in the Divine economy judgment becomes punishment, chastisement, and necessarily so; it is nevertheless God's strange work, His strange act."[1] So our Lord's action involving Peter and the cursing of the barren fig tree may appear strange to us, yet it is central to the Lord's lessons on judgment that He delivers to His disciples.

The events of the last days of the Lord Jesus before His crucifixion form a major theme of the Gospel records. Peter's development at the hands of Jesus, up to this moment never far from His conscious thoughts, now assumes a more subtle and deliberate subplot to the dominating force of the Lord's sacrificial death on the cross. We find ourselves occupied with the Lord's last days, not only to learn what He has in store for Peter the rock but also to enter into that holy of holies, within the veil, to witness His blood atonement. Christ's heart is heavy with the weight of our sins that He must bear on the cross. We must not allow ourselves to lose sight of the Lord's increasing heaviness of soul as He moves among His own disciples and friends as well as confronts the religious opposition in Jerusalem that seeks His end. We continue with the Lord's final days of ministry in Perea before He returns to Bethany and Jerusalem.

Brushing past the distressed rich young ruler as he withdraws in sorrow from the Master, a speedy messenger approaches Jesus with an urgent message from His beloved friends at Bethany near Jerusalem.

---

[1] G. Campbell Morgan, *The Gospel According to Mark* (1927), p. 251.

The news is grim. Lazarus, in whose house Jesus found shelter when in Judea, is frightfully ill. "Master, would You come immediately?" is the plea. "He whom thou lovest is sick" (John 11:3). Despite the urgent plea, however, the Lord remains in Perea for two more days, saying, "This sickness is not unto death, but for the glory of God, that the Son of God might be glorified thereby" (v. 4). The disciples, no doubt including Peter, stand mute at the Lord's strange conduct. The message said simply, "The one You love is sick." Could it be that in love the Lord refrains from rushing to His friend's side? For two days the Master lingers, then He announces to His disciples that He will go to His friend's bedside. "Let us go into Judaea again" (v. 7). Because Bethany is in the immediate neighborhood of Jerusalem, the site of Christ's most recent danger, His disciples protest. "Master, the Jews of late sought to stone thee; and goest thou thither again?" (v. 8). But they resign themselves to exposure to danger, Thomas giving voice to their general pessimism. "Lord, if You must go, then let us go with You so we can die with You." Since the disciples do not comprehend His statement of Lazarus's "sleep," Jesus must plainly tell them, "Lazarus is dead" (v. 14).

Martha is the first to confront Jesus on His arrival to Bethany. Rushing out to meet Him, she forsakes all thoughts of the Lord's incomparable love and compassion and rather reproaches Him. "If You had been here, my brother would not have died." She cannot bring herself to understand the loving Lord's delay in the face of her emergency; certainly she is not able to understand that the Son of God will be glorified through this experience. But four days have elapsed[2] and Lazarus is now dead. This is all that concerns Martha. "Thy brother shall rise again," Christ assures her, speaking with a distinctive certainty of life beyond the grave. Soon after, her sister Mary joins them and Christ, scarcely able to control His emotion, asks where the dead body of His friend has been laid. On approaching that symbol of the last enemy to be conquered, our loving Lord weeps.

In brotherhood of human woe,
Incarnate Deity has wept
And mingled tears with sisters' grief
Beside the grave where brother slept.[3]

—Bob Jones

---

[2]One day for the messenger to reach Jesus; two days of delay; the final day for Jesus to travel to Bethany.

[3]Bob Jones, "Christ, the Elder Brother," *Rhyme & Reason* (1981), p. 28.

"Jesus wept." What sublime condescension. All who are present are doubly moved. "Behold how he loved him," observe the mourners and others gathered at the house of the dead. What happens next is a story well known. At Christ's bidding, the dead man arises and comes forth, not a loathsome corpse, but a living man![4]

The beginning of the end

"Then many of the Jews which came to Mary, and had seen the things which Jesus did, believed on him. But some of them went their ways to the Pharisees, and told them what things Jesus had done" (vv. 45-46). The extraordinary nature of Christ's miracle, coupled with Bethany's proximity to Jerusalem, brings instant notoriety to the event, serving only to increase the spreading hostility of the ruling Jewish powers against Him. "Then gathered the chief priests and the Pharisees a council, and said, What do we? for this man doeth many miracles. If we let him thus alone, all men will believe on him: and the Romans shall come and take away both our place and nation" (vv. 47-48). Caiaphas, the high priest, who held his office at the appointment of the Roman government, and Annas, his father-in-law, meeting with the Sanhedrin, talk seriously about how to put an end to Christ (v. 53). By an overwhelming majority, a sentence of death is passed on Jesus, but the method to be employed is still much in doubt. Perhaps they have assassination in mind, for violence always lurked just under the surface in that ancient society. Since the Jews had no power for capital punishment, it would be difficult, they must have reasoned, to convince Pontius Pilate that the Prophet from Galilee had done anything worthy of death. But they must try.

"Jesus therefore walked no more openly among the Jews; but went thence unto a country near to the wilderness, into a city called Ephraim, and there continued with his disciples" (v. 54). With trouble imminent, Christ turns northward where He finds solace with Peter and his companions in a small village. The Lord's example of patiently enduring suffering and persecution, which Peter will describe in later years in his epistle, will leave an indelible impression on Peter. With a price placed on His head by the Jewish rulers in Jerusalem, no place, not even Ephraim, is safe for long in that small country. All too soon for Peter and his friends, these last few days of quiet pass away and now begins the final journey to the cross, the story of which has echoed down through the world ever since. It is the beginning of the end. Down from the slope of Ephraim onto the high road from Jericho walks Jesus,

---

[4]Tradition says that Lazarus lived another thirty years with his sisters.

mingling with the bands of Passover pilgrims, His face steadfastly set toward the cross. Only He knows the full extent of this journey and how it will end.

Having been raised from the dead, Lazarus becomes Bethany's most famous citizen. "Then Jesus six days before the passover[5] came to Bethany, where Lazarus was which had been dead, whom he raised from the dead" (12:1). The Mount of Olives, standing between Bethany and Jerusalem, hides the Holy City from it. At Bethany, therefore, Christ and His disciples part from the great bands of pilgrims heading for Jerusalem. The worshipers will continue on another mile or two, seeking lodging in the city or erecting tents in the Kidron Valley, which lay between Jerusalem and the Mount of Olives. At what would be a farewell meal at Bethany, Mary interrupts the gathering with a loving gesture as she anoints Jesus' feet with "very costly" perfumed oil, wiping the oil from His feet with her own hair. The effect is sublime, the house filling with the odor of the oil's perfume. When rebuked by Judas Iscariot, who grumbled about such a waste, Mary hears the Lord Jesus graciously intercede for her. "Let her alone: against the day of my burying hath she kept this" (v. 7).

> There art thou known—where'er the Book of Light
> Bears hope and healing, there, beyond all blight,
>   Is borne thy memory, and all praise above;
> Oh! say what deed so lifted thy sweet name,
> Mary! to that pure silent place of fame?
>   One lowly offering of exceeding love![6]

> —F. Hemans

The end is near, and in a prophetic gesture of love Mary bestows on the Lord an unspoken prayer of gratitude, in manner physical not unlike our own prayers that rise in gentle fragrance to the Father. By her loving heart—for love freely gives of itself—Mary stands forever in stark contrast to the greedy and resentful Judas, who, in giving in to his own evil impulses for gain, will sell innocent blood.[7] Crowds

---

[5]Hoehner holds that Jesus arrived at Bethany on Saturday before the Passion Week. He then outlines a chronology of events throughout that week that places the triumphal entry on Monday, rather than on the traditional Palm Sunday. See Harold W. Hoehner, *Chronological Aspects of the Life of Christ* (1977), p. 91. I will continue to follow the traditional chronology with the triumphal entry on Sunday, the cursing of the fig tree on Monday, and Peter's reaction to the cursing of the tree on Tuesday.

[6]F. Hemans, "The Memorial of Mary," *The Prose and Poetry of Europe and America* (1853), p. 461.

[7]By most reckonings, the price for which Judas sold Jesus was one-third the sum of Mary's sacrifice of love.

flood into Bethany to see the resurrected Lazarus for themselves. "Much people of the Jews therefore knew that he was there: and they came not for Jesus' sake only, but that they might see Lazarus also, whom he had raised from the dead. But the chief priests consulted that they might put Lazarus also to death; because that by reason of him many of the Jews went away, and believed on Jesus" (vv. 9-11). "The whole world is following Christ!" the Pharisees conclude and they will stop at nothing to eliminate Him.

Who is this?

On the "next day" (v. 12), which has come down to us as Palm Sunday of the Passion Week, Christ sets out from Bethany for Jerusalem. Sweeping around the south side of the Mount of Olives, Christ makes His way steadfastly toward Abraham's Mount Moriah as His "hour" looms nearer. "It is perfectly certain that from the commencement of His public ministry, [Christ] was perfectly conscious of the Cross. Through the three years of preaching, of working of miracles, of conflict, and of training His own, He moved with quiet dignity, and set determination, towards the Cross of His passion."[8] As the city comes into view, where He is to suffer so terribly in a few short days, Christ is overwhelmed with sorrow at the thought of the destruction that hangs over it. "Silent tears had coursed His cheeks at the grave of Lazarus—tears which neither thorny crown, nor scourging, nor crucifixion could make flow again—but for Jerusalem, the chosen city, the metropolis of His race, He could weep."[9]

And when he was come near, he beheld the city, and wept over it, saying, If thou hadst known, even thou, at least in this thy day, the things which belong unto thy peace! but now they are hid from thine eyes. For the days shall come upon thee, that thine enemies shall cast a trench about thee, and compass thee round, and keep thee in on every side, and shall lay thee even with the ground, and thy children within thee; and they shall not leave in thee one stone upon another; because thou knewest not the time of thy visitation (Luke 19:41-44).

Who o'er the herd would wish to reign,
Fantastic, fickle, fierce, and vain?
. . . .

[8]G. Campbell Morgan, *The Crises of Christ* (1903), p. 276.
[9]Quintin Hogg, *The Story of Peter* (1900), pp. 150-51.

THE MAKING OF A DISCIPLE

Thou many-headed monster thing,
O who would wish to be thy king?—[10]

—Sir Walter Scott

Now He is in the valley leading into the city and "much people that were come to the feast, when they heard that Jesus was coming to Jerusalem,[11] took branches of palm trees, and went forth to meet him" (John 12:12-13).The pilgrims from Galilee, who having heard among other things of the raising of Lazarus the previous month come out of their tents or temporary booths made of tree branches and greet Him with acclaim. At that moment, the two disciples, sent to a nearby village to procure a donkey for the Master, return with the beast in hand. Casting their garments on the colt, they set Jesus on the animal and then, moving through the valley toward the city, spread their clothing before Him. Waving branches and leaves they have cut from the nearby palm trees, the Galileans and others join the disciples in triumphant procession up from the valley and through the gates into the city, a "pageant of poverty."[12] "Save now,"[13] comes the shout—from the marchers leading the procession and from those trailing the joyous throng. "Blessed is he that cometh in the name of the Lord" (Mark 11:9). In His wise understanding of the Father's plan, the Lord knows

---

[10]Sir Walter Scott, *The Lady of the Lake* (1901), Canto Fifth, xxx. Scott's description of the fickle people of Stirling, wavering in loyalty between a tribal chief and a Scottish king, echoes the sentiment of the people of Jerusalem toward Christ.

[11]Hogg comments on the contrast between the Jerusalem of Christ's time and that of the beginning of the twentieth century: "Since those days the rebel and the Roman, the Greek and the Turk, the Crusader and the Mahomedan have combined to heap devastation upon devastation on the Holy City, till it has been more or less destroyed no less than some eleven times. He who would seek the pavements on which the feet of Christ actually trod would have to go twenty feet or more from the present surface, while in many cases the valleys themselves have to some extent been filled up with the accumulation of rubbish and debris. In Christ's time, however, the woods which were cut down by Titus to assist him in beleaguering the city were still growing; the temple with its foundation showing the marks of the Tyrian artisans hired from Hiram by King Solomon, with the rougher work of Nehemiah and the slighter but more elegant superstructure of Herod, was still standing, the white marble and gilded roof making the building an object of beauty as well as one of adoration to every Hebrew heart." Hogg, p. 150.

[12]Morgan, p. 256. "I suggest one method by which the meekness, the lowliness, the poverty, the absurdity, of this entrance may be understood. In imagination think, not as a Hebrew, but as a Roman; and think of the triumphal entry of a Roman emperor into his city; and then look at this pageant of poverty, lacking all the things usually associated with royalty and greatness. A procession of poverty, the scattering of the clothes the people wore, the broken branches of the trees, and the shouting of the Galilean mob! So He rode in the dignity of a great meekness . . . a pageant of poverty."

[13]"Hosanna!" Taken from Psalm 118:25.

that within a few short days, these shouts of glory and praise will revert to scornful hate. "Crucify Him! Crucify Him!" will echo and re-echo throughout the dusty streets still strewn with scattered hosanna branches. Though they cry "Save now," they have already refused the Messiah's salvation and have rejected Him as their Sovereign.

"All the city was moved" (Matt. 21:10) at the noisy procession, neighbor nudging neighbor asking, "Who is this?" The multitude continues to shout, as with one voice. "This is Jesus the prophet of Nazareth of Galilee" (v. 11). Dismounting from the beast of burden, the Lord Jesus makes His way to the temple—that place ordained of old where God would meet with His people. Standing to one side in the courtyard, the Lord "looked round about on all things" (Mark 11:11), gazing in particular at the re-energized merchants and moneychangers, whom only a few Passovers earlier and at the inauguration of His ministry, He had with righteous zeal driven from the scene. "Take these things hence," He had said on that first occasion. "Make not my Father's house an house of merchandise" (John 2:16). But once again the holy site looks more like a bazaar than the entrance to a place of prayer. Then Christ, looking up to heaven, gives voice to the prayer, "Father, glorify thy name," and from the sky comes the rumbling noise as of thunder. "I have glorified You, and will glorify You again!" (John 12:28). At day's end, the ebb and flow of emotions having taken their toll, the Lord Jesus returns to Bethany for His night's rest. The people of Jerusalem had for a long time rejected Him and His mission. Now symbolically, He rejects them, refusing to lay His head in rest within their city's walls. "Night has come upon Israel; the King has left them because of their unbelief. But He will return, and a remnant of Israel, in her darkest hour shall see Him and believe."[14]

During the next several days, Peter will be sorely tested. His reluctance to acknowledge the Lord's hour of suffering and death at Jerusalem began months earlier far to the north in Caesarea Philippi, when he sought to restrain the Lord from His appointment with the cross. During this Passion Week and in the power of his own flesh, Peter will once more attempt to turn aside the divine plan, but the ever-caring Christ will lovingly restrain him, pray for him, and lead him back to the fold; for on the other side of the cross and the grave lies a ministry of witness to Christ's resurrection. Only the post-resurrection indwelling Holy Spirit, whose presence and power gives spiritual discernment, will eventually clear the disciples' minds and strengthen their hearts.

[14]E. Schuyler English, *Studies in the Gospel According to Matthew* (1935), p. 151.

Writing years later, the apostle John records the disciples' belated acceptance of the Lord's actions. "These things understood not his disciples at the first: but when Jesus was glorified, then remembered they that these things were written of him, and that they had done these things unto him" (v. 16).

Nothing but leaves

On Monday morning, Jesus makes His way back toward Jerusalem. Being hungry, He seeks food on a fig[15] tree, where the abundance of leaves gives promise of finding the green first fruit of the new season. On closer inspection, He finds "nothing but leaves" (Mark 11:13), no fruit, "for the time of figs was not yet" (v. 13). Here was a tree that had failed in itself and becomes a perfectly just illustration of that which the Lord desired at the moment to teach.[16] Words of judgment follow from the Lord's broken heart as He voices disappointment at false profession: "No man eat fruit of thee hereafter for ever" (v. 14). "There is no more warrant for criticizing our Lord for destroying a tree for the purpose of teaching . . . than the plucking of the petals from a flower in a lesson on botany."[17] Why would people question the Lord's actions, or the evangelists' discernment for including this incident in their accounts? Some would hold even that it is not worthy of inclusion in Scripture. But they fail to see the lesson the Lord Jesus is teaching through parable and action. "The tree was the symbol, but the nation was in His mind."[18] Israel, God's nation, was barren. In the life of a nation, when faith perishes, the principle of life perishes, and the possibility of fruitfulness disappears. There was religious formality—the leaves—and one might expect to see "early" fruitfulness. But the Jews were not yet believingly fruitful. The cursing of the fig tree occurs before the Lord's cleansing of the temple in Jerusalem. Before day's end tomorrow, Christ will explain the meaning of the withered tree to Peter when he is emboldened to marvel at its speedy ruin. Christ's words of judgment on the false professing fig tree combined with its visible demise capture the attention of the disciples. "And his disciples heard it," Mark notes. They heard and they received from the Lord's lips a power-

---

[15]Gk. *sukon*. The fig tree differs from most other fruit trees in that its fruit is green and inconspicuous, concealed among leaves until near the time of ripening. If the promise given from a distance by the leaves be not fulfilled on approaching (Mark 11:13), "the tree is a *hypocrite*." *UBD*, p. 1136. It is the hypocrisy that the Lord cursed when He laid judgment on the fig tree.

[16]Morgan, p. 252.

[17]Morgan.

[18]Morgan, p. 258.

ful lesson on judgment—that privileges ignored become privileges
withdrawn.

With His heart full of pity for His nation, whose abundant privileges brought only empty profession, Christ, in an acted-out parable,
holds up the unproductive fig tree as an example of misused privileges.
It is important to notice the position in Mark's narrative that this incident occupies. It is one of Mark's interrupted accounts, in the middle of
which stands the record of the cleansing of the temple. "This is the clue
to its meaning. Like the cleansing of the temple, the story of the unfruitful fig tree has to do with judgment."[19] So we see that passing on
into Jerusalem, Christ visits the temple once more, this time clearing
out the moneychangers and sellers of beasts He had observed the previous day. The Pharisees again confront Him, and Christ rebukes them for
failing to believe in Him. With clarity and confidence, Christ teaches
once more by parables: There were two sons—one who promised to
serve his father and failed to do so, a second who refused but later repented and went and served his father. There was the husbandman who
rented out his vineyard and sought fruit, but the renters killed those
who came for the produce, including the farmer's own son. There was
the refusal of those invited to the great supper. "The cap fitted too well
not to be recognized."[20] The Pharisees and priests see that Christ includes them when He speaks of such hypocritical behavior and lost
privileges. They would have, no doubt, put an end to Him right then,
but they were not yet persuaded of the way to dispose of Him. So
Christ makes His way back to Bethany for another night's solace, much
of the night, no doubt, spent in fellowship and prayer with the Father.

As Peter retraces His steps to Jerusalem with Jesus the next day—
now Tuesday of the Passion Week—his quick eye spots the barren fig
tree, now withered, its leaves fallen, its bare branches giving no promise
of either shade or fruit. "Look, Master," says Peter, "the fig tree You
cursed has withered away." To which Christ gives the unusual response:
"Peter, have faith in God. You think it a great thing that the fig tree
should wither away. Obstacles as great as this hill on which the fig tree
grows shall wither away also before the one who can trust God."

The lesson is clear. When the Son of God came to Israel, His own
people, they rejected Him. They were as the fig tree, with a profession
but no fruit of their own. And that false profession brought the Lord's
condemnation. The Jews had indeed enjoyed privileges. From that nation sprang prophets and leaders whose words spoke of the great works

---

[19]*EBC* vol. 8, p. 726.
[20]Hogg, p. 155.

of God. But there is ever a woe spoken against the people who with great opportunities produce no results—nothing but leaves.

When shall these things be?

Later that day comes another opportunity for fresh teaching on judgment with special reference to the Jews. Simon Peter is again prominent. "And as he went out of the temple, one of his disciples saith unto him, Master, see what manner of stones and what buildings are here! And Jesus answering said unto him, Seest thou these great buildings? there shall not be left one stone upon another, that shall not be thrown down" (Mark 13:1-2). In His pronouncement, Jesus predicts that the temple buildings, so greatly admired by all, will be completely destroyed, with "not one stone left upon another," a prophecy fulfilled in A.D. 70, when the Roman general Titus destroyed the temple. By the time Jesus and the disciples reach the Mount of Olives, Peter and his brother, Andrew, together with the sons of Zebedee, have had time to ponder the Lord's heavy words of judgment. They inquire, "Tell us, when shall these things be? and what shall be the sign when all these things shall be fulfilled?" (v. 4). Clearly Peter and the others want some sure way to know that the destruction of the temple is about to occur and the end of the age is near. Refusing to offer eschatological signs, the Lord instead seeks to prepare them by exhortation and warning for the trials that lie ahead. His Olivet Discourse follows. "Judgment is sure; be prepared for it to come." Citing the danger of error and its insidious effects, the Lord issues a call to watchfulness. "But of that day and that hour knoweth no man, no, not the angels which are in heaven, neither the Son, but the Father. Take ye heed, watch and pray: for ye know not when the time is. . . . And what I say unto you I say unto all, Watch" (vv. 32-33, 37).

In His cursing of the barren fig tree, the Lord Jesus presents judgment in symbol, an acted-out parable. Through His Olivet sermon, He prophesies judgment realized. Through these lessons, the Lord seeks to teach Peter his one great need—faithfulness. The lesson of the fig tree is about inconsistency, about hypocrisy, about unreality in faith. It rebukes confession without conduct. To present outward goodness without genuine inward holiness is a terrible hypocrisy. "Creed and conduct should be exactly balanced."[21] The fruitlessness of the fig tree also reminds us of our great loss. To be fruitless is to be at "a permanent inability to help others."[22] Fruit is for blessing and usefulness in reproduction. A fruitless Christian is not a help; he is a dis-

---

[21]W. H. Griffith Thomas, *The Apostle Peter* (1956), pp. 52-53.
[22]Thomas, p. 53.

tinct hindrance. As Jesus linked faith to fruitfulness, so we observe that one great secret: It is faith that links us to God and gives vitality to our Christian experience. Faith receives from God and produces fruitfulness. "Have faith in God" (Mark 11:22).

Implications for Discipleship

1. *The Lord expects fruitfulness.* As Jesus looked upon the fig tree profuse with leaves, He expected to receive from it fruit. He expects no less from believers today. The ultimate goal in discipleship is to aid and guide the Christian in his growth to maturity and to equip him so that he is capable and challenged to reproduce himself in other converts. Such a disciple is, in Hadidian's words, "a multiplier,"[23] one who is committed to the task of reproducing his life in someone else, who in turn will reproduce himself in a third spiritual generation. "You" are the first generation, "the disciple" is the second generation, and "the disciple's disciple" is the third generation. "And the things that *thou* hast heard of *me* among many witnesses, the same commit thou to *faithful men,* who shall be able to teach *others* also" (II Tim. 2:2). Here we see *four* generations! The apostle Paul, Timothy, faithful men, and others. For someone to be able to reproduce himself, he must know how to lead an unbeliever to Christ, how to ground the new believer in the Christian faith, and how to challenge and train the new believer to conduct his own discipling ministry. A multiplier helps his disciple reproduce himself spiritually in someone else. What does this remind us of? It reminds us of the three phases of a discipling ministry—saved, growing in Christlikeness, equipped to serve.

2. *Be careful not to expect fruit too early.* Mark informs us, "the time of figs was not yet." The tree had a profession, but no possession of genuine fruit. It was too early. We know the inferior quality of "hot-house" tomatoes compared to the fully ripened fruit from the vine. Is it possible to press a young Christian into spiritual service too quickly, before he has the spiritual and personal strength to meet the challenge? The apostle Paul warns of thrusting responsibility of leadership too quickly on a new convert, a "novice," one who has

---

[23] Allen Hadidian, *Discipleship* (1987), p. 36.

been "newly planted."[24] As reasonable as it is to expect fruit from a believer in an appropriate amount of time, we should be careful not to demand spiritual development beyond the individual's capacity. Nature observes this pattern. First the blade, then the stalk, then the full head of grain.[25] False enthusiasm may limit a disciple's development. We must accurately assess our disciples' needs and structure their level of involvement accordingly. We will find, of course, that there will be those who will be similar to those rebuked in the Epistle to the Hebrews. "For when for the time ye ought to be teachers, ye have need that one teach you again which be the first principles of the oracles of God; and are become such as have need of milk, and not of strong meat" (5:12). But we should thank God for those who develop and mature along a steady path of growth and who show aptitude for evangelism and teaching.

3. *Challenge the disciple's faith.* "Be constantly having faith in God,"[26] Jesus implores His disciples. All that Christ ever did was in dependence on the blessed Holy Spirit, who continually empowered the words He spoke, the prayers He uttered, the miracles He performed, the life He lived. Thus, when He cursed the fig tree, reasons Wuest, the Lord Jesus, exercised faith that the Holy Spirit would empower Him to accomplish the task and in so doing pressed home the necessity of faith to the disciples.[27] Jesus shows us that faith in God should be constant, the normal attitude of our hearts. Faith is not to be a sudden emotion or isolated act. We should be constantly having faith in God. That kind of faith will move mountains, seeing in its exercise the effect as potentially fulfilled.

---

[24]I Tim. 3:6.
[25]Mark 4:28.
[26]Mark 11:22.
[27]Kenneth S. Wuest, *Mark in the Greek New Testament* (1957), p. 224.

THE MASTER PREPARES TO LEAVE

Beginning with the supper scene in the upper room, the Lord Jesus devotes an increasing amount of time to preparing His disciples for when He will no longer be with them on earth. He has told them of His impending death at Jerusalem and also that resurrection will follow. Soon He must leave them to return to the Father in heaven, so He will ask the Father to send another Comforter, the Holy Spirit, who will continue to teach them of Him. Before the Lord's final hours on earth are completed, the apostle Peter will suffer his disastrous fall, only to recover through the Lord's loving and gentle restoration to fellowship and service.

IN THE UPPER ROOM

Thou shalt never wash my feet (John 13:8).

> *From the table now retiring,*
> *Which for us the Lord hath spread,*
> *May our souls, refreshment finding,*
> *Grow in all things like our Head.*
>
> *His example while beholding,*
> *May our lives His image bear;*
> *Him our Lord and Master calling,*
> *His commands may we revere.*
>
> *Love to God and man displaying,*
> *Walking steadfast in His way,*
> *Joy attend us in believing,*
> *Peace from God, thru endless day.*

> *—John Rowe*

Setting: Jerusalem, Thursday, April 2, A.D. 33
Scripture: John 13:1-35

Like the alternating lights and shadows on the Urim and Thummin on the breastplate of the high priest of old, the story of our Lord's final hours with His beloved disciples proceeds "radiant with glory, and yet almost terrible with deep darkness."[1] The apostle John, who has said very little about the special relations of Jesus with the apostles up to this point, brings us inside the upper room to witness these special moments. "Now before the feast of the passover, when Jesus knew that his hour was come that he should depart out of this world unto the Father, having loved his own which were in the world, he loved them unto the end" (John 13:1). The Lord has uttered His final word to the outside world. He is with those He "loved unto the end," having shown His love to them in every conceivable way. Not selfishly engrossed with His own sorrows or with the anticipated joy of reuniting with the Father, Christ finds room in His heart for His disciples. His love for them "burns with extraordinary ardor."[2] Throughout this scene of dramatic interchange, Peter again draws forth our attention, though our

---

[1] G. Campbell Morgan, *The Gospel According to John* (n.d.), p. 227. "For the devout student of the oracles of God, the wonders of this section [i.e., John 13-17] never ceases."

[2] A. B. Bruce, *The Training of the Twelve* (n.d.), p. 342.

173

fuller focus must remain on the Lord Jesus as He ever moves toward the cross.

We are told nothing of Jesus' whereabouts on Wednesday of the Passion Week, the Scriptures being respectfully silent. Perhaps He spent these last hours in deep contemplation of the immense task that still lay before Him. Wednesday night the Lord lays Himself down to rest for the last time on earth. His next sleep will be in the tomb. The following morning,[3] the disciples discuss among themselves how the Master plans to observe the Passover, possibly expecting Him to take it at Bethany rather than inside Jerusalem, where His safety is gravely in question. It is Christ's selection of Peter and John for a special mission (the only occasion in the Gospels in which we see these two disciples acting together at the Lord's bidding) that resolves the question. The Lord directs the two trusted disciples to go into Jerusalem, where they will meet, He tells them, a household slave[4] carrying water from one of the springs in the city to his master's house. They are to follow the servant and, entering the same building he enters, they are to ask the owner of the house the location of the guest chamber. He will show them "a large upper room furnished and prepared" (Mark 14:15). This is where Peter and John are to make things ready and where Christ will partake of the Passover meal with His disciples.[5] Why the apparent secrecy? Why are these two—Peter and John—favored by the Lord for this special task? Why not give the assignment to Judas Iscariot, who

---

[3]Thursday, April 2, A.D. 33. Harold W. Hoehner, *Chronological Aspects of the Life of Christ* (1977), p. 143.

[4]Conspicuous because he was a man, this chore usually performed by women?

[5]Whether this meal was the actual Passover has been debated. It appears that this "Last Supper" occurred on the same night of the Lord's arrest in the garden. If so, the meal was then on Thursday night, the Crucifixion taking place on Friday, after the arrest and trial of the Lord. The Synoptics indicate that Jesus did intend to eat the Passover with His disciples (Matt. 26:18; Mark 14:14; Luke 22:11), though no mention is made of the Passover lamb. Hoehner presents both sides of the discussion, concluding that this meal was indeed the Passover, noting that much of the difficulty involving the Synoptics and the Gospel of John can be removed by showing that it was generally accepted that different calendars for reckoning the Passover were used by various groups and regions. It is tenable to conclude that the Galileans (and thus Jesus and His disciples) reckoned from sunrise to sunrise while the Judeans reckoned from sunset to sunset, thus allowing Jesus and His followers to observe the Passover while the Jews, who refused to enter the Praetorium so as not to defile themselves, later in the day could still be eligible to slay the animals for those Judeans who reckoned from sunset to sunset. Hoehner, pp. 76-90. In reaching his conclusion, Hoehner makes extensive use of the scholarly work of Joachim Jeremias, *The Eucharistic Words of Jesus*; A. J. B. Higgins, *The Lord's Supper in the New Testament*; and George Ogg, "The Chronology of the Last Supper," *Historicity and Chronology in the New Testament*.

seems to have borne some responsibility for the welfare of the small group since he handles the finances? We can only speculate at the Lord's concerns. Perhaps He desires to keep the location of the room secret, particularly to Judas, who is, after all, conspiring with the Lord's enemies in Jerusalem. If Judas knows where the Passover is to be kept, it will be easy enough for him to arrange for Christ's arrest at the house of the upper room. Luke tells us directly that Judas was duplicitous, that Satan having entered into him, "he went his way, and communed with the chief priests and captains, how he might betray [Christ] unto them. And they were glad, and covenanted to give him money. And he promised, and sought opportunity to betray him unto them in the absence of the multitude" (Luke 22:4-6). Had Judas been successful in betraying Jesus in the upper room, Hogg laments, "we should have had no Last Supper, no last discourse . . . while the disciples would have no chance to provide for their own safety by flight."[6] For His own reasons, therefore, the Lord sends Peter and John on their errand, and the arrangements are completed as Christ had instructed. Who "the goodman of the house" (Mark 14:14) was, who thus placed his upper chamber at the Lord's disposal, we do not know.[7] It must have been someone friendly to Him, though it is also difficult to imagine that anyone in a close relationship with the Lord Jesus would have failed to provide the customary comforts as the washing of feet, which, as the story unfolds, are left to neglect.[8] But with so many pilgrims crowding into the city, their Passover needs, in addition to those of the residents of Jerusalem, meant that household help could have been scarce.

How dare You wash my feet?

As the disciples are about to take their places at this last Passover, the "eternal squabble"[9] about precedence once more breaks out.

---

[6]Quintin Hogg, *The Story of Peter* (1900), p. 171.

[7]According to some traditions, it was Joseph of Arimathea; according to others, the upper room was in the house occupied by John Mark's mother, Mary.

[8]To provide a setting for the Passover meal in the upper room, Hogg describes its probable interior. "The walls of the upper room would probably be white, and the room itself would contain only the most necessary articles of furniture. In the centre of it would be a mat kept scrupulously clean, before treading on which the guests would remove their sandals so as to pass over it with bare feet. In one corner of the room would stand a large copper basin, filled with water for the purpose of ablution, and in the centre of the mat would stand a very low table, probably painted some bright colour. Round three sides of this table would run either cushions or setees for the accommodation of the guests. Each of these cushions or setees would be large enough for three persons, and the seat of honour was the central place of the central setee." Hogg, p. 173.

[9]Hogg.

Annoyed, perhaps, at being passed over in the matter of obtaining the upper room, Judas Iscariot asserts his right as treasurer of the disciples to take one of the places next to the Master, providing him ease of partaking of the same elements of the meal as the Lord Himself. At Christ's right reclines John, making it normal for him to rest on the bosom of his Lord. Farther, then, to Judas's left lay Simon Peter, the other disciples wrangling over the final positions toward either end of the low table. His "hour" has now come. The Lord Jesus knows that He is about to depart from this world to reunite with His Father in supernal glory. He had shown His love to His disciples in every conceivable way. John says that "Jesus knowing[10] that the Father had given all things into his hands, and that he was come forth from God, and went to God; He *riseth*" (John 13:3-4). Rising from His reclining position at the meal,[11] the Lord Jesus removes His outer garments, girds Himself with a towel—the sign and badge of a slave—and, going round the perimeter of the gathered men, begins to wash their feet individually. Judas,[12] for one, raises no protest, though the Lord's humble service must have aroused some fast-fading honor from the better side of his nature, if only as a reproach to the evil part he knows he is playing. But when Christ comes to Peter, the impulsive, warm-hearted apostle cannot bear to see his Master perform a menial task for him. Leaping from his seat, he cries out in protest, "How dare You wash my feet?" To which Christ sternly replies, "Peter, if I don't wash you, you have no part in Me." Then with a bound to the other extreme, Peter exclaims, "Then don't just wash my feet; wash my hands and my head. Wash all of me!" Our back-and-forth, prone-to-exaggeration disciple has done it again!

Jesus must further explain: "He that is washed[13] needeth not save to wash[14] his feet, but is clean every whit" (v. 10). The one who is bathed does not need to bathe again; he needs only to wash his feet. Christ's

---

[10]Morgan terms this the "causative consciousness" of Jesus, that is, the consciousness that led Him to the action recorded here, p. 229. "Too often the death of Jesus is spoken of as a martyrdom, the heroic surrender to the inevitable circumstances. There is no scintilla of truth in that view of the Cross. The New Testament accounts all reveal Him as moving with mien and attitude of One carrying out a Divine programme; His soul troubled, but always seeing through the gloom to the glory," p. 230. W. H. Griffith Thomas also notes this moment of "high consciousness" of the Lord Jesus, that He was conscious of (1) sovereign power, "had given all things," (2) divine position, "came forth from God," and (3) glorious prospect, "back to God." Yet He humbled Himself. *The Apostle Peter* (1956), p. 54.

[11]KJV "supper being ended" (v. 2) is "during supper," ASB.

[12]Legend has it that Jesus went to Judas first.

[13]Gk. *louo*, "a complete washing."

[14]Gk. *nipto*, "to wash a part of the body." Also in vv. 5, 6, 8. The meaning of Jesus is clear in His choice of two different Greek words. "The work of Christ draws

allusion is, of course, to the practice of bathing at the public bath-houses, where, after cleaning one's entire body, the person was obliged, out of necessity, to rinse off his dusty feet, made so by his return walk from the bathhouse. Peter is already a disciple. His standing is "secured and assured."[15] But he needs daily cleansing from defilement.

Peter's responses during this exchange with the Lord, rather than reflecting intense devotion, reveal serious misunderstanding, if not actual disobedience. By his vehement refusals, Peter resists once again, as he had earlier at Caesarea Philippi, the Lord's purposes. In both responses, Peter asserts his own judgment and thus shows "incipient disobedience."[16] His first response—"Lord, *You* would wash *my* feet?"—is inconsistent with the Lord's dignity and purpose, for if He had not humbled Himself, there would be no incarnation, no sacrifice, no salvation. Peter's second reply—"You shall *never* wash my feet!"—is an affront to Christ's Lordship. Peter's objections compromised the whole sum and substance of Christianity, his first sweeping away Christ's whole state and experience of *humiliation*, and the latter not less certainly sapping the foundation of Christ's *lordship*.[17] This is no exaggeration. If Jesus may not wash the feet of His disciples because it is beneath His dignity, then with equal reason objection may be taken to any act involving self-humiliation. "In short, incarnation, atonement, and Christ's whole earthly experience of temptation, hardship, indig-nity, and sorrow must go if Jesus may not wash a disciple's feet."[18] No less clearly is Christ's lordship at an end if a disciple may give Him or-ders, and say, "You shall never wash my feet." Peter's reversion to being "Satan" is in full bloom. He would not submit to the Lord's de-sires because his own moral senses and judgment tell him it is wrong to do so. He makes his own reason and conscience the supreme rule of conduct. By this he compromises the principle that says that the will of the Lord, once known, whether we understand the reason or perceive its goodness, shall be supreme. To be Christ's disciple, we are told to leave father, mother, and all else dear; Peter's principle would therefore tell us, "I won't do such a thing." To be born again, we are to eat His flesh and drink His blood; Peter's principle would tell us, "I don't wish to follow those dark sayings of the Master." Christ says we must give

---

a permanent line between those who have been cleansed and those who are not clean. There is need, however, for washing from incidental defilement and for the Christian's continuing growth in grace." *EBC* vol. 9, p. 138.

[15]Thomas, p. 56.

[16]Thomas.

[17]Bruce, p. 346.

[18]Bruce.

the kingdom of God first place in our thoughts; Peter's principle says, "In my present situation that is impossible, so I will set this requirement aside."

To be in Christ's kingdom is to receive Him for who He is and what He claims the power to perform. Obedience is the secret to discipleship. But if the Son of God may have no part with us, then we can have no part with Him. If Christ does not wash us, we have no part in the salvation He brings, no part in Him or His kingdom. If we do not submit to His divine purposes, we fail to acknowledge Him as Lord. Both are necessary. Jesus is Savior and He is Lord. Jesus' stern declaration brings Peter to his better senses, or rather "unreason in an opposite direction."[19] The idea of being cut off from the Master's favor through his waywardness drives Peter in sheer fright to the opposite extreme of overdone compliance. "Lord, wash my whole body—hands, feet, head, and all." There is still a sad lack of balance in Peter's character, swinging like a pendulum from one extreme to another. But we know he is sound at the core and after a due amount of mistakes, he will become a disciple with discernment by and by, writing of our abundant entrance "into the everlasting kingdom of our *Lord and Saviour* Jesus Christ,"[20] no longer challenging either the Lord's humiliation or His lordship.

While correcting Peter, the Lord cites the sad exception that "ye are not all clean" (v. 11). One was far from it. Though He does not name him, Jesus knew[21] of Judas Iscariot's evil intentions. Nor does He say in what respect that one is unclean; the disciples are left with a riddle that is not answered until the Lord plainly says later "one of you shall betray me" (v. 21). We must not pass from this scene without reflecting on its meaning for sinners today. Unless we are cleansed by the blood of the blessed Lord Jesus, we too shall have no part in Him. Unless the gospel of the saving grace of Christ has done its cleansing power in us, we have no right to claim any part of Him. And with regard to our necessity for daily cleansing, does not the word of Christ tell us that those who have knelt at the foot of the cross and have come to know the saving merit of that sacrifice still need the daily

---

[19]Bruce, p. 349.

[20]Second Pet. 1:11; see also 2:20, 3:2, and 3:18, where Peter speaks of Christ as Lord and Savior.

[21]Gk. *oida,* "know," is generally used by John to denote certain knowledge of a fact rather than experiential acquaintance with a situation or person. It is connected with Jesus' supernatural knowledge of His origin, destiny, or circumstances. The total impression by the use of *oida* is that Jesus completely understood what He was doing and that God's program for Him was not simply a series of accidents He had to meet fortuitously. "The concept fits with John's general picture of him as the divine Son of God, who came to perform the Father's will." *EBC* vol. 9, p. 139.

cleansing from worldly defilement that comes to all as we move about in this sinful world? Our faithful God will forgive our sinful stains of daily defilement as we confess them to Him.

I have given you an example

Our Lord now applies what He has just taught by His surprise foot washing. Returning to His place at the table, after laying aside the servant's badge and donning His own garment once more, He presents to them a question. "Do you know what I have done?" The disciples' discernment, as we have seen from the first days at Bethabara, has developed slowly. He has just told them that He loved them in every conceivable way, yet they still do not comprehend the intensity of His love for them. Over and over He has also demonstrated the nature of His humility in dealing with them. The Lord has even now told Peter that he does not know what is being done. "What I do thou knowest not now; but thou shalt know hereafter" (v. 7). For Peter, "hereafter" is but moments away. So that all may hear and learn, the Lord tells them, "Ye call me Master and Lord: and ye say well; for so I am. If I then, your Lord and Master, have washed your feet; ye also ought to wash one another's feet. For I have given you an example, that ye should do as I have done to you" (vv. 13-15). What has He done for them?[22] He has just stripped Himself of dignity and has taken the lowly station of a slave. All this to serve them. This is the predicted "hereafter." Peter now knows the Lord's intentions. He is among them as one who serves. It is therefore the Lord's powerful example of humble service, when He clothed Himself with the knotted garment of a slave, that will lead Peter again to write, "Yea, all of you be subject one to another, and be *clothed with humility:* for God resisteth the proud, and giveth grace to the humble. Humble yourselves therefore under the mighty hand of God, that he may exalt you in due time" (I Pet. 5:5-6).

The Lord completes His thought. "Verily, verily, I say unto you, The servant is not greater than his lord; neither he that is sent greater

---

[22]Certain segments of the Christian church take the Lord's words quite literally, choosing to observe foot washing as a ritual as carefully as the Lord's Supper and baptism. The "example" that the Lord speaks of does not, it seems to me, necessarily imply that believers are to perpetuate foot washing as an ordinance. The Lord's Supper and baptism both picture the gospel in some measure; foot washing does not. The "example" the Lord seems to be teaching implies an emphasis on one's inner attitude of humble and voluntary service of others, whatever form that service may take for believers today. The only other allusion to foot washing in the NT is in I Timothy 5:10, where it does not refer to a regular custom but seems to allude to charitable work toward the poor. *EBC* vol. 9, p. 137.

THE MAKING OF A DISCIPLE

than he that sent him. If ye know these things, happy are ye if ye do them" (John 13:16-17). Referring once again to His own mission given to Him from the Father, of which He was constantly conscious, the Lord now includes His disciples in the endeavor of servanthood. The true nature of the Christian life is serving others. For those willing to take this humble role upon themselves, Jesus promises great blessing.

Lord, who is it?

Though he does not record the actual Passover feast, John continues his account of that memorable night by remembering incidents that must have spoken to his own heart. Jesus startles the assembled Twelve with a dreadful announcement: Someone from their own midst will "betray" Him. This is not the first time the Lord spoke of His betrayal. He had announced it a year earlier after His hard demands on those who sought to follow Him.[23] But the disciples had not taken it to heart, as they had dismissed so much of His attempt to prepare them for the future, though on that earlier occasion Peter confessed his confidence in the divine mission of the Lord Jesus. Now, however, the hostility of the Jewish leaders in Jerusalem brought what seemed a remote implication into the realm of an immediate possibility. Though fully aware of Judas's impending betrayal, it still weighs heavily on the Lord so that He is "troubled in spirit" (v. 21), displaying the same agitation within that He experienced at the grave of Lazarus (11:33). The disciples do not know how to take this announcement or how to deal with His obvious agitation. They simply stare at one another until Peter, with his usual straightforwardness, suggests that John, who is nearest to Jesus, ask the Lord to identify the traitor. Perhaps Peter contemplates some preventive action if he learns in advance who the person might be who will betray the Lord. Leaning on the Lord's bosom, the apostle of love turns to intercede: "Lord, who is it?" (v. 25).

Jesus gives no specific identification. He simply indicates that the offender will be the one to whom He gives the special morsel He dips into the dish in front of Him. "He it is, to whom I shall give a sop, when I have dipped it. And when he had dipped the sop, he gave it to Judas Iscariot, the son of Simon" (v. 26). We must not lose sight of the custom in that day. For the host to select such a morsel from the main dish and give it to a guest would be a mark of courtesy and esteem.[24] For the disciples to see Jesus give a special morsel to Judas would mean that Jesus regarded him as a friend in whom He had confidence.

---

[23] John 6:70.
[24] *EBC* vol. 9, p. 140.

180

It is His "own familiar friend" in whom He trusted, as David did Ahithophel—one who ate bread with David, yet who rose up against him.[25] By His action, the Lord speaks a dual message: to Judas, He knows perfectly well what the traitor intends to do; to the disciples, He maintains a veil of ambiguity without openly disturbing them of what lies ahead. "That thou doest, do quickly" (v. 27), Jesus pleads after Satan enters Judas following the morsel of friendship. The Lord is clear. Judas makes the choice; He ratifies that choice with His own authority. It is as though the Lord is saying to Judas, "I have offered you the symbol of friendship, but you have made your own choice. What you intend to do, do it now." For Judas, it is now or never. The plot is "discovered." For it to succeed, the rulers must act at once! In its obliqueness, the Lord's action is, nevertheless, an open invitation to Judas to renounce His treachery. It is, lamentably, also the Lord's recognition that in the end, the deed will be done. Conscious that the time has come for His sacrifice, Jesus ushers Judas toward his own selfish end.

In little more than six weeks hence, Peter will preach to the people in Jerusalem about the cross to which Judas had betrayed Jesus. He was "delivered," Peter says, "by the determinate counsel and foreknowledge of God" (Acts 2:23). "Evil will deliver up Christ, but the infinite love and compassion of God will over-rule that betrayal, so that it becomes the very means by which redemption is provided for a race. Thus Judas, and the devil behind Judas, are seen under the control of God. He was over-ruling all. Expelled was evil, and so compelled to accomplish God's own program."[26] It is night, "night outside; night also inside the heart of Judas![27] and the Satan-inspired Judas has gone into his own "night" (v. 30) to carry out the purposes of darkness. Jesus now will continue His intimate ministry with the eleven who remain.[28]

Love one another

At this pivotal moment in the Lord's ministry, when it appears that the worst has come, He is nevertheless to be "glorified." John continues: "Therefore, when he was gone out, Jesus said, Now is the Son of man glorified, and God is glorified in him. If God be glorified

---

[25]Ps. 41:9. In David's case, the allusion is to the traitor Ahithophel (II Sam. 17:1-14). This is the verse Jesus applies to Judas Iscariot in v. 18.

[26]Morgan, p. 238.

[27]William Hendriksen, *Exposition of the Gospel of John* (1970), p. 250.

[28]With the departure of Judas, Jesus begins His long farewell discourse with His remaining disciples. His statement about His "glorification" is about to take place and this farewell section extends all the way through the end of His prayer in John 17.

in him, God shall also glorify him in himself, and shall straightway glorify him" (vv. 31-32). This very moment, which seems to spell "defeat, dishonor, and disaster,"[29] the Son of man is actually glorified! And God is glorified in Him. "The two are inseparable. Whenever we think of Christ's suffering, we never know what to admire most: whether it be the voluntary self-surrender of *the Son* to such a death for such people, or the willingness of *the Father* to give up such a Son to such a death for such people."[30] The Father and the Son glorify each other, for though they are two persons, they are one in essence.

Knowing that in a few short hours the intimate association with His disciples that has marked the last three years will end, never to be resumed in that same earthly fashion, Christ speaks to them as "little children" (v. 33).[31] Though still spiritually immature, they are nonetheless precious to Him, as dear children. By His death, resurrection, and ascension, He will go back to the Father. That is why they cannot follow Him: Yet they will follow Him "afterwards" (v. 36), after they die. Not so for those unbelieving Jews; they will die in their sins.[32] Although the disciples will no longer rejoice in the visible presence of the Lord, they will still be able to enjoy one another's visible presence. "A new commandment I give unto you, That ye love one another; as I have loved you, that ye also love one another. By this shall all men know that ye are my disciples, if ye have love one to another" (vv. 34-35).[33] The commandment to love one's neighbor is, of course, found in the OT.[34] Love for God and for one's neighbor is, in fact, the summary of the law.[35] But the *newness* of the precept here announced stems from this fact: they are to love one another *as He loved them!*[36] How has Christ loved them? John has already told us of Christ's constant love for them to the end (13:1), how He loved them in every conceivable way. That is

---

[29]Hendriksen, p. 250.

[30]Hendriksen.

[31]Gk., *teknia*. The only occurrence of this word in the Gospels.

[32]John 8:21.

[33]Holden cites a tradition that says that John in his old age was carried into church at Ephesus every Lord's Day, just to say, "Little children, love one another." Questioned as to its constant reiteration, the old man could reply only, "Because this is the Lord's sole command. If we fulfill this there's nothing more to be done." J. Stuart Holden, *The Master and His Men* (1953), p. 78. Of course, the Lord did give us other commands, among them the worldwide proclamation of the gospel, but the spirit of this tradition captures the essence of John's emphasis on loving one another, particularly in his epistles.

[34]Lev. 19:18.

[35]Mark 12:29, 31.

[36]Hendriksen, p. 253.

to be their pattern too. Genuine, self-sacrificing love for others is to mark the true disciple. "This is the way people will know you are My disciples; they will see how you love one another genuinely and completely!" Tertullian, writing at the end of the second century, said, "It is mainly the deeds of a love so noble that lead many to put a brand on us. 'See,' they say, 'how they love one another,' for they themselves are animated by mutual hatred; 'see how they are ready even to die for one another,' for they themselves will rather be put to death."[37] The measure to which believers love one another is the measure by which unbelievers will see genuineness in Christianity.

> *He serves thee best who loveth most*
> *His brothers and Thy own.*[38]

Implications for Discipleship

1. *Jesus Christ is Savior and Lord.* As Jesus began to teach the significance of His work on the cross, He also expounded other stringent conditions for those who would continue as disciples in a deeper, committed sense. In various settings, Jesus said that a disciple must deny himself, take up his cross, follow Christ, lose his life, not be ashamed of Christ, and hate his family and his own life.[39] The nature of these commitments and the fact that they were directed primarily to those who were already His close followers show that they are conditions of a deeper relationship with Jesus as Lord and Master, not conditions of salvation. They represent a progression in the revelation of God's will that must be accepted if a believer will continue in the path of discipleship. This is the reason that Jesus was so firm in dealing with Peter's refusals. Peter placed his own opinions above the revelation of Jesus as Savior and Lord. When a believer replaces the known revelation of God's will with his own knowledge or experience, he places himself in the dangerous position of having Jesus say, "If you will not have part in Me, I will have no part in you." By the Lord's own teaching, we see that discipleship is something that is very costly to the Christian.

---

[37]Tertullian, *Apology XXXIX*, quoted by Hendriksen, p. 254.

[38]John Greenleaf Whittier, "Our Master," *The Poetical Works of John Greenleaf Whittier* (1892), p. 232.

[39]Matt. 16:24-27; Mark 8:34-38; Luke 14:26-33.

To be a disciple in the broadest sense is to be a follower, or learner, of Jesus Christ. In the narrower sense used by Christ later in His ministry, it meant to be fully committed to follow Him and to learn from Him in a life of self-denial and obedience to His Word. The stringent conditions Christ attached to this latter sense of discipleship must not be made conditions of salvation[40] but should move us who are Christians further into God's will.

2. *Discernment takes time to develop.* The disciples' discernment developed slowly. The Bible clearly presents mature discernment as a necessary component to the believer's growth in the Lord. Christians of "full age," through continued practice of making spiritually sound decisions, grow stronger in their ability "to discern both good and evil" (Heb. 5:14). Peter's immature resistance to the Lord Jesus pointed up his need for further development in spiritual discernment, to build on what Jesus said of him earlier— that flesh and blood did not reveal the truth about His deity to Peter, but rather it was the Father in heaven who gave that discernment to him. Yet it is not time alone that will produce discernment. I have witnessed new converts, particularly from campus evangelism ministries, who grew exceedingly rapidly in their Christian experience, often outpacing believers who had been Christians since childhood. These newer converts uniformly manifested a strong sense of obedience to the Lord and a sincere love for His Word that brought about substantial spiritual growth over a relatively short period of time. I was amazed at the spiritual insights such new converts displayed. Disciplers who work with new converts have an obligation to maintain that same focus on obedience, not to allow self to interfere with the Lord's will, as Peter sought to do in the upper room.

3. *True leadership consists of character, knowledge, and skills.*[41] In His upper room discourse, the Lord Jesus stressed those character qualities and leadership skills the disciples would need to fulfill the task before them. "The basic ele-

---

[40]This is commonly termed "lordship salvation."

[41]Bill Hull, *Jesus Christ Disciple Maker* (1984), p. 213. The Lord's intimate conversations with His disciples in the upper room mark the beginning of the fourth and final aspect of His discipleship training as outlined by Hull.

ments taught by Jesus in His upper room discourse—humility, love, confidence, effective prayer, obedience, understanding of the Holy Spirit, and fruitfulness—are a combination of character traits resulting from applied knowledge. When put into practice, they are ministry skills."[42] When Jesus got down on His knees to wash the disciples' feet, it made a lasting effect on Peter. He heard from the Lord Jesus that the one who seeks to lead must be willing to serve. Peter also heard that the Lord's disciples are to love others, for He knew that the love of Christians for one another is a most powerful form of evangelism. When we care for others, we show to unbelievers that we truly follow God. And we cannot serve God without remaining in constant contact with Him through prayer and fellowship in His Word. In all this, the Holy Spirit must superintend our conduct, providing encouragement in times of trial or discouragement. The three years Peter and the others spent with the Lord Jesus were not to be in vain. We shall see the fruit of their labors in due time.

[42]Hull.

SUPREME FAILURE

I know Him not (Luke 22:57).

In the hour of trial, Jesus, plead for me,
Lest by base denial I depart from Thee;
When Thou seest me waver, with a look recall,
Nor for fear or favor suffer me to fall.

—*James Montgomery*

Setting: The upper room, the Mount of Olives, and various locations throughout Jerusalem; Friday of the Passion Week, A.D. 33

Scripture: John 13:33-38; 18:1–19:42; also Matt. 26:26–27:66; Mark 14:22–15:41; Luke 22:31–23:56

With Judas Iscariot now gone into the night to complete his dark deed of treason, an atmosphere of freedom and intimate interchange of thought and expression replaces the tense moments that earlier have marked the scene. Christ turns to His loyal men and speaks to them in loving words preserved for us in John 14-16, perhaps continuing to relieve their anxieties as they walk through the city streets toward the Mount of Olives. "Let not your heart be troubled. . . . I go to prepare a place for you. . . . I will come again. . . . I will not leave you comfortless. . . . Because I live, ye shall live also. . . . My peace I give unto you. . . . I am the vine, ye are the branches. . . . Continue ye in my love. . . . Ye are my friends, if ye do whatsoever I command you. . . . Ye have not chosen me, but I have chosen you, and ordained you, that ye should go and bring forth fruit. . . . Be of good cheer, I have overcome the world."

John also takes us into those holiest of moments when in chapter 17 Jesus pours out His soul in His high priestly intercession for His own. "Father, the hour is come. . . . I have finished the work which thou gavest me to do. . . . I have manifested thy name unto the men which thou gavest me out of the world. . . . I pray for them. . . . Sanctify them through thy truth. . . . Father, I will that they also, whom thou hast given me, be with me where I am." His blessed reunion with the Father, which Jesus so tellingly anticipates, is to be the believer's portion too. As the Father is in the Son and the Son in the Father, we also will be one with Him and participate in His glory! What wondrous prospects awaiting the child of God are brought before us for our meditation by these closing expressions of love from the Lord Jesus.

But now to Simon Peter. We come now to that moment in Peter's story when, forgetful of the Lord and full of himself, he falls prey to Satan, taking a course that we regret ever happened. Scripture gives us the details, showing us the dark side as well as the bright, in contrast to human biographers who "draw a veil of charity"[1] over the defects of those they chronicle. The incidents involving Peter multiply during these last hours as we follow the Lord's arrest, trial, and crucifixion. We walk on holy ground as we leave the upper room, cross the ravine of the brook Kidron to the Mount of Olives and Gethsemane's garden. The scenes about to unfold fill the final chapters of all four Gospel accounts.

I'm praying for you

The Lord Jesus has tarried long with Peter and the others in the upper room as friends often do before a final departure. He does not leave, however, until He speaks prophetic words of solemn warning to them all, but especially to Peter. During these precious moments with His men, the Lord describes His imminent death as a journey He must take, a journey, He says, in which they cannot follow Him. "Little children, yet a little while I am with you. Ye shall seek me: and as I said unto the Jews, Whither I go, ye cannot come; so now I say to you" (John 13:33). "Not follow You?" bursts in Peter, "Why not?" Affirming that he will lay down his life for the Lord's sake, Peter will not allow the Lord to proceed on that long journey, nor will he leave his Master to walk any dark valley alone. To this Christ replies with solemn warning: "Will you lay down your life for My sake? See! It is already late at night. The cock shall not crow before you deny that you know Me." Simon has been given a warning and we can only speculate that if he had heeded the admonition, what a different sequel would follow. But all former lessons on self-confidence appear to be lost on Peter as he vehemently asserts his readiness to sacrifice his own life as companion to the Lord Jesus on His journey. "If all You speak of is a dangerous journey, then You can count on me to die for You," he protests. Our rash and impetuous disciple once again demonstrates a weakness of spirit that will allow the Evil One to take advantage of him if our ever-present help in time of trouble does not intercede for him. Instead of pleading with Christ, "Lord, keep me," Peter asserts his own self-confidence. "Wherefore let him that thinketh he standeth take heed lest he fall" (I Cor. 10:12).

---

[1] W. P. T. Wolston, *Simon Peter* (1926), p. 107.

Supreme Failure

And not for signs in heaven above
Or earth below they look,
Who know with John His smile of love,
With Peter His rebuke.[2]

—John Greenleaf Whittier

Luke adds a darker hue to the Lord's grave words. Addressing Peter by his pre-conversion name, a sign perhaps that Peter is reflecting too much of the old Simon and not the stability of the rock, Jesus warns, "Simon, Simon, behold, Satan hath desired to have you, that he may sift you as wheat" (Luke 22:31). While speaking directly to Simon, Jesus declares that a sifting process is upon them all.[3] What Jesus reveals about Satan's actions toward God's people is highly instructive. "Satan has obtained you by asking"[4] is the real force of the Lord's caution: "Listen, Simon," Jesus warns, "Satan wants you and all the others so that he may ruin you." The Lord starkly reveals Satan's evil intent directed toward them all, which the Devil had previously tried unsuccessfully with Job,[5] an evil craving, we must admit, that continues unabated toward the saints of God to the present hour. Satan's demonic purpose is to usurp the authority of God over His people and to destroy every ounce of their spiritual relation with the Father. He would render worthless, if he could, our devotion and enslave us in his own hellish ends. But, praise to God, Satan is also under God's authority. Though he lusts for the hearts and souls of men, he can go no further than God permits; He cannot "sift" unless God allows. As with his request over Job, the Devil "cannot touch a hair upon the back of a camel that Job owns, until he has God's permission to do it."[6] He has no power to snatch any child of God from the Father's hand.[7] So the Lord makes use of His tool, Satan, to break Peter of his self-confidence. Wolston takes us forward to Peter at Pentecost—restored and happy in the love of the Lord Jesus—testifying to the risen Christ and preaching with Holy Spirit power so that three thousand souls are brought to Christ, the Devil now "heartily sorry" that he had not left Peter alone in the high priest's hall. "But

---

[2]John Greenleaf Whittier, "Our Master," *The Poetical Works of John Greenleaf Whittier* (1892), p. 231.

[3]"You" is plural in Greek, referring to all the disciples. Jesus speaks "a word in season to all, and concerning all." A. B. Bruce, *The Training of the Twelve* (n.d.), p. 471.

[4]ASB, or "asked to have you."

[5]Job 1:11.

[6]G. Campbell Morgan, *The Gospel According to Luke* (1931), p. 247.

[7]John 10:28-29.

for that bitter experience [Peter] would never had been enough broken down, humbled, and self-emptied, for the Lord to use him in that marvelous manner."[8]

Despite the tremendous spiritual pressures Peter will face as he contends with the wiles of the Devil, the Lord Jesus assures him of His intercessory presence and power. "But I have prayed for thee,[9] that thy faith fail not: and when thou art converted,[10] strengthen thy brethren" (v. 32). Not only does Satan ask for him but also the Lord asks in prayer for Peter. What a startling revelation! "A man, Simon, and the Devil and Christ both praying for him. Satan asking to have him and sift him and destroy him. Christ standing as his Bondman, asking that his faith shall not fail."[11] The Lord's prayer is that Peter's faith will not fail. It would appear that this is precisely what fell to Peter—he lost faith. But such is not the case at all. Let it be said that Peter's faith, though it may have suffered an eclipse, did not fail;[12] nor did his love for the Lord fail.

This entire ordeal, which we know so well, rather than disqualifying Peter for future service, will actually result in an increased responsibility. Jesus expects His frail disciple to become strong in grace, and thus able and willing to help the weak. Because of his experience—a supreme failure brought about through his own lapse— Peter will one day speak with forceful conviction that although the Devil, "as a roaring lion," seeks to destroy the people of God, he is to be resisted "stedfast in the faith" (I Pet. 5:8-9). When he turns around and faces the Lord's full embrace of forgiveness, he will find that he has the capacity to provide strength for other believers who suffer persecution and temptations. We must not lose sight of this encouraging word as forecast by Jesus. Peter will fail through weakness, but not through loss of faith. Peter still boasts, however, replying that he is ready to go with Him—to prison or even death! To which the Lord repeats His alarming deadline: "I tell thee, Peter, the cock shall not crow this day, before that thou shalt thrice deny that thou knowest me" (Luke 22:34).

---

[8]Wolston, p. 109.

[9]Singular in Greek. The Lord speaks directly to Peter in His warning and encouragement.

[10]Not converted in the sense of salvation, but "turned again" (ASB) in that Peter is better prepared because of the experience to establish other believers as strong in the faith.

[11]Morgan, p. 248.

[12]The verbal phrase "thy faith fail not" (Gk., *me eklipe*) probably means "may not give out" or "may not disappear completely" (as the sun in a total eclipse). If this is correct, then Jesus' prayer was certainly answered. Peter's denial, though serious

They sang a hymn

At last this prolonged night meeting draws to a close. The disciples rise from their couches and, before departing, sing the final selections of the Great Hallel Psalms,[13] which were appointed for the closing of the national festival. Their words and melodies constitute the last hymn of praise sung by Christ on earth. With that music in His ears, Jesus enters the valley of the shadow of death, for immediately afterward we find Him in Gethsemane. The words of these Hallel Psalms strike us as singularly beautiful and appropriate. "Our God is in the heavens: he hath done whatsoever he hath pleased. . . . The sorrows of death compassed me. . . . O Lord, I beseech thee, deliver my soul. . . . Thou hast delivered my soul from death. . . . The stone which the builders refused is become the head stone of the corner. This is the Lord's doings; it is marvelous in our eyes. This is the day which the Lord hath made. . . . Blessed be he that cometh in the name of the Lord. . . . O give thanks unto the Lord, for he is good: for his mercy endureth for ever."

"When Jesus had spoken these words, he went forth with his disciples over the brook Cedron, where was a garden, into the which he entered, and his disciples" (John 18:1). With the psalms of victory still ringing in His ears and heart, Jesus leads His group of eleven out into the moonlit streets of Jerusalem, leaving the city by what is now known as St. Stephen's Gate and climbing the path He often trod across the brook Kidron towards the Mount of Olives. Somewhere on the slope of the hill was a walled-in olive grove, bearing the name Gethsemane, or "olive press," perhaps belonging to a friend of the Lord's and thus accustomed to constant use. He may have sometimes slept in that same olive grove during the warmer months of the year, when sleeping out in the open was pleasant enough.[14] As He makes His way eastward out of the city, He could have continued on the road all the way back to Bethany, but instead He turns to the left towards this friendly garden. On the way Peter receives one more warning—

---

and symptomatic of a low level of faith, did not mean that he had ceased, within himself, to believe in the Lord. Nevertheless, his denial was so contrary to his former spiritual state that he would need to "return" (Gk., *epistrepho*) to Christ.

[13]Pss. 113-118. These six hymns of praise were sung at the three great feasts of the Jews: Passover, Pentecost, and Feast of Tabernacles. At the Feast of the Passover, the Great Hallel was divided into two parts—Pss. 113 and 114 were sung before the feast, Pss. 115 to 118 after the meal. It was this second section that was the "hymn" (Matt. 26:30) sung by the Lord Jesus and the disciples.

[14]Quintin Hogg, *The Story of Peter* (1900), p. 184. His narrative of the arrest and trial of the Lord Jesus provides the general flow of thought throughout the remainder of the chapter.

more prophetic than reproachful—that before the morning breaks, he will be tested and found woefully short. "All ye shall be offended because of me this night," Christ warns,

> for it is written,[15] I will smite the shepherd, and the sheep shall be scattered. But after that I am risen, I will go before you into Galilee. But Peter said unto him, Although all shall be offended, yet will not I. And Jesus saith unto him, Verily I say unto thee, That this day, even in this night, before the cock crow twice, thou shalt deny me thrice. But he spake the more vehemently, If I should die with thee, I will not deny thee in any wise. Likewise also said they all (Mark 14:27-31).

Peter protests, as did they all, that even if their Master's worst fears are somehow realized, they will not allow Him to die alone. How wrongly they trust their own failing hearts and ambitions.

Judas knew the place

Jesus passes out of the moonlit hillside into the dark shade of the olive grove, His men following close by. He tells eight of them to rest while He goes on a little farther with Peter, James, and John—the chosen three of the Twelve, who have seen Him raise the daughter of Jairus and have witnessed His glories on Mount Hermon. These three will now see His solitary agony prior to Calvary. They will see for themselves the cup of suffering their Master must drink, and with what baptism He must be baptized, a baptism James and John so lately claimed to be able to share.[16] Peter, too, must know how painful that path will be that he has claimed to tread with his Lord. Leaving the three by themselves and asking them to watch, Christ moves on a few yards farther and engages in a prayer that, like the vicarious sacrifice to follow, He must accomplish alone. Falling prostrate, He cries "Abba, Father, all things are possible unto thee; take away this cup from me: nevertheless not what I will, but what thou wilt" (Mark 14:36). No one of us can ever realize that bitter agony in the garden. And let us be certain of one fact—the Lord does not shrink from approaching death. We dare not confuse His agony and prayer to the Father with a fear of death. Many people—frail women and harmless children—have endured death bravely for many humanitarian and Christian causes. Believers from all ages have counted it joy to suffer for Christ's sake. No, our Lord knows every ingredient in that cup, and in the garden of the oil press, sorrow presses hard on His own soul as He com-

---

[15]Zech. 13:7.
[16]Matt. 20:22-23.

mits Himself to the Father's will. He knows that God will pour out His wrath against sin in that cup. He consents to drink it, for that is what He came to earth to do. Planned from all eternity, Christ knows this hour is the supreme purpose for His entrance into the world.

Coming back to find His three dear disciples sleeping, Christ speaks in sad surprise, "Simon, sleepest *thou?*" reminding Peter of his promise to walk with Him, to follow Him wherever He goes. Once this trio had slept on the Mount of Transfiguration; now again with the Master praying, they sleep. The visit is repeated, yet they sleep on. When Christ comes the third time, the moment for action has arrived. "Rise," He says, "he that betrayeth me is at hand" (v. 42).

"And Judas also, which betrayed him, knew the place: for Jesus ofttimes resorted thither with his disciples. Judas then, having received a band of men and officers from the chief priests and Pharisees, cometh thither with lanterns and torches and weapons" (John 18:2-3). "Judas . . . knew the place." Is there a more sobering or suggestive expression in all of Scripture? Judas finds it possible to fulfill his deed of betrayal because he has utmost familiarity with the Lord's prayerful devotion and fellowship with the Father. "Judas . . . knew the place." Of all the possible places for the Lord to be found, Judas knew most surely that Jesus would be in the Father's presence in that garden of prayer. Think of what is involved in these words. Days and nights in closest intimacy with the Son of God, spiritual teaching direct from His lips, personal witness of deeds of mercy and power, gentle rebuke, high appeal and tenderest love—that was the teaching Judas betrayed in Gethsemane. He knew the place; he had prayed there and had heard Christ pray. He had been taken into closest fellowship with the Christ of glory, yet the end of it all is to be treason and betrayal! Judas knew the place and now he enters through the dark shadows of the olive trees, the subdued hum of accompanying militia voices his guard, their weapons gleaming in the midnight light of torches and lanterns. The darkness of the grove offers cover for escape, if escape is desired.

Judas, in order to prevent all possible mistake as to the identity of the man they seek, has told the officers beforehand that he will indicate their victim by giving Christ a kiss. He might have spared himself the trouble. No thought of escape is in the Lord's mind. Walking back toward the small entrance to the garden grove so as to meet the advancing company, He stops apparently at the gate through the wall and asks, "Whom do you seek? If you seek Jesus of Nazareth, I am He; let these other men go their way." To Judas comes no condemnation from Jesus; only a question—"Betrayest thou the Son of man with a kiss?" (Luke 22:48)—a question that seems to have sunk into the wretched man's heart, for the next time we read of him he is his own victim on the path to self-destruction.

Once more Peter pushes impetuously forward, not stopping to ponder the consequences. The disciples have but two swords among them and one of them is in Peter's hand. As the first few of the armed band come through the opening in the wall, Peter, half dazed perhaps by his sleep and unaware of the overwhelming contingent accompanying the traitor, strikes a random blow, wounding the ear of one of the servants of the high priest. "Put up your sword, Simon," says Christ. "Do you think I need the meager help of such a few poor men? I could call not twelve Galilean peasants but more than twelve legions of angels if I would." Then, as a final act of earthly healing, the Lord repairs the wound Peter has inflicted with the wild swing of his sword.

Bitter tears

The hour is about midnight. No effort seems to have been made by the armed guard to capture Peter or any of the other disciples. If the mouth of their leader is stopped, His disciples can do little or nothing, the captors must think. So they lead Christ down the familiar slopes of the Mount of Olives, across the brook Kidron once more, through the gates of the silent city, to the palace of the high priest, where some members of the Sanhedrin have kept watch awaiting the completion of the arrest.

The palace of the high priest no doubt had been built on the plan usually followed in the construction of an eastern house—that of a large quadrangle surrounded on three sides with buildings with a high wall, separating the entire palace from the street, the fourth side of the quadrangle. In the center of this high wall was a large gateway, opened wide on all important occasions or when any large number of people wanted to find their way into the quadrangle but usually kept shut. Individual visitors would be admitted through a small door at one side of the great gateway. A servant would be in attendance to give or refuse entrance to the buildings inside the wall. The "hall"[17] of the high priest's palace, therefore, was in reality the large open courtyard enclosed by the buildings and of sufficient size and ventilation to the sky to allow for open fires. To this complex, Jesus is brought to appear first before Annas,[18] who, though he has been replaced by his son-in-law Caiaphas by the Roman governor, nevertheless still has very great

---

[17]Luke 22:55 (Gk. *aule*), "an open space, an uncovered court or hall of a house." Also an open "sheepfold" in John 10:1, 16.

[18]Hanan, or Annanas, as he is called by Josephus.

authority, exercising much of the influence attached to the office of the high priest. This is the first of six different trials Christ will receive this Friday morning.[19]

Arriving at the great gates leading into the courtyard, the Lord's captors find the gates thrown open and ready for them to enter. But as soon as the troop enters, the gates are closed and barred, the only means of entrance now being the small door to the side. One of the disciples, possibly John,[20] was acquainted with the family of the high priest and coming to the smaller door obtains entrance with no difficulty at all. Peter, however, arriving somewhat later because he had followed at a distance, tries to enter but is refused. John intercedes for him and the girl[21] in charge of the gate allows Peter in, where he finds himself in the large courtyard surrounded by the various rooms and apartments.

At that moment Annas is questioning Christ concerning His disciples and His teachings. Jesus answers, "I spake openly to the world; I ever taught in the synagogue, and in the temple, whither the Jews always resort; and in secret have I said nothing. Why askest thou me? ask them which heard me, what I have said unto them: behold, they know what I said" (John 18:20-21). By this time Caiaphas is ready with a small committee of the Sanhedrin to hold a more formal, though still private and irregular, trial. Search is made for some kind of evidence on which they can convict Jesus. They are certain that the Roman governor will never sanction a death warrant being signed on a matter of pure religious speculation. At last some men come forward with a wrong-headed and contradictory testimony of what Christ had said about destroying the temple. In response to prodding by Caiaphas,

---

[19]There is first this examination before Annas (narrated in John 18). Then He is brought before Caiaphas (Matthew, Mark, and Luke give this account), with both of these confrontations taking place before daybreak. In the early morning, Christ then appears before the Sanhedrin (Luke 22:66), followed by His first appearance before Pontius Pilate. When Pilate hears that Christ is a Galilean, he sends Him to Herod Antipas, who is in Jerusalem at the time. Herod having no success in obtaining any response from Jesus, sends Him back to Pilate for the final condemnation. The narrative for the last three aspects of Jesus' trial is found in Luke 23.

[20]John modestly often refers to himself as "that disciple," or "this man," or "the disciple whom Jesus loved." There are specific occasions when John is singled out—the incident at the Last Supper, when love took him deeper into the Master's counsels; the incident at the cross, when Jesus committed to him as the only one who had not forsaken Him the care of His mother; and his identifying the Lord Jesus on the shore after the miracle of fish after the Resurrection. More often we see him sharing experiences with others—with Peter and James on the Mount of Transfiguration and in the house of mourning and death; and in the Garden of Gethsemane. In Acts John continues in the company of Peter rather than embarking on his own agenda.

[21]MacDuff cites a tradition that her name was Balilla. J. R. MacDuff, *The Footsteps of St. Peter* (1887), p. 202.

Christ affirms that He is indeed the Son of God. This is sufficient for the high priest. Tearing his robe, he cries out, "He has spoken blasphemy." Christ is thereupon bound and taken across the courtyard, to a chamber occupied as a guardroom, to await the dawn, when the Sanhedrin are to be specially summoned and a more formal trial can take place.

In the meantime, Peter has found his way to the fire in the middle of the courtyard and is warming himself. Though he had said he was "willing to die" with the Lord Jesus, he fled from Him in the garden. Now sitting down with the Lord's captors, can we expect anything more than what takes place? Truth be known, Peter had fallen terribly even before he sat at the fire in the courtyard.[22] The servant girl who had admitted him at the walk-in gate, now relieved of her duty, taking a closer look at his face, asks him if he is one of the disciples of the prophet of Galilee. "I don't understand your asking me such a question," Peter replies. Thinking the question an awkward one, he retreats a little distance from the fire and sits in the shade thrown by the archway beneath which he entered.[23] Here, after a while, he is again scrutinized by one of the girls who has charge of the gate and who accuses him of being Christ's disciple. This time Peter gives a more emphatic denial: "So far from being His disciple, I do not even know the man." Piercing the quiet of the early morning air, a rooster crows, the herald of the coming dawn.

Peter once more finds his way back to the fire, apparently joining in the conversation so that his unfriendly behavior might not attract attention to himself. His rough Galilean language, which betrayed him in the misuse of Hebrew gutturals, attracts notice, however, and once more he is questioned by one of the guards, a relative of the man Peter had wounded in the ear. Then Peter, with a sense of personal peril upon him, and losing all control of himself, bursts out into oaths and blasphemy, cursing the name of his Master and denying all knowledge

---

[22]Bruce notes four elements missing in Peter's spiritual strength: (1) A lack of forethought that took him by surprise. He went to Gethsemane without any definite idea of what was coming, though Jesus had warned him several times. (2) A lack of clear perception of truth since his faith in the Messiah was still entwined around a false theory of His mission. (3) A lack of self-knowledge since Peter only imagined how strong and loyal he would be, but when the test came, he failed. (4) A lack of discipline that experience provides. As experience in war is one great cause of the coolness and courage of veteran soldiers in the midst of battle, so the Christian warrior must gain victories in similar spiritual battles. "Even Frederick the Great ran away from his first battle." *The Training of the Twelve* (n.d.), pp. 468-71.

[23]Hogg supplies vividly imaginative details of these encounters by Peter with his questioners, pp. 199-200.

of Him. Poor Peter! Old habits return so readily! Sailors, I am told, are great swearers and so probably are fishermen. What had been Simon's style of language by the Sea of Galilee, before the Lord had called him, comes out again. I suppose the last thought in his mind was that his words would fall on the ear of Christ, but while the curse is yet upon his lips, once more the cock crows in the neighborhood of the palace. The tramp of many feet breaks the stillness of the night. Peter looks up to see that the guard is taking Christ bound from the house of Caiaphas to the guardroom, beating Him the while and laughing at Him. There is a wonderful pathos in what follows. Think of it! "And the Lord turned and looked upon Peter." That night Christ has been betrayed by one friend and deserted by all. He has been beaten and mocked by His countrymen, towards whom His heart goes out in infinite pity, and now, as if to make the cup of His trouble run over, He hears His chosen friend deny Him with a curse.

G. Campbell Morgan relates the following personal reminiscence:

It was on an August Sunday, a good many years ago now. I happened to have nothing to do in London on that Sunday. I went in the morning to hear Father Stanton. He was an Anglican, with much in his service which did not appeal to me at all. He preached that Sunday morning from the text, 'He looked round about upon all things, and went out.' Something he said at the close gripped me. He was talking about the eyes of Jesus, of how He looked about upon the Temple, of how He looked at many things; and he came to this, He looked at Peter and broke his heart. Then, leaning over his desk, he said, 'Don't ever forget that the look of Jesus, however wonderful, would have been no good, if at that moment Simon had not been looking his way.' Did you ever think of that? It is perfectly true. It reveals Simon to me again, vulgar, profane swearer, base denier, and yet underneath, loving Jesus, keeping his eye on Him; and so the watching eyes of Simon saw the love glance in the eyes of Jesus.[24]

. . . the forsaken Lord
Looked *only, on the traitor . . .*
And Peter, from the height of blasphemy—
"I never knew this man" —did quail and fall,
As knowing straight that God; and turned free
And went out speechless from the face of all,
And filled the silence, weeping bitterly.

[24]Morgan, p. 254.

THE MAKING OF A DISCIPLE

I think that look of Christ might seem to say—
"Thou Peter! art thou then a common stone
Which I at last must break my heart upon,
For all God's charge to His high angels may
Guard my foot better? Did I yesterday
Wash thy feet, my beloved, that they should run
Quick to deny Me 'neath the morning sun?
And do thy kisses, like the rest, betray?
The cock crows coldly.—Go, and manifest
A late contrition, but no bootless fear!
For when thy final need is dreariest,
Thou shalt not be denied, as I am here;
My voice to God and angels shall attest,
Because I know this man, let him be clear."[25]

—Elizabeth Barrett Browning

Not waiting for the third and more formal trial of Jesus before the Sanhedrin, Peter deserts the palace courtyard for the streets of the city. Aimlessly he wanders, no doubt, until with sudden affection he makes his way back to Gethsemane's garden. Going through that same small gate on Olivet, he throws himself down full length on the very spot of his Master's agony,[26] and with his tears washes again the plot of earth still fresh with the sweat of blood. There he "wept bitterly." Alas! for Peter. Can we not enter into some of his thoughts as he lay sobbing on the side of Olivet? Had he not three times, only the previous day, promised his Master that he would "go with Him to prison or to death"; that he would "in no wise offend Him"; that if "all deserted Him" he would stand fast; and three times during that same night had he not failed in his own promises? "I do not know the man," he falsely claims, and yet he must have thought during those bitter hours of his own private "Gethsemane," of all that Christ had meant to him—from being taken as a mere fisherman to being a witness of the "most wonderful life the world had seen."[27] Peter has sinned, yet Peter can and will be forgiven. Our God does not change: "If we confess our sins, he is faithful and just to forgive us our sins, and to cleanse us from all unrighteousness" (I John 1:9).

---

[25]Abridged from "The Look" and "The Meaning of the Look," *Sourcebook of Poetry,* (1968), pp. 141, 142.

[26]F. B. Meyer, *Peter: Fisherman, Disciple, Apostle* (1950), p. 103.

[27]Hogg, p. 203.

We must pause long enough to note the stark contrast between Peter and Judas Iscariot. That Peter did not fall as Judas irrevocably fell is due to the fact that Peter is genuinely a child of God. Judas, at the core of his being, has been all along a child of Satan. Therefore, we can say that Peter could never have sinned as Judas sinned, nor could Judas have repented as Peter repented,[28] though we must hasten to acknowledge that there is no sin ever committed by another that we in our sinful adamic condition cannot also commit under the proper provocation. We have the same resource as Peter. The Lord had prayed for him, that his fall would not be ruinous. And it is in Peter's repentance, immediately after his denials, that we see the Lord's prayers answered. Not in Peter's earnestness of heart did this repentance spring, but through God's Holy Spirit and His guarding providence is this change produced. But for the rooster crowing, the Lord looking on His disciple, and the tender mercy of the Father in heaven, who can tell how far Peter would have gone down the path to self-destruction and ruin? By grace he was delivered, as are we all.

The Hour

Early that same morning Christ is taken from the guardroom of the palace across the bridge that then spanned the Tyropean Valley,[29] accompanied by His accusers, to the audience hall of Pilate. Summoned early and perhaps not wholly surprised at some special demand being made on his time at the Passover, Pilate at first tells the Jews to take such a case as this and deal with it according to their own law. The Jews remind Pilate that the right of capital punishment has been withdrawn from them and therefore they can act only through him. During the progress of the trial, Pilate sends Christ to Herod Antipas on the grounds that He belongs to Herod's province in Galilee. Herod, finding that he can get nothing out of Christ, returns Him to Pilate, with the result that the Sadducees finally have their wish as the formal order goes out to the guard: "Go, soldier, prepare the cross." Then comes the sad scene at Calvary. His "hour" has come—the last bitter cry of all when with His last breath Christ bows His head in sacrificial, atoning death. And where is Peter all this time? Hanging about, no doubt, on the outskirts—"troubled, repentant, miserable."[30]

---

[28]Bruce, p. 476.

[29]That valley, on the western edge of the old city, is now filled up with the debris of various destructions of Jerusalem so as scarcely to exist. In Christ's day, however, the Tyropean Valley was deep and wide enough to warrant a suitable bridge.

[30]Hogg, p. 208.

Then comes the earthquake and the rending of the tombs. The high priest at his evening sacrifice is startled by the veil of the temple being torn in two pieces. A centurion, who has seen many a death on the battlefield, struck by the patient endurance of Jesus, cries aloud, "Surely this is the Son of God!" Though Judas betrayed the Lord Jesus and Peter denied Him, the Lord's crucifixion is the means of bringing bold affirmation from Joseph of Arimathea and Nicodemus. Long have these two been secret disciples of Christ. No sooner has life left the body of the dead Christ than Joseph goes boldly to Pilate and asks permission to take it down from the cross. It is nearly sunset, and Pilate, having satisfied himself that Christ is really dead, gives an order for the deliverance of His body to Joseph. Perhaps Joseph's intervention spared Christ's body from being cast into the Valley of Hinnom with the dead carcasses of the two thieves who died in the same crucifixion. The time is short. The Jewish Sabbath begins at sunset. They are able just to wrap the body of their Master in a linen sheet doused with an assortment of spices used for embalming and to lay it in the rock-cut tomb, which Joseph had prepared for his own use. They intend, no doubt, to finish the rites of burial more perfectly as soon as the Sabbath passes. They then "rested the Sabbath day according to the commandment" (Luke 23:56). Peter, meanwhile, is left to himself, sustained for the next three days by that last look of love from the Lord.

Implications for Discipleship

1. *Experience is integral to a believer's spiritual ministry of encouragement.* In His wisdom and sovereignty, God brings into our lives those experiences He knows will develop us as stronger believers. Our ministry to others demands it.

> Blessed be God, even the Father of our Lord Jesus Christ, the Father of mercies, and the God of all comfort; who comforteth us in all our tribulation, that we may be able to comfort them which are in any trouble, by the comfort wherewith we ourselves are comforted of God. For as the sufferings of Christ abound in us, so our consolation also aboundeth by Christ (II Cor. 1:3-5).

As painful as his failure was to Peter, it enabled him to comfort and strengthen his brothers and sisters, as he writes in his first epistle: "But the God of all grace, who hath called us unto his eternal glory by Christ Jesus, after that ye have suffered a while, make you perfect, stablish, strengthen, settle you" (I Pet. 5:10).

2. *Intercessory prayer has power.* The Lord Jesus assured Peter of His intercessory prayer on his behalf. The Lord's ministry of intercession continues for all believers. "Wherefore he is able also to save them to the uttermost that come unto God by him, seeing he ever liveth to make intercession for them" (Heb. 7:25). Those converts we disciple also have tremendous spiritual needs that provide us an opportunity to minister to them through our intercessions for them. We should pray *for* our converts in the quiet of our own closets, and we should pray *with* our converts so that they see and hear prayer modeled before them. In this way, they will sense our burdens and concerns for them too.

3. *Failure is not final.* Peter's experience is a paramount example in this regard. We are exceedingly familiar with the details of his failure in the crucial moments of the Lord's arrest and trial. He wisely mourned over his failings, but then he also responded to the Lord's loving restoration. He made steppingstones out of his stumbling blocks. While his failure teaches us to hate sin, his restoration holds out hope for every sinning child of God. Sin is to be feared and abhorred. Sin already committed is to be confessed and forsaken. We must not trifle with temptation, yet if a believer sins, he has an advocate with the Father, Jesus Christ the righteous. Therefore, despair not. Forsake your sins, and find mercy with God. He will abundantly pardon and restore.

STEPS UPWARD

And Peter (Mark 16:7).

Out of the depths I have cried to Thee, O Lord.
Lord, hear my voice!
Let Thine ears be attentive
To the voice of my supplications.
If Thou, Lord, shouldest mark iniquities,
O Lord, who could stand?
But there is forgiveness with Thee,
That Thou mayest be feared.

—Ps. 130:1-4 (NASB)

Setting: Jerusalem, Sunday, April 5, A.D. 33
Scripture: Matt. 28:1-17; Mark 16:1-8; Luke 24:1-35; John 20:1-29

While the city rests, the religious opposition to Christ continues to busy themselves to avoid any possibility that the Lord's disciples will steal away His body and then spread a false report that He has risen from the grave. Perhaps they remembered the words of Christ when He compared Himself to Jonah[1] and gave other indications of a resurrection,[2] for they go to Pilate and beg him to set a guard over the great stone that has been rolled to the sepulchre. Pilate treats them roughly since he is still disturbed by the predicament forced on him, but he grants permission for their own guard, also cautioning them to make the tomb as secure as possible. Something more is taking place as well. Silently and without warning, that last Sabbath day of the old economy gives way to a new day—what we now observe as the "Lord's Day," Sunday, the first day of the week. Of course, no one is aware of this event at the moment, but a new deliverance, greater than that of the original Passover, has been accomplished. The Lord's promise is now realized: "I am the resurrection, and the life: he that believeth in me, though he were dead, yet shall he live: and whosoever liveth and believeth in me shall never die" (John 11:25-26).

And what of Simon Peter, whom we left sobbing tears of repentance in that blessed garden on the Mount of Olives?[3] Peter has sunk

---

[1]Matt. 12:41.

[2]Matt. 16:21; 17:23; 20:19.

[3]Some of the early Latin hymns allude to a legend that through his life Peter never again heard a cock crow without weeping. A. H. Broadus, *Commentary on the Gospel of Matthew* (1886), p. 554.

to the lowest depths,[4] but he does not remain there. After his fall, he rises again. After his wandering, he returns to the fold. After his lapse comes a fresh start. We know the story well. No part of Peter's history is more familiar than that of his dreadful downfall and tender restoration. Out of his deep misery, he cries to the Lord and finds forgiveness in Him. Though conscience-stricken at his desertion and denial of the Master in His time of need, Peter receives special assurances from his Lord. Let us mark his steps upward that first Resurrection Sunday as that last Sabbath passes, the tomb guarded and secure, the disciples crushed, frightened, and scattered.

That Resurrection morning

The narrations of the visits to the garden tomb by the various men and women contain several strands that we must weave together to behold the finished tapestry of that first Resurrection morn. With the Sabbath now ended and before sunrise on Sunday morning, a group of women, including Mary Magdalene, come to the tomb with spices and ointments to anoint the body of Jesus. Though the Lord spoke repeatedly of His resurrection from the dead after three days, no such hopes linger in the hearts of these faithful ones. They can think only of the impossibility that faces them—finding someone capable of rolling the stone away from the sepulchre [5]so that they may attend to the body of their dead Master. As they come within sight of the tomb, they are horrified to find that the stone is already pushed to one side of the opening. Who has desecrated the Master's tomb? Mary Magdalene, perhaps indignant that the priests or others have stolen the body, comes no closer to the tomb. She runs instead back to the apostles with her terrible news, telling them that thieves have come by night and removed the body of Jesus from its place of rest. The other women, whom Mary Magdalene has left, proceed toward the sepulchre, where a heavenly messenger consoles them. "Be not affrighted," says the angel, "Ye seek Jesus of Nazareth, which was crucified: he is

---

[4]The steps of Peter's downfall have been variously stated, the primary ones being these: (1) His self-confidence and loud professions of fidelity; (2) his lack of watchfulness, particularly in the garden; (3) his rash swing of the sword when taken off guard; (4) his middle course between lagging self-confidence and following Jesus from a distance to the trial scene; (5) his courage to venture into danger, yet lacking enough courage to overcome it; (6) his denials when asked if he were one of Jesus' disciples; (7) his final denial with oaths and curses when frightened by repeated inquiry.

[5]A large circular stone was placed in front of the opening to the sepulchre. Since such stones were usually set in a sloping track, it would have been easy enough to push down the slope to cover the opening. Once established in place, however, it would have been difficult to remove. It would have to be rolled back up the incline or lifted out of the groove and removed. *EBC* vol. 8, p. 787.

risen; he is not here: behold the place where they laid him. But go your way, tell his disciples *and Peter* that he goeth before you into Galilee: there shall ye see him, as he said unto you" (Mark 16:6-7). Upon hearing the initial news from Mary Magdalene but not the angel's subsequent word to the women, Peter and John[6] run rapidly to the sepulchre, missing contact with the women returning from the tomb. John, being the younger of the two, outruns Peter, but he does not enter the tomb, perhaps fearing defilement if he touches the dead body. But when Peter enters the sepulchre, he finds the linen cloth in which the body had been wrapped lying empty, and the napkin, which had been around His head, folded together in a place by itself.[7] Peter and John do not tarry at the sepulchre, so Peter does not yet hear the touching words "and Peter" from the women or that the disciples, including himself, are to meet with Jesus in Galilee.

With broken heart, Mary Magdalene makes her way slowly back to the burial scene, arriving after Peter and John leave.[8] As she kneels in mourning at the tomb, a voice speaks to her from behind, "Woman, why are you weeping? Whom do you seek?" Her energies expended, she neither turns around nor rises from her knees, imagining the voice to be that of the keeper of the garden in which the tomb is located. "If you have taken Him away," she sobs, "tell me where you have laid Him, and I will carry Him away." In her weakness, Mary's love for the Lord still knows no bounds. By herself she would carry His heavy body away to a rightful rest. Love "hopeth all things." And then from His lips comes the familiar entreaty, "Mary," and the woman whom Christ had redeemed from sin is the first, among the disciples, to see her risen Lord.

---

[6]The only friend Peter seems to have consorted with during those dark hours following the Lord's crucifixion may have been John, perhaps staying at John's place of residence in the city, along with Mary, the mother of Jesus (John 19:27). We read nothing of Peter's activities until after Christ's resurrection and his journey to the tomb with his friend that Sunday.

[7]When Lazarus rose from the dead, he brought his burial garments with him. He would need them again. But for Christ, when He arose, death had no more dominion and He left them in the empty tomb.

[8]Wolston: "Neither Peter nor John are held to the spot by the same attachment to the Lord as marked Mary . . . out of whom He had cast 'seven demons' (Mark 16:9), and personal love for her deliverer was her characteristic. The two disciples, on the other hand, 'saw and believed,' and then 'went away again unto their own home.' . . . Satisfied that Jesus was risen, they go away to *their own home.'* They had one, without Jesus; Mary really had none, save the spot where she had last seen her Saviour; and therefore, when the others had gone, she 'stood without at the sepulchre weeping." W. P. T. Wolston, *Simon Peter* (1926), pp. 125-26.

Later on that same day, Peter again visits the tomb, perhaps to reassure himself that it is indeed empty, and departs, "wondering in himself at that which was come to pass" (Luke 24:12). At some later time this Lord's Day—we know not when or where—Peter himself has an interview with the Lord. Of the details of this meeting we have none, though the fact is told by two different writers. Luke tells us that when on that same Sunday evening the two disciples come back from Emmaus and find the apostles in the upper room, they are met with the news, "The Lord has arisen indeed, and hath appeared unto Simon."[9] Writing to the Corinthian believers some twenty to thirty years later, the apostle Paul confirms that Christ appeared unto Cephas[10] and then to the Twelve. We search in vain throughout Peter's "Gospel" as delivered to us through Mark for any reference to this solemn meeting. Nor does Peter himself refer to this encounter in his own epistles. But there are some things too sacred to be told even to a best friend. Some things are best kept secret between a believer and his God. So the veil is drawn over the seeking Shepherd as He restores the soul of His straying lamb.

What steps does the Lord Jesus take to restore His disciple? We know already that He had prayed for Peter. We have also seen that the Lord's look of love brought genuine grief and shame to Peter. In a few short hours Jesus will appear to Peter in private, a most touching occasion of confession and forgiveness. Subsequently, when they come together again in Galilee, the Lord will delicately remind Peter of his loud protests of fidelity, and while no longer claiming superiority to others, Peter will earnestly state his love for the Lord. After the coming of the Holy Spirit at Pentecost, Peter's upward climb reaches a climax with his bold confession of Christ before the Sanhedrin and the nation. No longer cautious and afraid, he confronts the opposition with a convincing affirmation of the saving power of Jesus Christ of Nazareth.[11] These steps along the road to recovery are there for us to understand how the Lord restores an erring disciple and how we, with God's help, may find hope, forgiveness, restoration, and complete joy in loving fellowship with our Lord. Let us follow them with Peter.

Out of the depths

We return once more to Christ's trial and Peter's defection at the prodding of the Lord's enemies in the courtyard of the high priest.

---

[9]Luke 24:34.
[10]I Cor. 15:5.
[11]Acts 4:13.

Peter's foul words denying he ever knew Christ have but left his lips and "the second time the cock crew. And Peter called to mind the word that Jesus said unto him, Before the cock crow twice, thou shalt deny me thrice. And when he thought thereon, he wept" (Mark 14:72). Peter's weeping is the first sign of his genuinely repentant heart. He "thought" on his conduct, he "wept" over it, and he left to take care of the matter alone with his God. Thought, sorrow, action—all three elements produce the "godly sorrow" that issues in repentance. "For godly sorrow worketh repentance to salvation not to be repented of: but the sorrow of the world worketh death" (II Cor. 7:10). True repentance is a change of mind that issues at once in a change of life direction. Peter is on the path to genuine repentance, though at this moment he has no hope ever to see his Lord and Master again. If his denial of the Lord is his last deed in the Master's presence, so much the more he must pour out his soul in godly sorrow in seeking forgiveness from his God.

Can we not enter into some of those "thoughts" as he lay sobbing on the side of Olivet? Has he not three times, only the previous day, promised his Master that he would go with Him to prison and to death? That he would not in any way offend Him? That if all deserted the Lord, he would not? And three times during that same night Peter had failed in his promises? "I do not know the man," he swears with an oath. Are these the thoughts that flood his mind and soul? Or perhaps his thoughts return to those first full days of acquaintance and friendship with the Lord Jesus. He may have thought of the gracious words and life of the Lord that drew him to the Master. His own response to the Lord's call from fishing for fish to catching men's souls alive. The feeding of the five thousand . . . the walk on the water . . . the restoration of his mother-in-law . . . the raising of Jairus's daughter and Lazarus . . . the entrancing parables and sermons . . . the Master's own words of blessing on his confession of faith in the Christ. Those incredible scenes and so much more could have been the fountain from which flowed reminders to Peter of God's great mercies and forgiveness. He had been privileged to join fellowship with the most wonderful life ever to live here on earth!

There are two "repentant" souls that awful day. One was Peter, the other Judas Iscariot. The conscience of neither could let him rest. But with Judas, his "repentance"[12] is mere remorse at unintended consequences. Not expecting that the confrontation with Jesus would end in His death and ashamed at his own involvement in the plot, he rejects

---

[12]Matt. 27:3-4.

any use of the blood money he has received to betray the Lord Jesus. With the thirty pieces of silver clutched in his hand, he bursts into the presence of the priests and cries, "I have sinned in that I have betrayed the innocent blood" (Matt. 27:4). Judas's trail of horrors is easily marked: avarice and thievery,[13] betrayal and remorse, suicide and perdition.[14]

These two disciples, Peter and Judas, though each a disaster, end the day poles apart. Peter recovers from his failure; Judas does not. Called and trained by Jesus, as were Peter and the other disciples, Judas had all the advantages enjoyed by the others. He knew and saw Jesus. He heard Jesus' teaching about mammon, for example, yet when tempted by avarice, he collaborates with the enemy with premeditated determination. "Peter slid into his pit; Judas looked at his and deliberately jumped in."[15] He learned too late that there are men who value friendship as a tool for their own ends only to throw it aside when the deed is done.

What makes Peter different from Judas? The Lord Jesus spoke of them both as "Satan"[16] and they both turned against Him in the hour of trial. But, while they both sorrowed deeply, the similarities end right there. For Peter, his sorrow is a humble and loving repentance; though Judas says, "I have sinned,"[17] he suffers only the pangs of remorse, not true repentance. He ends his own life, while Peter finds forgiveness and lives a long life of usefulness to his Lord.

And Peter

As the angel explains the Lord's absence from the grave to the women, the heavenly being speaks a special word regarding Peter.

---

[13] John 12:6.

[14] "His own place," Acts 1:25.

[15] David W. Gill, *Peter the Rock* (1986), p. 122.

[16] Matt. 16:23; John 6:70.

[17] Spurgeon preached a sermon titled "Confession of Sin—A Sermon with Seven Texts" in which he takes Judas's phrase, "I have sinned," and traces it though the Bible: All these said, "I have sinned." Pharaoh, whom Spurgeon called the hardened sinner (Exod. 9:27); Balaam, the double-minded man (Num. 22:34); Saul, the insincere man (I Sam. 15:24); Achan, the doubtful penitent (Josh. 7:20); Judas, the repentance of despair (Matt. 27:4); Job, the repentance of a saint (Job 7:20); the prodigal, the blessed confession (Luke 15:18). Regarding Judas, Spurgeon writes, "Here is the worst kind of repentance of all; in fact, I know not that I am justified in calling it repentance; it must be called remorse of conscience. But Judas did confess his sin, and then went and hanged himself. Oh! that dreadful, that terrible, that hideous confession of despair. Have you never seen it? If you never have, then bless God that you never were called to see such a sight." *Sermon No. 113*, pp. 967-80. Delivered at the Music Hall, Royal Surrey Gardens, January 18, 1857. AGES Software CD, Master Christian Library.

"But go your way, tell his disciples *and Peter* that he goeth before you into Galilee: there shall ye see him, as he said unto you" (Mark 16:7). The angel's word reveals God's gracious provision for Peter's special need. "Go, tell His disciples and Peter." And Peter. "How these two little words would linger like a strain of music in his soul. How they would follow him every step in his way back to his native Galilee, haunt his sleeping and waking hours, and prove to be a bright gleam in his lonely watches on the night sea."[18] Peter is singled out because he has denied Jesus and thus needs assurance that he is not excluded from the company of disciples. On hearing any invitation from the risen Lord through intermediary means, such as the women or other disciples, Peter may have been justified in thinking that he is not included. "I have denied Him and forsaken Him. Surely He does not mean to include me anymore. I am no more a true disciple." On the contrary, the Lord's message is "and that includes Peter too."

> *Lord Jesus, who would think that I am Thine?*
>   *Ah! who would think*
> *Who sees me ready to turn back or sink*
>   *That Thou art mine?*
>
> *I cannot hold Thee fast though Thou art mine;*
>   *Hold Thou me fast,*
> *So earth shall know at last and heaven at last*
>   *That I am Thine.*[19]
>
> —Christina Rossetti

Even if Peter felt like hanging himself, as Judas did, he didn't do it! He might have been tempted to drown his misery with the Lord's captors at the courtyard fire, but he didn't. Instead, he remembered his rash words; he wept about his failure; he stayed among his fellow disciples, whether embarrassed or not.[20] This is critical to Peter's restoration; when he hears the words "Peter, the Lord desires to meet with all the disciples in Galilee, and he specially said to tell you about this," he does not think of the message as so many idle words. He accepts them in the spirit that the Lord meant them to be received. Nor did the others rebuke Peter, their acknowledged leader, for his past conduct. If Jesus has a message for them, then Peter must be included too, but the Lord must make that perfectly clear to Simon.

---

[18]J. R. MacDuff, *The Footsteps of St. Peter* (1887), p. 213.

[19]Christina Rossetti, "Hold Thou Me Fast," *Rhyme & Reason* (1981), p. 158.

[20]Gill, p. 124.

The Lord has appeared to Simon!

This first Easter abounds with wild swings of emotion. For one moment a gloom and darkness surrounds everyone because the loving Lord is sealed in the tomb. But then the women report that He is risen from the dead! How can this be true? The two disciples journeying back to Emmaus from Jerusalem epitomize this emotional quandary.

"What are you talking about that makes you so sad?" asks the stranger who joins them in their walk.

Cleopas[21] is first to respond. "What makes You ask that question? Are You the only one in Jerusalem ignorant of what has been going on the last several days?"

"What things?"

"About Jesus of Nazareth. He was a prophet mighty in deed and word before God and all the people," continues Cleopas.

"But the chief priests and our rulers passed a death sentence on Him and have crucified Him," the other explains.

"We had so much faith in this Jesus of Nazareth," Cleopas adds. "We really believed that He would redeem Israel.[22] And now it is three days since His crucifixion and we are confused."

"Yes, because several women we know went to His tomb early this morning and came back with astonishing news, telling all of us that they had seen a vision of angels who told them that Jesus is alive!"

"So several others went to the tomb and, true enough, it was empty, just as the women had said."

"But they never saw Jesus," interrupts Cleopas.

The stranger cannot restrain himself any longer. "O fools, and slow of heart to believe all that the prophets have spoken: ought not Christ to have suffered these things, and to enter into his glory?"[23] He did not stop with these words but continued to explain that Messiah's sufferings were predicted in their own Scriptures. They listened as He traced the messianic note of all the prophets, showing them that He was Isaiah's child-king with a shoulder strong enough to bear the government; that He was Jeremiah's branch of righteousness, executing righteousness and justice throughout the land. He was Ezekiel's plant of renown, giving shade and fragrance; that He was Daniel's stone cut without hands, smiting the image, becoming a mountain, and filling

---

[21]Not to be confused with Cleophas (Gk., *klopas*), the husband of Mary, the sister of Christ's mother (John 19:25).

[22]Luke 2:25, 38.

[23]Luke 24:25-26.

all the earth.[24] "He expounded unto them in all the scriptures the things concerning himself" (Luke 24:27).

Arriving at their destination, Cleopas and his companion urge the Stranger to stay with them for the night. "Abide with us,"[25] they plead. "It is late in the day." To which the Stranger consents. "And it came to pass, as he sat at meat with them, he took bread, and blessed it, and brake, and gave to them. And their eyes were opened, and they knew him; and he vanished out of their sight" (Luke 24:30-31).

> *The new acquaintance soon became a guest,*
> *And made so welcome, at their simple feast*
> *He blessed the bread, but vanished at the word,*
> *And left them both exclaiming—"'Twas the Lord!*
> *Did not our hearts feel all he deigned to say—*
> *Did they not burn within us by the way?"*[26]

> *—William Cowper*

Eyes that had been providentially shut[27] are now opened to their amazement.

> Did not our heart burn within us, while he talked with us by the way, and while he opened to us the scriptures? And they rose up the same hour, and returned to Jerusalem, and found the eleven gathered together, and them that were with them, saying, The Lord is risen indeed, and *hath appeared to Simon.*

---

[24]G. Campbell Morgan, *The Gospel According to Luke* (1931), p. 278.

[25]Morgan (pp. 279-80) rightly points out that Henry F. Lyte's hymn "Abide with Me" carries the connotation "Come in, and take care of me, come in, and look after me." He does not disparage the great hymn; but that is not what the men asked of the Lord, Morgan explains. What they asked for was the opportunity to care for Him, not for Him to take care of them. Having expressed these sentiments in a message in his church in London on one occasion, a woman who heard his remarks felt impressed to compose another poem, similar to "Abide with Me," in which she gave expression to the heart desire of the men. In part, the poem reads:

O Jesus, come, and likewise with us stay,
    We'll give Thee welcome on Thy lonely way;
Our lives at Thy disposal we will place,
    With acts of love Thy sorrow deep to chase.
Abide with us, and treat us as Thy friends;
    Thus may we for past coldness make amends;
Our door to Thee be always open wide;
    Come in, and ever with us now abide!

[26]William Cowper, "The Pilgrims of Emmaus," *The Prose and Poetry of Europe and America* (1853), p. 493.

[27]Luke 24:16. The Lord chooses not to reveal Himself to Cleopas and his companion until their souls were made ready to receive and believe Him.

And they told what things were done in the way, and how he was known of them in breaking of bread (vv. 32-35).

Here is the wonderful fact that thrilled them all. "The Lord Jesus has appeared to Simon!" Simon! The man who had openly denied the Lord!

Concerning this private meeting[28] between Jesus and His erring disciple we have no further details, but we can have no doubt as to its object and purpose. The risen Master remembers Peter's sin. He knows how troubled Peter is in mind and heart because of it. So the Lord Jesus desires, without delay, to let him know he is forgiven. And out of delicate consideration for the offender's feelings, Jesus arranges for this loving act of restoration to be alone and private.[29] Oh, our gracious Lord! Peter has made many mistakes and they are there in the Word for all to read. But that blessed interview when Simon Peter bares his heart to Jesus is something that is left between Peter and his loving Lord, "too intimate, too precious, to be revealed to others."[30] In that meeting, all the sin and the shame of Peter's denial are dealt with by the Lord, settled and put away forever. Morgan provides imaginative touches to the Lord's words:

> Simon, do you remember how, six months ago, I told you I must die and rise? And, Simon, you were so terrified at the dying that you never heard about the rising. Simon, do you remember that I warned you, because you did not trust Me, you would go down to the depths! But I prayed for you, that your faith should not fail, and it never failed. Now, Simon, do you understand why I went to the Cross? I am the living Lord, and your sins are forgiven.[31]

Oh, this much is certain. The Lord indeed appeared to Peter. That is the glory of the story.[32]

---

[28]Some have conjectured that Jesus met alone with Peter at the house where he and John took residence in Jerusalem, John and Jesus' mother, Mary, being gone from the home. See, for example, Morgan, *The Gospel According to Luke*, p. 281.

[29]It is necessary to Peter's later ministry that he be restored both publicly and privately. Public denial will be followed by public reinstatement. "The *disciple* has to be restored privately; the *apostle* must be restored publicly." W. H. Griffith Thomas, *The Apostle Peter* (1956), p. 72.

[30]E. Schuyler English, *The Life and Letters of Saint Peter* (1941), p. 105.

[31]Morgan, p. 281.

[32]Martin Luther found himself overwhelmed by the Lord's forgiveness of Peter: "If I could paint a portrait of Peter, I would write on every hair of his head forgiveness of sins." Quoted by Broadus, p. 554.

Be sure that if you have sinned, there is someone seeking you, "not to slay you, but to save you";[33] not to condemn, but to bless. The difference between deliverance and ruin, purity and vice, heaven and hell, may rest on whether you allow the Lord Jesus to find you as He sought out and found Peter. And if, as a believer, you are going to suffer, it is much better, as Peter later writes, to suffer for doing good, for being faithful to Christ, than for doing evil and bringing it on yourself. The maturer and wiser apostle Peter counsels that Christians must lay "aside all malice, and all guile, and hypocrisies, and envies, and all evil speakings" (I Pet. 2:1). In our struggles to be holy as God is holy,[34] we may fall. But if we humble ourselves under God's mighty hand, He will lift us up. God has not changed.

O the bitter shame and sorrow!
That a time could ever be
When I let the Savior's pity
Plead in vain; and proudly answered,
All of self, and none of Thee!

Yet He found me: I beheld Him
Bleeding on the accursed tree:
Heard Him pray: Forgive them, Father!
And my wistful heart said faintly,
Some of self, and some of Thee!

Day by day His tender mercy,
Healing, helping, full and free;
Sweet and strong, and ah! so patient,
Brought me lower, while I whispered,
Less of self, and more of Thee!

Higher than the highest heaven,
Deeper than the deepest sea;
Lord, Thy love at last hath conquered;
Grant me now my supplication—
None of self, and all of Thee![35]

—Theodore Monod

---

[33]Quintin Hogg, *The Story of Peter* (1900), p. 218.
[34]I Pet. 1:15-16.
[35]Theodore Monod, "O the Bitter Shame and Sorrow," *Hymns of Truth and Praise* (1971), p. 530.

Implications for Discipleship

1. *Confront an opposing individual privately.* Earlier in His ministry, the Lord Jesus called Peter "Satan" because of his opposition to the Lord's destiny with the cross. Often we are faced with individuals who oppose the work of God or His workers. Paul instructed Timothy to be gentle when confronting and correcting such individuals.

> And the servant of the Lord must not strive; but be gentle unto all men, apt to teach, patient, in meekness instructing those that oppose themselves; if God peradventure will give them repentance to the acknowledging of the truth; and that they may recover themselves out of the snare of the devil, who are taken captive by him at his will (II Tim. 2:24-26).

The only prudent manner for giving such correction is in a personal confrontation, as the Lord Jesus did with Peter. Humbly lay out the problem, give the person a chance to explain, and then—quietly but firmly—show that person from Scripture what is wrong.[36] Once you have made your point, withdraw from the scene as soon as courtesy allows, rather than staying to argue his point, thus avoiding foolish arguments and quarrels. It is interesting that the Greek verb *zogreo* ("taken captive") is found elsewhere in the NT only in Luke 5:10 and means "to catch alive," the ministry the Lord Jesus called Peter to perform, catching men alive for Him. Satan is not to be their master; the Lord Jesus is to be their true Master.

2. *Backsliding must be dealt with appropriately.* Jesus prayed that Peter's faith would not fail. It didn't. Peter remained a true believer; but he had to deal with his backsliding. When dealing with a Christian in a backslidden condition, it is often more convenient to place the source of his deficiency in the fact that he has "never been saved." Thus, all that is thought necessary is an immediate and "truer" confession of Christ as Savior. While it is important to recognize a false profession for what it is, it is equally as problematic to fail to see backsliding for what it is. To confound back-

---

[36] Robert C. Anderson, *The Effective Pastor* (1985), p. 161.

sliding with a lack of conversion is to couple it with a faulty remedy—pray and ask Jesus to be your Savior. It is quick, convenient, and lauded in many circles, including youth camps. What is needed for the backsliding believer, youth or adult, is not a quick solution, but the painful and humiliating path of recovery shown in Peter's restoration. There must be the painful admission of sin and the humility of a genuine repentance that manifests itself in separated, holy living. This is a longer path to victory than is the false help of convincing oneself "I never was really saved, so I will now get saved," but it deals properly with the underlying weight of a besetting sin.

3. *Avoid the "Judas procedure" in dealing with erring brothers.* What Judas did after his failure could lead only to defeat, not recovery. He repented to the enemy, but not to God. He died a rebellious, self-centered, punitive suicide, what Gill terms the "Judas procedure,"[37] which is to punish and destroy rather than to heal and restore. The Lord's method is to reach out and rescue from drowning, not to club someone because of his lack of faith. Our prescription and procedure for helping a fallen believer to recover cannot be punitive and vindictive anymore than it can consist of ignoring and avoiding the problem. "Brethren, if a man be overtaken in a fault, ye which are spiritual, restore such an one in the spirit of meekness; considering thyself, lest thou also be tempted" (Gal. 6:1).

---

[37]Gill, pp. 122-23.

PETER'S FUTURE

When thou shalt be old (John 21:18).

In our joys and in our sorrows,
Days of toil and hours of ease,
Still He calls, in cares and pleasures,
"Christian, love Me more than these."

—Mrs. Cecil F. Alexander

Setting: Sea of Galilee, a short time after the Resurrection, A.D. 33
Scripture: John 21:1-25; also Luke 24:36-53

We left the eleven, including Peter, gathered back in Jerusalem, just having heard the uplifting news from the two companions of Emmaus. They told the anxious listeners that the risen Jesus met with them while they walked back from Jerusalem, then stayed to visit with them in their home, all the while opening up the Scriptures to them and showing how they spoke of Christ. If Peter spoke up, he could have related his own testimony of meeting with the Lord. "I went back to the empty tomb, saw again for myself the linen clothes laid aside, and left once more, wondering in my own mind what it all meant.[1] But then while I was home alone, John and Mother Mary being gone, the Lord came to me and spoke such words of comfort and encouragement that I knew He still considered me His disciple. How gracious He was to me, my blessed Lord. When I told this to the others, the disciples began to spread the message, 'The Lord has appeared to Simon! The Lord has appeared to Simon!'"

Suddenly and without warning, no door opening, no lock loosening—for the doors were bolted for fear of the Jews—Jesus appears before them all. How strange! How terrifying! "And as they thus spake, Jesus himself stood in the midst of them, and saith unto them, Peace be unto you" (Luke 24:36). "He *Himself.*" Not a ghost, not a vision, not an invention of distressed and imaginative minds—the Lord Himself. He speaks words of peace. And then in no uncertain manner, the Lord demonstrates the literal nature of His resurrection. He stands among them with the same hands, the same feet, but now with the wounds so clearly visible.

The shame He suffered left its brand
In gaping wound in either hand;

---

[1] Luke 24:12.

Sin's penalty He deigned to meet
Has torn and scarred His blessed feet;
The condemnation by Him borne
Marred His brow with print of thorn.
Trespass and guilt for which He died
Have marked Him with a riven side.

Mine was the shame, the penalty;
The sin was mine; it was for me
He felt the nails, the thorns, the spear.
For love of me the scars appear
In hands and feet and side and brow.
Beholding them I can but bow
Myself in living sacrifice
To Him who paid so dear a price.[2]

—Bob Jones

As if to doubly prove the reality of His presence, the Lord asks, "Do you have anything here to eat?" Quickly they find a piece of broiled fish and some honey, which He heartily consumes. He then gives to all assembled in that upper chamber a discourse similar to that which thrilled the companions on the road to Emmaus. "These are the words which I spake unto you, while I was yet with you, that all things must be fulfilled, which were written in the law of Moses, and in the prophets, and in the psalms, concerning me" (v. 44).

Luke tells us that having made this declaration, He then opened their minds "that they might understand the scriptures" (v. 45). The Lord Jesus disentangles their minds[3] so that what had previously been tangled, blurred, or indistinct becomes clear and sharply focused. They understand as never before the significance of the Lord's suffering and death. And with their new understanding the Lord also gives a commission to preach the message of hope—repentance and remission of sins! A message that will become the daily occupation of these disciples.

Omitting all the intervening days from the Resurrection to the Ascension, Luke records in this final chapter of his Gospel the Lord's blessed return to glory.[4] But there is one special aspect of this interim that still concerns Peter. To this we are indebted entirely to John, who in the last chapter of his Gospel records for us the touching scene.

---

[2]Bob Jones, "Scarred," *Rhyme & Reason* (1981), p. 163.
[3]"Opened" is from Gk. *dianoigo*, "to thoroughly open up."
[4]Luke 24:49-53.

Matthew reminds us that our Lord had given the disciples the assignment to meet Him in Galilee,[5] and after a few more days spent in Jerusalem, the eleven proceed north to their home region. What mountain it is or the exact day on which the interview takes place, we do not know. Probably it is the occasion the apostle Paul cites as the Lord's having been seen by the "five hundred brethren at once" (I Cor. 15:6). It is during this same time in Galilee that the Lord Jesus completes Peter's restoration.

I'm going fishing

In the three years that Simon Peter has traveled with the Lord, he has been taught many lessons. Has he learned them? He has been taught that the Lord expects unquestioning obedience under every circumstance. He has seen Christ's majesty and glory revealed and has been assured as to His coming in power to reign. He has had demonstrated to him the need for daily cleansing and watchful living. He has seen Satan as a formidable foe who is to be resisted in the Faith. Only the power of Christ and His intercession will guard the disciple in the hour of temptation. He has been taught that nothing is too hard for the Lord, that His Word never fails, that His promises are sure, that His love is unceasing, and that His forgiveness is available to all who call out of a contrite and repentant heart. But there must be more than intellectual assent to spiritual truths. To affect the life, truth must reach the heart. That is what the Master must now accomplish before He returns to the Father in heaven.

We commonly approach the scene before us as we open this last chapter of the Gospel of John as one of deserved rebuke by the Lord of His erring disciple. But this is not the case at all. In what we are about to witness between the Lord and Peter, "there is far more laughter than tears, far more hope than despair. If it has a shade of night, it has more of the radiance of morning."[6] The disciples have gone north to Galilee as the Lord instructed. While waiting to meet with Jesus, seven of them, led by Peter, go on another night of fishing. "After these things Jesus showed himself[7] again to the disciples at the sea of

---

[5]Matt. 28:10, 16.

[6]Clovis G. Chappell, *Sermons on Simon Peter* (1959), p. 68.

[7]The expression "shewed himself" ("manifested himself," ASB; see also v. 14), stresses the idea that "Jesus is no longer dwelling with men as He had done before. He suddenly appears on the scene. Just as suddenly He disappears again. But while He is with them, they see Him as their resurrected and glorious Lord, though not always immediately." William Hendriksen, *Exposition of the Gospel of John* (1970), p. 478.

Tiberias;[8] and on this wise showed he himself. There were together Simon Peter, and Thomas called Didymus,[9] and Nathanael of Cana in Galilee, and the sons of Zebedee, and two other of his disciples. Simon Peter saith unto them, I go a fishing. They say unto him, We also go with thee" (John 21:1-3). Five we know by name—Peter, Thomas, Nathanael, James, and John; and, probably, from their intimate connection with the others, the remaining two are Philip and Andrew. Peter's actions in leading the others back to fishing are seen by many as further backsliding on his part, but need not be interpreted that way. The disciples have seen the risen Lord with their own eyes, they have a direct command from Him to meet with Him in Galilee, and now they have time on their hands. Since they no longer have a common purse among them from which they can draw what is necessary for their simple needs, naturally enough they would revert to their original trade to meet these needs. Peter, taking the initiative as usual, proposes to try his hand again at fishing one evening. The others agree. So the old boat is launched, the sail hoisted, and the nets (the identical ones they were mending when Peter received his first call from the Master two years earlier?) are lifted onboard. While all this takes place, we could ask ourselves if Peter allows his mind to dwell on the eventful scenes of the past two years as he recalls his blessed companionship with the Master. Is his heart yet warm with the loving words of restoration spoken to him in secret by the Lord Jesus? What more is in store for Peter and the others as they await the promised meeting with the Master in Galilee?[10]

The associations are too close and vivid for Peter not to remember that terrible night on this same lake when, in the midst of the storm, Jesus appeared to them on the water and Peter, flushed with excitement at seeing his Lord, begged to go to Him on the water. "They went forth, and entered into a ship immediately; and that night they caught nothing" (v. 3). Again they toil in vain, as on the night preceding that first miraculous catch of fish, when Christ called them to be fishers of men. The faint promise of the coming day begins to illumine the

---

[8]Another name for the Sea of Galilee. See also John 6:1. It is thought that John used this name as being more familiar to nonresidents in Palestine than the indigenous name of Sea of Galilee or Sea of Gennesaret. *UBD*, p. 1094.

[9]From the Aramaic meaning "Twin." Out of this name has grown the tradition that Thomas had a twin sister named Lydia. Another tradition has it that he was a twin brother of our Lord, identified as Judas in Matt. 13:55.

[10]Gill calls this incident in John 21 "stage two" in Peter's recovery. David W. Gill, *Peter the Rock* (1986), p. 125.

lake and shore now. This time they see, not a figure on the waves but a solitary stranger on the shore, but it is too dark for them to distinguish his features. They see only that the stranger has stopped and now calls to them.

"Boys, you don't have any fish, do you?"[11]

"No."

"Cast the net on the right side of the boat and you will find some."

They follow the stranger's advice, thinking perhaps that one more attempt at casting the net will be no more futile than their nightlong efforts have been; and it may be worthwhile. Worthwhile indeed! The result is such a haul that they cannot get all the fish into the boat. Then John, "that disciple whom Jesus loved" (v. 7), with a ready memory of a similar scene two years previously, whispers to Peter, "It is the Lord." Peter, impetuous, loving, sometimes blundering, grabs his fisher's coat,[12] which he had laid aside to give him more freedom in working, and throws himself into the waves, swimming to shore, desiring once more to embrace the one who died and rose again and promised to meet with him in Galilee. Once more to look on that loving face and fellowship with the one who had been so ready to speak forgiveness. Coming to shore, he runs to Christ, only to see that a small fire of charcoal has been lit and preparations are underway for breakfast. "Come and dine,"[13] the Lord invites, though "none of the disciples durst ask him, Who art thou? knowing that it was the Lord" (v. 12). John adds that this appearance of Jesus on the shore of the Sea of Galilee is the third time that Jesus manifested Himself to His disciples, the two previous occasions being in the locked room in Jerusalem, with and without Thomas present.[14]

---

[11]The Lord's question assumes a negative answer. The KJV "children" is from *paidion*, a childling (of either sex), i.e. (properly), an infant, or (by extension) a half-grown boy or girl; figurative of an immature Christian. James A. Strong, *Greek Dictionary of the New Testament* (n.d.). Hogg prefers "lads." Quintin Hogg, *The Story of Peter* (1900), p. 238.

[12]"For he was naked," explains John, meaning that Peter had only his undercloth-ing. Ambrose, quoted by MacDuff, sees in Peter's donning of his tunic an act of be-coming reverence to his Master. MacDuff, p. 225. This lesson must not be sacrificed to the present Christian public in which casual attire and contemporary music pro-mote a pernicious attitude of irreverence toward God and lightheadedness toward His holy Word. Peter cared how he presented himself to his Lord and so does the earnest disciple today.

[13]The word means to break fast, the first meal of the day.

[14]A close count of the Lord's appearances after His resurrection will show that this appearance in Galilee was actually the seventh appearance. Apparently what John meant by "the third time" is linked to the word "disciples." This was the third time that Jesus appeared to His official group of disciples, who were often designated as the Twelve. *EBC* vol. 9, p. 200. Hendriksen lists twelve specific occasions when the

Do you love Me?

The seven and Jesus once more sit down to a meal together, partaking of the fish Jesus has prepared as well as fish from their own fresh catch. In earlier days, at the miraculous feedings of the multitudes with the fish and loaves, the Lord Jesus had taken what the disciples had provided and had multiplied it and used it to meet the needs of many. Here once again He shows that He seeks to multiply and bless their efforts as He requests them to "bring of the fish which ye have now caught" (v. 10). After He is gone from their presence, He will continue to do the same as they witness for Him—bless their valiant efforts—though they are unaware as yet what direction those efforts will take them.[15] As the breakfast continues, they enjoy sweet fellowship with the one whom they love and worship now more than ever before.

The meal over, Christ gets to the heart of His mission on the shore. He asks His apostle, "Simon, son of Jonas, lovest thou me more than these?" (v. 15).[16] The ASB rightly notes that the word "love" in this exchange between Peter and the Lord Jesus represents two different Greek words.[17] In His first two questions, the Lord uses

---

Lord appeared to people post-resurrection, noting that there may have been several others, but how many we do not know (cf. Acts 1:3). Hendriksen, pp. 477-78.

[15]*EBC* vol. 9, p. 200.

[16]The *EBC* notes the ambiguity of the Lord's question and suggests three possible solutions: (1) Do you love me more than these other men do? (2) Do you love me more than you love these men? (3) Do you love me more than these things—the boats, the fish, etc.? *EBC* sets aside the third solution as "least probable" and seeks a choice between the first two alternatives. "In view of Peter's boastful promise that whatever the others did he would not fail, the former (*i.e.*, the first) alternative seems more likely, p. 201.

[17]The Greek words are forms of *agapao* and *phileo*. Hendriksen has written a lengthy yet careful footnote on these two words and their usage in this passage. He notes that we are compelled to proceed on the basis of the Greek text as we have it, not the Aramaic conversation that occurred between Jesus and Peter. It is the Greek text that is inspired. Is the difference in word usage merely stylistic, or do these two words convey meanings that differ to some extent? And does the point of the story hinge on this difference? My own opinion is that since this incident is integral to the Lord's complete restoration of Peter, there is adequate reason to suppose that Peter now has a less optimistic view of his strengths and loyalty, which the Lord brings out with His pointed questioning. Among the reasons Hendriksen cites in favor of a distinction in meanings is the fact that Peter chooses his synonym not once, but twice in succession. Hendriksen then shows by an "up-to-date" illustration how nuances of meaning often affect a conversation.

Q. "You have recommended this person, but do you actually know him?"
A. "Yes, I am acquainted with him."
Q. "Do you know him?"
A. "I am acquainted with him."
Q. "*Are* you acquainted with him?"

a form of *agapao*, which signifies a wider type of love that involves the deliberate assent of a person's will. Peter, in all three of his responses, uses a more restrictive word of friendship, a word that means to be fond of an individual, to have affection for someone as a matter of sentiment or feeling. Thus *agapao*, is chiefly related to the head; *phileo* to the heart.[18] The Lord Jesus subsequently adopts Peter's word in His third question to the apostle. Since the ASB follows the KJV in translating both words as "love," any inferences drawn from the nuances inherent in the original text must be less than dogmatic. The unique circumstances surrounding this particular confrontation, however, seem to present ample reason to believe that a full understanding of the interchange between the Master and His disciple is possible only by acknowledging the variations in meanings.

Can we incorporate the Lord's intentions or motivations into His actual recorded words? What would His question sound like? "Simon, son of John, not many days ago you professed that although all deserted Me, you would not. What do you say now? Do you love Me more than these?"[19] The word Christ uses for "love" is a strong one, suggestive of deep, abiding affection that seeks the highest good in the one loved. It is the word used of the love of God the Father that led Him to give His Son for the salvation of the world. Peter, however, responds with a word more indicative of human affection, friend to friend. Their conversation is thus, with only Peter's lesser word for love changed:

> So when they had dined, Jesus saith to Simon Peter, Simon, son of Jonas, lovest thou me more than these? He saith unto him, Yea, Lord; thou knowest that I am fond of thee. He saith unto him, Feed my lambs. He saith to him again the second time, Simon, son of Jonas, lovest thou me? He saith unto him, Yea, Lord; thou knowest that I am fond of thee. He saith unto

---

The man frowned when this third time he was asked, "Are you acquainted with him?" He answered, "Now, listen! You know us well enough to realize that he and I are really acquainted with each other."

Hendriksen explains: "Thus *to really know* a person is one thing; *to be acquainted with* that person is not quite so strong, does not necessarily imply such a high degree of intimacy or familiarity." To the Bible student familiar with the passage before us, the above illustration fittingly applies, the Lord using the stronger word for love, while Peter, accommodating his more pessimistic view of his professed loyalty, uses the weaker or lesser word. See Hendriksen's complete footnote in his *New Testament Commentary: Exposition of the Gospel of John*, pp. 494-500.

[18]No doubt this is the reason Strong suggests that *agapao* is the "cooler" of the two words.

[19]Hogg, p. 239.

him, Feed my sheep. He saith unto him the third time, Simon, son of Jonas, art thou fond of me? Peter was grieved because he said unto him the third time,[20] Art thou fond of me? And he said unto him, Lord, thou knowest all things; thou knowest that I am fond of thee. Jesus saith unto him, Feed my sheep (vv. 15-17).

The obvious purpose of our Lord's repeated questioning of Peter's love is to tell Peter that He still loves him and has not cast him out. Remember, this personal encounter with Peter is one more step in his restoration by the Lord Jesus. To lose sight of this is to miss the underlying meaning of this post-resurrection interchange. For if we knew nothing of Peter's life between his denial and Pentecost, we might be tempted to ask, "Why is Peter still the Lord's chief spokesman throughout the early chapters of the Book of Acts? How can a man who has sinned so lately and so deeply stand forth as the chief witness for the risen Lord? Did he not deny the Lord profoundly? Should we not look for another leader, one not stained by crass denial?" Of course not, for the Lord's dealings with Peter on this occasion show to us the degree to which Peter has matured in his fidelity to the Lord. And the Gospel writers, supported by the apostle Paul, tell us enough of Peter's story to see that Christ Himself restored Peter to the position that otherwise he might have thought he had forfeited. Peter has learned his lessons well. "Never again could he say, 'More than these.'"[21] But he is a new man now. He is still a leader, of course, and still "affectionate, demonstrative, energetic, and outspoken, but no longer proud, self-confident, and boastful."[22] Should we not say, therefore, that Peter is now "converted" as the Lord promised through His prayer? Converted from self-confidence to humble distrust of his own strength,[23] now equipped and destined to "strengthen his brethren." The man who has "fallen most deeply, and learned most thoroughly his own weakness, is, or ought to be, best qualified for strengthening the weak, for feeding the lambs."[24] Notice that the Lord's question is this: "Do you love Me deeply and sacrificially?" The Lord did not gauge Peter's repen-

---

[20]"We read that Simon was grieved that the Lord Jesus asked him the third time. His grief was not, I think, because of the change in the form of the word, but because the Lord asked him thrice. What grieved him? Simon Peter was reminded of the fact that three times he had denied the Lord in the presence of others." E. Schuyler English, *The Life and Letters of Saint Peter* (1941), pp. 108-9.

[21]W. W. Fereday, *Simon Peter* (n.d.), p. 102.

[22]English, pp. 106-7.

[23]J. R. MacDuff, *The Footsteps of St. Peter* (1887), p. 218.

[24]A. B. Bruce, *The Training of the Twelve* (n.d.), p. 518.

tance by the weight of his tears of sorrow. Tears may accompany salvation and repentance, but they are no proof of it. Simply put, the Lord asks, "Do you love Me?"

Let us recount the Lord's dealings with His erring disciple: First, there was the look from Christ at His trial. Then there was the special message to Peter, sent by the Lord when He first appeared to the women, followed by the personal encounter, and then toward evening the session with all in the upper room, all on that first glorious day of resurrection. Then there was the advice to return home to Galilee, and finally this early morning breakfast on the lake shore followed by the restoration of his commission. What grand faith the Lord Jesus places in His loyal disciple. Christ's mission with Peter was not "to crush him, but to save him; not to drive him away, but to restore him."[25]

There may have been need for the Lord to ask Peter if he loved Him, but there is no need for us to ask if Christ loved Peter. Of course He did. He loved him—and loves us—with an everlasting love. God has not changed since those days when the Master was on this earth. F. B. Meyer tells that Charles Kingsley desired that these three words should be engraved on the tomb that held the mortal remains of him and his beloved wife—*Amavimus, Amamus, Amabimus*—we loved, we love, we shall love. But the love of Jesus in its past, present, or future, only eternal ages will reveal. So why do we speak of tenses, when we speak of God's love? It is eternal, ageless, timeless. Before time began, and when time has ceased to be, Love *is*.[26]

> *O Hope of every contrite heart!*
> *O Joy of all the meek!*
> *To those who ask, how kind Thou art!*
> *How good to those who seek!*
>
> *But what to those who find? Ah, this*
> *Nor tongue nor pen can show;*
> *The love of Jesus, what it is,*
> *None but His loved ones know.*[27]

> —*Bernard of Clairvaux*

There is no break in the past and present when it comes to the love of God for His own. The one who sought Peter seeks for us today, questioning us and commissioning us anew. Peter may well

---

[25]Hogg, p. 243.

[26]F. B. Meyer, *Peter* (1950), p. 107.

[27]Bernard of Clairvaux, trans. by Edward Caswall, "Jesus, the Very Thought of Thee," *Church Service Hymnal* (1948), p. 103.

have thought, "I have broken the fellowship. I am no longer one of His friends, certainly not His apostle." But Peter has learned that although he has relaxed his grip on the Lord, Christ has not forsaken him. Peter might have ceased to recognize that love, but the Master's love continued, unaffected by Peter's actions. "Repelled it lingered, reviled it blessed, being persecuted it endured, being defamed and evil-entreated it remained patient through all wrongs, loving on and on until it won back the erring heart and filled it with blessedness."[28] May we never limit, distort, or curtail the love of God that flows to us. His love is not an echo of ours, but ours is the echo of His.

What is that to you? Follow Me.

This then is Peter's public restoration. Not merely is it a restoration but it is also a special charge, a recommissioning to shepherd God's flock. What could be greater proof of the Lord's confidence in His servant? But God's grace extended to Peter does not end with a new and precious commission. Peter's past is forgiven; his present fellowship with the Master is restored; but what of his future? The humbled and now pliable disciple, trained to serve by the Master, still must face two great experiences before he will go forward as the apostle Peter. He will witness the Ascension of the Lord Jesus Christ and then partake of the gift of the Holy Spirit on the day of Pentecost. These await us as we leave the Gospels and enter the Book of Acts.

John concludes his Gospel with the Lord's further word to Peter about his future—a new responsibility, a new danger, and a violent death.[29] It is paraphrased for us in a sermon by Stanley in one of his "Sermons in Palestine":

> *"Verily I say unto thee, when thou wast young*, when thou wast a fisherman's boy on the shores of the Galilean Lake, *thou girdest thyself* in thy fisher's coat, *and walkedst* over these hills and valleys, *wither thou wouldst: but when thou shalt be old*, as years and duties and infirmities increase, thou shalt stretch forth thy hands, even on the cross of martyrdom, *and another*—the Roman executioner—*shall gird thee* with the bonds of imprisonment, *and carry thee whither thou wouldst not*, even to the place where thou must glorify God by thy death."[30]

---

[28]Hogg, pp. 244-45.

[29]*EBC* vol. 9, p. 202.

[30]MacDuff, p. 238, quoting Stanley in his *Sermons in Palestine*, p. 59.

He had failed when following Christ in the energy of the flesh; now he will follow Him[31] through the will of God. If Peter is to follow Christ, he would have to follow Him to his own cross.

"Follow Me." It is not as if Peter will continue to walk beside the Lord Jesus as he has the past three years. Those days are ended. What Jesus means is "Be my disciple and apostle, and as such follow me in service, in suffering, and in death (by being willing to endure affliction and even martyrdom for my sake)."[32] It was a renewed call to discipleship and to the duties of the apostolic office.

Peter continues to be himself. "Then Peter, turning about, seeth the disciple whom Jesus loved following; which also leaned on his breast at supper, and said, Lord, which is he that betrayeth thee? Peter seeing him saith to Jesus, Lord, and what shall this man do? Jesus saith unto him, If I will that he tarry till I come, what is that to thee? follow thou me" (vv. 20-22). Without a doubt, John is meant here. Having heard the call to Peter, John also follows, for they are intimate friends.[33] Peter's instructions become John's too, and Peter shows natural concern for his friend. A moment ago Jesus had predicted Peter's death; now what about his friend John's? The Lord's enigmatic answer tells us that it is enough for us to know our own path; we are not called on to inquire about our brother's. "What shall this man do?" is too often on our lips, asking questions of our Lord that we have no need to ask. The Lord's reply is also a rebuke to Peter. "Leave your brother alone, Peter, and follow Me. Keep your eye on Me, not your brother." No matter where we find him, Peter is still the same impetuous man. "Discretion had little part in his composition, while warmth ever marked him."[34] No doubt it is Peter's affection for John that prompts his innocent question, but the Lord turns Peter's attention to his own responsibility to follow the Master. Jesus' reference to His return ("till I come") is one of the few clear allusions to the Second Coming in

---

[31]The command, "Follow me," is a present imperative, which literally means "keep on following me."

[32]Hendriksen, p. 490, quoting J. H. Bernard.

[33]We have been studying Peter's character and personality to a great extent. There is merit in also comparing Peter's life with that of his intimate friend John. As the "disciple of love," John was not a soft, effeminate, sentimental type, the sort of man Holden describes that "walks delicately, speaks mincingly, thrills emotionally, and disgusts other men by his affectations." For Holden, love is "a thing that has iron in its blood and strength in its hands and feet; true love has energy in its mind and courage in its heart. And loyalty that takes no thought of cost is the breath of its life." J. Stuart Holden, *The Master and His Men* (1955), p. 74.

[34]W. T. P. Wolston, *Simon Peter* (1926), p. 139.

John's Gospel. Jesus offers a supposition, not a promise,[35] of John's long life, though some in the early church took the Lord to mean that John would not die until the Lord returned.

"Follow Me" is abundantly plain. May we heed the Lord's call to the fullest, to please and serve Him until He returns from glory.

> *Jesus calls us; o'er the tumult*
> *Of our life's wild, restless sea,*
> *Day by day His sweet voice soundeth,*
> *Saying, "Christian, follow Me."*[36]
>
> —Mrs. Cecil F. Alexander

Implications for Discipleship

1. *A Christian is a follower of Christ.* Christian discipleship means following Jesus Christ.[37] "Follow thou me" was the Lord's command to Peter, first issued two years earlier at the seashore and now restated following Peter's recovery from failure. After warning Peter that he will one day meet with imprisonment and death, Jesus reaffirms His original and permanent challenge, "Follow Me." His recovery completed, Peter is up and walking in the Lord's footsteps. Recovery, for Peter or for any other disciple, does not mean perfection. As they rose to leave, Peter asks, "What about him?" pointing to John. Jesus rebukes Peter mildly, "What is that to you? Follow Me." Even the recovering, forgiven disciple is not free from the old nature. "There are weaknesses even during recovery," notes Gill, but "these do not cancel out the value or significance of the great work God is doing in a life being put together again. Keep moving! Follow Jesus."[38]

2. *Understanding Scripture depends on yieldedness to God.* Jesus opened the understanding of the two disciples on the road to Emmaus; then He opened the understanding of the disciples hid in the upper room. Through His explanations of the OT Scriptures, they came to understand how they spoke of Christ. God has given us His Spirit so that we

---

[35]*EBC* vol. 9, p. 203.

[36]Mrs. Cecil F. Alexander, "Jesus Calls Us," *Church Service Hymnal* (1948), p. 124.

[37]Gill, p. 43.

[38]Gill, p. 128.

might have the capacity and ability to read, study, and understand His holy Word. "But ye have an unction from the Holy One, and ye know all things. . . . But the anointing which ye have received of him abideth in you, and ye need not that any man teach you: but as the same anointing teacheth you of all things, and is truth, and is no lie, and even as it hath taught you, ye shall abide in him" (I John 2:20, 27). Don't get the wrong idea from John's writing. He is not saying that there is no place for Christian teachers; after all, the Holy Spirit dispenses the gift of teaching to believers and all Christians have a command to teach. But inherent in John's words is the truth that every believer has the capacity and ability, by the Holy Spirit, to gain spiritual truth for himself from the revealed Word. Christians do not need to rely on "secondhand" thoughts from someone else; they are gifted by the Holy Spirit to learn for themselves from His Word.

> But as it is written, Eye hath not seen, nor ear heard, neither have entered into the heart of man, the things which God hath prepared for them that love him. But God hath revealed them unto us by his Spirit: for the Spirit searcheth all things, yea, the deep things of God. For what man knoweth the things of a man, save the spirit of man which is in him? even so the things of God knoweth no man, but the Spirit of God. Now we have received, not the spirit of the world, but the spirit which is of God; that we might know the things that are freely given to us of God (I Cor. 2:9-12).

Because the Holy Spirit knows the mind of God and because we have the Holy Spirit dwelling within, we have the capacity also to know the mind of God. This is a tremendous promise to the individual believer, not to be diminished by an attitude that says, "I don't get anything from the Bible when I read it." God's Word is there for our edification and delight.

3. *Advice and counsel concerning "God's will" must be carefully given.* Jesus rebuked Peter for his attempt to delve into His future plans for John. Christian leaders are often tempted to assume the place of God in giving advice and

counsel. Godly advice based on Christian experience is helpful for the young disciple. What is not proper is for the discipler to assume God's stead by implying or stating directly, "This is God's will for you," unless, of course, the counsel revolves around a clear violation of Scripture. For example, some pastors claim it is their right and duty to inform each young person in their church who he or she should marry. Any other choice not approved by the pastor is therefore not God's will for the individual, or so the pastor asserts. The temptation to control others always exists in a discipling relationship. Care must be constantly exercised to make certain unhealthy or unscriptural habits are not formed in these relationship.

4. *The wise discipler prepares his disciple for the future.*
Since the time had almost arrived for the Lord to return to heaven, He sought to prepare Peter for the future. How near he was to the Lord, how close he followed the Master during difficult moments, would determine the strength of his testimony. We cannot be with our converts forever, but we must energize them to "follow Christ," for that is true Christianity; that is Christlikeness.

5. *Shepherding is the peculiar task of ministers of the gospel.*
Peter's threefold denial is met by the threefold questioning from the Lord, "Lovest thou me?" And Peter's three responses are met each time with a commission to shepherd the people of God. "Be a shepherd to my people," the Lord says to Peter. "Represent Me, the Good Shepherd. Take My place. I place into your hands My dearest treasure, My flock for which I laid down My life."[39] What greater mark of trust could the Master give to Peter than this commission? It must have filled Peter with a sense of mission that remained with him to the end. He would later write to other elders: "Feed the flock of God which is among you, taking the oversight thereof, not by constraint, but willingly; not for filthy lucre, but of a ready mind; neither as being lords over God's heritage, but being ensamples to the flock. And when the chief Shepherd shall appear, ye shall receive a crown of glory that fadeth not away" (I Pet. 5:2-4).

---

[39]Chappell, p. 68.

SERVING THE MASTER

From the time of the Lord's ascension to the emergence of the apostle Paul as the dominant force in the early church, Simon Peter leads by word and example. After taking responsibility to fill up the roster of the Twelve, he preaches a powerful sermon at Pentecost, leads in the opposition to the religious elite in Jerusalem who seek to restrain the Christians' witness, and brings the gospel to the gentiles. By his confession and action, he uses, in the power of the Holy Spirit, those keys of authority promised by the Lord Jesus Christ.

TAKING THE LEAD

Peter stood up in the midst of the disciples (Acts 1:15).

> Go forth to serve, as Jesus went,
> To minister to men;
> A messenger from heaven sent,
> To do His work again.

> *—A. H. Ackley*

Setting: Jerusalem, May A.D. 33
Scripture: Matt. 28:16-20; Luke 24:44-53; Acts 1

The time between the Lord's resurrection and ascension must have had an important and profound influence on Simon Peter. Those great forty days, to be followed by the ten days after the ascension until Pentecost, were filled with appearances and instructions from the Master, enabling the apostle to understand more clearly what before had been dark, cloudy, or mysterious. During this interim, Peter will come to understand more fully the Lord's purpose and will assume the leadership role the Master Teacher intended for His disciple. The "many infallible proofs" (Acts 1:3) of the reality of the Lord's living presence among them following His resurrection comprise the final chapters of the Gospels as well as the first of the Book of Acts.

"Keep your eye on Me, not on John or another brother," the Lord Jesus counsels Peter—now restored and commissioned by Christ to shepherd His flock—as they depart the shores of the beloved Galilean lake for the final time. While still in Galilee, they join the others who obeyed the Lord's invitation to meet with Him "in a mountain in Galilee." We do not know the "mountain" where this meeting took place; perhaps it was one of those ridges on the northeastern side of the Sea of Galilee, where Jesus had so often taught the people. The gathering must have been large, no doubt the one Paul refers to when Christ appeared "to five hundred brethren at once."[1] Though such a gathering might possibly have occurred in Jerusalem, the followers there numbered only one hundred twenty, as we learn later from Acts. Since the Lord had spent most of His ministry in Galilee, it would be natural that the largest number of His followers would live there also;

---

[1] I Cor. 15:5-6. Paul also pointed out that most of these people were still alive when he wrote his letter to the Corinthians, a not-so-subtle suggestion that if anyone doubted the authenticity of Christ's bodily resurrection, there were still plenty of witnesses!

so this is undoubtedly the meeting Paul notes and Jesus promised following His resurrection.

Go ye

Who are the followers of Christ who meet together with the Lord Jesus on that slope for this parting moment? If we allow our memories to retrace the earthly ministry of the Lord, we remember those whose lives He touched in a special way: the Twelve, now eleven, who had accompanied Him for over three years; Jairus, whose daughter Christ raised from her bed of death; the woman with the blood disease, now whole physically and spiritually; the maniac from Gadara, now restored, clothed, and in his right mind; Mary of Magdala; Peter's wife's mother; the lepers, the infirm, the needy. All these, and hundreds more willing now to eat of His flesh and drink of His blood, form the Lord's last congregation in Galilee. Some of them recognize Him at once and worship Him.[2] Others hesitate in doubt until they too become convinced that it is truly Christ and that His resurrection from the grave is real. To all of them Christ delivers His singular parting message, His "Great Commission"[3] as recorded in Matthew 28:18- 20. "And Jesus came and spake unto them, saying, All power is given unto me in heaven and in earth. Go ye therefore, and teach all nations, baptizing them in the name of the Father, and of the Son, and of the Holy Ghost: Teaching them to observe all things whatsoever I have commanded you: and, lo, I am with you alway, even unto the end of the world. Amen."

Christ speaks first of His authority. "All power [authority][4] is given unto to me," He assures His followers. At the beginning of Jesus' ministry, Satan had tempted Him with the power and glory of the kingdoms of this world.[5] To obtain them, Satan said, all Jesus had to do was to bow to him. But He resisted the Devil and the monster fled. Now Christ affirms what is rightfully His, not through compromise with Satan, but through obedience to the Father's will.[6] Forsaking

---

[2]Matt. 28:16-17.

[3]Thomas says these words were called "the Marching Orders of the Church" by the duke of Wellington, for they constitute a divine warrant for all types of Christian service and witness. W. H. Griffith Thomas, *Outline Studies in the Gospel of Matthew* (1961), p. 464. Noting that four times in the original the word "all" is used in these verses, Thomas speaks of (1) the secret of service—"all authority," v. 18, ASB; (2) the scope of service—"all the nations," v. 19, ASB; (3) the substance of service— "teaching . . . all things," v. 20*a*; (4) the strength of service—"I am with you all the days," v. 20*b*, Gk.

[4]Gk. *exousia*, "power, authority, right."

[5]Matt. 4:8-10; Luke 4:5-8. Satan will not be the "prince of this world" forever (John 12:31).

[6]John 5:22, 26-27, 30.

the broad path leading to destruction, the Lord Jesus trod the narrow path of suffering and death. With the Father's authority now entrusted to Him, Christ issues His command: "Go ye therefore." Since the disciples will stand in great need of this authority as their witness for Christ begins and develops, the Lord assures them at the very outset of this divine enablement. What an encouraging prospect for all believers who go forward as ambassadors in the name of Christ. They do so, convinced of His message, filled with His power, and sustained by His blessed presence!

Christ also speaks of the universal extent of their work. They are to "make disciples"[7] of all nations, or as Mark gives it, "preach the gospel to every creature" (Mark 16:15). Then through baptism, these new converts are to identify themselves in an obedient relationship with Christ.[8] Having made disciples and baptized them, it would be most natural that the disciples would teach these new learners everything previously given to them by Christ to guide His followers. The command "teaching them to observe all things whatsoever I have commanded you," though directed here to the disciples, is not to be limited to them alone. The apostle Paul, speaking of Christ's gifts to the church, includes the gift of teaching,[9] indicating its mandate for the continuing edification ministry of the local church.

Christ completes His commission with this promise: "I am with you alway." In the account of the three young men in ancient Babylon thrown into the flaming furnace for their refusal to bow to the heathen king, the men walked unhurt in the fire for they were in the presence of one "like the Son of God" (Dan. 3:25). What a foretaste of what believers have come to know and experience in the midst of their own trials by fire, literal or otherwise. Daniel also knew the Lord's presence when cast into the den of lions for his loyalty to God. Others too knew

---

[7]KJV "teach," Gk. *matheteuo*, "to enroll as a disciple, to instruct, to teach." The word "implies practice as well as intellectual formulation. That is, the disciple does not just have certain ideas and opinions; he or she behaves in certain ways, living out those ideas. The Christian disciple is one trained and taught by Jesus Christ, one who 'follows after' Jesus. . . . Christian discipleship means following Jesus Christ." David W. Gill, *Peter the Rock* (1986), pp. 41-43.

[8]To be baptized in the name of the Father, the Son, and the Holy Spirit is the full expression of the believer's unity with God in salvation.

[9]Rom. 12:7; I Cor. 12:28-29; Eph. 4:7-12. Teaching, or edification, as a function of the local church is supported with abundant NT concepts: (1) Christ commanded us to teach (Matt. 28:19-20). (2) The Holy Spirit gives the gift of teaching (I Cor. 12:11). (3) The early church taught its new converts (Acts 2:42; 14:21). (4) Paul taught Timothy and commanded him to teach others also (II Tim. 2:2). (5) Ability to teach is a qualification for a bishop (I Tim. 3:2), while false doctrine is to be refuted with sound teaching (I Tim. 1:3; 4:6; 6:3).

God's presence in trials—Jacob at Bethel, the psalmist in the valley of the shadow of death. Believers in every generation have faced intense adversity and great opposition and, though they stood alone, they knew God was with them and that through God's reassuring presence they could endure. To be with God is to be in the majority. "Don't be afraid sometimes to find yourself in a minority, for every great cause has been in a minority once."[10]

Tarry ye

Two great experiences still await Peter before he goes forward as the powerful apostle and leader of the early church. He is to be witness to the ascension of the Lord Jesus back to heaven, and he is to be partaker of the gift of the Holy Spirit at Pentecost. The opening chapters of the Book of Acts introduce us to these two events as Peter takes the lead in the infant church, rallying the disciples, preaching the gospel, confronting the council, exercising discipline, and demonstrating a life wholly committed as a witness to Christ.[11] For the moment, however, we return to Luke 24, where we left the disciples still in Jerusalem on that first Resurrection Sunday, for Luke does not mention the Lord's appearances at the Sea of Galilee or the mountain appointment. We continue with his abbreviated account of the closing days of the Lord's ministry among His disciples. Addressing those gathered in the upper room that first Lord's Day, the Lord explains, "These are the words which I spake unto you, while I was yet with you, that all things must be fulfilled, which were written in the law of Moses, and in the prophets, and in the psalms, concerning me" (Luke 24:44). "The law of Moses . . . the prophets . . . the psalms." The whole of the OT Scriptures spoke of Him, Jesus says, giving His stamp of approval on the OT Scriptures from beginning to end. Then we read that He "opened . . . their understanding, that they might understand the scriptures" (v. 45). I have no doubt that Simon Peter, here assembled with the others, receives from the Lord's lips that fuller and deeper grasp of His person and work that will form the foundation for his powerful witnessing of Christ in the Book of Acts—from his insight into Joel's prophecy to application of David's explicit references to the holy one who would come, die, and be raised up again.

---

[10]Quintin Hogg, *The Story of Peter* (1900), p. 255.

[11]Stewart Custer adopts this theme, witness to Christ, for his commentary on the Book of Acts. The early believers, Custer shows, were "not just spectators; they testified to the Lord Jesus Christ." Stewart Custer, *Witness to Christ: A Commentary on Acts* (2000), pp. xviii, 4.

The Lord goes on to say, "Thus it is written, and thus it behoved Christ to suffer" (v. 46). God's great love for man demanded that Christ suffer and die if sinners are to be brought to salvation. There is but one door to heaven, and that entrance is a person, the Good Shepherd, who gave His life for His sheep. As a result of that vicarious death on the cross and that glorious resurrection from death, "repentance and remission of sins should be preached in his name among all nations, beginning at Jerusalem" (v. 47). Begin, says the Lord, "at the very worst spot, the spot where they would not have Me, the spot where they scorned and spit upon, and slew Me; begin there, but go out to all nations."[12] "Ye are witnesses of these things," He reminds them. But there is one thing more. "Behold, I send the promise of my Father upon you: but tarry ye in the city of Jerusalem, until ye be endued with power from on high" (vv. 48-49). Witnesses . . . power from on high . . . tarry in Jerusalem.

"Go ye . . . tarry ye." The Lord Jesus had commanded them to go into all the world; now He also says to wait in Jerusalem. What can this possibly mean? The words will linger in their minds and hearts after He is gone. "And he led them out as far as to Bethany, and he lifted up his hands, and blessed them. And it came to pass, while he blessed them, he was parted from them, and carried up into heaven" (vv. 50-51). Thus, Luke describes in his Gospel what he relates in greater detail later in Acts: "And they worshipped him, and returned to Jerusalem with great joy: and were continually in the temple, praising and blessing God" (vv. 52-53).

The promise of the Father

In His intimate conversations with the disciples in the upper room before His death, the Lord Jesus confided that it was necessary[13] that He go away, for if He did not go away, "the Comforter will not come unto you" (John 16:7). Christ would ask the Father and He would give them "another Comforter, that he may abide with you for ever" (John 14:16). Jesus identifies that Comforter as "the Holy Ghost, whom the Father will send in my name" (John 14:26). It is for this "promise from [His] Father" that the Lord Jesus instructs His disciples to "tarry ye in the city of Jerusalem" (Luke 24:49) so that they may "be endued with power from on high."

---

[12]W. T. P. Wolston, *Simon Peter* (1926), p. 144.

[13]KJV "expedient," Gk. *sumphero*, lit. "to bear together," thus (fig.) "conducive, better for, expedient, profitable."

Now let us now turn more fully to the Acts of the Apostles. The Lord has been taken up, as we have seen in the end of Luke and re-stated with a little more detail in the first of Acts. Introducing his sequel to Theophilus, Luke sounds the refrain with which he closed his Gospel.

> The former treatise have I made, O Theophilus, of all that
> Jesus began both to do and teach, until the day in which he
> was taken up, after that he through the Holy Ghost[14] had
> given commandments unto the apostles whom he had chosen:
> to whom also he shewed himself alive after his passion by
> many infallible proofs, being seen of them forty days, and
> speaking of the things pertaining to the kingdom of God: and,
> being assembled together with them, commanded them that
> they should not depart from Jerusalem, but wait for the prom-
> ise of the Father, which, saith he, ye have heard of me. For
> John truly baptized with water; but ye shall be baptized with
> the Holy Ghost not many days hence (Acts 1:1-5).

In these opening verses, we see the four factors that provide the major emphasis that runs throughout the Book of Acts: the Lord's mandate to witness, the ministry of the apostles, the indwelling power of the Holy Spirit, and the continued presence of the ascended Lord.[15] The mandate is clear. Believers are to go into all the world to preach the good news that Jesus saves. Fulfillment of that mandate rests not only on our obedience to Christ's command to evangelize but also on His living presence in heaven and the sure promise of His return. The reality of Christ's ascension will assure His disciples that He will be with them as He promised. We take that same promise, "Lo, I am with you alway," as true because our Savior is a living Lord.

We read here that the Lord, after His resurrection and before His ascension, was seen of His disciples for "forty days, and speaking to them of the things pertaining to the kingdom of God." Why forty? Because forty was the full time of probation and testing. These forty days allow for the most absolute testimony to the truth and validity of His resurrection.[16] We may also infer that as Jesus teaches during the forty days following His resurrection, He validates His messiahship

---

[14]All that Christ said and did was "through the Holy Ghost." Wolston adds: "I believe we see here what the Christian will be in the eternal state—full of the Holy Ghost, and acting entirely by Him," p. 145.

[15]*EBC* vol. 9, p. 253.

[16]We have recorded in Scripture that the Lord was seen ten times in His resur-rection body, five times on the first day of the week, and five times afterward.

with them and also interprets additional OT Scriptures from the perspective of His resurrection. Most importantly, He brings to the forefront their responsibility to bear witness to what has happened among them in fulfillment of Israel's hope.[17]

This time being over, the Lord tells them not to leave Jerusalem but to wait for the promise of the Father He told them about. Thus, the stage is set for what follows. The disciples are to leave to God the matters that are His concern—when the kingdom will be restored to Israel—and are to take up the mandate entrusted to them. "But ye shall receive power, after that the Holy Ghost is come upon you: and ye shall be witnesses[18] unto me both in Jerusalem, and in all Judaea, and in Samaria, and unto the uttermost part of the earth" (v. 8).[19] Here the mandate to witness that stands as the theme for the whole of Acts is explicitly set out. It comes as a direct commission from Jesus Himself—in fact, as Jesus' last words before His ascension and, therefore, as one that is final and conclusive. The concentric geographic setting, so explicit that it stands as the Spirit-inspired outline for the Book of Acts—Jerusalem, Judea and Samaria, the uttermost part of the world—shows the mission of the church in its witness to Jesus succeeding at Jerusalem (Acts 2:42–8:3) and throughout Judea and Samaria (8:4–12:24), and its progress until it finally reached the imperial capital of Rome (12:25–28:31). Salvation, "like a shining river, could go out to the ends of the earth, beginning at the guiltiest spot of all, but ever widening and flowing out and on until, thank God, it reached the benighted Gentiles."[20]

This same Jesus

The scene suddenly changes. "And when he had spoken these things, while they beheld, he was taken up; and a cloud[21] received him out of their sight. And while they looked stedfastly toward heaven as he went up, behold, two men stood by them in white apparel; which also said, Ye men of Galilee, why stand ye gazing up into heaven? this

[17]This is what Luke 24:25-27, 44-49 reveals as the content of Jesus' post-resurrection teaching, and this is what Acts elaborates in what follows. *EBC* vol. 9, p. 254.

[18]The concept of "witness" is so prominent in Acts (the word in its various forms occurs some thirty-nine times) that everything else in the book should probably be subsumed under it. *EBC* vol. 9, p. 256.

[19]Thomas suggests this brief outline for v. 8. (1) Our great work—witnessing; (2) our great field—the world; (3) our great need—power; (4) our great provision—the Holy Spirit; (5) our great secret—waiting on God.

[20]Wolston, pp. 145-46.

[21]Jesus as the ascended Lord is enveloped by the Shekhinah cloud, the visible manifestation of God's presence, glory, and approval. *EBC* vol. 9, p. 258.

same Jesus, which is taken up from you into heaven, shall so come in like manner as ye have seen him go into heaven" (Acts 1:9-11). They have ascended the well-known slopes of Olivet with the Master. With hand outstretched in blessing, the Master parts from them and they see Him no more. "The man Jesus vanished from sight, but the Christ did not depart."[22] Jesus had promised to be with them and us, even to the end of the age. The body in which He began to do and to teach passed out of their sight. It did not cease to be, but for their sakes it vanished to make way for the "body," His church, in which He would continue to do and to teach. "The days of limited service were over, the days of unlimited service were about to begin."[23] Jesus' new body, though not yet come to birth and power, waited for the coming of the Holy Spirit at Pentecost.

Peter, with upturned eyes, might wonder where his Lord has gone, for he has been witness of a life like none other on earth—the Son of God become man. But he will soon reap the fruit of the Master's final words: "Expedient for you that I go away . . . promise of the Father . . . Comforter . . . Holy Spirit . . . witness . . . Jerusalem . . . Judea and Samaria . . . the ends of the world . . . tarry . . . endued with power . . . not many days hence."

How could it be expedient for the church to lose its risen Lord? Why would it be necessary for the apostles to lose their great Teacher? The two angels at the ascension scene had assured them that "this same Jesus, which is taken up from you into heaven, shall so come in like manner as ye have seen him go into heaven" (v. 11). And now what does that all mean? Peter and his friends wind their sad way down from the slopes of Olivet to return to the city;[24] on their right lies Gethsemane, on their left the road by which but a few weeks previously Christ had made His triumphal entry. Crossing the Kidron, they ascend the slope of the hill towards Jerusalem, talking no doubt of their great loss, and of the Master's final commission, though still pondering His instructions. They were to go, the Master had said, to Jerusalem, and wait until, in "not many days," they would receive power from on high.

---

[22]G. Campbell Morgan, *The Acts of the Apostles* (1924), p. 22.

[23]Morgan.

[24]The "sabbath day's journey" (Acts 1:12) that the rabbis allowed the Jews to travel was little more than half a mile. In Joshua 3:4 they found a rule for this distance—two thousand cubits separated the people from the ark of the covenant when they marched over the Jordan. Taking this distance between the people and the tabernacle as proper, the rabbis concluded that is was right to travel just that far on the Sabbath.

What this power is they scarcely have a clue, but their orders are to wait for it. There are but one hundred twenty in all, for the majority of Christ's followers are in the northern province of Galilee, which had been the main scene of His labors. In some room—we know not which, but probably it is the same as that in which they had taken the Last Supper—they meet together for the first time to pray in the name of Christ. "Whatsoever ye ask in my name" had been the promise, and from that little room in Jerusalem first goes forth that now universal prayer: "And this we ask for Jesus' sake."

Peter leads

In keeping with his portrayal of Peter, Luke here presents Peter as taking the lead among the apostles. The Master is gone and the focus shifts in Acts to the centrality of the apostles and their ministry, another of Luke's emphases in Acts. Under God's direction, the apostolic band will regain its full number as Peter moves to fill the void created by Judas's defection and suicide. In addition to the eleven, the women, Mary, and Jesus' brothers in that upper room,[25] others also were there at various times for prayer and supplication; for we are told their number is now one hundred twenty. Jesus' brothers were never with Him during the days of His earthly ministry, but now we find them assembled with the others and all of them "with one accord" (v. 14) as "confidence in each other is the basis of a new fellowship."[26]

Having returned to Jerusalem from the scene of the ascension, the apostles lack one thing—the full complement needed for their witness within Jewry.[27] Taking the initiative, for he is now more than the first name on the list of apostles, Peter rises in their midst to speak. "Scripture must be fulfilled," he begins. "Judas Iscariot, who was one of us, is no longer among us, having fallen by his own transgression that he

---

[25]The use of the definite article in speaking of "the room" (*to hyperoon*) and the emphatic place these words have at the beginning of the clause suggest that the room was well known to the early Christians—perhaps the room where Jesus and his disciples kept the Passover just before His crucifixion (Mark 14:12-16). Perhaps it was the room where He appeared to some of them after He rose from the dead (Luke 24:33-43; cf. John 20:19, 26). Or, though this is more inferential, it may have been a room in the home of Mary, John Mark's mother, where the church later met (Acts 12:12). *EBC* vol. 9, p. 260.

[26]Morgan, p. 19. He also notes their confidence in the Lord that He is able to bring the purpose of God to a final consummation (Acts 1:6-7), and their confidence in the OT Scriptures, as Peter interpreted "the present by Scriptures from the past."

[27]*EBC* vol. 9, p. 260. Custer: "To the Jew the number 12 referred to the people of God. There had been 12 patriarchs, 12 tribes, 12 stones of memorial at the crossing of the Jordan (Josh. 4:3). The 12 apostles were plainly intended to be the new people of God (Matt. 10:1-5). To have only 11 meant that the image was broken." Custer, p. 11.

might go to his own place." Quoting from Psalms 69 and 109, Peter applies these passages to their present predicament. "For it is written in the book of Psalms, Let his habitation be desolate, and let no man dwell therein: and his bishoprick let another take" (v. 20).

Peter then authorizes that the replacement be chosen from the ranks "of these men which have companied with us all the time that the Lord Jesus went in and out among us" (v. 21), someone who had been a disciple from the time of "the baptism of John, unto that same day that [Christ] was taken up from us," someone "ordained to be a witness with us of his resurrection" (v. 22).

> An apostle, then, was not an ecclesiastical functionary, nor just any recipient of the apostolic faith, nor even the bearer of the apostolic message; he was a guarantor of the gospel tradition because he had been a companion of the earthly Jesus and a witness to the reality of his resurrection because the risen Lord had encountered him.[28]

They then select two men who meet the qualifications—Justus and Matthias—and turn to look to the Lord for the expression of His choice. Following Jewish tradition, they cast lots and Matthias is chosen.[29] Only one man, not both, are chosen, for as the symbolism failed when it lacked one apostle, so too would it fail if there were one too many. Therefore, prayer is offered to the Lord for His selection between the two men.

Just a few days

The ascension day passed, and Friday came, the one-week anniversary of Christ's crucifixion. Surely today the promised "power" would come, but the late afternoon sun sank as evening enveloped

[28]An interesting question is often raised. Why was not James replaced after he was martyred? The reason is that James had faithfully functioned as a witness to the reality of Jesus' resurrection for some fifteen years before he was killed. By that time, the church was growing beyond the apostolic dimension, and since there is no such thing as apostolic succession, that apostolic ministry was not to be repeated. *EBC* vol. 9, p. 265.

[29]In taking the lead in this matter, Peter bases his action on the clear teaching of the Word of God as well as a practice culturally accepted at the time. I have no doubt that God approved the action, founded as it was on His own Word. *EBC* notes that Peter's action illustrates for us sound hermeneutical methodology that distinguishes between normative principles and culturally restricted practices in the progressive revelation of the Bible. We are exhorted as Christians to "search the Scriptures" and "to know what is the will of the Lord"—exhortations that are normative. But the early church's midrashic exegesis and the practice of casting lots were methods for interpreting the OT and determining God's will used at that time, and we need not be bound by them today. *EBC* vol. 9, p. 266.

them and no message came. The next day was the Sabbath. Surely He would send "rest" to their hearts on the Sabbath rest. But that, too, passed, to be succeeded by the new Sabbath of the Christian dispensation—the Lord's Day, the day of His resurrection. What day could be more fitting for the coming of the Comforter, for the presence of the power of the Most High? But that day, too, passed, and, with weary watching, they counted off the Monday and the Tuesday and the Wednesday of the next week. Then Thursday dawned on them, the complete week after His ascension. He had promised His blessing in "not many days." Has He forgotten His promise? That cannot be true; they must repel all suggestion to doubt. So still they wait and pray. They have been waiting now nine days, for the second Sabbath has come since the Lord had parted from them. Why should this delay take place? Were not men perishing for the need of a Savior? Had they not been told to go preach to all nations? With such a work before them, why tarry? Strange must seem to them the unexpected delay, yet still they wait and still they pray.

Implications for Service[30]

1. *The Master is gone; the disciple must continue His work.*
   The Lord Jesus had planned from the beginning that His disciples would continue His ministry on earth after He returned to the Father. He had told them earlier: "Verily, verily, I say unto you, He that believeth on me, the works that I do shall he do also; and greater works than these shall he do; because I go unto my Father" (John 14:12). Through the power of the Holy Spirit, the Comforter, the disciples are to obey the Master's command to evangelize the world. This is the task the Lord assigned to them at the beginning, to catch men alive for God. There comes a time in the master-disciple relationship that the teacher steps aside and the disciple assumes more complete responsibility for his work and witness to Christ. When the master teacher is aware of this necessary eventuality, he will proceed to prepare his disciple for this next phase of the disciple's development.

2. *Every witness needs the power of the Holy Spirit.* Following His mandate to evangelize the world, the Lord also prom-

---

[30]Now that we have entered the phase of Peter's life in which he is serving the Master following his period of discipleship training, it is more appropriate to draw implications for our own service from Peter's actions as he witnesses for Christ in the Book of Acts.

ised that the Father would send the Holy Spirit to empower them in their labors. Personal charm and persuasion are not sufficient for the disciple maker. Spiritual tasks demand spiritual power, the enabling grace of the Holy Spirit working in the life of the witness as well as convicting and regenerating the sinner. To learn to work with the Holy Spirit in the spiritual ministry of snatching sinners from a burning hell is our admission that in ourselves we can do nothing. Or as Jesus reminded us: "I am the vine, ye are the branches: he that abideth in me, and I in him, the same bringeth forth much fruit: for without me ye can do nothing" (John 15:5).

3. *Aware of the need for action, Peter took the initiative.* Peter's prompt, energetic decision is consistent with what we now know of Peter from the Gospels. What we see in Acts 1 is a transformation of an impetuous nature, one that acts first and thinks later, to one that takes the lead when action is appropriate and necessary. Scripture must be followed, Peter asserts, and the full complement of disciples must be restored. He has also learned the lesson of true servanthood. A servant sees a need and, without being told, relieves that need. The servant of Christ is quick to obey the Word of God.

4. *God's will is to be sought in all matters.* How to know God's will is a pressing concern for young disciples. After Peter draws the attention of the others to the teaching of the OT Scriptures, he counsels them concerning the replacement for Judas Iscariot. They then follow the culturally accepted norm for discerning God's will, the casting of lots. Believers today often find themselves asking about the use of other means of discerning God's will, that is, practices that range from those generally acceptable (favorable circumstances or a settled peace) to those of questionable use (allowing the Bible to open to a random passage). Our first priority in determining God's will must always be a clear understanding of relevant Bible teaching on any matter. We must remember, however, that culturally accepted means to assist us in identifying God's leading will vary between Christian communities, but these are only secondary and supportive. They must never violate the clear teaching of Scripture.

PENTECOSTAL POWER

They were all filled with the Holy Ghost (Acts 2:4).

The Comforter has come,
The Comforter has come!
The Holy Ghost from heaven—
The Father's promise given;
O spread the tidings 'round,
Wherever man is found—
The Comforter has come!

—Frank Bottome

Setting: Jerusalem, Sunday, May 24, A.D. 33[1]
Scripture: Acts 2:1-47

They wait and pray, the one hundred twenty unified and obedient followers, there in the upper room. It is early morning on the second Lord's Day after the ascension and fifty days now since the Master resurrected to life from the tomb. It is also the morning of the Feast of Weeks, kept, as its name "Pentecost" showed, just fifty days after the earlier Feast of the Wave Offering, when the first few ripe heads of barley were waved by the priest before the Lord in anticipation of the coming harvest.

Under Moses and the old economy, God had ordered that His ancient people observe seven great national festivals, or feasts, each year.[2] These feasts, described in Leviticus, the third book of Moses and Israel's instructions for the worship of Jehovah, picture for the Christian church today the blessings that Christ brings to believers. Those great festivals began, as Israel's national history began, with the Passover in Egypt, observed in memory of the night the death angel "passed over" the houses that had the blood-sprinkled doorways.[3] This feast symbolizes the death of the Lord Jesus Christ as the Lamb of God.[4] The last Passover of the old economy had now been celebrated on that climactic day when Christ died. A second feast, that of unleavened bread, took place the day after the Passover[5] and speaks of our

---

[1] Harold W. Hoehner, *Chronological Aspects of the Life of Christ* (1977), p. 143.
[2] Lev. 23:1-44.
[3] Exod. 12:13.
[4] I Cor. 5:7; I Pet. 1:19.
[5] Exod. 12:14-20.

remembrance of Christ's death.[6] Next came the Feast of the Wave Offering, last kept on the day of Christ's resurrection, when He became the "first fruits"[7] from the dead, led captivity captive, and robbed the grave of its sting. The next feast, fifty days later, would be Pentecost.[8]

The Comforter comes

While these fellow believers, men and women together, pray and enjoy the sweet and heavenly unity of fellowship with one another (Acts 2:1), "suddenly," the sound of a mighty wind fills the entire room where they are assembled. Flames appear over each, which, as they watch, take the shape of divided tongues of fire flashing brightly above their heads. "And they were all filled with the Holy Ghost" (v. 4). The house was filled and they were filled! The "promise of the Father," so patiently pondered during those "few days" following the ascension, has come upon them. That promised baptism, not of water as with the Baptist, but of the Holy Ghost from the Father in heaven, is now their privileged portion. The Comforter has come!

Pentecost is the "kernel of Christianity,"[9] the day of the coming of the Holy Spirit personally to earth to abide in the believer. By the death of the Lord Jesus, the way had been laid open back to God. Sin had been put away, the grave opened, death annulled, the Lord having ascended to the right hand of the throne of God. The way was thus prepared for the Holy Spirit to come to earth to take the place of Jesus and to reproduce the life of Jesus in His disciples. Thus is brought into being that organism—promised by Jesus Christ following Peter's great confession at Caesarea Philippi—His church, to which the gates of hades would hold no lasting resistance. Earlier, on His resurrection day, the risen Lord had announced His provision of the Holy Spirit and the apostles' commission to proclaim the forgiveness of sins.[10] Now at Pentecost we witness the historic fulfillment of that announcement. The Spirit, who baptized them all into the body of Christ, de-

---

[6]I Cor. 11:23-26.

[7]I Cor. 15:20.

[8]The remaining three feasts were the Feast of Trumpets, which speaks prophetically of the still future blessing of the Jews at the end of the church age (Isa. 18:3, 7; 27:12-13); the Day of Atonement, which teaches us not only that Christ died for our sins on the cross but also that our sins are completely removed (Heb. 10:10, 17), to be remembered no more by God (Jer. 31:34); and the Feast of Tabernacles, or Booths, during which time the Israelites were to live in tents, in observance of the years of wilderness wanderings when the people of Israel lived in tents, yet always in God's care. This feast speaks of the final rejoicing of all God's people of every age and time, when the kingdom of God is set up on the earth (Rev. 21:3).

[9]W. T. P. Wolston, *Simon Peter* (1926), p. 147.

[10]John 20:22-23.

scended with great announcement, but He Himself was unseen and unheard. The Spirit was not the boisterous wind, for that was but a signal to attract listeners. Nor was He the fire, for that symbol but pointed to their empowerment. But as the wind blows where it will and we do not see it, only its effects, so is everyone born of the Spirit.[11] The trusting believers are now indwelt by the blessed Holy Spirit, and the most marvelous sight of all is that these Spirit-filled believers begin "to speak with other tongues, as the Spirit gave them utterance" (v. 4).[12]

The noise and the rumor of what has suddenly happened flows into the streets of Jerusalem, and a large number of people rush to the temple area where the disciples have now gone seeking wider accommodation for the increasingly curious crowd. Before long the gathering included "devout men out of every nation under heaven," dumbfounded to hear powerful witnesses for Christ speaking in their own languages "the wonderful works of God" (v. 11). In this temporary reversal of Babel, the apostles, empowered by the Holy Spirit, speak in all sorts of languages that they had never learned, and all the various nationalities who were in the city came up to hear about Jesus of Nazareth. God "rang the bell,"[13] so to speak, in a remarkable way just to gather souls to hear of His Son. Blessed, indeed, are the ways of the God of all grace.

Some of the gathering crowd, not understanding the strange tongues, regard the proclamations as drunken babblings. But others, recognizing them, ask honestly, "What does all this mean?" and marvel at the miracle taking place. Now comes that opportunity for which Peter and the disciples have been trained by the Master—the need of testimony and explanation. Will they be equal to the task, these Galileans who have spent their last three years in Jesus' presence, receiving from Him their understanding of the Word of God? "Harder tasks few men have had to undertake," observes Morgan, sensing something of the gravity of the situation thrust upon these unlearned men, "than that which fell to the fishermen of Galilee."[14]

---

[11]John 3:8.

[12]The Jews were familiar with certain signs as proofs that God gave when He wanted to call attention to the fact that He was speaking directly from heaven (Exod. 19:18; I Kings 19:11-12). On the day of Pentecost, the rushing mighty wind, the tongues of fire, and the voice of the Holy Spirit speaking through the disciples in other languages were all proofs, or signs, that what was occurring was from God. In the next few chapters of Acts, the Holy Spirit is given to different groups under different conditions, but never twice in exactly the same way (Acts 2:38; 8:17; 9:17; 10:44-46; 19:6). The tongues of fire never appeared again. After the first century, all the signs ceased.

[13]Wolston, p. 148.

[14]Quintin Hogg, *The Story of Peter* (1900), p. 273.

"But Peter, standing up with the eleven" (v. 14), so as to be seen by all, lifts up his voice to speak loudly and clearly[15] to proclaim the message of God to the unsettled crowd. Yes, it is Peter, who but two months previously, zealous, but lacking "somewhat in ballast,"[16] slithered into the courtyard of the palace and cowered before a servant girl. At that critical moment, Peter failed ignominiously, not once, but three times over. Are we witnessing the same man, telling with flashing eye and unfaltering lips the story of Christ to the crowd? Can the Peter of the palace be the same Peter of Pentecost? Indeed it is, but there is also a profound difference now. In the high priest's hall, where we saw him denying the Lord, Peter was "full of himself."[17] Now we see him "full of the Holy Ghost." A man full of himself, God must humble; a man full of the Holy Spirit is someone God can trust and use for His glory.

Peter's first sermon

Listen to Peter. "Ye men of Judea, and all ye that dwell at Jerusalem, be this known unto you, and hearken to my words" (Acts 2:14). There is something perfectly uplifting in the bold way in which Peter now speaks. He possesses such a sense of the Master's love and forgiveness that he can stand up now and face the whole world, if necessary, for his beloved Master. Peter is unapologetic, speaking with "all boldness," as Luke puts it in another place.[18] The sermon is that of a man with truth now woven into every fiber of his being. He is absolutely persuaded that this truth must be accepted if any sinner is to be converted. Led, I am sure, by the Holy Spirit, Peter includes in this first sermon several elements that comprise all powerful preaching of the gospel. First, he establishes a point of contact with the people, noting their false accusation of drunkenness. Then turning to the OT Scriptures, he cites the prophecy from Joel that forcefully explains what is transpiring. His masterful handling of the Scriptures includes not only the prophet Joel but also the quotations and allusions from the Psalms, all of which he uses to exalt Christ, another essential in preaching. Peter offers no apology for his accusation that those who now hear him are responsible for the death of Jesus of Nazareth, though he also acknowledges that their actions are but a part of the broader purpose of "the determinate counsel and foreknowledge of God" (v. 23). He concludes with a scathing denunciation of their actions and the sufficiency of Christ for salvation. "Therefore let all the house of Israel know as-

---

[15]That is the sense of the Greek construction.
[16]Hogg, p. 274.
[17]Wolston, p. 142.
[18]Acts 4:29.

suredly, that God hath made that same Jesus, whom ye have crucified, both Lord and Christ" (v. 36). To this Jesus of Nazareth, whom God has raised up, "we all are witnesses" (v. 32), Peter stresses, affirming with unhesitating lips his commitment to the Lord's final command, "Ye shall be witnesses unto me" (1:8). And so, as the voice of the fisherman sounds through the morning air,[19] the murmurs and the questioning gradually cease, and the hearers gather closer together to listen to a man speaking with the authority of sincere conviction and in the power of the indwelling Spirit.

Listen to Peter as he continues: "These are not drunken, as ye suppose, seeing it is but the third hour of the day. But this is that which was spoken by the prophet Joel" (2:15-16). Whether it was with a serious intent that would brush aside a frivolous accusation to get to the essential burden or with a sort of twinkle in his eye, Peter points to the sky to show that it is too early for men to be drunk. The Jews did not break their fast before the morning sacrifice, and there-fore they had not eaten, much less drunken. "It's only nine o'clock in the morning," says the apostle, hastening directly to show that they stand in the midst of prophetic fulfillment. The prophet Joel had spoken of this very time.

> And it shall come to pass in the last days, saith God, I will pour out of my Spirit upon all flesh: and your sons and your daughters shall prophesy, and your young men shall see vi-sions, and your old men shall dream dreams: and on my ser-vants and on my handmaidens I will pour out in those days of my Spirit; and they shall prophesy: and I will shew wonders in heaven above, and signs in the earth beneath; blood, and fire, and vapour of smoke: the sun shall be turned into dark-ness, and the moon into blood, before that great and notable day of the Lord come (vv. 17-20).

Peter says, as it were, "This is the first installment of the prophecy of Joel," showing now his mastery of the Scriptures as he cites the prophet. Peter is careful not to say that it is the complete fulfillment of Joel, for the prophecy anticipates the return of the Lord Jesus Christ "in the last days" when it will all be fulfilled exactly as prophesied. But the point of Peter's reliance on the prophet is to remind his hearers of what Joel prophesied: "And it shall come to pass, that whosoever shall call on the name of the Lord shall be saved" (v. 21). God will keep His timeless promise of salvation and deliverance, notes Custer:

---

[19]Hogg, p. 275.

"It does not matter whether it is Joel's day, or Peter's day, or our day, or the future Day of the Lord; God will save all who call upon Him in truth."[20] That means that for those living today, now is the day of salvation and deliverance. If you refuse to take Christ now, if you miss salvation now, it will not come to you later when the Lord comes to set up His kingdom upon the earth. That issue will have already been settled.[21] The day of blessing of which Joel speaks is for the future. At that time, all present rejecters of Him will be judged, not blessed.

Peter then goes on to witness strongly and effectively for the Lord: "Jesus of Nazareth, a man approved of God among you by miracles and wonders and signs, which God did by him in the midst of you, as ye yourselves also know" (v. 22). Peter speaks of those things he has seen and heard from the Master Himself. He speaks of what Jesus had been doing—how on every hand He blessed people, as the crowd well knew. But then what a change Peter makes! He strikes boldly at their guilt. "Him, being delivered by the determinate counsel and foreknowledge of God, ye have taken, and by wicked hands have crucified and slain" (v. 23). What a terrible, scathing indictment! They are guilty of the murder of their Messiah and rejection of the Son of God! Only seven weeks before, they had refused to have the Lord and had chosen Barabbas, a robber and murderer, instead of Him. They had cried, "Away with him, crucify him," even though Pilate, the Roman governor, had declared Him innocent. All sinners have this same guilt on their heads. They have not nailed Him to a cross with their hands, but their sins placed Him there. The mob said, "Let Him be crucified." Sinners today repeat the refrain in their refusal to convert to the Savior. Peter's solemn charge is laid before us all.

But the man whom the world refused, God has raised from the dead and seated at His own right hand. Peter could remind his hearers that they had crucified the Lord of glory, but He could not be held by death. He went into it, came up from it, annulled its power, and set its captives free.

---

[20]Stewart Custer, *Witness to Christ* (2000), p. 25. See also his study of the Greek word for save (*sodzo*) in the NT, especially its theological development in Acts. He also shows that all the verbs (Rom. 5:9-10; 10:9-13; Eph. 2:8-9; I Tim. 2:4) are in the passive voice in Greek, showing once again that the believing sinner trusts Christ and allows God to save him. We must be saved by the Almighty or be lost forever.

[21]A current series of novels, the Left Behind Series, by Tim LaHaye and Jerry B. Jenkins, has stirred renewed interest in the end times, and I rejoice at the many people who have professed coming to Christ as a result of reading these books. One feature of the series, however, is problematic to many Bible students who view the novels as offering a "second chance" for salvation to people "left behind" after the rapture of the church, a view that must be reconciled with the biblical warning that "today is the day of salvation."

For David speaketh concerning him, I foresaw the Lord always before my face, for he is on my right hand, that I should not be moved: therefore did my heart rejoice, and my tongue was glad; moreover also my flesh shall rest in hope: because thou wilt not leave my soul in hell, neither wilt thou suffer thine Holy One to see corruption. Thou hast made known to me the ways of life; thou shalt make me full of joy with thy countenance (vv. 25-27).

Then Peter shows how Psalm 16 could not refer to David when it said, "Thou wilt not leave my soul in hell; neither wilt thou suffer thine Holy One to see corruption." David indeed had seen corruption, for they laid him in his grave. But for the risen Lord, death held no claim, "whereof," Peter says, the eleven nodding their approval, "we all are witnesses" (v. 32).

Peter continues with his account of the exaltation of Christ. "Therefore being by the right hand of God exalted, and having received of the Father the promise of the Holy Ghost, he hath shed forth this, which ye now see and hear. For David is not ascended into the heavens: but he saith himself, The Lord said unto my Lord, Sit thou on my right hand, until I make thy foes thy footstool" (vv. 33-35). The work of redemption is complete, the power of Satan has been broken, and the Holy Spirit has come to tell us this and that the Lord now sits on high until He makes His foes His footstool. In the meantime, He is gathering out a people for His name. Israel put the Lord in a tomb. God has placed Him on His throne in glory.[22]

What shall we do?

Peter unfolds the truth that the King is in heaven, and in doing so, he unlocks the door of salvation for those Jews and proselytes hearing the gospel of the saving grace of Christ for the first time. Prejudice is swept aside as Peter's voice, along with those voices of his fellow witnesses, are overcome, first with a single cry bursting from the lips of one man, then finding its echo among the many: "Men and brethren, what shall we do?" (v. 37).

Indeed, what should they do? Listen to Peter's invitation. "Repent, and be baptized every one of you in the name of Jesus Christ for the remission of sins, and ye shall receive the gift of the Holy Ghost" (v. 38). "What we have witnessed to of the salvation that is in Jesus Christ, you too may have," Peter assures the people. Remission of sins and the

---

[22]Wolston, p. 152.

indwelling of the same Holy Spirit, who has performed such remarkable wonders in the disciples, is the Father's gift to all who will repent of their sins and be baptized as believers[23] in the name of Jesus Christ. Peter then adds, "Save yourselves from this untoward generation" (v. 40). But you say, "How can I save myself?" By coming to Jesus, who is the living Savior, and in doing so be free from the judgment to be poured out on this world. "You are in the wrong company this day," Peter asserts. "Come out from among them and be converted."

Do you remember that at the first the Lord had said to Peter, when He called him to follow Him, "Henceforth thou shalt catch men"? We hear nothing of Peter's catching men alive until here in Acts 2, but then what a catch! Three thousand people in one day! That was the effect of the first gospel sermon. Without pomp or ritual, the gospel proves to be the power of God to salvation to all who will believe. And first to the Jews, though it is not limited to them, for they are told that God's power is not limited to one particular people but that the promise is "unto you, and to your children, and to all that are afar off, even as many as the Lord our God shall call" (v. 39).

The new church grows

This remarkable chapter of Acts begins with the tongues of fire sitting on the believers. Here at the end we see the fire of the Holy Spirit doing its work in the three thousand people who, convicted of their need of a Savior, bow in submission to the Lord Jesus Christ, confessing their sins. They heard the gospel, surrendered their life-long prejudices and convictions, believed in Jesus of Nazareth, repented of their sins, and were baptized. Will not these thousands of Pentecost converts one day rise in judgment against any today who, with full knowledge of the gospel of grace, continue to refuse to call upon God for salvation?

What follows is instructive. "And they continued stedfastly in the apostles' doctrine and fellowship, and in breaking of bread, and in prayers" (v. 42). Peter and the others continued to instruct these new converts (the word "doctrine" means "teaching"). Christ's chosen disciples are now discipling others. "The apostle's teaching" no doubt

---

[23]By his answer, "repent, and be baptized" (v. 38), Peter does not teach "baptismal regeneration." Custer properly shows that Peter commands his hearers to "repent" (2nd person sing.), an action that includes one's change of heart and thinking and presupposes true faith. Then each one who has thus repented and believed should "be baptized" (3rd person sing.). One who is a repentant believer should publicly confess Christ as Savior "on the basis of the forgiveness of sins," that is, because he has repented and been forgiven. This same Greek construction is found in Matt. 12:41, where the men of Ninevah "repented on the basis of the preaching of Jonah." Custer, p. 29.

refers to a body of material considered authoritative because it was the message about Jesus of Nazareth proclaimed by these true apostles. It undoubtedly included a compilation of the words of Jesus, some account of His earthly ministry, passion, and resurrection, and a declaration of what all this meant for man's redemption. As revelation progressed throughout the NT era, the teaching must have included new insights into the OT Scriptures that these Jews brought into Christianity from their previous religious life. In addition to obeying the teaching of the apostles and the Word of God, these early Christians sought fellowship among one another, the definite Greek article in "the fellowship" implying that there was something distinctive in the gatherings of these early believers. Their proclamation of Jesus as Israel's promised Messiah and the Lord of all set them apart in Jerusalem as an identifiable assembly. And in their practice of breaking bread and praying, they participated in direct worship of God. Again using the definite article, Luke speaks of "the prayers," suggesting formal prayers, primarily Jewish, but increasingly Christian in character. The chapter concludes with these new converts participating in service for God as they assist others in their needs, witness to Christ in the temple, and praise God continually.[24]

God could have brought about no more auspicious beginning to His church than what we see as Peter, using the keys to the kingdom, preaches the gospel to those in Jerusalem. But this is just the beginning of the outreach that will come in obedience to the Lord's command. There is still more of Jerusalem and Judea, then Samaria, and finally the uttermost parts of the globe. God is at work, and Christ's presence, through His Holy Spirit, as He promised, will energize and fill His waiting disciples.

Let ev'ry Christian tongue proclaim the joyful sound:
The Comforter has come![25]

Implications for Service

1. *Believers need the filling of the Holy Spirit for effective service.* Though I have focused on Peter and his preaching

---

[24]These early Christians received instruction in the Word of God, fellowshiped with the people of God, worshiped the person of God, and expressed their faith in the work of God. These four elements—*instruction, fellowship, worship, and expression*—are vital ingredients to any local assembly. And through all these activities, *evangelism* is prominent as God's people witness to Christ and the Lord adds to the church those being converted.

[25]Frank Bottome, "The Comforter Has Come," *Great Hymns of the Faith* (1968), p. 161.

at Pentecost, the Scripture tells us that "they were *all* filled with the Holy Spirit," not just Peter. Through Peter's preaching and the witnessing of the others as well, three thousand people converted to Christ that day. What God did at Pentecost is available for all believers. The crowd's mistaken criticism that the disciples were drunken men should remind us of the apostle Paul's exhortation to the Ephesians not to be "drunk with wine, wherein is excess; but be filled with the Spirit" (Eph. 5:18). Jesus had promised His people that "when the Comforter is come, whom I will send unto you from the Father, even the Spirit of truth, which proceedeth from the Father, he shall testify of me: and ye also shall bear witness, because ye have been with me from the beginning" (John 15:26-27). The Spirit-filled Christian testifies of Christ, not of himself. After analyzing Peter's five messages found in Acts, Gill observes that in all of them, Peter "does not spend time promoting or analyzing 'speaking in tongues,' the exemplary love of Christians or reforms in local laws limiting religious freedom. He promotes the person of Jesus Christ."[26] That is what a Spirit-filled Christian will do—promote and glorify the Lord Jesus Christ, for that is what the Spirit has come to do.

2. *Converts need biblical instruction and fellowship with other believers.* Those who converted to Christ and were baptized "continued stedfastly in the apostles' doctrine and fellowship, and in breaking of bread, and in prayers" (Acts 2:42). As soon as it is feasible, new converts should be enrolled in regular Bible study, particularly with other Christians. It can be in a small Bible study group in a home or apartment,[27] since that is one location that may pose little threat to new converts, but effort should be made to bring them into the fellowship and teaching of a local church as soon as possible. Peter also urged baptism as a vivid symbol

---

[26]David W. Gill, *Peter the Rock* (1986), p. 141.

[27]When compared to a one-on-one discipling encounter, the small group has several values, according to Hadidian. (1) The small group provides those in the group an opportunity for close fellowship with more than one person. (2) Friendships are developed. (3) It provides the disciple an emotional home where he is accepted. (4) It provides an opportunity for members to develop a sensitivity toward one another. (5) It gives the disciple greater exposure to God's personal working in people's lives. Allen Hadidian, *Discipleship* (1987), pp. 135-37.

of their conversion to Christ. Their repentance and faith must be demonstrated by action. Baptism is not a work that earns salvation, but it is an act of obedience that symbolizes one's public identification with the person and work of the Lord Jesus Christ in dying for our sins and rising again for our justification; for the very symbol of baptism derives from the resurrection of Jesus Christ. Baptism is thus a statement to all that we leave all to follow Christ, that we are dead to ourselves and the world and alive unto God. Baptism, church membership, continued Bible study, and fellowship with God's saints—these are the Lord's design for growth.

3. *The church is a community of disciples composed of all those who have believed on Jesus for salvation.* In this sense, discipleship is not optional; nor is it confined only to those who are extremely committed to Christ. And discipleship is not limited to those who have been called to leadership and ministry. When a person converts to Christ and is saved, he is brought into the body of Christ, a community "that defines its expectations, responsibilities, and privileges in terms of discipleship."[28] In the wonderful events of Pentecost, we see the Lord's disciples testifying in the power of the Holy Spirit and bringing others into a saving relationship with Christ. Hadidian defined discipleship to include the concept that the trained disciple should mature to the point that he is equipped to reproduce himself in a spiritual third generation.[29] That is what we witness in the lives and testimonies of these Spirit-filled believers in Acts. The result of discipling is that God's work will continue for future generations. When we teach for discipleship, as much is carried on by example as by what we say. The educational ministry of the local church takes on tremendous importance if believers are to continue in the apostles' teaching, as did the early converts at Pentecost. The challenge for our churches is to develop teachers and leaders who are willing to give of themselves in life and preparation to discipleship training.

---

[28]Michael J. Wilkins, *Following the Master* (1992), p. 271.
[29]Hadidian, p. 29.

255

4. *Effective preaching and witnessing exalts Christ.* By godly instinct and Holy Spirit enablement, Peter focused on Jesus Christ in his preaching—who He is and what He came to do, especially as He is presented in the OT Scriptures. A well-known Bible conference speaker, who preached regularly in various churches and Christian camps, remarked that wherever he was on Sunday mornings, he preached on some aspect of the person and work of Jesus Christ. What a powerful focus to sustain in one's preaching for a lifetime of ministry—to exalt Christ every Sunday in his sermon. Pastors, evangelists, and teachers would do well to consider what this godly man had already settled for himself—that his preaching should exalt Christ and not self.

LIVING FOR CHRIST

Such as I have give I thee (Acts 3:6).

Lord, help me live from day to day
In such a self-forgetful way,
That even when I kneel to pray
My prayers shall be for others.

—*Charles D. Meigs*

Setting: Jerusalem, A.D. 33
Scripture: Acts 3:1–4:33

During the ten days of waiting after the Lord's ascension, we saw Peter take his first steps of leadership in the choice of Matthias to replace Judas Iscariot. After the Holy Spirit came to indwell believers at Pentecost, we saw Peter, "the Spirit-filled Evangelist and Apologist,"[1] witness of Christ through his first Christian sermon. Now comes Peter's first miracle, one of the "greater works,"[2] which Jesus promised His disciples would accomplish in His absence after the arrival of the Comforter from the Father. "Now Peter and John went up together into the temple at the hour of prayer, being the ninth hour. And a certain man lame from his mother's womb was carried, whom they laid daily at the gate of the temple which is called Beautiful, to ask alms of them that entered into the temple; who seeing Peter and John about to go into the temple asked an alms" (Acts 3:1-3).

The allusions in the Gospels and the Book of Acts to the associations of Peter with John, the son of Zebedee, afford a striking illustration of what Griffith Thomas calls "the power and blessing of true friendship."[3] Peter, possessor of an impulsive nature, is counterbalanced by John's calmer disposition. Peter's intense zeal, which makes him a natural leader, is matched by John's loving devotion, which gives him added spiritual perception. Thus possessing two very different natures, the two men—Peter the older, John the younger lad—find in their friendship a fellowship of kindred spirits that nourishes each other's strengths and compensates for one another's weaker tendencies. Their fellowship now ripens further after Pentecost as they continue united in their service for the Master, "the combination of age and youth,

---

[1]David W. Gill, *Peter the Rock* (1986), p. 138.
[2]John 14:12.
[3]W. H. Griffith Thomas, *The Apostle Peter* (1956), p. 122.

together with their different personal characteristics, [making] an ideal association for the promotion of their Master's work."[4]

The two friends set out for the temple to pray at one of the Jews' appointed times. We must remember that the Christian church only slowly cast aside its "Jewish swaddling clothes."[5] Still essentially Jewish in background, the early church continued those beliefs and practices long associated with the coming of the Messiah, adding to convictions the certainty that the promised one had now come. The convincing proof of this was that Christ had risen from the dead. The liberation of the church from these Jewish remnants remained for Paul to enunciate in his ministry, though as we continue our study of Peter, we shall see him broadening his grasp of the "one fold" of which the Master spoke, notwithstanding his continued struggles against his own national prejudices. Thus, it was natural enough that Peter and the others would, in the early days of the church, keep the Jewish feasts, attend the Jewish services, and behave themselves, to a great extent, as ordinary members of their race, including "the prayers" and daily communion in the temple area as we see at the end of chapter 2.

The Jews held to three periods of prayer, each of which was attributed to one of the patriarchs—Abraham, Isaac, and Jacob. The morning prayer, from 6:00 A.M. to 9:00 A.M., which was said to have been started by Abraham, was the "third hour" of the day (the Jewish day began at 6:00 A.M.). Then there was the time of the noon prayer, from 9:00 A.M. until noon, said to have been started by Isaac, and corresponding to the "sixth hour" of the day. Finally, there was the "ninth hour," from noon until 3 P.M., said to have been started by Jacob. It is at this third period of prayer, the ninth hour, that we find Peter and his friend John on their way to the temple area to pray.

The Beautiful Gate

Approaching the temple area, they enter the large courtyard known as the court of the Gentiles, the only gathering place where non-Jews were allowed throughout the temple complex. In this courtyard all the buying and selling took place. Moneychangers erected their tables to provide exchange from Roman coins into temple currency. Those selling doves and other animals for sacrifice also set up their booths in this large open court. It was here that Christ taught and, as Hogg suggests, great stones still lay around, some ready to be fitted into their places, others having been rejected by the builders and laid aside, but

---

[4]Thomas. See pp. 122-26 for further development of their friendship from their earliest associations as fishing partners to their work for the Lord in Acts.

[5]Quintin Hogg, *The Story of Peter* (1900), p. 277.

which just a few months earlier the people had taken up for the purpose of stoning Jesus.[6] Around the court of the Gentiles ran a covered walkway, its cedar roof supported by handsome Corinthian columns. On the roof of the walkway patrolled Roman soldiers with immediate access to the fortress of Antonia, where lived the Roman garrison, always ready to quell any disturbance. Continuing westward, Peter and John climb a flight of steps leading from the court through a grand archway into what was known as the court of the women. Across the entrance of this second court ran a low barricade on which was written in three languages an absolute prohibition to any foreigner to proceed any farther. At the west end of this court of the women, another flight of steps led up to a still smaller and higher court, the court of the priests, from which those permitted could enter the small white building that was the temple proper.

As they approach the beautiful archway,[7] with the intent to enter the court of the women, Peter and John encounter a crippled beggar, whose friends had brought him that day, as they had daily year after year, to seek alms from those entering the temple area. If you have seen any of these beggars outside Roman Catholic churches in Europe, as I have, you can easily picture the scene. Here he is, lying in his rags, a horrible contrast to the splendor of the gate and of the temple itself, wailing out his monotonous appeal for a stray coin. Dare we ask this question? If he had been here for so long, had he witnessed any of Christ's teachings and ministries in the temple? If so, did he associate these Galilean fishermen with Jesus of Nazareth? He certainly must not have cried out for help from Jesus; otherwise, the Lord would have healed him. Nor do we discern in him any sense of belief in the Messiah. His only concern seems to be to obtain a few coins during his daily round of begging.

No money, but . . .

That those in dire circumstances often have low expectations confound many. Rather than reaching out in expectation of an improved life through the ministry of these followers of Jesus of Nazareth, the beggar continues to wallow in what for the last forty years has been his crippling condition. Seeing the two apostles, he begs for the usual

---

[6]Hogg, p. 278.

[7]To placate the Jews over whom he ruled, Herod the Great had built much of this temple, including the Beautiful Gate. The gates to this archway were especially choice—in material and workmanship, size and weight. Over sixty feet high, it took twenty men to open and close them. They were covered with the famous "Corinthian brass," hence the designation as "the gate Beautiful."

handout with customary low expectation that any will heed his cry. But when Peter engages the man and demands him to "look on us," the crippled beggar's heart must have leaped at the prospect of reward. Just as suddenly it droops, however, with Peter's admission that "silver and gold have I none" (v. 6). Peter confesses, however, that though he has no money, "What I have, I will give to you." What a powerful possession it is—the indwelling power of the Holy Spirit of God and the Master's own promise to bless and extend Peter's service. Peter's faith is revived in the Master's power working through him. Flushed with the joyful reception of his pentecostal message, Peter invokes his Master's name and once more in faith announces healing to the man. Without hesitation, Peter boldly commands, "In the name of Jesus of Nazareth, rise up and walk."[8] Then, taking the man by the right hand, Peter lifts him up, "and immediately his feet and ancle bones received strength" (v. 7). Peter knows that it is not through his own power or by his authority that he commands healing, but in fulfillment of that commission on the mountain when the authoritative Lord Jesus promised His presence and power as Peter served Him. What Peter possesses, he is willing to give on behalf of others. Note the contrast to the Master Himself. The Lord Jesus had told the leper, "*I will*, be thou clean." To another paralytic, we hear "*I say unto thee,* Rise up and walk." Peter, the Master's servant, with no power of his own, but acting in faith "in the name of Jesus," heals the crippled beggar.

Why do you marvel at this?

The Beautiful Gate never looked more beautiful to the healed cripple than this day when, with Peter and John, he enters through it for the first time—"walking, and leaping, and praising God" (v. 8). After the time of prayer concludes, the disciples and the former cripple pass out through the court of the Gentiles, only to find that the news of Peter's miracle has spread throughout the temple area, causing a wondering crowd to gather at "Solomon's porch,"[9] the open corridor, or portico, running along the eastern wall of the temple complex. Seeing the commotion because of the healing, Peter steps forward to speak to the

---

[8]Many writers, commenting on the words of Peter, the alleged first pope, to the cripple, cite in one form or another an incident alleged to involve Thomas Aquinas. Going into the room of Pope Innocent IV, Aquinas found the pope surrounded by some of the great treasures that made the Roman Catholic Church wealthy. "You see," said the pope with a smile, "the days have gone by when the head of the church has to say, 'Silver and gold have I none.'" "Yes," was the reply of Thomas Aquinas, "as have also the days in which he could say to crippled men, 'Rise up and walk.'"

[9]The temple built by Herod the Great was surrounded on all four sides by a covered walkway or colonnade. The walkway on the east side, leading into the court of

crowd. "Ye men of Israel," he begins, "why marvel ye at this? or why look ye so earnestly on us, as though by our own power or holiness we had made this man to walk?" (v. 12). Disclaiming all personal credit for the miracle, he points to the one who but recently ascended to heaven. Peter tells the crowd that it is this same Jesus—whom they had rejected and killed—who had healed the cripple at the gate Beautiful. It was Christ the Messiah, Christ crucified, Christ glorified, Christ healing.[10] That is Peter's Spirit-filled message, once again reminding the people of their own condemnation. It was not only that they had rejected the Messiah but also that they had "desired a murderer" to be given to them. To reject the Prophet of Nazareth was bad, but to prefer Barabbas to Him was to add insult to their hate. "The Giver of Life was to be crucified, the taker of life set free."[11] But God raised Him up from the dead and "we are witnesses of this," proclaims Peter once more. Sounding a generously tender yet faithful note and speaking as a Jew to his countrymen, he allows that "through ignorance ye did it, as did also your rulers" (v. 17), but then urges them to repent "and be converted, that your sins may be blotted out, when the times of refreshing shall come from the presence of the Lord" (v. 19). "Repent of your iniquities," Peter warns, "that your sin may be blotted out by God's grace."

Once again Peter discloses his Spirit-led understanding of Scripture as he exalts the person and work of Christ. All people, including those hearing his message,[12] must face the one of whom the prophets—from Moses through Samuel and onward—spoke. To these Jews, children of the prophets and of the covenant (v. 25), belong the promise of

---

the women, was called Solomon's Colonnade because of a tradition that Solomon had a similar portico in the same area. Built on a platform or high retaining wall, Solomon's "porch" was a place for people to walk and talk, for teachers to share their learning. It was about fifty feet wide and had three separate rows of columns made of white marble. The columns were about forty feet high. Carved cedar beams formed the roof, and on the floor were mosaic stones, all in the latest Hellenistic architectural style. V. Gilbert Beers, *The Victor Handbook of Bible Knowledge* (1981), p. 537.

[10]Hogg, p. 285.

[11]Hogg, p. 286.

[12]Thomas suggests some personal characteristics of a Spirit-filled man, as Peter most evidently demonstrates in his preaching. (1) *Sympathy* (v. 4)—Peter prompts the crippled man to look on him, thus demonstrating a sympathetic understanding of the man's condition. (2) *Frankness* (v. 6)—Peter admits he has no money. (3) *Boldness* (v. 9)—Peter claims healing for the man in the name of Jesus of Nazareth. (4) *Humility* (v. 12)—The miracle is not of his own power and he does not claim what belongs to God. (5) *Faithfulness* (vv. 13-16)—Peter plainly preaches against sin. (6) *Generosity* (v. 17)—He makes the best of their position, acknowledging their ignorance, yet not excusing it either. (7) *Tactfulness* (vv. 22-26)—He tries to win their support by using their Scriptures and his tone is loving and attractive. "Impertinence is not faithfulness," nor is hardness of attitude. Thomas, pp. 86-87.

blessing given to their patriarch Abraham. Peter addresses them: "Unto you first God, having raised up his Son Jesus, sent him to bless you, in turning away every one of you from his iniquities" (v. 26). Declaring God's judgment on all who refuse to hear God's ultimate Prophet, Jesus Christ, Peter nevertheless assures them of His divine love for all. We are impressed this second time with the boldness of speech from this disciple who once failed his Lord. The answer must be the indwelling Holy Spirit. As Jesus promised, the Holy Spirit is guiding Peter into all truth and bringing all things to his memory. Hence, the clarity and force of his preaching and teaching. "The Master, the Word, and the Spirit, thus filled the disciple and used [Peter] for the glory of God."[13]

Opposition follows blessing

Following the first Christian sermon and Peter's first miracle, we see the first organized opposition to Christianity from those who thought they monopolized religion in Jerusalem. Peter's attitude and spirit throughout the trying experience show another aspect to this Spirit-filled man as he stands for the truth. Before the pious but threatened leaders of Judaism now stand the unlettered fishermen from Galilee, led by none other than Simon Peter. The priests, the captain of the temple, and the Sadducees all fall on them, "being grieved that they taught the people, and preached through Jesus the resurrection from the dead" (4:2). How dare this untaught fisherman sit in Moses' seat and give instruction on religious matters? Yet here is Peter, speaking with fervent heart, his message taken in by the people held in rapt attention, the irrefutable testimony of the healed cripple by his side!

A call is made to the garrison in the Tower of Antonia and in a few minutes the apostle's sermon is interrupted by the arrival of armed soldiers who disperse the crowd and arrest Peter and John. The hour is late, now about 6:00 P.M., the time of the evening sacrifice, and not convenient for the Sanhedrin to assemble that night; so Peter and John have their first experience of imprisonment that the Lord Jesus had warned them would be the inevitable result of the preaching of the gospel. And what is the charge against them? First, they "taught the people," and second, they ventured to preach "through Jesus the resurrection from the dead." Our disciples have learned well from their Master, who received sinners and preached to the harlot and the publican as well as to the Pharisee and the scribe, so that the "common

---

[13]Thomas, p. 87.

people" heard Him gladly. We are learning at the very beginning of Christianity that it is a faith for the common people, not the religionists. Christianity is for the people, to get them to God. That is what Peter and the others are attempting as they "witness to Christ" and His resurrection. Their gospel is that of the death, burial, and resurrection of Jesus Christ, who is now exalted at the Father's right hand. There is power in that message, and the enemies of Christ now see that power manifested in the powerful preaching of His devoted ones. Here is Peter, with rough Galilean speech, proclaiming the simple yet profound truths of the kingdom of God, and the religionists will have none of it.

Rather than resort to argument against the apostle's teaching and preaching, the Jews take up the old weapon of persecution. They will suppress and kill the messenger rather than answer him. But the Sadducees and others had tried that earlier with Christ. They thought to silence and suppress Him, yet here stands before them one of His disciples, confronting them with the same message of resurrection from the dead! Well, Peter and John are placed securely in prison[14] and the next day, for the first time, they face the Sanhedrin,[15] the very same council that only recently had condemned Jesus to death. They had slain the Master. Could His servants expect any mercy? To face this formidable assembly, with its reputation for learning, is no light task for two seemingly poorly trained fishermen from Galilee. Even so, these two disciples hold in their hearts the truth of the gospel, which the Sanhedrin in their wisdom have never fathomed. "The Word had been made flesh, and dwelt among them; and the fishermen had caught sight of His glory, while the priest had seen nothing but the carpenter."[16]

---

[14]"hold," v. 3.

[15]The Sanhedrin (Gk. *synedrion*, from the Aramaic word for "council") was the ruling body of ecclesiastics in Judaism who controlled its religious and political life up to the overthrow of the Jewish commonwealth in A.D. 70. Its origin is uncertain. The rabbis held that it began with the seventy elders who advised Moses (Exod. 24:1), but no evidence exists of the persistence of any organized council from the time of the Exodus. The first clear reference to an organized body is in the time of Antiochus the Great (223-187 B.C.). It had a membership based on age and wealth, over which the high priest presided. Membership in the Sanhedrin was limited to Israelites of pure blood and was held for life. Its jurisdiction was limited to Judea. It made final decisions in cases relating to the interpretation of the law and acted in criminal cases, subject to the approval of the Roman governor. It served as his advisory council on Jewish affairs and provided a central government during the years when the nation had been largely stripped of any real independence. Merrill C. Tenney, *Wycliffe Dictionary of Theology* (1960), pp. 471-72.

[16]Hogg, p. 298.

The morning interrogation by the Sanhedrin begins with a formidable company of questioners—rulers, elders, scribes, Annas the high priest, with many of his own kin, as well as Caiaphas, John, and Alexander. They pose a single question: "By what power, or by what name, have ye done this?" (v. 7). They make no attempt to deny that indeed a miracle has brought wholeness to the crippled man. Their searching question goes to the heart of their opposition, for as Sadducees they held no belief in the supernatural. There must be a rational explanation for this occurrence. "You are poor Galilean peasants. You must be acting in the name of some greater power. Tell us who it is."

Peter and John, the doer and the thinker, stand before the council. But now a third man stands with them. We do not know if the healed man spent the night with the two disciples in the hold, but he stands before them "whole" (v. 9). Filled with the Holy Spirit, Peter once more takes the opening given to him, this time focusing on their demand to know in whose "name" they have healed the man. "Ye rulers of the people, and elders of Israel," Peter begins, "if we this day be examined of the good deed done to the impotent man, by what means he is made whole; be it known unto you all, and to all the people of Israel, that by the name of Jesus Christ of Nazareth, whom ye crucified, whom God raised from the dead, even by him doth this man stand here before you whole" (vv. 8-10).

Peter is by no means finished. Drawing on an allusion to the Psalms,[17] and perhaps pointing to several building stones cast aside nearby, Peter further explains that the stone rejected by the builders is now the chief cornerstone in God's building. "This is the stone which was set at nought of you builders, which is become the head of the corner. Neither is there salvation in any other: for there is none other name under heaven given among men, whereby we must be saved" (vv. 11-12). Completing his witness of Christ, Peter tells his hearers that there cannot be salvation in any other than the one chosen by heaven, that God saves men through this stone, which they have rejected. There is nothing in the entire story of Peter in the Gospels and Acts that is more uplifting and encouraging than to witness his transformation from cowering denier in the palace to bold apologist before his accusers in the council. His "boldness" (v. 13) is not simply bravery; it is outspoken clarity of thought and powerful statement of fact and Scripture. In his preaching to his accusers, there is no mistaking the meaning of his message, for it contains "an almost blunt and defi-

[17]Ps. 118:22.

ant enunciation, that arrested attention, and compelled men to listen."[18] Peter's bold and powerful message, coupled with the personal testimony from the healed man, provide proof that God is at work, proof that cannot be denied; for the accusers agree among themselves that Peter and John "had been with Jesus." That is, they had walked and lived with the Master, Jesus of Nazareth, and what they spoke and did in His name came from a personal acquaintance, an intimate knowledge, and an abiding fellowship with the Christ of God. Having nothing with which to refute Peter's message, they "clear the court" and confer among themselves as to what they should do next, acknowledging that something notable has occurred, for all Jerusalem now is aware of what has happened. "We cannot deny it" (v. 16), they confess.

What to do? Calling the two apostles back into their council, they issue a command. Peter and John are not to speak or teach ever again "in the name of Jesus" (v. 18). "Surely these poor, timid men will have no backbone to stand up for Jesus of Nazareth," the council may have reasoned, "just as they forsook Him when He was crucified. We will just threaten them and let them go; they will not bother us again." A bad conclusion, certainly, for Peter abruptly asserts, "We cannot but speak the things which we have seen and heard" (v. 20), reminding their accusers all are accountable to God, the higher judge. Peter's only concern is that he and John "do right" in the sight of God, that they obey Him when opposed by God's enemies. "Is it right?" is Peter's criteria. Does not this dictum extend to our lives today? A life molded around this principle—do right—will be a godly life, one that pleases the Father in heaven. In any question, we must ask, not what is convenient nor the most profitable nor even the pragmatic, but what is right.

Throughout his defense, Peter demonstrates to all that God is real (v. 19), Christ is precious (vv. 10-12), and the Spirit is powerful (v. 8).[19] With further threats, but no actual punishment, the council releases the apostles, fearing any adverse reaction from the population at large, "for all men glorified God for that which was done" (v. 21). Ask any resident or even pilgrim in Jerusalem that day, and you would have learned that all the city knew that God had wrought a beautiful miracle at the beautiful gate.

Give us boldness!

If the Sanhedrin council imagines that they have seen the last of a troubling minority, they are terribly mistaken. Heading directly to their

---

[18]G. Campbell Morgan, *The Acts of the Apostles* (1924), p. 128.

[19]Thomas, p. 90.

own company of believers, Peter and John report "all that the chief priests and elders had said unto them" (v. 23). They immediately commit themselves anew to the God of heaven.

Lord, thou art God, which hast made heaven, and earth, and the sea, and all that in them is: who by the mouth of thy servant David hast said, Why did the heathen rage, and the people imagine vain things? The kings of the earth stood up, and the rulers were gathered together against the Lord, and against his Christ. For of a truth against thy holy child Jesus, whom thou hast anointed, both Herod, and Pontius Pilate, with the Gentiles, and the people of Israel, were gathered together, for to do whatsoever thy hand and thy counsel determined before to be done. And now, Lord, behold their threatenings: and grant unto thy servants, that with all boldness they may speak thy word, by stretching forth thine hand to heal; and that signs and wonders may be done by the name of thy holy child Jesus (vv. 24-30).

What powerful praying! It is not surprising that following their prayer, the building in which they are praying convulses, the Holy Spirit once more fills them with power, and they continue to speak the Word of God—again "with boldness" (v. 31)—witnessing to the Lord's resurrection with great power. "And great grace was upon them all" (v. 33).

Years later John would write:

That which was from the beginning, which we have heard, which we have seen with our eyes, which we have looked upon, and our hands have handled, of the Word of life; (for the life was manifested, and we have seen it, and bear witness, and shew unto you that eternal life, which was with the Father, and was manifested unto us;) that which we have seen and heard declare we unto you (I John 1:1-3).

Peter could have said the same. And this is his testimony before the council:

"I have stood in the presence of one who spoke as no man ever spoke. I have seen this life violently ended and then risen from the grave. I communed with Him after you had done your worst to Him. I have seen Him received back into glory and now bear within me His blessed Holy Spirit. I stand here as a witness to Christ and His resurrection. I can but tell you the things I have seen and heard."

Implications for Service

1. *Personal evangelism is as important as mass evangelism.* On the day of Pentecost, Peter experienced the thrilling results of mass evangelism when three thousand turned to Christ. This is still one method for reaching sinners—mass meetings conducted in churches and civic auditoriums. The second is personal evangelism in which we deal with the individual. To open the Scriptures and present Christ to one person and then to see the light of the glorious gospel shine in his face and rest in his heart is an equally thrilling experience. This is a wonder that is within the grasp of every believer's experience. Perhaps you think that there is nothing you can do for Christ. God has not called you into the Christian ministry. You cannot speak to great congregations. But you can speak to one person. You can say to a friend or neighbor, "What I have I give to you too," just as Peter did with the lame man. And you can lead that person to newness of life in Christ. Christians possess what this sin-cursed world needs—the message of hope and salvation in Jesus Christ.

2. *Persecution follows blessing.* Peter and John engaged in a deed of compassion that brought healing to a man who had been afflicted for over forty years. Yet the religious establishment in Jerusalem refused to give God the honor or to accord these men special praise because they had done their ministry "in the name of Jesus of Nazareth." They were not sanctioned by the religious monopoly in Jerusalem; therefore, they must be punished. Peter later writes:

> And who is he that will harm you, if ye be followers of that which is good? But and if ye suffer for righteousness' sake, happy are ye: and be not afraid of their terror, neither be troubled; but sanctify the Lord God in your hearts: and be ready always to give an answer to every man that asketh you a reason of the hope that is in you with meekness and fear (I Pet. 3:13-15).

Believers may expect persecution in this world, even when they act righteously by following God's Word. But godly conduct in the midst of accusation and persecution will cause

others to ask about our faith in God and our commitment to
His Word. The opportunity to speak for God will follow, as it
did with Peter and the others as they witnessed with renewed
enthusiasm to the grace of God in their lives.

3. *Believers support each other through fellowship and prayer.*
   Peter and John enjoyed rich fellowship together in their
   service for the Lord Jesus. Perhaps they learned this as they
   went forth two by two as disciples for the Master. They certainly knew one another from their days of fishing together.
   There is power in the mutual support that comes through
   fellowship and prayer with other believers. It is through this
   time together that we are able to edify one another, as the
   Scriptures exhort us to do. We need each other and we need
   the Lord. The prospect of walking together to the place of
   prayer should cheer our flagging spirits every day.

PETER'S LONG SHADOW

The shadow of Peter passing by (Acts 5:15).

Not every day the preacher's soul is fired,
But when the spark is there, foundations quake
And mountains move. Then sinful hearts, inspired
By judgment fears, to penitence awake.
Spirit anointed, most imperfect clay
Becomes a golden vessel for God's Word,
Which, overflowing, heals and cleans away
Black doubt and hind'ring fear. Then Christians stirred
Know rushing mighty wind, baptizing fire,
Speaks such a preacher with a prophet's tone,
By love consumed, revival his desire,
Blessed beyond measure, pulpit then a throne.

Give to this preacher now the heavenly pow'r
My people wait. Make this the shining hour.

—Bob Jones

Setting: Jerusalem, A.D. 33
Scripture: Acts 4:34–5:42

During His intimate conversations with His disciples before the Crucifixion, the Lord Jesus warned that they should expect no less persecution as servants of the Master than what the Master receives. "The servant is not greater than his lord. If they have persecuted me, they will also persecute you" (John 15:20), He predicted. They will be persecuted, said Jesus, "for my name's sake" (v. 21) because those who oppose Him neither know Him nor believe in Him. Peter has now seen this animosity firsthand for speaking "in His name." If he ever doubted the Lord's forecast, he should no longer. And if Peter is at all surprised by the frenzied opposition from the religious elite of Jerusalem, he does not show it. Rather, he boldly, clearly, and forcefully takes the lead, empowered by the Holy Spirit, in witnessing for Christ. His long shadow of influence—both symbolically and literally—now takes the form of exerting serious disciplinary remedy within the early church in Jerusalem; shortly we shall see his extended healing ministries among the needy in outlying cities throughout Judea.

Leaving the Sanhedrin council, Peter and John go directly to the assembly of believers in Jerusalem to join them in prayer—not to have the opposition removed but to ask for boldness to continue to preach and teach, to bear witness to the risen Lord. Real danger produces earnest prayer, a type of praying that brings results no formula prayer has ever produced. The entire assembly, rather than being intimidated by the danger just experienced by the two apostles, are filled with Christian enthusiasm, brotherly love, and compassion for one another. The thick clouds that have lowered on them drive them closer to each other. They begin to see their persecuted brothers and sisters in the Lord as ones to whom they must extend helping hands. All the believers, holding loosely the things of this world, throw much of their individual worth into one common fund so as to provide assistance for the needs of all.

We must not err on this point. Some point to this practice of the infant church and call it "Christian communism." That is unfortunate, for communism abolishes all private property by force, imposes a compulsory redistribution of wealth, compelling all workers to place their possessions and earnings in a common purse. These private contributions of personal property to the general welfare of the church were not compulsory and should not be thought of as a universal requirement within the body of Christ. Remember, Mark's mother retained her house in Jerusalem, to which Peter will later resort when released from prison.[1] Naturally enough, those who saw fit to do so received praise for their deeds, as did Barnabas, who was commended for his gracious spirit of giving. This "son of consolation," as he is renamed by the apostles,[2] who afterward will be a companion of Paul on his missionary endeavors, had land and sold it. He then brought the proceeds from that sale into the general fund.[3] Out of this fund a certain amount would be laid aside for the rooms and meals that they had in common. Some would also be given to the apostles and their fellow workers. Also those who were in destitute condition—the sick or the widowed—would have their needs met through this fund. Though only Barnabas is specifically mentioned as giving to this fund, there must have been others who provided similar contributions

---

[1] Acts 12:12.

[2] There is no question of the prominence of the apostles in the early life of the church. Those who converted their possessions into currency and other goods laid all this "at the apostles' feet" (4:35, 37). Joses is "surnamed Barnabas" by the apostles (v. 36). At this time they are the spiritual and temporal guides of the infant church, a position clearly acknowledged and accepted by the church. This authority was intended only for the foundation of the church however (Eph. 2:20), for they could have no successors. The qualification for apostleship was unique and necessarily limited (Acts 1:21-22).

[3] Acts 4:34-37.

from their possessions. Perhaps Barnabas was the first, however, and the others follow his example. Thus, side by side with Barnabas's gift is another, one of "acted falsehood,"[4] that calls for immediate and drastic discipline from the apostle Peter. His shadow of influence and leadership lengthens.

Why has Satan filled your hearts?

The striking contrast between the end of Acts 4 and the first part of Acts 5 should prompt serious examination of the extraordinary event. At the end of chapter 4, the believers are unified in their loving and sacrificial care. A little bit of heaven shines through their compassionate concern for one another. With the first word of chapter 5— "big, black and ugly," as Hogg describes it—the "trail of the serpent comes across the new Eden."[5] As the fall in the garden forever altered its original state, so the work of Satan in the hearts of Ananias and his wife threatens the early church with a danger that the Sanhedrin's threats of prison and excommunication could not effect. "*But* a certain man named Ananias, with Sapphira his wife, sold a possession, and kept back part of the price, his wife also being privy to it, and brought a certain part, and laid it, at the apostles' feet" (5:1-2). The real source of danger to the church is always more potent from within the assembly than from without. The shedding of blood by martyrs has not corrupted the church. Lives wasting away in dark, filthy prisons have not fostered backsliding of the faithful; rather they have enhanced the spiritual vitality of believers. But the "humble worm kills the tree which the hurricane tests in vain."[6] And, therefore, we must give earnest heed to the story about to unfold and the lessons it provides the church of God about dealing with rot from within the individual heart as well as that within the assembly.

Among the early followers are a husband and wife—their names are recorded for us—Ananias and Sapphira. Were they present in the upper room while the one hundred twenty waited for Pentecost? Did they witness for Christ at Pentecost or did they come to Christ at the first preaching of Peter? Had they already made sacrifices in behalf of other believers in the infant assembly? Were they among those strong enough to pray for boldness to continue to witness of the risen Christ, even after the council's threats? None of these questions matter. For some time now, their enthusiasm for God has died out and worldly

---

[4]F. B. Meyer, *Peter* (1950), p. 144.
[5]Quintin Hogg, *The Story of Peter* (1900), p. 310.
[6]Hogg.

avarice has crept into their souls. That was all the vacuum Satan needed to plant his divisive ideas. Since everyone praised Barnabas for his generous spirit, Ananias and Sapphira crave the same for themselves, posing to appear more devoted than they really are. So they conspire together to sell their plot of land but to keep the selling price secret. From this sale they will give a portion to the church, withholding for their own use the remainder. At this point we must remind ourselves that Ananias and Sapphira are absolutely within their rights to sell what they want to sell, to give what they want to give. No one would criticize them for giving only a portion of the proceeds. The trouble comes—and this is when Satan's hand is seen—when they seek praise for having given up *all*, while actually retaining a measure for themselves. Their scheme looks reasonable and harmless enough, but God will not be mocked. Though they profess to give all to God and His church, they keep back part, evidently no small amount; but small or large, their sin brings God's judgment and apostolic discipline.

Peter does not take lightly the action of Ananias and Sapphira. He sees their hypocritical conduct as inspired of Satan and as a lie to the Holy Ghost and to God. What he faces is a case of deliberate deceit, an affront not only to the Christian assembly but more importantly to God. In the infant church, such deceit would be spiritually disastrous, for there can be no trust in one another where there is any sign of deception. Like Achan's sin that brought defeat in battle, the sin of Ananias and Sapphira now jeopardizes the entire mission of the church at its start. But notice how Peter, acting with supernatural knowledge taught by the Spirit and apostolic authority, confronts, first of all, Ananias with the challenge: "Why has Satan filled your heart to lie to the Holy Spirit and to retain part of the price of the land you sold?" We see at once Peter's discernment that the couple's actions are a sin against the blessed Holy Spirit of God. The apostle reminds Ananias that he had every right to dispose of his property as he chose, and even after he sold it, he had the right to donate what portion he chose. Instead of publicly and forthrightly announcing that he is giving only a portion of the full amount for which he received remuneration for the sale of the property, Ananias presents the gift as the full amount, keeping for himself and his wife a significant portion.

What reason does Ananias have to do this and therefore to lie to God the Holy Spirit, Peter contends. Peter echoes the Master, who taught that what comes out of a man is what defiles him, for from the heart proceeds all that is evil.[7] Ananias saw the temptation coming and opened the door and invited it in, made it welcome, made it his own. Outwardly, he joined in prayer, in praise, in fellowship; outwardly, he broke bread and drank the cup. But his sin in secret grieved the blessed Holy Spirit. Ananias in appearance did as Barnabas—an act of Christian compassion. In reality, there is a stark difference. Avarice is certainly seen on the surface of the matter, but hidden deep within the inner man is profound hypocrisy. Ananias's great evil that threatens the infant church is the superficiality of an appearance of godly consecration, but he lacks the genuine experience, which should cause alarm to any wayward child of God who thinks to pacify himself with the notion that God is unconcerned about such hypocrisy.

Peter says simply, "Thou hast not lied unto men, but unto God" (v. 4), the God who was in the midst of their assembly, and He has detected the sin. "And Ananias hearing these words fell down, and gave up the ghost" (v. 5). As he sinks to the floor in a dying faint, what burning thoughts must possess Ananias as he realizes at this very moment that God knows all about him, and God has judged his sin. Ananias dies because God will have true spirituality, not hypocritical pretense, in His people. This is a solemn moment. God's infant church must maintain its purity so that it may increase in size and strength and fulfill its commission to go to the ends of the world. Three hours later, after Ananias has been carried out for burial, his wife Sapphira appears. Just why Ananias is buried so quickly and why his wife is not told seems strange, though we are not told enough about the circumstances to offer any explanation. Without hesitation, Peter inquires of her, "Did you sell the land for a certain amount of money?" When she asserts her agreement with the figure, with deliberate and even defiant lying, Peter proclaims her doom, identical to that of her husband.

God must be intolerant of evil in His assembly. He judges among them simply because He lives among them. He cannot allow evil where He dwells, and the more His presence is manifested and realized, the more intolerant He is of that which is unholy. It cannot be otherwise. God is holy and He will have holiness among His saints. Peter will later write in his first epistle that believers are to be holy, for their Father God is holy. Ananias and Sapphira pretended to follow an impulse of the Holy Spirit, but they actually disregarded His presence. And they fell dead in that presence. Peter asked, "Why has Satan *filled* your heart?" When we are filled with the Spirit, there is

---

[7]Matt. 15:18-20.

no space left for the filling of Satan. The presence of God in the midst of His people is a truth of deepest importance. Whether Ananias and Sapphira were truly converted cannot be known for certain. Outwardly, they were members of God's assembly on earth, but they were hypocritical in their profession of commitment to God. As a result God's hand came upon them in judgment.

Do you remember Peter's amazement at the suddenness with which the fig tree withered under the curse of Jesus? What did Jesus condemn? False profession and hypocrisy: His actions spoke a profound object lesson to the Jews who refused Him, though He was in their midst. Peter now nurtures that same fervor to condemn hypocrisy that the Lord taught him as he administers discipline in the infant church. The sin of Ananias and Sapphira is still with us today. It is attempting, by confession of mouth, or deed of hands, or song of lips, to make things appear as they are not—to profess but not to possess. Our churches function today with leaders ordained by the Word of God—pastors, teachers, evangelists—and not what was present at its founding—apostles and prophets; otherwise, there might be many dead men and women at the end of our services. But perhaps that is to our shame. That God allows hidden sins to continue in anyone's life is no testament to our vitality, but perhaps more to the worldliness that afflicts the church of God. He still knows, and He will still judge for "some men's sins are open beforehand, going before to judgment; and some men they follow after" (I Tim. 5:24).

As a result of God's immediate and decisive judgment on Ananias and Sapphira at the hand of the apostle Peter, "great fear came upon all the church, and upon as many as heard these things" (Acts 5:11). The entire incident of apostolic discipline becomes an "indelible warning regarding the heinousness in God's sight of deception in spiritual and personal matters."[8] The tremendous and overwhelming aspect of this incident, that which fills us with awe, is not the death of Ananias and Sapphira. Rather, it is the purity of the church that demands such a drastic judgment. That small but growing company of believers is the body of Christ, His chosen instrument for accomplishing His purposes on earth. When sin enters that divine fellowship, Christ's apostle, himself fully yielded to the Holy Spirit, does not hesitate to do the work of Christ, his word of condemnation and judgment meant for the glory of Christ and the purity of His body.

---

[8]*EBC* vol. 9, p. 314.

Peter's shadow

Fear and power—these are the consequences of Peter's action. The assembly of God's people and also those outside the church are greatly moved by the catastrophe. All feel God's presence, and as a result, the Christians continue to assemble at Solomon's porch in the temple complex. The Jews who continue in their unbelief, however, hesitate to associate too closely with the Christians, while responsive Jews seek company with the believers, place their faith in the Lord, and are added to the church. The lesson we must learn from this solemn scene is that God's eye is constantly on us and that He eventually deals with hypocrisy and lack of reality in our lives. He may not judge as swiftly as in the days of the infant church, when purity demanded such action, but the earnest believer knows that the Lord knows us and will search us out. With the psalmist we must plead, "Search me, O God, and know my heart: try me, and know my thoughts: and see if there be any wicked way in me, and lead me in the way everlasting" (Ps. 139:23-24).

As a result of the Holy Spirit's pruning the branches of the young Christian vine, the work of God grows stronger and "by the hands of the apostles were many signs and wonders wrought among the people" (Acts 5:12). At the beginning of His own earthly ministry, the Lord Jesus healed those brought to Him—those with various diseases and torments, those possessed with demons, those who were lunatic, those who were crippled and palsied, "great multitudes of people from Galilee, and from Decapolis, and from Jerusalem, and from Judaea, and from beyond Jordan" (Matt. 4:25). We now see the same ministry among His apostles. Thus "signs and wonders," the exercise of the spiritual gifts of healing of which we read in I Corinthians 14, are on display. We read,

> And by the hands of the apostles were many signs and wonders wrought among the people. . . . Insomuch that they brought forth the sick into the streets, and laid them on beds and couches, that at the least *the shadow of Peter* passing by might overshadow some of them. There came also a multitude out of the cities round about unto Jerusalem, bringing sick folks, and them which were vexed with unclean spirits: and they were healed every one (Acts 5:12, 15-16).

Peter thus is greatly used of the Lord, as His messenger, both for the healing of bodies and the blessing of their souls. Early in his association with Jesus, Peter had witnessed the healing of the woman with the issue of blood, who grasped the hem of Jesus' cloak. Jesus said that "virtue," or energy, had gone forth from Him on that occasion. Now Luke tells us of something of the same extraordinary situations involving Peter in which even Peter's shadow is used by God to bring about healings. Whereas the healing of the solitary crippled man at the gate Beautiful originally aroused the wrath of the Sadducees, now we learn that such a miracle is being repeated over and over by the apostles throughout Judea. Little wonder that bitter opposition arises once again from the Sadducees as the "smouldering embers of their jealousy burst into fire."[9] They had tried imprisonment of Peter and John once before with no success. Now they arrest the Twelve with hope of better success at stopping their growing popularity with the people and cast them all into a public prison. But the Lord will not allow Satan to put a stop to the glorious work of God's servants. In His providence, God watches over His work and, acting through the ministry of angels, frustrates the plans of those opposing His grace. "Go, stand and speak in the temple to the people all the words of this life" (v. 20), commands the angel. "And when they heard that, they entered into the temple early in the morning, and taught" (v. 21).

Peter and the others give immediate heed to the angelic injunction and go to the temple to preach. Meanwhile, the council gathers again and sends officers to have the apostles brought out from prison to appear before the council once more. The officers go but return immediately when they learn that although the prison was secured and the guards in place, nevertheless, within the prison itself the prisoners are nowhere to be found. Our imagination must dwell on the scene of the empty cell for a moment—the great door to the prison house, the dark room within, the emptiness, the dampness—while all the while outside the cell pace the sentinels in their diligent care of . . . nobody, except the scurrying rats that infested all such dwellings. If you had asked these guards what they were doing, they would have responded that they were performing a great task for the religious elite Sadducees, that inside were dangerous people capable of insurrection and sedition. Yet they guard a prisonerless room, for the angel from God has delivered the prisoners from their dungeon. Well might the council be puzzled and wonder "whereunto this would grow." The council had reckoned on dealing with the apostles; they had not realized that they must also deal with the God of the apostles. This is the way with the world. The council's confusion is compounded when at the same moment others come in to tell the council that "the men whom ye put in prison are standing in the temple, and teaching the people" (v. 25).

---

[9]Meyer, p. 147.

Again the council issues arrest warrants for the disciples, who are taken without violence, for the council remain afraid of arousing the animosity of the people at large.

We must obey God

As they stand once more in the presence of the council, Peter and the disciples hear the words of the priest. "Did we not straitly command you that ye should not teach in this name? and, behold, ye have filled Jerusalem" with teaching about Jesus (v. 28). Peter's reply, as he speaks again for all the apostles, shows settled purpose that the Sadducees did not desire to know the truth. His accusers are utterly opposed to God. "We ought to obey *God* rather than men" (v. 29). These religious elites of Judaism, opposed as they were to God and His program, had been set aside by God, judged by God to receive no more light. And where any religious body seeks to oppose Christ, the believer must indeed obey God rather than any man who stands on opposite sides from the eternal God.

Peter once more boldly presses home their sin, saying, "The God of our fathers raised up Jesus, whom ye slew and hanged on a tree. Him hath God exalted with his right hand to be a Prince and a Saviour, for to give repentance to Israel, and forgiveness of sins. And we are his witnesses of these things; and so is also the Holy Ghost, whom God hath given to them that obey him" (vv. 30-32). Peter implies that the apostles are all ready to die for the faith that is in them. He faithfully delivers the Word of God as he preaches of the "God of our ancestors . . . you killed Jesus and hanged Him on a tree . . . God has exalted Him . . . He is now the Savior of the world . . . repent . . . receive forgiveness for your sins . . . we are true witnesses to the risen Christ . . . God will give to you His Holy Spirit if you obey His gospel." But the antagonists do not repent, taking counsel rather how to kill Christ's disciples also. Gamaliel, a Pharisee and therefore not one of the dominant faction,[10] his reputation for scholarship and his ancestry earning him a position second to none on the council, stems the tide for the moment with his call to moderation.

---

[10]Pharisees were in the Sanhedrin, but their presence during these earliest days of the infant church seems to be more of a moderating influence on the antagonism of the Sadducees. It is the Sadducees, that is, "the high priest and all that were with him" (v. 17), who took the official action against the apostles the second time, arresting them and thrusting them into the public jail, from which the angel delivered them. While the Sanhedrin did not have the authority under Roman jurisdiction to inflict capital punishment on the apostles, undoubtedly they would have found some pretext for handing these men over to the Romans for such action, as they did with Jesus, had it not been for the intervention of the Pharisees, as represented particularly by Gamaliel.

Gamaliel does not seem willing to allow the Sadducees to carry their hatred toward the apostles and the doctrine of the Resurrection to such a mad conclusion as the slaying of the apostles. In a plea for fairness, if not justice, he seeks to counter the Sadducean leadership who have carried their animosity to the extreme. He speaks persuasively as he reminds the council of the fate of several upstarts, Theudas and Judas of Galilee, who came to a sudden end without any success. His advice is to wait and see. If the thing is of men, it will be overthrown. But if it is of God, they cannot overthrow it for they will find themselves fighting against God. Gamaliel's counsel relieves the tension of the moment, placates the council for yet another time, though for the first time the apostles are flogged with forty stripes save one before being released.

Undeterred by the beatings and threats—in no wise depressed or dejected—the disciples rejoice that they are counted worthy to suffer "for his name" (v. 41). One senses that there is now in the apostles' actions "nuances of defiance, confidence, and victory."[11] Peter and the rest continue nonetheless to teach and preach Jesus Christ every day in the temple and throughout Jerusalem, just as they began to do at the end of Acts 2 after Peter's message on Pentecost.

Implications for Service

1. *Spiritual perception is the result of fellowship with God.*
   Peter exercised a miraculous gift of spiritual perception when he detected the hypocrisy of Ananias and Sapphira. Even apart from miraculous gifts, a great deal of spiritual discernment is possible for the Christian. It is the result of fellowship with God and is a mark of a growing experience with Him. "And this I pray," Paul told the Philippians, "that your love may abound yet more and more in knowledge and in all judgment; that ye may approve things that are excellent; that ye may be sincere and without offence till the day of Christ" (Phil. 1:9-10). Paul prayed that the believers would grow in their ability to discern things that differ. Mature Christians, by regularly using their ability to discern, grow even better at discerning good and evil, as the Hebrew Christians were encouraged to do (Heb. 5:14). Such discernment saves a Christian from error and enables him to "try the spirits" (I John 4:1-2; 2:20).

---

[11]*EBC* vol. 9, p. 325.

2. *God demands holiness in His church.* God is holy and
therefore His people must also be holy. Peter repeats this
demand in his first epistle. "But as he which hath called
you is holy, so be ye holy in all manner of conversation;
because it is written, Be ye holy; for I am holy" (I Pet.
1:15-16). A church can be ruined in spirit or unity by the
sinful conduct of one or two individuals. As was the case
with Achan when he caused the camp of Israel to fail in
combat because of his hidden sin, blessing can be withheld
from all because of the sin of one. God's prescription is to
"purge out therefore the old leaven, that ye may be a new
lump, as ye are unleavened. For even Christ our passover is
sacrificed for us" (I Cor. 5:7). "Follow peace with all men,
and holiness, without which no man shall see the Lord"
(Heb. 12:14).

3. *Spiritual power is a great blessing.* After the hypocrisy was
purged from the assembly, power came upon the church
once again. The power of Satan gave way to the power of
the Holy Spirit. "The spirit of life triumphed over avarice,
the spirit of truth over hypocrisy, the spirit of holiness over
sin, and the Church went forward blessed and made a
blessing."[12] The record in Acts 5 shows many miracles by
the apostles (v. 12), testimony by the people (v. 13), great
additions to the church (v. 14), the remarkable healing influence of Peter (v. 15), and blessing spreading to the entire
region (v. 16). "Thus did God overrule sin to His own
glory."[13]

4. *Christians must learn to work with the Holy Spirit.* "We are
witnesses of these things that have happened," said the
apostles, "and so is the Holy Spirit." This is exactly what
the Lord had promised would be their experience. When
the Holy Spirit was come, He would bear witness of Christ
and they too would bear witness of Him because they had
been with Him from the beginning. We have the Lord's
own promise that we may count on the corroborating affir-
mations of the Spirit of Truth. It is the "Spirit and the
Bride" that say, "Come." The church empowered by the

---

[12]W. H. Griffith Thomas, *The Apostle Peter* (1956), p. 96.
[13]Thomas, p. 95.

Holy Spirit bids the unconverted world to come to Christ. This great discovery made by Peter that day is of immense importance to us all. When we are appalled by the resistance of the human heart to the gospel of the grace of God, we must remind ourselves that ours is a partnership with the God of heaven, the Holy Spirit.

> The child's finger may be able only to strike one note after another with one finger on the piano keys, but who will break his heart over such a trifle, when a master of music sits beside her accompanying each of her notes with magnificent thrilling chords, and is able to turn over her mistakes into profounder harmonics?[14]

We must never allow the thought that we are workers together with the Holy Spirit to fade from our minds as we witness for Christ. We will also want to be certain that we speak only those truths that the Holy Spirit has already given in His Word and that He will bless with His divine stamp of approval.

---

[14]Meyer, pp. 148-49.

BEYOND JERUSALEM

Peter passed throughout all quarters (Acts 9:32).

Proclaim to ev'ry people, tongue and nation
That God in whom they live and move is love:
Tell how He stooped to save His lost creation,
And died on earth that man might live above.

—*Mary A. Thomson*

Setting: Samaria, Lydda, and Joppa, between A.D. 33 and 40
Scripture: Acts 8:1-25; 9:32-43

Peter and his friends continue to teach and preach Jesus Christ in the temple, undeterred by the threats of the high priest and the council—their opposition, for the moment, muted, but not extinguished. After returning from the council, Peter is occupied with an internal problem of the infant church. With the increase in adherents to the gospel come further demands for help from the common fund, especially for those with no means of support. Though a larger portion of the believers are lifelong Jews of Palestine,[1] a second group composed of Greek-speaking Jews of the Diaspora, who have settled in Jerusalem,[2] are also converts to Christ. Each group of believers, because of their differing backgrounds, may have tended to harbor prejudices formed before conversion. Such attitudes are, sadly enough, often carried over into the Christian experience, and thus the "Grecians" find themselves at odds with the "Hebrews" because their widows are thought to be unfairly treated in the daily provisions dealt out within the Christian community. With the company so large, the apostles find it impossible to tend to the material needs of the flock as well as fulfill their spiritual responsibilities.

Faced with a situation demanding utmost care and Christian tact, the apostles, no doubt with Peter as a prominent force, though Luke does not mention it, call on the believers in general to nominate seven "deacons,"[3] or servants, whom the apostles will ordain to assist at the

---

[1] "Hebrews" (Acts 6:1) who spoke Aramaic.

[2] "Grecians," v. 1, or Hellenists. Hellenistic Jews who did not respond to the Christian message were very hostile to Paul after his conversion (Acts 9:29-30). Those who did respond made good material for missionaries, especially to the Gentiles (Acts 11:20). *WDT*, p. 268.

[3] Gk., *diakonos*, Phil. 1:1. Though the word "deacon" is not found in this passage in Acts 6, it is generally understood that this action by the apostles comprises the institution of the office of deacon in the church. Though created to relieve a temporary

relief tables, thus freeing the apostles for the essential work of praying and preaching the Word of God. The selection of seven believers who are also Greek-speaking Jews shows the wisdom of all concerned in handling a potentially explosive matter—all the deacons being chosen from among those who bring the complaint! The action brings harmony and increased power to the early church so that "the word of God increased; and the number of the disciples multiplied in Jerusalem greatly; and a great company of the priests were obedient to the faith" (Acts 6:7).

Scattered abroad

No sooner do the deacons—men "of honest report, full of the Holy Ghost and wisdom"—begin their service ministry than one of them attains particular notice. Stephen, "full of faith and power," is used of God to perform great wonders and miracles among the people. This brings renewed persecution from the council, to the end that Stephen, whose name means "crown,"[4] wins the first martyr's crown. Incensed at the powerful deacon's sermon denouncing their sin, the unsaved Jews stone Stephen to death. The Christlike manner of Stephen's death produces a profound and lasting effect on at least one disciple of Gamaliel, for "you can hear the echo of Stephen's voice in almost every one of the speeches of Paul of Tarsus."[5] Still a young man, Saul assents to the stoning by guarding the robes of the outraged Jews hurling the deadly rocks. There follows a great general persecution against the saints,[6] but with results far different from what the persecutors intend. Multitudes of Christians flee Jerusalem to avoid the persecution, but as they depart, they take with them the gospel message. Wherever they go, they preach Christ. The infant church is outgrowing its Hebrew swaddling clothes[7] as it scatters beyond

---

need, "the officers proved of value, and in due course settled into an established order," *WDT*, p. 156.

[4]Gk., *stephanos*.

[5]Quintin Hogg, *The Story of Peter* (1900), p. 334.

[6]Acts 8:1-4.

[7]F. B. Meyer sees in Acts 6-10 five stages of progress in extending the gospel to the Gentiles. To overcome Jewish prejudice toward the heathen, God moved in several steps to bring Peter and the other Jewish believers to the point of accepting Gentiles into the family of God. (1) The resolution of the dispute between the Hellenist Jews and the Hebrews; (2) the martyrdom of the young Hellenist Stephen; (3) Philip's mission to Samaria; (4) the conversion of Saul of Tarsus and his call to preach to the Gentiles; (5) Peter's vision from heaven at Joppa when God told him not to call unclean what He had cleansed. Anticipating the final phase of this progression—the appearance of the messengers from Cornelius to Peter—Meyer asks, "Was some new development of the Divine pattern at hand which [Peter] must realize for himself and

Jerusalem to Judea and Samaria. It is as though a large fire has broken out, and its sparks are soon to set the entire forest into a roaring blaze.

We follow "one of the embers"[8] of that fire, a man named Philip, not the apostle but a second deacon ordained by the apostles to look after the poor within the church.[9] While the apostles remain in Jerusalem to attend to the affairs of the "mother" church, Philip takes the message of Christ north into Samaria. Had not the Lord commanded them to witness for Him, not only in Jerusalem but also in Judea and Samaria, and even to the ends of the world? Indeed He had, and how perfect are His ways in carrying out this plan. Knowing how some of His people would react to severe persecution, God ordains that as the opposition increases, some will flee Jerusalem and take with them the Christian message.

That is how we find Philip preaching Christ in Samaria "and the people with one accord gave heed unto those things which Philip spake, hearing and seeing the miracles which he did. For unclean spirits, crying with loud voice, came out of many that were possessed with them: and many taken with palsies, and that were lame, were healed. And there was great joy in that city" (8:6-8). Through the power of Christ, Philip provides physical healing as did the martyr Stephen. More importantly, he brings to the people the good news, spiritual healing for their souls. And with the gospel comes great joy in the city. True joy always accompanies the reception of the gospel, when sinners convert to Christ. Yes, when a sinner comes to God in repentance and faith, he is overwhelmed with his sense of sin and judgment on his soul. Sorrow, contrition, regret, confession—all these come into play as the sinner forsakes his old life and clings to Christ for eternal life. The gospel, when it is received, removes all sorrow, regret, and shame and replaces these with His joy in our hearts. Though we have greatly sinned, we have been even more greatly forgiven. When that revelation comes to the believer's soul, there must needs be "great joy" in the life. But when God's people allow the world to seep into their experience, they find their joy replaced with callousness. They possess enough of Christ so that they do not now enjoy the world, but, unfortunately, they also possess too much of the world to enjoy Christ.

others?" The question is answered with Peter's call to preach to Cornelius. *Peter* (1950), pp. 153-58.

[8]Hogg, p. 335.

[9]Acts 6:5.

Simon Magus and Simon Peter

Among Philip's converts in Samaria is one called Simon, a magician of sorts who bewitched or amazed people with his powers, so much so that he earned the name "great one" (v. 9), hence the more familiar name "Simon Magus."[10] Simon Magus is more than a mere trickster, for use of satanic powers seems to be the only way to account for his success at his magical arts. His great power is met by an even greater power—the dynamite of the gospel of Jesus Christ. Simon Magus "himself believed also: and when he was baptized, he continued with Philip, and wondered, beholding the miracles and signs which were done" (v. 13). And herein lies our troubles with properly assessing Simon Magus. Was he a true believer? When Luke writes that he "believed," should we take this in the same manner in which he writes in the previous verse that the other Samaritans also "believed"? Or is his a supreme case of profession of belief without true possession of eternal life? The Scripture tells us that this practicer of satanic arts believed, was baptized, and continued with Philip. The gospel is not fettered. All who call on the name of the Lord are saved. Did Simon Magus truly call on the Lord? Do his subsequent actions show a converted soul given over to the strong inclinations from his former life? Or does the record show through his actions that Simon never truly converted to Christ? A hint of Simon's problem comes with Luke's caution about him, that as he continued with Philip, Simon Magus "wondered, beholding the miracles and signs which were done." If indeed Simon Magus is now a believer, he nevertheless presents a serious problem to the assembly in Samaria, enamored as he is with the spectacular. If he is not a true disciple, he must be exposed as a fraud. It will be up to Simon Peter to deal with the matter with apostolic authority.

The tidings of blessing in Samaria reach Jerusalem that "Samaria had received the word of God" (v. 14). What the Lord Jesus promised in Acts 1:8 is coming to pass. The gospel is now penetrating the prejudices and deep animosities latent within the Samaritans, a significant extension of Christianity beyond Jerusalem. To show the importance of this event, the apostles in Jerusalem send[11] Peter and John to Samaria

---

[10]Justin Martyr says that Simon Magus was born at Gitton, a village in Samaria. The many subsequent fantastic stories concerning Simon Magus, however, are without merit. *UBD*, p. 1027.

[11]Note, "they sent" (v. 14) Peter and John. There is no supremacy of Peter here. The action of the apostles in Jerusalem "sheds a clear light on (Peter's) relation to other apostles. They acted together as a body." W. H. Griffith Thomas, *The Apostle Peter* (1956), p. 103.

to investigate and authenticate this good news. When the two apostles arrive there, they immediately pray for the believers that they also might receive the Holy Spirit for, Luke explains, "as yet he was fallen upon none of them: only they were baptized in the name of the Lord Jesus" (v. 16). Then as Peter and John lay their hands on the believers, they receive the gift of the Holy Spirit.

Clearly these Samaritan believers received the Holy Spirit separate from their conversion, unlike the experience of those who believed Peter's preaching at Pentecost, when he urged the people to repent, be baptized, and receive the gift of the Holy Spirit.[12] But with the Samaritans, it takes the intermediate agency of Peter and John to bestow the Holy Spirit, a unique gift operating through them and the other apostles that even Philip is not able to bestow. When we recall that the Jerusalem Jews regarded the Samaritans as second-class residents of Palestine, an attitude that the Samaritans returned toward the Jews, we begin to understand the marvelous workings of God in the spread of the gospel during these early days of the church. In His wisdom, God chose to use Philip, a Hellenist, to evangelize the Samaritans, for Philip shared some of the same attitudes of rejection at Jerusalem as did the Samaritans. It is not too difficult to imagine a scenario in which, if the apostles sought to evangelize Samaria, they would face the same hostilities the disciples faced when they proceeded through their land with the Lord Jesus on the way to the cross. So God uses Philip to preach the gospel in Samaria with attendant great success.

It is also not difficult to imagine that if the Samaritan believers had received the Holy Spirit at Philip's preaching, there could have arisen a rift between the two camps of Christianity. So God withholds the Holy Spirit, the apostles send Peter and John to authenticate Philip's ministry, and the unity of the church is maintained and indeed strengthened. In His wisdom and grace, God attests to the genuineness of the work in Samaria, showing the Samaritan believers to be part of the Christian church, through this miraculous bestowal of the Holy Spirit on them.[13] God worked in such a way that the gospel is received by the Samaritans and they are welcomed by the church at Jerusalem. Oh, the ways of God are past finding out!

Simon Magus's response to this bestowal of the Holy Spirit is one of those tragic stories that accompany the preaching of the gospel

---

[12] Acts 2:38.

[13] This limitation of unique power to the apostles shows the impossibility of any apostolic succession. Such claims could only be proved today by similar "apostolic success." Thomas, p. 104.

throughout the world. Whenever God is at work, Satan is present to duplicate the blessing. "And when Simon saw that through laying on of the apostles' hands the Holy Ghost was given, he offered them money, saying, Give me also this power, that on whomsoever I lay hands, he may receive the Holy Ghost" (vv. 18-19). Simon's offer to pay for the ability to confer the Holy Spirit through the laying on of hands[14] is immediately condemned by Peter, consigning Simon Magus and his money to hell. "But Peter said unto him, Thy money perish with thee, because thou hast thought that the gift of God may be purchased with money" (v. 20). With spiritual insight, Peter tells Simon that his heart is not right with God, is full of bitterness, and is captive to sin. New converts often bring into the Christian experience debilitating habits and attitudes that must be rejected and replaced with devotion to the truth. Simon appears not to desire any change of lifestyle after his supposed conversion. Peter counsels him to repent of his wickedness and to pray to the Lord. Perhaps God will forgive him for having such a thought in his heart. But Simon asks lamely, "Peter, you pray to the Lord for me that nothing of what you have said will happen to me." Did Simon Magus ever repent and genuinely respond to God, thereby becoming a new creature in Christ? We do not know. He is "like a buoy, affixed to a sunken rock by the hand of God, to keep passing ships off it."[15] He is a solemn warning to all false professions. Indeed he was baptized, professed to follow Christ, and sought entrance into God's assembly in Samaria; but he remained in the gall of bitterness, not the joy of the Lord. The soul of the true child of God rejoices in Christ, our object, our guardian, our coming Lord.

Fifteen days with Paul

After the solemn encounter with Simon Magus, Peter and John, while returning to Jerusalem, preach in many villages of the Samaritans, cheering the people on the way. "And they, when they had testified and preached the word of the Lord, returned to Jerusalem, and preached the gospel in many villages of the Samaritans" (v. 25). But before we hear more of Peter's ministry, we learn of the conversion of Saul of Tarsus, afterwards called Paul, an event that probably took place soon after Peter's return to Jerusalem. The story of Paul's conversion is well known—how he sought to persecute Christians, securing authorization to travel to Damascus to capture them and

---

[14]Simon's effort to obtain sacred, or spiritual, functions by a bribe has come down to us as our word "simony," the buying or selling of sacred or spiritual things, such as sacraments.

[15]W. T. P. Wolston, *Simon Peter* (1926), p. 192.

bring them back to Jerusalem. On the way, however, he meets the risen Christ and is gloriously converted, Ananias of Damascus being instrumental in bestowing on Paul the Holy Spirit. Paul immediately begins to testify of Christ and before long furious Jews drive him out of Damascus. He escapes over a city wall in a basket. By his own reckoning, after three years, Paul journeys to Jerusalem.

> But when it pleased God, who separated me from my mother's womb, and called me by his grace, to reveal his Son in me, that I might preach him among the heathen; immediately I conferred not with flesh and blood: neither went I up to Jerusalem to them which were apostles before me; but I went into Arabia, and returned again unto Damascus. Then after three years I went up to Jerusalem to see Peter, and abode with him fifteen days. But other of the apostles saw I none, save James the Lord's brother (Gal. 1:15-19).

What took place in these fifteen days is not recorded for us in God's Word. But what could have transpired during that fortnight between two Christian brothers? Two weeks is certainly long enough for Paul and Peter to get to know one another and to develop a loving, Christian friendship, though the believers at Jerusalem were not eager to commit themselves to this former persecutor. "And when Saul was come to Jerusalem, he assayed to join himself to the disciples: but they were all afraid of him, and believed not that he was a disciple.[16] But Barnabas took him, and brought him to the apostles, and declared unto them how he had seen the Lord in the way, and that he had spoken to him, and how he had preached boldly at Damascus in the name of Jesus" (Acts 9:26-27). Barnabas comes to Paul's rescue and when confidence is gained, communion is assured. Peter is not one to harbor suspicions and he takes Paul to his heart as "our beloved brother Paul" (II Pet. 3:15). How much of the Lord's life does Paul hear from Peter? And how Paul must have thrilled Peter with his own testimony of how he met the risen Christ on the road to Damascus. Here they are—Peter and Paul—two saints of God who fill memorable pages of God's Word and who now together enjoy fellowship with one another because of their Lord.

The fifteen days Paul spends with Peter are not idle days. "And [Paul] was with them coming in and going out at Jerusalem. And he

---

[16]This is another instance, found throughout Acts and the Epistles, in which the believers are identified as "disciples." Saul is now a follower of Christ—a believer, a Christian, a disciple.

spake boldly in the name of the Lord Jesus, and disputed against the Grecians: but they went about to slay him" (vv. 28-29). With a ready audience, Paul witnesses boldly, especially to the Hellenistic Jews, or Grecians, residing now in Jerusalem. Once again Paul is persecuted for his testimony, as in Damascus, and so to save his life, the brethren send him away to Tarsus, his hometown. "Then had the churches rest throughout all Judaea and Galilee and Samaria, and were edified; and walking in the fear of the Lord, and in the comfort of the Holy Ghost, were multiplied" (v. 31). The churches have rest because their chief persecutor is now a Christian.[17] Through the witness of many believers—including Stephen and Philip and now Paul—the church grows and is edified. Believers multiply in Galilee in addition to Judea and Samaria. Through the Spirit of God, His people are responding in a magnificent work of spreading the Christian message beyond Jerusalem to all regions of Palestine.

Simon Peter and Simon the tanner

Peter too travels throughout various regions beyond Jerusalem, eventually ministering to the "saints"[18] at Lydda[19] in the plain of Sharon on the Mediterranean coast of Palestine. At Lydda Peter meets Aeneas, a paralytic who has been bedridden for eight years, whom Peter heals with a word. "Aeneas, Jesus Christ maketh thee whole: arise, and make thy bed" (v. 34). The instantaneous healing of the man brings further interest in the preaching of the gospel so that "all that dwelt at Lydda and Saron saw him, and turned to the Lord" (v. 35). The gospel continues to spread beyond Jerusalem, extending now the length of the maritime plain from Joppa to Mount Carmel, with Caesarea on the coast as its geographic center.

Now there was at Joppa a certain disciple named Tabitha, which by interpretation is called Dorcas: this woman was full

---

[17]Robertson says that this peace in Palestine also came about as a result of the order from Caligula in A.D. 39 for his statue to be set up for worship in the temple in Jerusalem, an action that diverted the anger of the Jews away from the Christians. A. T. Robertson, *Epochs in the Life of Simon Peter* (1939), p. 221.

[18]The first mention of believers as "saints" in the NT. "Saints" are not those canonized by the Roman Catholic Church. All who are born of the Spirit and washed in the Savior's blood are saints. They are set apart to God as belonging to Him by redemption.

[19]Lydda (modern Lod), twenty-five miles northwest of Jerusalem, appears only here in Scripture. St. George, patron saint of England and hero of the legendary slaying of the dragon, was martyred at Lydda in A.D. 303. There is a Greek Orthodox Church of St. George located in Lod. In A.D. 415 the council that tried Pelagius for heresy met in Lydda.

of good works and almsdeeds which she did. And it came to pass in those days, that she was sick, and died: whom when they had washed, they laid her in an upper chamber. And forasmuch as Lydda was nigh to Joppa, and the disciples had heard that Peter was there, they sent unto him two men, desiring him that he would not delay to come to them (vv. 36-38).

At Joppa,[20] ten miles from Lydda and thirty-five miles northwest of Jerusalem, lived a disciple[21] named Dorcas,[22] known for doing good and helping the poor, especially destitute widows. When she dies, the believers at Joppa send to Lydda with a message for Peter: "Come at once," with no explanation given as to their expectations involving the apostle and their beloved sister, though God certainly is at work in moving Peter from Lydda to Joppa. Peter has been instrumental in several healings, as we have already seen, and he even pronounced the death sentence on Ananias and Sapphira. But raising people from the dead has not been a part of his ministry, though he was present as one of the inner circle when Jesus raised Jairus's daughter from the dead. Now as Christ's apostle and empowered by the Holy Spirit, Peter responds to the urgent call and, in conduct reminiscent of the Lord raising the little girl, Peter speaks these words: "Tabitha, arise." When Dorcas opens her eyes, Peter takes her by the hand, helps her to her feet, and presents her alive to the believers standing nearby. As a result of this exceptional exhibit of God's mercy and the Holy Spirit's power, now outside of and beyond Jerusalem, "many believed in the Lord" (v. 42).

The stage is set for Peter to open the door to the Gentiles. He has ministered in a broad swath beyond Jerusalem, observing firsthand the Samaritans' reception of the gospel, as well as the gospel taking root up and down the coast of Palestine. "And it came to pass, that he tarried many days in Joppa with one Simon a tanner" (v. 43). As the work of God continues to grow in Joppa, Peter resides with a man called Simon, who no doubt worked at his trade in his home, where Peter is staying. The rabbis considered tanning an unclean trade and

---

[20]Modern Jaffa, a suburb of Tel Aviv ("Japho" in Josh. 19:46). Joppa was the ancient seaport of Jerusalem, possessing the only natural harbor on the Mediterranean from Egypt to Ptolemais (Acts 21:7; OT Accho, Judg. 1:31), eight miles north of Mount Carmel. Through Joppa, Solomon brought cedar beams from Lebanon to build the temple (II Chron. 2:16). Jonah sailed to Tarshish from Joppa (Jon. 1:3).

[21]Gk., *mathetria*, the only feminine form of the word "disciple" in the NT.

[22]Gk.; Heb. Tabitha. Both names mean "gazelle." Near the Russian monastery in Tel Aviv is a tomb said to be that of Tabitha. V. Gilbert Beers, *The Victor Handbook of Bible Knowledge* (1981), p. 559.

Peter's lodging with such a man, presumably now a believer also, shows that Peter is not overly scrupulous in observing Jewish ceremonial traditions. God continues to break down Peter's prejudices so that when the messengers come from Cornelius, Peter is ready to enter at once to the obviously open door to the Gentiles.

Implications for Service

1. *Be prepared to deal with backsliding.* If Simon Magus was never truly converted to Christ, we would have good reason to understand how he could revert to his old ways. If he was born again, he furnishes a vivid warning of the danger a Christian faces when he fails to gain victory over besetting sins. In some ways, it is more difficult to deal with a backslidden Christian than it is to deal with a person who is not yet converted. Recovery from backsliding requires a long and consistent hunger and thirst for righteousness, a process in which old habits and lifestyles are put off and new habits and attitudes are consistently followed. The backsliding believer has this promise from the Word of God: "There hath no temptation taken you but such as is common to man: but God is faithful, who will not suffer you to be tempted above that ye are able; but will with the temptation also make a way to escape, that ye may be able to bear it" (I Cor. 10:13).

2. *The church of Jesus Christ is as broad as the world.* Peter has learned some valuable lessons—that the gospel is for everyone, no matter their background or standing. This lesson is about to be put to the ultimate test in the request from Cornelius for Peter to come to his house to speak to him. But as he has gone beyond Jerusalem to Judea, Samaria, the plain of Sharon, and surrounding countryside, he has found God at work in the hearts of people. God has His "saints" in all places, and those of us who have been fortunate to travel a bit to other parts of the globe and to fellowship with believers from all ethnic backgrounds thrill at how God is able to bring us all together into His one body. What must heaven be like!

3. *There is a prepared place for a prepared Christian.* In some ways, Peter is unaware of the preparation he is experiencing. He is busy about the Father's business, but in it all God is

preparing His apostle for a most important task—opening the door of the gospel to the Gentile world. Peter will take the keys and walk through that door because he has been faithful in the small tasks God has already given him.

SURPRISING LESSONS

God hath shewed me (Acts 10:28).

Heir of heaven Thou has made me,
Bought me with Thy precious blood;
Took the form of man upon Thee
That I might be child of God.

So, my song must swell the chorus
While the angels' praises ring;
I, poor sinner, saved and pardoned,
Have more cause than they to sing.

—Bob Jones

Setting: Caesarea and Jerusalem, A.D. 40
Scripture: Acts 10:1–11:18

Believers today have a special interest in this portion of the Book of Acts, for it shows the manner in which God opened the door of salvation to all—Gentiles as well as Jews. We cannot say with certainty that no Gentile found his way to Christ during the seven or eight years following Pentecost. It is highly probable that others had been brought to Christ. This particular case involving Cornelius, however, "arrested attention, provoked controversy, and finally brought the apostles and the Church to a recognition of the larger meaning of the work of Christ."[1] That God saw fit to use Simon Peter as the central figure in this historic event only magnifies the sovereign grace of the Lord Jesus, who called him to be His disciple. The disciple in the making is now the apostle serving. The same apostle whom God used to preach the first great gospel sermon to his countrymen at Pentecost is now selected to do a similar service for God to the Gentile world. Surely here we get the simplest possible explanation of the "keys" that the Lord Jesus said Peter would hold. It certainly was given to him, in a most obvious way, to open the kingdom of heaven to Jew and Gentile alike, certainly what the Lord meant when He spoke of Peter as the key bearer of the church.[2] God's hand, directing and sustaining, can be seen on all the participants in the scene about to unfold before us—on the eager military captain who senses his personal need for more spiritual light and on the servant of God who brings that light to him.

---

[1]G. Campbell Morgan, *The Acts of the Apostles* (1924), p. 263.
[2]Quintin Hogg, *The Story of Peter* (1900), p. 371.

Since the inception of the church at Pentecost, God has moved unalterably forward to this moment—imperceptibly at times, but always toward the ultimate purpose of opening the door of faith to the Gentiles. God is going to use Peter[3] to bring about this mission, but He does not lead him to a great change in his thinking about the Gentiles all at once, though as a Christian "his inherited prejudices were gradually wearing thin."[4] Peter must have had some sense that the Gentiles would be eligible for the kingdom of God, but it may never have occurred to him that they would come in some other way than by becoming Jews first and then Christians. Step by step God leads Peter to widen his views of the Christian faith. We noted the beginnings of this openness to the Gentiles when Hellenist Jews, with Peter's direction and approval we may be certain, were appointed as the first deacons of the church at Jerusalem. Then came the great apology of one of the Hellenists, the young deacon Stephen, and his subsequent martyrdom. Those who listened to his burning words could not escape the argument that throughout their history, the chosen people had resisted God's Holy Spirit. Peter must have sensed the "breath of a new age"[5] as it fanned the cheeks of those who heard Stephen, and the door opened a little wider for admission of the Gentile world to the church of Jesus Christ. Then with astounding success came the preaching of the gospel in Samaria and the approval of the mission there by Peter and John, who were sent from Jerusalem to examine the spread of the gospel. Peter witnessed for himself the unfolding of the purpose of God in that region and, seeing no need for further oversight, returned to Jerusalem, but on the way also preaching in the villages of the Samaritans—again a further unfolding of God's plan. God's purpose for the Gentiles accelerated still further at the conversion of Saul of Tarsus, whom God commissioned to go directly to the Gentiles. Subsequently, Paul meets up with Peter in Jerusalem, and for two weeks these two pillars of the early Christian church recount the Lord's dealings with them—Paul, called to be an apostle to the Gentiles; Peter, to the Jews. Finally, Peter now resides at Joppa with a tanner, one whose trade was despised by the Jews, since the handling of the skins of dead and unclean animals was to a scrupulous Jew hopelessly unclean.[6] Recent events at Lydda and Joppa provide Peter

---

[3]Robertson calls Peter "the liberator of the Gentiles." A. T. Robertson, *Epochs in the Life of Simon Peter* (1939), p. 220.

[4]*EBC* vol. 9, p. 387.

[5]F. B. Meyer, *Peter* (1950), p. 155.

[6]Robertson, p. 224.

with still further proof that God is determined to expand His church, now to all the regions of Palestine: Jerusalem . . . Judea . . . Samaria. Could the reach of the gospel to the world and the Gentiles be far off?

In this "Pentecost of the Gentiles,"[7] the middle wall of partition separating Jews from Gentiles will come down. The God-given levitical laws, with their dietary regulations, guaranteed Israel's separateness from all the other nations, for they were to be His peculiar treasure, His kingdom of priests, His holy nation. The Jews viewed Gentiles as strangers and foreigners, aliens from the commonwealth of Israel and to the covenants of promise. Gentiles were without God and without hope. If they ever desired entrance to God, they would have to "travel round by the tents of Abraham and the wilderness of Sinai."[8] With their heritage of centuries of obedience to the laws of Moses, Peter and the other converted Jews will learn that Gentiles can be saved and become members of the church without observing certain ordinances of the law. For all Gentiles this is about to change, and radically so. No longer will it be thought that "except ye be circumcised after the manner of Moses, ye cannot be saved" (Acts 15:1). Peter and Cornelius will be brought together by a sovereign God, and from their encounter a clear path to the new and living way will open to the Gentiles. Peter will learn that "the uncircumcised body was nothing; that the prepared heart was everything."[9] The message will be for all—Jew and Gentile alike—that sinners are made nigh by the blood of Christ. Christ has reconciled all to God. All are one body in Christ.[10]

Cornelius in Caesarea

There was a certain man in Caesarea[11] called Cornelius, a centurion[12] of the band called the Italian band, a devout man, and one that feared God with all his house, which gave much

---

[7]Hogg, p. 371.

[8]Meyer, p. 160.

[9]Hogg, p. 381.

[10]This is the "mystery" God revealed to Paul as expounded in Eph. 3:1-12. This NT mystery is not something odd or spooky, but God's secret until He revealed it. In this case it is the secret, or mystery, that Gentiles would be in the same body as Jews. God had promised that Gentiles would be blessed (Gen. 12:3), but no one knew how that would take place. God revealed to Paul that the Gentiles should be fellow heirs and of the same body as believing Jews.

[11]Built by Herod the Great and named for Augustus Caesar, Caesarea Palaestinae (to distinguish it from Caesarea Philippi) was as Gentile as Joppa was Jewish. "When Herod built, you had no need to fear too much shoddy [work]." Hogg, p. 373.

[12]A centurion was a noncommissioned officer, roughly equivalent to a captain today, in command of a group of soldiers within a Roman legion. Cornelius

alms to the people, and prayed to God alway. He saw in a vision evidently about the ninth hour of the day an angel of God coming in to him, and saying unto him, Cornelius. And when he looked on him, he was afraid, and said, What is it, Lord? And he said unto him, Thy prayers and thine alms are come up for a memorial before God. And now send men to Joppa, and call for one Simon, whose surname is Peter: he lodgeth with one Simon a tanner, whose house is by the sea side: he shall tell thee what thou oughtest to do (Acts 10:1-6).

Cornelius, the Gentile centurion, enters the scene to complete the picture of God's purpose. The Scriptures call him "a devout man," one who "feared God with all his house," who "gave much alms," and who "prayed to God alway." Here is a benevolent man, very interested in others as well as his own spiritual needs. His domestic help regard him as a "just man," one who "feareth God" and "of good report among all the nation of the Jews." He is an awakened man—pious, prayerful, God fearing, but still anxious for his soul. If someone had asked him at his home in Caesarea, "Are your sins forgiven?" he would have had to say, "No," because the testimony of the gospel and the preaching of forgiveness to the Gentiles had not yet gone forth.[13] Cornelius, strongly religious, but still unconverted, is nevertheless assured by the angel who interrupted his praying that God is listening to his prayers, observing his generous giving, and leading him along to Himself. "God does not despise the untutored seeking of a needy soul."[14] God has read his heart and acknowledges what Cornelius desires—light.[15]

---

commanded a cohort of Italians separate from the legionary soldiers. Many Bible scholars have noted that all four centurions who are mentioned in the NT are spoken of favorably. It is said of the centurion who lived at Capernaum that he loved the Jewish nation and built them a synagogue. The centurion at the Lord's crucifixion proclaimed, "Surely this was the Son of God." Of the centurion who accompanied Paul to Rome, Luke speaks only of courteous conduct toward Paul. And here at Caesarea, we meet this centurion who is God fearing and searching for truth.

[13]W. T. P. Wolston, *Simon Peter* (1926), p. 204.

[14]Stewart Custer, *Witness to Christ* (2000), p. 139.

[15]Morgan cites Cornelius as an example of the truth to which John draws attention in the first chapter of his Gospel, that there is a "light, which lighteth every man" (John 1:9). Cornelius stands in contrast to the Gentiles described by Paul (Rom. 1:18-19), who had not obeyed the light they possessed. Cornelius had been true to the light that was within him. He had followed it and had become a worshipper of the one true living God. But he had not passed into the fulness of that light. He needed spiritual enduement; he needed Christ. Morgan, p. 266.

The angel informs Cornelius that he is to send a message to Simon Peter, who resides with Simon the tanner at Joppa. Angels are not strangers to our house and address. They know exactly where to find Peter. "He shall speak to you," the angel says, and we should note that it is God's purpose to use another believer, a Christian, to spread the message of the good news, for angels have never known the joy of salvation that believers possess. What God asks Cornelius to do is to listen to words, not do good works. Words of the gospel, not good works of the flesh. Many people think that if they are to be saved, it will be through their good works. God's salvation is in the message of the cross; it is words, not works. "No man was ever yet saved by his own *works*: and no man was ever saved without believing *words*—the words of God."[16]

No sooner does Cornelius hear the message from the angel than he does as he is bidden, having learned the value of promptness in military matters and now applying this same to his earnest desire for spiritual help. "Immediately I sent for you," he tells Peter later. He does not wait even one day. The angelic visit comes at the ninth hour, or 3:00 in the afternoon. By noon the next day the three messengers are at Simon the tanner's house in Joppa, some thirty miles down the seacoast of the Mediterranean.

Peter in Joppa

Peter had come to Joppa because of Dorcas and the other disciples there. Since there were already "disciples" at Joppa who asked for Peter's help regarding Dorcas, how did they come to be there? We learn of a possibility from Philip's ministry after Peter and John left him in Samaria. The Holy Spirit came to Philip and instructed him to leave the successful ministry of the gospel there and meet a man in the desert wilderness near Gaza. Philip obeys the Spirit and meets the Ethiopian treasurer, who converts to Christ and is immediately baptized by Philip. The Ethiopian continues on his way home, while the Holy Spirit whisks Philip away and he is then "found at Azotus: and passing through he preached in all the cities, till he came to Caesarea" (Acts 8:40). Since Joppa is located in that maritime plain leading up to Caesarea on the coast, it is entirely possible that Philip evangelized the people of Joppa, making it possible for an enclave of disciples or believers to be present and functioning, among whom would have been Dorcas and her friends.

---

[16]Wolston, p. 206.

And when the angel which spake unto Cornelius was departed, he called two of his household servants, and a devout soldier of them that waited on him continually; and when he had declared all these things unto them, he sent them to Joppa. On the morrow, as they went on their journey, and drew nigh unto the city, Peter went up upon the housetop to pray about the sixth hour: and he became very hungry, and would have eaten: but while they made ready, he fell into a trance, and saw heaven opened, and a certain vessel descending unto him, as it had been a great sheet knit at the four corners, and let down to the earth: wherein were all manner of fourfooted beasts of the earth, and wild beasts, and creeping things, and fowls of the air. And there came a voice to him, Rise, Peter; kill, and eat. But Peter said, Not so, Lord; for I have never eaten any thing that is common or unclean (10:7-14).

On a previous occasion, Peter had told the Lord Jesus "Not so," that the Lord could not and should not go to His death at Jerusalem. But Jesus had to squelch that voice of Satan seeking to turn Him aside. And even now, Peter retains that hint of rebellion, but it gives way soon enough to God's gentle threefold persuasion.

In Cornelius we have a truly earnest seeker! No sooner does the angelic messenger depart than the centurion summons two household servants and a guard and directs them to leave immediately for Joppa so that they might bring Peter back to him. Following the road south by the seashore, they travel a portion of the thirty-mile distance that evening and, after sleeping at a convenient place, the three men arrive at Joppa the next day. Cornelius will not be kept waiting for long. The wild olive is about to be grafted.

Meanwhile, in Joppa God is preparing His apostle for this encounter with the eager and seeking Cornelius. Peter goes to his housetop to pray at noon, but God interrupts his praying too in the form of a vision of animals assembled on a sheet dropped from heaven. This collection of animals, doubtless those most familiar to Peter—quadrupeds, reptiles, fowls tame and wild—were mingled indiscriminately, both "clean and unclean." Peter hears the command. "Rise, Peter, kill and eat." True to his heritage, Peter replies, "I have never eaten anything that is unclean," with the clear intention that he would never do so either.[17] But the message from the sovereign God is strange indeed, an

---

[17]Jewish scruples regarding clean and unclean food were deeply ingrained. The uncanonical historical books tell of the dreadful privations to which the Jews submitted in the time of the Maccabees, accepting slow death rather than violating their law by eating forbidden meats. J. R. MacDuff, *The Footsteps of St. Peter* (1887), pp. 460-61.

"almost inscrutable riddle."[18] "What I have cleansed, do not call common[19] or unclean." Not once, nor twice, but three times this interchange between God and Peter takes place. Then the sheet containing the animals withdraws to heaven and Peter is left pondering the meaning of this "new apostolic manifesto."[20] "Don't call unclean what God has cleansed. . . . What has God cleansed? What should I not call unclean?"

At this moment, Peter hears a call from downstairs that messengers are at the gate asking for him. But God has already prepared His apostle. "While Peter thought on the vision, the Spirit said unto him, Behold, three men seek thee. Arise therefore, and get thee down, and go with them, doubting nothing: for I have sent them" (vv. 19-20). Peter now catches an inkling of what the vision means. The strange vision . . . an immediate request from three messengers . . . an assurance to go with them . . . don't doubt . . . God says He has sent them. What can he do but obey? Under the Jewish law, God had forbidden the Jew to mingle with the Gentile. Now that the Lord has showed Peter that that day has passed—what God has cleansed, he is not to call common or unclean[21]—he hurries down the outside stairway, calls the men inside, and provides lodging for them in the house. As morning ushers in the next day, Peter heads for Caesarea and Cornelius, but not before engaging several Christian brethren to accompany him. They will serve as witnesses to Peter's venture, though Peter himself knows only that the centurion desires to obey the angel's warning bidding him to "hear the words of Peter." Wholehearted and prompt obedience is so characteristic of Peter![22]

Peter and Cornelius in Caesarea

While Peter and his companions journey northward, Cornelius summons his household. Eager that his own family as well as close friends join him to hear what Peter has to say, the centurion assembles them awaiting Peter's arrival. As Peter enters, Cornelius reverences him, but the apostle is quick to reject any such worship, lifting him to his feet and saying, "Stand up; I myself also am a man" (v. 26). How unlike the one who today pretends to the succession of Peter in the

---

[18]*EBC* vol. 9, p. 387.

[19]Gk., *koinos*.

[20]MacDuff, p. 461.

[21]"Later, when Mark writes his Gospel, he will inject a remark (an anacoluthon) that reflected Peter's later insight about the teaching of Jesus concerning inward and outward defilement, 'making all meats clean' (Mark 7:19). But for the moment Peter was hopelessly puzzled." Robertson, p. 225.

[22]W. H. Griffith Thomas, *The Apostle Peter* (1956), p. 112.

church of Rome, who receives and encourages worship from his followers. The house is full of souls whom God is about to bless, "prepared soil for Peter's sowing."[23] Peter explains his presence among these Gentiles: "Ye know how that it is an unlawful thing for a man that is a Jew to keep company, or come unto one of another nation; but God hath showed me that I should not call any man common or unclean" (v. 28). "God has showed me," declares Peter. The one who thrice denied the precious Lord Jesus, who received the threefold question of love from the Master, has learned the thrice-offered message of the breaking down of distinctions. He now knows the key to the difficult vision he pondered on the rooftop in Joppa. When Peter had gone down and obeyed, he began to comprehend quite clearly that God's grace was going to flow to the ends of the earth. Allowing the eager soul to first express its need, Peter probes Cornelius to find out the purpose of his call. Why does Cornelius want him there in his home? Cornelius then tells his story: His praying . . . the angelic visitor . . . the commendation of his attention to spiritual concerns . . . the instruction to send for Peter at Joppa. Now that Peter has arrived, Cornelius explains, they are all present "before God, to hear all things that are commanded thee of God" (v. 33).

What a ready audience for Peter to address! Even before he begins to preach, he knows that there is before him not one scoffer, not one dull or uninterested hearer. Cornelius, obeying God's warning, has gathered for the preacher of the gospel a company of earnest seekers, longing only to know the truth. "We are all present before God to listen to you," reminds Cornelius. "Anxious listeners make earnest preachers; longing hearers make it easy to preach."[24] Peter treats these Romans as he has the Jews—as sinful men, offering them Jesus as their only hope of forgiveness for sin.

Peter begins with his recently acquired stance that God does not show racial preferences and moves directly to presenting the life and ministry of Jesus Christ:

> God is no respecter of persons . . . The one who fears God and
> works righteousness is accepted with Him . . . Peace is by
> Jesus Christ, whom God anointed with the Holy Spirit and
> power . . . He did good because God was with Him . . . We wit-
> nessed what He did . . . But the Jews killed Him and had Him
> hung on a cross . . . God raised Him up from the dead . . . We

---

[23]Robertson, p. 226.
[24]Wolston, p. 211.

have seen Him with our own eyes . . . We ate and drank with Him . . . He has commanded us to preach to the people . . . He told us to testify that He will judge the living and the dead . . . If you believe on Him you will receive remission of sins.

His theme is evident: God with us, God for us, and God in us. God was with us in the life of Jesus of Nazareth, who went about doing good. God is for us because the one whom man refused God raised from the dead. And God is in the one who believes in Christ, for He sends the Holy Spirit to indwell the believing and repentant sinner. Christ is risen, preaches Peter: Men killed Him, God raised Him, we have seen Him. He will judge you; believe and receive remission of your sins. This last call "struck like a thunderbolt into the consciousness of the assembled Gentiles, releasing their pent-up emotions and emboldening them to respond by faith."[25]

"While Peter yet spake these words, the Holy Ghost fell on all them which heard the word. And they of the circumcision which believed were astonished, as many as came with Peter, because that on the Gentiles also was poured out the gift of the Holy Ghost. For they heard them speak with tongues, and magnify God" (vv. 44-46). At that moment, these Gentiles received the seal of God, the Holy Spirit, and God also providentially authenticated the Spirit's coming by the same sign of tongues as at Pentecost.[26] The gift of tongues at Pentecost was no doubt distinguishable languages because they were immediately recognized as dialects then current. But here in Cornelius's house "an outburst of foreign languages would have fallen on untuned ears and failed to be convincing."[27] What takes place with these Gentile converts now baptized and sealed by the Holy Spirit is probably what the apostle Paul expressed as being ecstatic utterances when writing to the Corinth-

---

[25]*EBC* vol. 9, p. 394.

[26]This is the fifth time we see the Holy Spirit given in Acts and the second time that signs accompanied it. Notice that it is different from the other times. (1) The disciples at Pentecost received the Holy Spirit and spoke with tongues (2:4). (2) They were followed by the Jews who believed when Peter preached and who he said would receive the gift of the Holy Spirit (2:38). (3) The Samaritans believed and were baptized but did not receive the Holy Spirit until the apostles laid their hands on them (8:17). (4) Saul believed but received the Holy Spirit when the hands of Ananias, God's chosen representative, were laid on him, after which he was baptized (9:17-18). (5) The Gentiles in Cornelius's house received the Holy Spirit immediately when they believed and spoke with tongues before they were baptized. In Acts 19:6 is the final bestowal of the Holy Spirit. This is the last record of the gift of tongues as a sign of the presence of the Holy Spirit, the gift of prophesy also accompanying Paul's laying on of hands on the Ephesian believers.

[27]*EBC.*

ians, the sign of tongues being given primarily for the sake of the Jewish believers who had accompanied Peter. But the tongues experience of these Gentiles will also certify to the Jerusalem believers that the conversion of these Gentiles is entirely the work of God. None can revert to old prejudices and relegate these Gentile converts to that of second-class Christians.

Dare we ask ourselves what or whom does the Holy Spirit seal? What led to the coming of the Holy Spirit on those who heard Peter preach at Pentecost? They repented, believed the gospel, and were baptized. Who are the recipients of this blessing from the Holy Spirit in Cornelius's house? Again, those who believe in the Lord Jesus Christ. They have heard of Jesus, of His death and resurrection, the power of His name, that through His name is forgiveness of sins. In simple faith, they believe the word preached, and God gives them the Holy Spirit as His seal of their faith. God *with* us—that is the life of Jesus. God *for* us—that is the death and resurrection of Jesus. God *in* us—that is the gift of the Holy Spirit.[28]

Peter knows he cannot keep from these new converts their privileges as sons of God. "Can any man forbid water, that these should not be baptized, which have received the Holy Ghost as well as we?" (v. 47). No, he says, for they are forgiven, they have the Holy Spirit, and they must be acknowledged as members of the great household of God on earth, His body, His church. "The inward grace was ratified by the outward act [of baptism]."[29] In baptizing these Gentile believers, Peter and those who are with him confess that God in His sovereignty brings Gentiles into direct relationship with Jesus Christ, apart from any prior relationship with Judaism. Realizing the need to strengthen the newborn assembly in their faith, Peter remains for a time in Caesarea, perhaps even enjoying fellowship with Philip and his gifted daughters.

This is the second occasion on which Peter uses the keys of the kingdom of heaven as promised by the Lord Jesus, the first being when he spoke for God at Pentecost. Peter has never had any authority to allow or disallow anyone entrance to heaven. But through his faithful confession of Christ as Savior and Lord and through his powerful preaching of Christ's all-encompassing gospel, Gentiles, who once were far away from God and with no hope, are now brought near to God.

---

[28]Wolston, p. 215.
[29]Meyer, p. 166.

Peter in Jerusalem

Upon returning to Jerusalem, Peter discovers that reports of his action in Cornelius's house have preceded him and have stirred questions from other Jewish converts. God's people are both excited and perplexed. "And the apostles and brethren that were in Judaea heard that the Gentiles had also received the word of God. And when Peter was come up to Jerusalem, they that were of the circumcision contended with him, saying, Thou wentest in to men uncircumcised, and didst eat with them" (11:1-3). Within the church there is already forming a strong exclusivist party that afterwards will give the church much grief, obstinately insisting that Gentiles must submit to Jewish rites before admission into the assemblies. Therefore challenged by these men to give an account of his actions,[30] Peter rehearses the workings of God on behalf of the Gentile centurion and his household, explaining in conclusion that as he spoke to them, the Holy Spirit came upon the Gentile hearers as He had on the believers at Pentecost. "Then remembered I the word of the Lord," continues Peter "how that he said, John indeed baptized with water; but ye shall be baptized with the Holy Ghost. Forasmuch then as God gave them the like gift as he did unto us, who believed on the Lord Jesus Christ; what was I, that I could withstand God?" (vv. 16-17). Throwing the onus on his critics, Peter shows them that to withstand what took place would be to work against God. His argument is unanswerable. His critics are forced into silence. "When they heard these things, they held their peace, and glorified God, saying, Then hath God also to the Gentiles granted repentance unto life" (v. 18). The question is moot for the moment, but it will rise again in harsher realities when Peter joins in with the council in Acts 15. There once again, Peter will tell his wonderful story of God's grace showered on the Gentiles, reminding the brethren that God has broken the heavy yoke placed on their necks—that of the restrictive levitical system, that yoke that "neither they nor their fathers had been able to bear."[31]

---

[30]"Had [Peter] been invested with the absolute authority, with which the apostate Church has credited him, he would never have allowed his brethren to call him to account, would never have pleaded his case at their bar, would never have summoned witnesses to attest to his truth. He would have carried the matter with a high hand, and asserted his supreme and unassailable authority. Instead of this he appealed from men and from himself to God," Meyer, p. 167.

[31]Meyer calls his chapter on Peter and Cornelius "The Breaking of the Yoke." It is a masterful portrayal of God's deliberate movement to include the Gentiles in the church of Jesus Christ. Meyer, pp. 159-69.

The significance of Peter's opening the door of salvation to the Gentiles cannot be overstated. Though the Lord Jesus had established His church at Pentecost, the truth, or doctrine, of her oneness as His body had not yet emerged. In due course, the apostle Paul will be called to reveal that truth in his Epistle to the Ephesians. But the conversion of Cornelius and the other Gentiles showed that it was not necessary to become a Jew before being converted to Christ. To receive salvation one needed only to place his faith in Jesus Christ and repent of his sins. Those Jews who are slow to accept this truth will continue to plague the church. But the way has been opened and there is no turning back the gospel from spreading beyond Jerusalem, Judea, and Samaria to the ends of the world.[32]

Even Peter will lapse into his earlier prejudices when faced with the possibility of offending Jewish believers from Jerusalem. The fear of man will bring a snare to our beloved apostle, but his lapse is not permanent. God will still overrule in his life; his concluding years will be a tribute to the grace of God.

Implications for Service

1. *The goal of discipleship is to produce believers who will reproduce themselves in other Christians.* Christ called Peter to become a fisher of men and through his preaching and personal testimony, thousands converted to Christ, taking their place in the family of God. Christians are "saved to serve" and we take great encouragement from Peter's early ministry. Filled with the Spirit of God, as was Peter, and convinced that salvation is only in Jesus Christ, we have the same blessed privilege of proclaiming the good news of salvation. The Christian goal of perfection, of maturity in Christ, is not complete until we too allow the Lord to make us into fishers of men.

2. *God uses Christians, not angels, to preach His gospel.* The angel who spoke to Cornelius could only instruct him to send for Peter, who brought the gospel to him. Even when

---

[32]Thomas notes what Peter learned through this remarkable incident. (1) The significance of God's purpose. It broke down barriers and brought eternal blessings to the Gentiles, thereby realizing the Master's anticipations of "other sheep" (John 10:16). (2) The simplicity of God's plan. Its gradual development by means of the Samaritans and the eunuch; its natural development by the simultaneous though separate preparations of Cornelius and Peter. (3) The sufficiency of God's power. God arranged all the circumstances and accomplished all the results. "All so simple and natural, and yet so manifestly Divine." Thomas, p. 115.

Saul of Tarsus met the risen Lord on the road to Damascus, the Lord did not say to Saul, "Believe in me and be saved." He instructed Saul to continue into the city, and there another believer would tell him what he must do. Christians are God's ambassadors to the unsaved world. We cry out to them, "Be reconciled to God." As the angel knew Peter's address and told Cornelius where to go for him, are we in the place of the Lord's choosing and are we willing to go as He leads us? The marvelous truth is that as God moves on our hearts to obey His call to witness, He is at work preparing hearts to receive that message, as He did with Cornelius.

3. *Prejudice and bias should not prohibit Christians from proclaiming the gospel to all who need to hear it.* Christians must be concerned that old thought patterns and traditional thinking do not hinder them from proclaiming the gospel to others. God will use varying experiences to teach us, as He did Peter, that no person is to be called common; all are objects of God's love as shown in Jesus Christ.

4. *Being obedient to God brings its rewards.* Peter learned his surprising lesson concerning the gospel and the Gentiles by keeping his soul close to God, by keeping his mind open to God, and by keeping his will obedient to God—what Griffith Thomas calls abiding, attending, and acting.[33] Obedience to God and love to others are the ways we show that we are believers, that as Christians, we belong to God's family.

---

[33]Thomas, p. 116.

PETER'S LAST DAYS

And he departed, and went into another place (Acts 12:17).

His purposes will ripen fast,
Unfolding every hour:
The bud may have a bitter taste,
But sweet will be the flower.

—*William Cowper*

Setting: Jerusalem, spring, A.D. 44-49 and later
Scripture: Acts 12:1-19; 15:1-12; Gal. 1:18–2:14

The persecution in Jerusalem and Judea causing Christians to flee means that the gospel begins to spread to other regions of the middle east. One contingent of converted Jews make their way to Antioch in Syria, on the northeastern shore of the Mediterranean Sea, but they preach the gospel only to the Jews. It is not long, however, before various believers, arriving at Antioch from places such as Cyprus and Phenice, begin to proclaim the good news also to the "Grecians," the Hellenist Jews in Antioch. The results are tremendous as "a great number believed, and turned unto the Lord" (Acts 11:21). Hearing of the great impact of the gospel on this city, the church at Jerusalem sends Barnabas to investigate this growing ministry. Finding need of additional workers, Barnabas heads for Tarsus, seeks out Saul, and brings him to Antioch to assist in the work. These disciples with whom Paul and Barnabas minister are the first believers to be called Christians, a tribute the believers gladly receive, though given, no doubt, in derision. From this cosmopolitan congregation at Antioch the apostle Paul will eventually launch his missionary endeavors.

The relative quiet in Judea that allowed for the edification and growth of the church there[1] does not last long. Within a year or two after the conversion of Cornelius, the flames of persecution against Christians again burst forth. Adding to the misery of the Jerusalem believers, a great famine, as prophesied by Agabus, ravages the land. The compassionate believers in Antioch, many of them still having

---

[1]Acts 9:31. As noted earlier, some attribute this relative quiet at least partially to the distraction caused by Caligula when he endeavored to set up his image in the temple at Jerusalem. Now in addition to the lessening of the persecution of Christians, the distraction may also have contributed, at least partly, to the famine abroad, induced by the neglect of agricultural work in Palestine.

friends or loved ones in Jerusalem, call on Paul and Barnabas to take relief to them.[2]

The persecution arising in Judea comes at the instigation of Herod Agrippa I, grandson of Herod the Great and father of Herod Agrippa II, before whom Paul will one day be arraigned. "Now about that time Herod the king stretched forth his hands to vex certain of the church. And he killed James the brother of John with the sword. And because he saw it pleased the Jews, he proceeded further to take Peter also" (Acts 12:1-3). Agrippa spared no efforts to ingratiate himself with the Jews over whom he ruled, acting the part of an observant Jew whenever it would enhance his reputation. His efforts to "vex" the church to please the Jews usher in a new wave of persecution. One stark result of this headstrong drive against the Christians is the murder of the apostle James, brother to John and one whom Agrippa must have held prominent among the saints at Jerusalem.[3] These two brothers are the first and the last of the Lord's apostles to suffer martyrdom. James does not have a long ministry for the Lord Jesus, perhaps only some ten or twelve years after the Lord's crucifixion. During the Lord's earthly ministry, the mother of these two "sons of thunder"[4] pleaded for a place of honor for them in Christ's coming kingdom. "Are ye able to drink of the cup that I shall drink of?" the Lord asked.[5] Both responded with determination to drink of that same cup and to receive the same baptism as the Lord Jesus. Now comes the drinking of that cup by James. We are told nothing of the manner of his soul in the hour of his going forth to be beheaded, but the grace that sustained the first Christian martyr, Stephen, now sustains faithful James in his hour of trial.[6]

Peter in prison

Seeing that James's death pleases the Jews, Herod Agrippa apprehends Peter, intending to eliminate him too, except that any execution

---

[2]Acts 11:9-30.

[3]"It is hardly surprising that this unspectacular man was the first of the group to be martyred for Christ's sake. Herod was really afraid of the quiet power and influence of James. . . . And it was almost inevitable that Herod should put him out of the way, though in doing so he made a tragic mistake for himself. The body of such a man may mould in the grave, but his soul goes marching on! And its march means the downfall of Herod and all like him! In the end of the day it's the James's [sic] who'll sit on the Thrones!" J. Stuart Holden, *The Master and His Men* (1955), p. 54.

[4]Mark 3:17.

[5]Matt. 20:22.

[6]Morgan notes the sixfold work of Christ in James's life, by which the apostle saw *the power of Christ*—by miracle (Mark 5:37); *the glory of Christ*—by transfiguration (Matt. 17:1); *the love of Christ*—by forbearance (Luke 9:56); *the spirit of*

must be delayed by the arrival of Passover[7] and the accompanying Feast of Unleavened Bread. After the celebration of the Jewish holy days, Herod no doubt plans a grand public spectacle in executing Peter so that the Jews will be further ingratiated to him. He puts forth his hand against one of God's servants, really to exalt himself but also thinking that since Peter has so influenced the people around Jerusalem, he must be silenced as well.

> The politic Agrippa saw that this opening act of wanton cruelty 'pleased the Jews;' and that if he added the murder of the 'Rockman' to that of the 'Son of Thunder,' it would be like the removal of Jachin and Boaz from the support of the Christian Temple. Save Saul of Tarsus, no one of the surviving band of believers was so obnoxious as the intrepid son of Jonas. Quench this burning and shining light, and the lesser lights of the infant community would soon pale.[8]

What a security guard Herod orders for the apostle! Sixteen soldiers to guard one man! But then, had not Peter and the others escaped from prison when confined by the council? So Herod takes no chances with his captive. But Peter knows his life is in the Lord's hands, not Herod's. God can bring him out of his predicament if He so chooses. Peter knows God and sleeps peacefully; Herod knows not God and warily sets a watch on his prisoner. Of the two soldiers who guarded Peter, one was chained to him, another stationed a little farther off, at the prison door outside. Herod's excessive precautions are designed to make escape impossible to Peter. But Herod is leaving God out of his thinking. "What availed all his bolts, bars, sentinels, and 'two chains' upon his prisoner, if God stepped in?"[9] We shall see.

"Peter therefore was kept in prison: but prayer was made without ceasing of the church unto God for him" (v. 5). Two forces are at work. Peter is kept in prison, but the church prays. Opposition from the Evil One brings imprisonment to the apostle. Prayer by God's people seeks to unleash the power of God in behalf of His apostle. On the night before Agrippa's planned show trial of Peter, the angel of the Lord enters the cell where Peter soundly sleeps, no guard demanding, "Halt, who goes there?" Peter's two guardsmen continue their sleep, neither seeing

---

Christ—by compassion and correction (Mark 10:35); *the wisdom of Christ*—by revelation of the future (Mark 13:3f.); *the sufferings of Christ*—by witness of agony (Mark 14:33). G. Campbell Morgan, *Acts of the Apostles* (1956), p. 240.

[7]Gk., *pascha*.

[8]J. R. MacDuff, *The Footsteps of St. Peter* (1887), p. 485.

[9]Quintin Hogg, *The Story of Peter* (1900), p. 222.

the light now engulfing the prison nor hearing the angel's voice. "Arise up quickly," the angel instructs after arousing Peter with a touch. As he obeys the command, Peter's chains fall off his hands, clanking to the floor, but still failing to stir the insensible guards.

There is no hurry, for all is orderly. "Get dressed and tie up your sandals," the angelic visitor next commands and as Peter obeys, he hears further "and pull your cloak around you and follow me." Thinking he sees a vision and not yet realizing for certain that this is an angel at work, Peter nonetheless accompanies him. They pass the first and second guard safely without interruption and then, coming to the iron gate that leads out to the city, they see it open to them of its own accord. Leaving the confines of the prison,[10] they pass through one more street and then the angel is gone from him. Peter knows these streets so well that he has no further need for the angelic helper, and so he is left alone to ponder his miraculous escape.

Peter's bewilderment, brought about initially from being roused from his sleep, now changes over to increased sensibility. "And when Peter was come to himself, he said, Now I know of a surety, that the Lord hath sent his angel, and hath delivered me out of the hand of Herod, and from all the expectation of the people of the Jews" (v. 11). Acknowledging the gracious intervention by God, Peter takes time to consider his next action. After some thought, he proceeds to the house of Mary, sister to Barnabas and mother to John Mark. There, probably unknown to him, a number of believers have gathered late at night or now perhaps even early morning to pray for Peter's deliverance. After arriving at the house, Peter knocks at the outside gate in an effort to gain entrance. A young girl, Rhoda by name, approaches the gate in the wall:

"Who is it?"

"Please open the gate for me."

"Oh . . . it's . . . it's . . ." And Rhoda scampers back into the house without unlocking the gate.

" . . . it's Peter, dear brothers and sisters! Peter knocks at the outside gate!"

"You must be mad, Rhoda."

"Yes, Peter is in prison."

"You know we are here to pray for him. Don't interrupt our prayer to God."

---

[10]If Peter's imprisonment was in the Tower of Antonia, there would have been entrances to the fortress from both the temple mount and the city proper. The angel takes Peter through the entrance opening into the city street.

"But it's Peter. I heard his voice. He is at the gate."

"You are crazy. We tell you, it can't be Peter. Herod Agrippa has seen to it that he can't escape from the fortress."

"I know Peter's voice. I heard it. He's outside at the street."

"It can only be his angel."

But the knocking continues.

"Mary, you go to the gate and see who it is. Perhaps it is some neighbor in special need at this late hour."

"Or if it is a troublemaker, offer him a little of our food and send him away."

"Hello, who is it out there?"

"It is me, Peter. I can hear all of you inside the courtyard. Please open the gate." And when they finally open the gate, they are astonished to see that indeed it is Peter who stands before them—free from the chains that held him prisoner. They rejoice at the wisdom and sublime purpose of God, acknowledging that although James was killed, Peter is delivered. And who is to question the wisdom of God regarding His control of our lives? Whether He chooses to deliver or allow martyrdom, all is to accomplish His divine purpose and to reveal His matchless glory.

Beckoning to them to hold their questions, Peter describes his angelic visit and timely escape from Herod's hold. He then instructs them to explain everything to James, the Lord's brother, who is to assume a more prominent place as a pillar in the church at Jerusalem. Then Peter "departed, and went into another place" (v. 17).

Peter passes from the scene

At daybreak the soldiers charged with Peter's security are embarrassed to find that once again their prisoner is gone. Herod is even more exercised. Disgusted at the failure to locate the despised apostle, Herod commands that Peter's guardsmen be executed, after which Herod makes his way to Caesarea, where, in a short while, he meets an ignominious end. Under the judgment of God, he is smitten of the angel of God, is consumed of worms, and dies. Herod Agrippa's fleeting fancy and fame dissipates, but "the word of God grew and multiplied" (v. 24). The lesson should be obvious in this ugly scene brought about by degradation and sin. Though men devise their evil plans, God will have His way. And through it all He honors prevailing prayer. This account of Peter's remarkable experience in prison should encourage us to wait on God in "united, persevering, believing prayer."[11] No case

---

[11]Hogg, p. 228.

could seem more hopeless than that of Peter, yet God is sufficient for it. Has God changed? Should we not plead with God to teach us to pray so that we too may experience that deliverance of soul or body when imprisoned by the enemy?

Before we leave this portion of Luke's record of Peter, we should note the transition taking place. Peter passes off the scene and the apostle to the Gentiles, Paul, is about to take center stage in God's program. "And Barnabas and Saul returned from Jerusalem, when they had fulfilled their ministry, and took with them John, whose surname was Mark" (v. 25). From this we conclude that Paul was in Jerusalem at the time of Peter's imprisonment and deliverance. If this is so, we can understand the joy that would fill his large heart in seeing the beloved Simon Peter at liberty again—free to go about the Lord's work. Paul now becomes God's special vessel of the Holy Spirit's power and leading, and Peter, after a brief appearance once again in Jerusalem and also in Antioch, fades into that realm of conjecture in which we have no sure word of his whereabouts. His remaining work will be his two epistles, bearing his name and imprint of his own personal growth in knowledge and grace of the Lord Jesus Christ, his Master and now his Friend.

> O Jesus, I have promised
> To serve Thee to the end;
> Be Thou forever near me,
> My Master and my Friend;
> I shall not fear the battle
> If Thou art by my side,
> Nor wander from the pathway
> If Thou wilt be my Guide.[12]

> —John E. Bode

Peter and Paul

Very early in Christian history we find the names of Peter and Paul linked. Clement of Rome and Ignatius will couple them together soon after Peter and Paul have died. Churches and cathedrals today bear the names of both apostles, and frequently we see their statues standing side by side: Peter always with the keys, the symbol of his authority, and Paul always with the sword, the gladiator of the Word of God and the Gospel.[13] In many respects, Peter and Paul stand out

---

[12]John E. Bode, "O Jesus, I Have Promised," *Church Service Hymns* (1948), p. 331.

[13]A. T. Robertson, *Epochs in the Life of Simon Peter* (1939), p. 317.

from the rest of the leaders of the early Christian church, for, at least from a human point of view, early Christianity depended more on them than on any of the other leaders. We have seen how God used Peter to lead the disciples from the time of the Ascension until he now fades from the scene, unceremoniously going to "another place." In the remainder of Acts, Paul comes to the forefront as he inaugurates his expansive missionary tours to the regions beyond Jerusalem and Antioch. The personal contacts between Peter and Paul are not numerous in the Scripture portions that remain, but they are exceedingly important and instructive.

We have already noted their first meeting at Jerusalem three years after Saul's conversion.[14] Those fifteen days of hospitality and friendship must have given the two apostles deeply moving experiences, as each related to the other his varying impressions of their Master's fellowship.[15] The remaining contacts between these two men revolve around the question of receiving the Gentiles as legitimate converts into the church of Jesus Christ. Paul records just such a contact in Galatians 2. Luke gives his account in Acts 15 of the Jerusalem council, convened also to deal with the question. Serious study and discussion has sought to show, on the one hand, that these two events are identical or to prove, on the other hand, that they are separate incidents. I shall treat them as separate incidents, though I am more concerned that we obtain in these interactions between Peter and Paul an intimate look into the respect each held for the other.

As the apostle Paul preaches the gospel in Gentile countries, he experiences great opposition from narrow-minded Judaizing Christians from Jerusalem. He finds it necessary to confer with the apostles on this serious question, going to Jerusalem, as he writes, "by revelation."[16] God evidently revealed to Paul His will for unity in the church and confirmed to him, I am certain, His plan to continue the preaching of the gospel to all—Jew and Gentile alike. The outcome of that session is a clear yet frank recognition of the varying spheres of ministry given to Peter and to Paul. Paul states this to the Galatians, who were being subjected to influence from the Judaizers.

> When they saw that the gospel of the uncircumcision was
> committed unto me, as the gospel of the circumcision was

---

[14]Gal. 1:18. MacCartney writes two fascinating conversations that he imagines occurring between Paul and Peter as they meet for the first time in Jerusalem and later as they face death in Rome. Clarence Edward MacCartney, *Peter and His Lord* (1937), pp. 237-47.

[15]W. H. Griffith Thomas, *The Apostle Peter* (1956), pp. 127-28.

[16]Gal. 2:1-10.

unto Peter; (for he that wrought effectually in Peter to the
apostleship of the circumcision, the same was mighty in me
toward the Gentiles:) and when James, Cephas, and John,
who seemed to be pillars, perceived the grace that was given
unto me, they gave to me and Barnabas the right hands of
fellowship; that we should go unto the heathen, and they unto
the circumcision (Gal. 2:7-9).

Peter also participates in the deliberations by the leaders of the
church at Jerusalem to settle whether the Judaizing Christians were
right when they held that "except ye be circumcised after the manner
of Moses, ye cannot be saved" (Acts 15:1). The implication of this
teaching by these self-appointed regulators from Jerusalem is clear
that the Gentile Christians in Antioch and in all the other churches
established by Paul and Barnabas are not truly converted. It is during
this Jerusalem session that Peter recounts God's gracious choice to
use him to preach the gospel to the Gentile Cornelius.

And when there had been much disputing, Peter rose up, and
said unto them, Men and brethren, ye know how that a good
while ago God made choice among us, that the Gentiles by
my mouth should hear the word of the gospel, and believe.
And God, which knoweth the hearts, bare them witness, giving
them the Holy Ghost, even as he did unto us; and put no difference between us and them, purifying their hearts by faith.
Now therefore why tempt ye God, to put a yoke upon the neck
of the disciples, which neither our fathers nor we were able to
bear? But we believe that through the grace of the Lord Jesus
Christ we shall be saved, even as they (vv. 7-11).

And with that word of testimony, Peter affirms God's work by
Paul and Barnabas among the Gentiles with the result that the pro-
ceedings conclude with a strong commendation of Paul's ministry.

On one other occasion—whether before this Jerusalem council or
later—Peter visits Paul in Antioch of Syria, perhaps to express appreciation of the famine gift brought by Paul and Barnabas.[17] Peter's first attitude on arrival is complete unity with Paul and the Gentile Christians.
But after other Christians come from Jerusalem, Peter abruptly changes
course and adopts a narrow and unchristian attitude toward the Gentile
believers. Despite the clear conclusions from the recent conference, the
Jerusalem Christians were still "honeycombed with Judaism,"[18] and evi-

---

[17]Thomas, p. 128.
[18]W. W. Fereday, *Simon Peter* (n.d.), p. 170.

dently Peter fears loss of prestige on his return if he is seen associating with the Gentiles abroad. The situation is so grave, for even Barnabas is drawn into sharing Peter's attitude, that Paul confronts Peter publicly about his conduct and rebukes him for his hypocrisy. Once again both men acknowledge God's purposes for them—that Paul has been called to the Gentiles while Peter has a special ministry to the Jews of the Dispersion. It would appear from the biblical record that both Peter and Paul realize that "Christianity is to be without a doubt a world-wide religion based on the acceptance of the Lord Jesus Christ through faith."[19] We see from their handling of this sensitive issue surrounding the Gentiles and the lack of claim on them by the Jewish law, that Peter and Paul have no difficulty in accepting one another and rejoicing in God's plan for each of them.

Through incidental references in Scripture we capture some of the interplay between the two apostles. In his extended section on personal rights in I Corinthians, Paul notes that he has the same right as Peter to take a Christian sister as a wife,[20] though his purpose is to show that he chose not to exercise that right, as he chose not to be supported by the Corinthian believers. "This incidental reference to Simon Peter shows clearly that Paul is familiar with the preaching work of Peter and rejoices in it. . . . But this one word by Paul shows that . . . the rift at Antioch was completely closed."[21]

Peter is not without praise of Paul. In his second epistle, Peter speaks of Paul as his "beloved brother," who has in the wisdom given to him written to the people, though some things are "hard to be understood, which they that are unlearned and unstable wrest, as they do also the other scriptures, unto their own destruction" (II Pet. 3:16).[22] It is clear that Peter regards Paul's epistles as a definite body of writings and on a par with the OT Scriptures. Peter rises above pettiness to a noble spirit in which he recognizes the greatness of Paul, who now towers over him throughout the Christian world. There is not a hint of suspicion or jealousy on the part of Peter toward this apostle to the Gentiles.

---

[19]Thomas, p. 130.

[20]I Cor. 9:5. Paul calls Peter "Cephas" in this passage and in I Cor. 1:12.

[21]Robertson, pp. 256-57.

[22]"But Paul might have returned the compliment and said that there were some things in the Epistles of Peter also which are hard to understand." MacCartney, p. 235. I assume MacCartney means such matters as Peter's references in his first epistle to election (1:2), Jesus preaching to the spirits in prison (3:19), and baptism (3:21) and, in his second epistle, tartarus (2:4), righteous Lot (2:7), the ancient world (3:5-6), and the dissolution of the present world (3:12).

Throughout their associations, Paul acknowledges Peter's prominent and important position as an apostle of the Lord. For all of Peter's failings, we see him in perfect harmony with Paul in matters of principle and Scripture. How different they are in temperament, in social circumstances, in intellectual power; yet God makes room for both of them, for each is an important part of the Lord's plan. Whatever differences they encountered, they faced them openly and squarely. At the same time, they approached one another lovingly and in Christian grace. Our Christian heritage is so much the richer for the fellowship and experiences these two giants of the faith shared with one another.

Peter and Rome

We left Peter, following his marvelous deliverance from prison, moving on to "another place," though we know not the location, for the Scripture is silent. Our only hint of Peter's movements is to be found in his first epistle, which he sends to scattered Jewish Christians in "Pontus, Galatia, Cappadocia, Asia, and Bithynia" (I Pet. 1:1). He speaks of being "at Babylon" (5:13) when he concludes his words of encouragement. During all the years following the Lord's ascension, Peter is seen in Jerusalem or Samaria or Joppa or Lydda or Caesarea or some other part of Palestine. Up to the time of the council at Jerusalem, there is not one trace that he passed beyond the borders of his native land in ministering for Christ. He appears briefly at Antioch of Syria, but then he is gone from the biblical record, except for his interest in those regions to which he writes his epistle. Why would he seek to encourage these believers if he has not had previous acquaintance and fellowship with them, perhaps being instrumental in their conversion to Christ and feeding them as the flock of God? And is "Babylon" a symbolic reference to Rome? I am inclined to think not. That "Babylon" does not mean Rome is sufficiently proved by the fact that the symbolic name was not given until the Book of Revelation, the Apocalypse, was written at a much later period. And even if Peter had made that connection between Babylon and Rome beforehand, it is unlikely that he would have used it in an ordinary epistle and in connection with these ordinary salutations at the end of his epistle.[23]

The question of Peter's presence and then his eventual martyrdom in Rome is linked in most minds with the assumptions of Roman Catholics that Peter was the founder of the church at Rome, followed by an unbroken line of popes who have thus carried on through the ages the exclusive power of the keys committed by Jesus to Peter and by him

---

[23]Fereday, p. 175.

to his successors. In their attempt to deny this assumption by the Catholics, others move to deny that Peter was ever in Rome so as to disprove any claim that Peter was the first pope. We have dealt with the false claim that Peter was the first pope when studying our Lord's commendation of His apostle at Caesarea Philippi. Peter's position as pope rests on legends and Roman Catholic tradition, not scriptural revelation.

Did Peter ever find his way to Rome? We must admit that he does not appear to be there when Paul writes his epistle to the Romans, which was around A.D. 57. It seems unlikely that Paul would omit his name from the long list of greetings at the end of the epistle if Peter were in the assembly at Rome. And since there is already an established church there when Paul writes, it cannot then be claimed that Peter founded the church at Rome. Nor is it likely that Peter was in Rome during Paul's first Roman imprisonment, if we can judge by the absence of any mention of Peter in Paul's Prison Epistles.[24]

There are, however, other testimonies to Peter's presence in Rome and though possessing varying value, they all agree on the main idea that Peter did visit Rome on one or more occasions. The so-called First Epistle of Clement (about A.D. 95 or 96) seems to say that Peter suffered martyrdom in Rome, and Ignatius of Antioch (about A.D. 115), writing to the church at Rome, says, "Not as Peter and Paul do I command you," though he does not say that Peter had been in Rome. Iranaeus (about A.D. 190) speaks of Peter and Paul as having founded the church at Rome, a position which I have shown to be seriously in doubt. Eusebius quotes Clement of Alexandria (about A.D. 200) as saying that Peter followed Simon Magus to Rome and quotes Origen (about A.D. 252) as saying that Peter was crucified at Rome head downwards. Tertullian (about A.D. 200) is the first writer who speaks of Peter's death by crucifixion during Nero's reign. "Out of this welter of tradition the one thing that seems to have support is the fact that Peter at one time or another went to Rome."[25] The most likely time is after Paul's departure from Rome (A.D. 63) and after A.D. 64 when Nero began his persecution.

---

[24]Eph., Phil., Col., Philem., written during A.D. 60-63. Robertson holds that there are several places in these epistles in which Paul could hardly have escaped mentioning Peter's name, if he were in Rome: Phil. 2:19-30; Philem. 23; and especially Col. 4:10-14, in which Paul commends Mark to the Colossians and sends Mark's greetings. "It would seem a positive discourtesy for Paul to overlook Peter after speaking so kindly of Mark," Robertson adds, noting that Mark was with Peter for some time "in Babylon" (I Pet. 5:13), but "surely this was not the time," Robertson, p. 315. As I noted above, I am not convinced, as Robertson appears to be, that Peter's "Babylon" is a symbolic reference to Rome.

[25]Robertson, p. 318. The testimonies I have cited relating to Peter's presence in Rome are a summary of Robertson's compilations.

Whether Peter suffered martyrdom at Rome, we have already noted Origen's reference to Tertullian, who says that Peter was crucified upside down, confessing that he was not worthy to be crucified in the same manner as the Lord Jesus. There are also archeological inscriptions in Rome that make reference to the deaths of Peter and Paul. Ambrose gives the legend of Peter's death preserved in the words of *Quo Vadis?* The story is that some Christians at Rome persuade Peter to flee from Rome to escape Nero's wrath. At the gate of the city, as he flees, Peter meets the Lord Jesus and says to Him: "Lord, where are You going?" The risen Christ replies, "I go to Rome, there once more to be crucified." Shattered and embarrassed by the Lord's words, Peter returns to the city to be crucified.[26] What we have in Scripture are the Lord's inspired words to Peter: "Verily, verily, I say unto thee, When thou wast young, thou girdedst thyself, and walkedst whither thou wouldest: but when thou shalt be old, thou shalt stretch forth thy hands, and another shall gird thee, and carry thee whither thou wouldest not. This spake he, signifying by what death he should glorify God" (John 21:18-19). Peter has lived to be an old man. He has borne witness to Jesus as Christ and Lord. He goes into the presence of the Christ whom he loves and has served so faithfully and if that was by means of the martyr's death at Rome, then so be it.

"And so we take our leave of thee, thou generous, impulsive, wayward, impetuous, yet true-hearted man of God! We have come to know ourselves better through our acquaintance with thee, and even thy backsliding has shown us new depths of mercy in the heart of Christ."[27] God's purpose for Peter has unfolded before us, bitter buds yielding at last to the sweet fragrance of the mature flower.

Implications for Service

1. *Be faithful until the Lord calls you home.* During that time of intense persecution of Christians by the Romans, many believers were martyred for the cause of Christ, including, if the accounts are true, the apostle Peter. Jesus promised these martyrs in the Book of Revelation, "Fear none of those things which thou shalt suffer: behold, the devil shall cast some of you into prison, that ye may be tried; and ye shall have tribulation ten days: be thou faithful unto death, and I will give thee a crown of life" (Rev. 2:10). Peter has shown his faithfulness up to and including his martyrdom.

---

[26]Robertson, p. 320.

[27]W. M. Taylor, quoted by Robertson, p. 321.

God promises the "crown of life" to all who tread the martyr's path. The faithful Christian, laboring in the will of God, is immortal until his job is done on earth. The Devil cannot defeat you, death cannot overtake you, until God is finished using you for His purpose.

2. *Continue in intercessory prayer for God's saints.* Peter was held in prison, but God's people made specific prayer for him. Though they were slow to acknowledge that God had answered their prayers, the saints in Mary's house rejoiced at the release of Peter. They had shared in the work of God in removing Peter from the grip of Herod. God's saints, including missionaries, pastors, Christian workers, and church leaders, need our prayers on their behalf. The early church was a praying church. Filled with the Holy Spirit, they effected great victories for God through their intercessory pleadings for their leaders and for one another.

3. *Learn to trust God's purposes as best.* These incidents involving James's martyrdom and Peter's deliverance from prison manifest God's sovereign control over all of human life. "James, the faithful apostle, is killed by an evil man in the will of God; Peter, a faithful apostle, is delivered against all odds in the will of God. No one should ask why God permits such. In His infinite wisdom, only God knows the answer."[28] God could have delivered James too, but He chose not to do so. We know God's will to be "good, and acceptable, and perfect" (Rom. 12:2). Our study of Peter should cause us to seek to know and follow God's will and leave all else in His hands.

---

[28]Stewart Custer, *Witness to Christ* (2000), p. 170.

EXHORTING AND TESTIFYING

Exhorting, and testifying that this is the true grace of God wherein ye stand
(I Pet. 5:12).

> *Oh, turn me, mold me, mellow me for use,*
> *Pervade my being with Thy vital force,*
> *That this else inexpressive life of mine*
> *May become eloquent and full of power,*
> *Impregnated with life and strength divine,*
> *Put the bright torch of heaven into my hand,*
> *That I may carry it aloft,*
> *And win the eye of weary wanderers here below,*
> *To guide their feet into the paths of peace.*
>
> *—H. Bonar*

Setting: "Babylon"[1] and possibly Rome,[2] between A.D. 63 and 68
Scripture: I and II Peter

Anticipating that Peter would deny Him during His trial, the Lord Jesus revealed to His disciple, "Simon, Simon, behold, Satan hath desired to have you, that he may sift you as wheat: but I have prayed for thee, that thy faith fail not: and *when thou art converted, strengthen thy brethren*" (Luke 22:31-32). Peter did indeed deny the Lord in a time of crisis, but he also repented and turned around—he was converted from a denying apostle to that of a restored and forgiven apostle with a new commission to feed God's flock. As leader in the early church in Jerusalem, Peter showed himself to be a confident, Spirit-empowered preacher of the gospel as well as a fearless and effective administrator. But his ministry to believers extends beyond his personal ministry to that of NT writer, for Peter is also the author of the two epistles that bear his name. That Peter has grown in grace and knowledge of the Lord Jesus is evident from the reading of these two letters, which abound in references to the shepherd's care for his sheep as well as the responsibilities of Christians toward the Lord and to other believers. Peter wrote his first epistle, he tells us, "*exhorting, and testifying that this is the true grace of God wherein ye stand*" (5:12). "Exhorting" is

---

[1] I Pet. 5:13.

[2] We have no reliable information for determining where II Peter was written, but since Peter traveled widely throughout Palestine, as well as Asia Minor and possibly Corinth in Greece, it is possible he may have written his second epistle from one of these locations, though Rome remains the probable choice because he is known to have been there.

from *parakaleo*, "to call near," the verb from which we obtain "paraclete," the name Jesus gave for the Holy Spirit. As the Holy Spirit is our Comforter, the one called alongside for comfort and aid, so the apostle[3] sends his brief letter to comfort persecuted Christians of Asia Minor. "Testifying" means "to corroborate, to attest further," from *epimartuereo*. Peter seeks to testify through his own experiences the true grace of God in which believers are established and in so doing to encourage them as they endure trials of faith. "Let me tell you what God has done in my life," Peter seems to be saying, "and let it be an encouragement to you in the midst of your trials and persecutions." We have followed Peter from his conversion to his extensive ministry throughout Palestine and beyond. He has found the Lord sufficient in every situation and trial. He now exhorts believers to cast their burdens on the Lord because he knows from experience that God cares for them. Thus, we find Peter's two letters filled with personal recollections of his life with the Lord as well as mature spiritual insights developed through a life of fellowship and devotion to God. We will trace how Peter's experiences with the Lord are reflected in his exhortations to believers in his two epistles, beginning with the exhortation that comprises the major theme of the first epistle.

The first epistle

From the early days of the church, there has been almost unanimous agreement that Peter is the author of the first epistle bearing his name.[4] As noted earlier, we know little of Peter's later life following his brief encounter with Paul at Antioch, but he must have traveled extensively after that incident, no doubt accompanied by his wife.[5] It seems likely that he made preaching visits to Asia Minor (now modern Turkey), including Galatia, where Paul also ministered, but especially the provinces that Paul did not visit—Pontus, Cappadocia, and Bythinia (1:1). I am inclined to think that he also made a longer visit to Babylon on the Euphrates, the "Babylon" from which he writes his first letter (5:13). If Peter ever arrived in Rome, it was in all likelihood after Nero began his intense persecution of Christians in A.D. 64, and while in Rome, Peter died a martyr's death in 67 or 68, after penning his second epistle.

---

[3]Peter calls himself "an apostle of Jesus Christ" in I Peter 1:1 and "a servant and an apostle of Jesus Christ" in II Peter 1:1.

[4]Thiessen cites extensive external evidence as well as internal proof of Petrine authorship. Henry C. Thiessen, *Introduction to the New Testament* (1955), pp. 279-82.

[5]I Cor. 9:5.

Many attempts have been made to outline I Peter, most of them
focusing on the idea of suffering. I prefer to identify the chapter content of I Peter as stressing the word "new."[6]

1. The New Birth (ch. 1)—our salvation
2. The New People (ch. 2)—as strangers and pilgrims
3. The New Way to Live (ch. 3)—submission
4. The New Way to Suffer (ch. 4)—for righteousness
5. The New Way to Serve (ch. 5)—in humility[7]

The following ideas are those that are most instructive in Peter's
writings because they reflect Peter's mature understanding of what the
Lord sought to teach him as a disciple.

Suffering and glory

With a masterful combination of doctrine and practical exhortation
throughout his first letter,[8] Peter offers hope to persecuted Christians
who face severe trials of faith as they experience "heaviness through
manifold temptations" (1:6). The major theme of his first epistle,
therefore, centers on suffering,[9] showing that, for believers, suffering is
part of the will of God. "Wherefore let them that suffer according to
the will of God commit the keeping of their souls to him in well doing,
as unto a faithful Creator" (4:19). He reminds them of the sufferings of
Christ (1:11; 5:1) and holds up Christ as an example in this regard.
"For even hereunto were ye called: because Christ also suffered for us,
leaving us an example, that ye should follow his steps" (2:21). He
admonishes them to expect suffering (4:12) and not to be troubled by it
(3:14) but to bear it patiently (2:23; 3:9), yes, even to rejoice in suffering (4:13), knowing that their brethren elsewhere suffer the same
things (5:9). Showing the value of suffering to the Christian, Peter
explains, "that the trial of your faith, being much more precious than
of gold that perisheth, though it be tried with fire, might be found unto
praise and honour and glory at the appearing of Jesus Christ" (1:7).
With practical insight, Peter warns that they should not bring suffering
on themselves through their own evil conduct (2:20; 4:15).

---

[6]See Appendix D for expanded outlines on I and II Peter.

[7]Adapted from the *Pilgrim Edition of the Holy Bible* (1952), p. 1615. I should
note that the section on submission is actually 2:13–3:13, and the section on suffering
is 3:14–4:19.

[8]From 1:13 to the end of his epistle, Peter deals mainly with exhortation, yet he
weaves in much doctrine because he bases his various exhortations on important doctrines. In his salutation (1:1-2), for example, Peter refers to the Trinity, election, sancti-
fication or holiness, and the atonement.

[9]Thiessen says there are some seven words for suffering that occur in I Peter, p. 279.

To Peter, suffering and glory go together. He learned this lesson well after he stumbled at Caesarea Philippi. Jesus had just commended him as "blessed" for his confession of His messiahship but immediately rebuked Peter as "Satan" when he sought to restrain the Lord from going to the cross at Jerusalem. Peter did not understand that before the Lord would enter the glory of His kingdom, He would first face suffering and death. First the suffering, then the glory; first the cross, then the crown. Peter now shows that he understands this spiritual reality. Notice how Peter blends it into his words of comfort to the believers as he speaks of the "*sufferings* of Christ, and the *glory* that should follow" (1:11). He encourages his readers to "rejoice, inasmuch as ye are partakers of Christ's *sufferings*; that, when his *glory* shall be revealed, ye may be glad also with exceeding joy" (4:13). As part of his "testifying" to the believers, Peter reminds them that he was "a witness of the *sufferings* of Christ, and also a partaker of the *glory* that shall be revealed" (5:1), a clear reference to his witness of the glory of the transfigured Christ on the mount. To some extent, Peter suffered for his faith in Christ, but more significantly he saw with his own eyes the suffering of fellow Christians. He witnessed also the sufferings of the Lord Jesus. But he also saw the glory of Christ and is now convinced that any suffering that believers experience in this life is but prelude to their future glory. The crown will not be won without the cross; neither will the believer's inheritance in glory be his without first the suffering that is a part of this earthly existence. Though their present experience is that of faith being tested, they will "be found unto praise and honour and glory at the appearing of Jesus Christ" (1:7).

The example of Christ

After Jesus had healed Peter's mother-in-law and scores of others, Peter proudly reported to the Lord that "all men seek for thee" (Mark 1:37). Jesus replied simply, "Let us go into the next towns, that I may preach there also: for therefore came I forth" (v. 38). And with that statement, He showed Peter that His mission was not to garner popularity with the masses. Christ's humility of spirit precluded any desire for prominence. By His example of perfect obedience to the Father's will—His all-consuming passion—the Lord Jesus showed He was not reluctant to commit Himself to the Father, for He knew God would judge righteously. Later, when in need of coinage to pay the temple tax, Jesus provided the shekel for Peter and Himself, demonstrating once again His humility, this time His submission to the temple demands on Jewish males. Peter also heard the Lord speak eloquently of the humility of a child and the need for unlimited forgiveness of those who would seek to be part of His kingdom.

Peter showed his greatest insight when at Caesarea Philippi he confessed Jesus as "the Christ, the Son of the living God" (Matt. 16:16).

Throughout his epistle, therefore, the deity of Christ dominates Peter's thinking as he applies to Christ OT passages used of Jehovah (2:3). To Peter, Jesus Christ is Lord (1:3), the spotless Lamb (1:19), our Pattern (2:21), our sin offering (2:24), our Shepherd and Overseer (2:25). Christ inspired the prophets (1:10), descended into hades to preach to the dead (3:19), ascended into heaven, and is on the right hand of God (3:22). He will come again in revelation of glory to bestow a crown of glory (5:4).

The most significant example of Christ that Peter cites is the Lord's patient endurance of suffering on the cross. This is Peter's second major encouragement to believers in this epistle, which is filled with references to Christ. Peter speaks of the "obedience and sprinkling of the blood of Jesus Christ" (1:2), the "Spirit of Christ" (1:11), and the "precious blood of Christ" (1:19). Then as he addresses servants, he encourages them to submit willingly to their masters, even to those who are "froward" (2:18), thus showing them that the new way to live is to endure suffering with a patient spirit, not in an attitude of revenge. Peter writes: "For even hereunto were ye called: because Christ also suffered for us, *leaving us an example,* that ye should follow his steps: who did no sin, neither was guile found in his mouth: who, when he was reviled, reviled not again; when he suffered, he threatened not; but committed himself to him that judgeth righteously" (2:21-23). Pointing out that such suffering by Christians may be God's will for them, Peter further tells them: "Forasmuch then as Christ hath suffered for us in the flesh, arm yourselves likewise with the same mind: for he that hath suffered in the flesh hath ceased from sin; that he no longer should live the rest of his time in the flesh to the lusts of men, but to the will of God" (4:1-2). In thus encouraging these persecuted believers, Peter offers the same encouragement as the writer to the Hebrews when he says, "For consider him that endured such contradiction of sinners against himself, lest ye be wearied and faint in your minds" (Heb. 12:3). Thus, Peter seeks to encourage these persecuted and fainting Christians with the example of Christ, who patiently endured the agony of the cross.

Submission

Intertwined with Peter's emphasis on humility is his unique teaching on submission. Peter urges his readers to "submit" to state and civil government (2:13), to extremely unkind masters (2:18), to leadership in the family (3:1, 5, 7), and to other Christians in general (3:8-12). Submission, the "new way to live," is peculiarly and essentially Christian, for in the NT world humility and submission were thought unworthy of manly conduct. "Christ thus introduced a new thought and a new aspect of character into the world."[10] Peter's call to submission to governmental authorities is specially instructive in light of his challenge to the Sanhedrin. "We ought to obey God rather than men" (Acts 5:29), Peter demanded, when the council, acting beyond their authority, sought to divert the apostles' Christian duty. Peter knew there was a legitimate role for government in the affairs of men, that power superseded only when it seeks to interfere with one's obligation to a higher authority— that of God Himself. So to Peter, there is to be no question on this point. "Submit yourselves to every ordinance of man for the Lord's sake: whether it be to the king, as supreme;[11] or unto governors, as unto them that are sent by him for the punishment of evildoers, and for the praise of them that do well. For so is the will of God, that with well doing ye may put to silence the ignorance of foolish men" (2:13-15). Peter shows that it is consistent with a Christian's religious duty to submit to the state and civil authorities, up to the point at which it becomes a sin to obey. God must be kept first in the believer's life, but that does not have to be inconsistent with his obeying civil authorities where proper. Such submissive conduct is not only the revealed will of God but also is used by God to silence opposition to the Christian.

Peter further implores Christian slaves to obey their masters, even those who mistreat them (2:18-20). The true characteristic of Christian submission is not fear of punishment but "that spirit of deference and respect which shows itself in unquestioning obedience."[12] Peter is specially insistent that Christian wives be submissive to their husbands, particularly those wives who are concerned about their unsaved husbands. Their "chaste conversation coupled with fear [or reverence]" would have a salutary effect on those pagan husbands who have heard the gospel message (3:1-6). They would be won to Christ, Peter explains, not with further spiritual lecturing or "nagging" but by the attractive behavior of their godly, Christian wives. Again citing the OT, Peter holds up Sara as a proper example of this needful yet productive submission by the wife. Christian husbands do not escape Peter's attention, however, for he exhorts them to dwell with their wives "according

---

[10]W. H. Griffith Thomas, *The Apostle Peter* (1956), p. 193.

[11]An injunction all the more remarkable when we remember that in all probability Nero was on the Roman throne when Peter wrote this epistle.

[12]Thomas, p. 197.

to knowledge, giving honour unto the wife, as unto the weaker vessel, and as being heirs together of the grace of life; that your prayers be not hindered" (3:7). Thus, Peter sees married life and spiritual development as compatible, not mutually exclusive, concerns. He then ends this section on submission with general counsel to believers instructing them to strive for unity, compassion, brotherly love, but especially courteousness, or humble-mindedness (3:8). Nor are Christians to seek revenge on nonbelievers because they have been called to something far better—the blessing of God on their conduct (3:9).

In the final chapter of his first epistle, Peter appeals to the younger men to "submit yourselves unto the elder" (5:5). This exhortation follows Peter's directives to the elders themselves and is couched in terms of mutual submission of all believers. "Yea, all of you be subject one to another, and be clothed with humility: for God resisteth the proud, and giveth grace to the humble" (v. 5). Peter presents a beautiful paradox for believers to follow: Each Christian is to be in submission to everyone else. This the Christian accomplishes by submitting in humility to God, placing himself "under the mighty hand of God" (v. 6), certainly a timely and comforting exhortation to those who were suffering persecution. When the Lord Jesus girded Himself with the servant's towel in the upper room and washed the disciples' feet, including the feet of the protesting Peter, He told them, "I have given you an example, that ye should do as I have done to you" (John 13:15). Having witnessed the beauty of that marvelous servant scene and understanding more fully its meaning, Peter now holds the Lord's example up for all to emulate. Christians, Peter says, are to be "clothed with humility" (I Pet. 5:5),[13] to take up the adornment of the lowly servant and be willing to do as Jesus did—humbly serve others.

Living stones

When the Lord's disciples first believed in Him and followed Him, they were still a part of that old dispensation in which John the Baptist ministered. At Pentecost, however, the Holy Spirit came to indwell them, so that when Peter writes to these first-century believers, he speaks of them as being "born again, not of corruptible seed, but of incorruptible, by the word of God, which liveth and abideth for ever" (1:23). Peter then describes Christians as "newborn babes" (2:2) and

---

[13]"Gird yourselves with humility" is how Robertson states the command, noting that "gird" is a rare word, found only here in the NT and meaning "to tie a knot, as of a girdle or apron." A. T. Robertson, *Epochs in the Life of Simon Peter* (1939), p. 287. Thus, Peter has in mind the Lord's girding Himself with the servant's towel in the upper room.

living stones (2:5) as well as "a chosen generation, a royal priesthood, an holy nation, a peculiar people" (2:9).[14] He also speaks of Christians as strangers and pilgrims whose citizenship is in heaven (2:11-12), weaving in the process a mosaic of OT quotations that shows his knowledge of Scripture and his ability to bring it to practical use in exhorting the believers.

To designate Christians as "living stones"[15] should carry special significance to Peter, for he received that new name meaning "rock" at his conversion. Now he reveals the further significance of Christians as living stones. "Ye also, as lively stones, are built up a spiritual house, an holy priesthood, to offer up spiritual sacrifices, acceptable to God by Jesus Christ" (2:5). As such, believers are built on their foundation stone, the Lord Jesus Christ, "a chief corner stone, elect, precious" (v. 6). But to those who refuse to obey Him, Christ is "a stone of stumbling, and a rock of offence, even to them which stumble at the word, being disobedient: whereunto also they were appointed" (v. 8).

Shepherding

Peter delivers special exhortations for the elders whom he addresses.

> The elders which are among you I exhort, who am also an elder, and a witness of the sufferings of Christ, and also a partaker of the glory that shall be revealed: feed the flock of God which is among you, taking the oversight thereof, not by constraint, but willingly; not for filthy lucre, but of a ready mind; neither as being lords over God's heritage, but being ensamples to the flock (5:1-3).

In addition to reminding his readers that he witnessed the Lord's sufferings on the cross, Peter also notes that he was participant at the glorious transfiguration of the Lord Jesus on the mount. Once again we see a dominant theme of I Peter—no glory without the suffering; no crown without the cross. Having established his credentials as an elder and an eyewitness, Peter charges the elders to shepherd the flock of God, using the very command that the Lord Jesus used of him in that postresurrection appearance at the Sea of Galilee.[16]

The elders are to do their pastoral work, not out of a sense of compulsion but gladly and freely, refraining from seeking shameful

---

[14]Though he speaks of believers by various designations (a temple, a priesthood, a sacrifice), Peter does not use the word "church" in either of his epistles.

[15]KJV, "lively." Gk. *zao*, "to live," hence, "quick," or "living."

[16]John 21:16.

gain. Peter is quick also to charge them not to lord their position and authority over God's people (Peter is clearly non-popish here) but to become models for the flock, for sheep will follow the shepherd, whether he be good or evil. From the Chief Shepherd they will receive the unfading crown of glory when He returns. Peter closes his first epistle with a reminder of God's constant care (5:7), the need for vigilance and resistance against our adversary, that roaring lion the Devil (5:8-9), and a final comfort that following suffering, God will perfect, establish, strengthen, and settle them (5:10). "Surely Peter has learned how to strengthen his brethren now that he has really turned back to the Master."[17]

A second epistle

After identifying himself as "Simon Peter, a servant and an apostle of Jesus Christ" (II Pet. 1:1), Peter notes that this is his "second epistle" (3:1), written, he says, to stir up the memory of his readers. They are to be "mindful of the words which were spoken before by the holy prophets, and of the commandments of us the apostles of the Lord and Saviour" (3:2). Peter wrote his first epistle to comfort and encourage persecuted believers. In his second epistle, Peter issues words of warning against the dangerous influence of false teachers. His antidote to false teaching is true spiritual knowledge, based on facts and communicated to the believer by the Holy Spirit. The grace and peace that Peter desires for his readers is "through the knowledge of God, and of Jesus our Lord" (1:2) "Know this," Peter warns (3:3). The key word throughout the epistle, therefore, is "knowledge," which in its various forms occurs twelve times.[18] Peter also links with this emphasis on knowledge the importance of remembering certain things (1:12-13; 3:1) or the danger of forgetting important truths (1:9; 3:8), thus showing the teachings of the Word of God as true and normative for the Christian life.

A brief outline for II Peter focuses on his three chapters:

1. First Things (ch. 1)
2. False Things (ch. 2)
3. Final Things (ch. 3).[19]

Experience and the Word of God

Identifying himself with all believers who "have obtained like precious faith" (1:1), Peter begins this epistle on the same note as he did

---

[17]Robertson, p. 287.

[18]1:2, 3, 5, 6, 8, 16, 20; 2:20, 21; 3:3, 17, 18.

[19]See Appendix D for expanded outlines for Peter's two epistles.

the first—with an emphasis on salvation. He assures his readers that God has given Christians "all things that pertain unto life and godliness, through the knowledge of him that hath called us to glory and virtue" (v. 3). That means that in salvation, believers become "partakers of the divine nature" (v. 4). When we are born into God's family, we receive God's own nature through faith in Jesus Christ. But while God has provided all for salvation, there remains for the Christian the responsibility to energetically furnish to his faith those qualities that develop one into a strong and fruitful believer—self-control, patience, godliness, brotherly kindness, love, but especially knowledge (1:5-7). Peter shows that it is the believer's responsibility to avail himself of these divine resources so that he will not be "barren nor unfruitful in the knowledge of our Lord Jesus Christ" (1:8).

What kind of knowledge does Peter stress? Is it a knowledge that comes as a result of personal experiences? Perhaps his readers may think so. Peter, therefore, proceeds to tell several personal experiences in vivid manner. Always ready to remind his readers, though they are well established in doctrinal and moral truth (v. 12), he considers it his duty to keep reminding them so long as he is in this "tabernacle." Making an allusion to his death using the metaphor of laying aside that tabernacle, or tent, Peter also knows that Christ's prediction about the manner of his death will soon come to pass. So he calmly faces his exodus, or "decease" (v. 15). Was it not the Lord's own exodus that formed the content of conversation with the heavenly visitors— Moses and Elijah—on the mount? Indeed, Peter's mind is now drawn to that experience that never left him—the Lord's glorious transfiguration on Mount Hermon. Having already alluded to this event in his first epistle (5:1), he now writes:

> For we have not followed cunningly devised fables, when we made known unto you the power and coming of our Lord Jesus Christ, but were eyewitnesses of his majesty. For he received from God the Father honour and glory, when there came such a voice to him from the excellent glory, This is my beloved Son, in whom I am well pleased. And this voice which came from heaven we heard, when we were with him in the holy mount (vv. 16-18).

"I heard that voice," Peter declares, "and I was with Christ on that holy mount." What a tremendous personal experience for the apostle! His was an experience all believers would want repeated for themselves.

Yet, Peter interrupts, "we also have a more sure word of prophecy" (v. 19). This is *the priority of Scripture.* Experience may be personal and profound, but the revealed Word of God takes priority over all experience. Christians judge their experience by the Word of God, not subordinating the Word of God to their personal experience. Christians "do well that ye take heed" (v. 19) to this revealed Word of God, given by inspiration through holy men of God who were moved, or carried along, by the Holy Spirit. Is there no room for personal experience? Yes there is, for we are to grow in grace and knowledge of Christ. But what we learn of Christ we learn from His Word. For Peter it is the revelation from God that is the priority.

False teachers

"But there were false prophets" (2:1) among God's people in the OT when the prophets ministered for God. Likewise, Peter warns, there will be false prophets among the people of God in our dispensation, but their path leads toward certain destruction with their final state worse than the first (v. 20). Those who follow them can expect nothing better. As the sure judgment of God was on the sinners of the OT (2:4-6, 15), so it will be on all false teachers. What was true in Peter's day is true today. Gullible people easily fall victims to charlatans who use religion for their own unseemly profit.

For Peter, proper knowledge is necessary to avoid being carried away with the errors of the wicked (3:17). He desires his readers to grow in grace and knowledge of Jesus Christ. This knowledge of Christ is, as Peter points out, knowledge of "the right way" (2:15) and the "way of righteousness" (2:21). Noah was a "preacher of righteousness" (2:5) and Lot was "righteous"[20] (2:7). In contrast, Peter calls these false teachers unrighteous men who walk after the flesh and despise the lordship of Christ. Self-willed, they do what angels fear to do—rail at dignities.[21] Their whole tone is that of conceited charlatans.[22] With solemn impressiveness, Peter acknowledges that it would have been better for them never to have known the way of righteousness than, knowing it, to turn from it, driving his point home with two illustrations—the dog returns to its vomit; the pig wallows in the mire. Having sinned and denied the Lord himself, Peter is specially concerned that his readers do not run the risk of deserting Christ for the heinous teaching of these deceptive preachers.

---

[20]KJV, "just."

[21]Presumptuous and arrogant, these false teachers "do not tremble when defaming those in exalted positions." Kenneth S. Wuest, *In These Last Days* (1954), p. 34. They scoff at the notion of either angelic help or satanic influence.

[22]Robertson, p. 306.

Last words

Peter was present when the Lord Jesus ascended back to heaven. He heard with his own ears the promise that "this same Jesus" shall return to earth. Years have passed. One by one the apostles have left the scene. Yet Jesus has not returned. Was that promise still true? What should these believers know concerning the Lord's promised coming? Acknowledging that the world has always had its scoffers, Peter assures his readers that "the Lord is not slack concerning his promise, as some men count slackness; but is longsuffering to us-ward, not willing that any should perish, but that all should come to repentance" (3:9). Peter presents the essential truth—Jesus is coming back in God's own time. God is patient with men so that all may come to repentance. "But the day of the Lord will come as a thief in the night" (v. 10), the very metaphor Jesus used in Peter's hearing.[23]

Peter's allusions to both OT and NT Scriptures in this short epistle, particularly in this final chapter, clearly indicate the necessity and value of God's revelation for growth in the Christian life as well as for defense against the dangers of false teachings. In a final appeal that is immensely practical, Peter writes that in view of the sudden and final dissolution of earthly things, we ought to live holy and godly lives, "looking for and hasting unto the coming of the day of God" (3:12). Peter's final word is that, with all this knowledge beforehand, we should not be carried away by the error of false teachers and preachers and thus fall from our own steadfastness. Rather, we must keep growing in grace and knowledge of the Lord Jesus Christ. Peter speaks of knowledge of "our Lord and Saviour" (3:18). Remember, it was Peter's failure to acknowledge Christ as Savior and Lord that prompted him to protest Christ's washing of his feet in the upper room. Now, however, Peter understands that Christ is both Savior and Lord, and intreats all to continue to gain that knowledge of Christ available to us through fellowship with Him in His Word. "There is no limit to one's growth," observes Robertson, "for Christ is too wonderful and too high for us to exhaust in a lifetime or in eternity."[24] Peter walked and talked with the Lord and learned much from Him. Peter lived a fruitful life that demonstrated his steadfastness to the Lord. His final words to us are our challenge: "grow in grace and the knowledge of our Lord and Savior, Jesus Christ" (3:18). And his final benediction expresses the essence of our fellowship with Christ in this life and the next:

"To him be glory both now and for ever. Amen"

---

[23]Luke 12:39; Matt. 24:43.
[24]Robertson, p. 311.

AFTERWORD

True to the Lord's prophetic insight, Simon became the Rock that Jesus saw him to be at conversion. Though slow in the making—for hard rocks are not made in a day—Peter learned how to become a fisher of men and in his subsequent years of ministry, caught many people alive for Christ. Though he denied the Lord at a crucial moment, he repented and following his restoration, he strengthened his brethren, as the Lord had prayed. He shepherded God's flock and fed the lambs committed to his care. He used the keys given to him by the Lord to open the door of Christ's church to all who would hear the gospel, repent, and be baptized. As an apostle who thought of himself as but an elder among others, Peter has been misappropriated in name by a false religious system that Peter would have scorned and repudiated. However, his life as revealed in the Gospels and the Book of Acts is an inspired record of imperishable words and deeds that enable every devout Christian to learn what it means to be a disciple and follower of the Lord Jesus Christ.

God has a plan and purpose for your life too. He seeks to change your name from child of disobedience to child of God. He gave His Son so that you might be brought out of the kingdom of darkness into the kingdom of the Son of His love. Christ seeks to make you into His fruitful and productive disciple. And though you may have failed Him—perhaps not as severely as did Peter, or perhaps a hundred-fold worse—still be assured that the Lord Jesus, at the Father's right hand, intercedes for you. We have an advocate with the Father—Jesus Christ, the righteous Son of God.

> *Dear heavenly Father: Through the life and ministry of Thy servant, Simon Peter, we have witnessed the most wonderful life that ever walked this earth—Thy Son, the Lord Jesus Christ. As you sought to make Peter a true and strong disciple, make us after Thy will and in Thine own image. Help us to cling only to Thee, not for what we are or even for what we may become, but for who Thou art. In Jesus' name, Amen.*

APPENDIXES

A HARMONY OF THE LIFE OF PETER

EVENT	MATTHEW	MARK	LUKE	JOHN
Meeting the Messiah				1:35-51
Call to service	4:18-22	1:16-20	5:1-11	
Healing of mother-in-law	8:14-15	1:29-31	4:38-39	
Jesus' popularity		1:36–2:12		
Choosing of the Twelve	10:2-4	3:13-19	6:12-19	
Woman healed, girl raised	9:18-26	5:22-43	8:41-56	
Feeding of five thousand	14:13-21	6:32-44	9:10-17	6:1-15
Walking on the lake	14:22-33	6:45-56		6:15-21
Question of unwashed hands	15:15-20	7:17-23		
Great confession and testing	16:13-28	8:27-38	9:18-27	
The Transfiguration	16:28–17:9	9:1-10	9:27-36	
Coin in the fish's mouth	17:24-27			
Forgiving a brother	18:21-35		17:3-4	
True discipleship	19:16–20:16	10:17-31	18:18-30	
Cursing of the fig tree	21:18-22	11:12-26		
Questions about the future	24:1-3	13:1-5	21:5-7	
In the upper room	26:17-30	14:12-25	22:7-30	13:1-35
Warning to Peter	26:31-35	14:26-31	22:31-38	13:36-38
In the garden	26:36-56	14:32-52	22:39-53	18:1-11
The denial	26:69-75	14:66-72	22:54-62	18:15-27
Resurrection and restoration	28:1-10	16:1-8	24:1-35	20:1-10
Called again				21:1-25
Replacing Judas Iscariot	Acts 1:1-26			
Preaching at Pentecost	2:1-47			
Healing the lame man	3:1-26			
Opposition	4:1-37			
Apostolic discipline	5:1-16			
Before the council again	5:17-42			
Simon Magus	8:1-25			

Appendix A

EVENT	MATTHEW	MARK	LUKE	JOHN
Expanded ministry	9:32-43			
Cornelius's conversion	10:1–11:18			
Deliverance from prison	12:1-19			
At the Jerusalem council	15:6-11			
Peter and Paul	Gal. 1:18; 2:1-21			

CHRONOLOGICAL TABLE OF CHRIST'S LIFE

Harold W. Hoehner

Christ's birth	winter 5/4 B.C.
Herod the Great's death	March/April 4 B.C.
Prefects began to rule over Judea and Samaria	A.D. 6
Christ at the temple when twelve	Passover, April 29, 9
Caiaphas became high priest	A.D. 18
Pilate arrived in Judea	A.D. 26
Commencement of John the Baptist's ministry	A.D. 29
Commencement of Christ's ministry	summer/autumn A.D. 29
Christ's first Passover (John 2:13)	April 7, 30
John the Baptist imprisoned	A.D. 30 or 31
Christ's second Passover	April 25, 31
John the Baptist's death	A.D. 31 or 32
Christ at the Feast of Tabernacles (John 5:1)	October 21-28, 31
Christ's third Passover (John 6:4)	April 13/14, 32
Christ at the Feast of Tabernacles (John 7:2, 10)	September 10-17, 32
Christ at the Feast of Dedication (John 10:22-39)	December 18, 32
Christ's final week	March 28 - April 5, 33
Arrived at Bethany	Saturday, March 28
Crowds at Bethany	Sunday, March 29
Triumphal entry	Monday, March 30
Cursed the fig tree and cleansed temple	Tuesday, March 31
Temple controversy and Olivet discourse	Wednesday, April 1
Christ at Passover, betrayed, arrested, and tried	Thursday, April 2
Christ tried and crucified	Friday, April 3
Christ laid in the tomb	Saturday, April 4
Christ resurrected	Sunday, April 5
Christ's ascension (Acts 1)	Thursday, May 14, 33
Day of Pentecost (Acts 2)	Sunday, May 24, 33

Hoehner, Harold W. *Chronological Aspects of the Life of Christ.* Grand Rapids: Zondervan Corporation, 1977. Used by permission.

APPENDIX C

BIBLE MEMORY SYSTEMS

Hood, Ron. *How to Successfully Memorize and Review Scripture.* Greenville, S.C.: Spiritual Success Institute, Inc., 1974.

A method for memorizing and reviewing Scripture verses; contains 108 verses every Christian should memorize; memory cards available.

Hummel, Rand. *Five Smooth Stones: Scripture Memory Plan.* Brevard, N.C.: The Wilds, 1991.

Three volumes of verses designed for young people.

Lewis, Norman. *Bible Themes Memory Plan.* Lincoln, Neb.: Back to the Bible, 1964.

Sivnksty, Jerry. *The Two-Edged Sword Memory Plan.* Maple Grove, Minn.: Nystrom Publishing Company, Inc., 1982.

Five separate books of memory verses: daily living, character, Bible doctrines, family, and teens.

Topical Memory System. Colorado Springs: The Navigators, 1957.

DISCIPLESHIP STUDIES FOR NEW CONVERTS

Berg, Jim. *Basics for Believers.* Greenville, S.C.: Bob Jones University Press, 1978.

Includes question and answer studies on eternal life, assurance, God's Word, temptation, prayer, witnessing, church attendance, dedication; also contains verses to memorize, a personal prayer journal, a Bible reading schedule for the NT, and memory verse cards.

Bible Helps and Witness Cards. Schaumburg, Ill.: Regular Baptist Press, n.d.

Sturdy plastic cards, suitable for carrying in a Bible, include Bible verses on assurance of salvation, facing temptations, growing as a Christian. Witness card includes the plan of salvation.

Appendix C

Burns, Ralph O. *Basic Bible Truths.* Schaumburg, Ill.: Regular Baptist Press, 1971.

Covers basic doctrines, gives suggestions for Bible study and Scripture memorization, and offers guidance for victorious Christian living.

Cook, Robert A. *Now That I Believe.* Chicago: Moody Press, 1977.

Short studies on important topics for new Christians. Answers questions, such as What happened to me? How long will this new-found joy last? How do I act like a Christian? How can I pray? Do I have to testify? What shall I do with my life?

Hamrick, Frank and Jerry Dean. *Milk for New Christians.* Rocky Mount, N.C.: Positive Action for Christ, 1972.

Question and answer studies on assurance of salvation, the importance of God's Word, how to study the Word, prayer, sharing your faith, baptism, the believer and the church.

Merrill, Darwin E. *New Life for Adults.* Colorado Springs: Accent Bible Curriculum, 1988.

A thorough new converts course designed to be taught as a 13-week series in Sunday school or a Bible study group; includes assignments for the new believer and additional lessons on Bible study and spiritual growth, Christian duties and responsibilities, how to have victory over temptations, and how to know God's will. A children's edition is also available.

Orr, William W. *Believer's First Bible Course.* Great Bend, Kans.: Glad Tidings!, 1992.

Bible teaching on basic doctrines plus how to study the Bible.

"The New Life in Christ," New Life Discipleship Series, Course 1. Valdosta, Ga.: The Mailbox Club, 1986.

Thirteen lessons for children complete with questions, daily quiet times and devotional guide, and selected subjects for discussion.

EXPANDED OUTLINES

First Peter

Introduction (1:1)

I. The New Birth (1:2-25)

   A. The foundation of our salvation (1:2)

      1. the election of God (v. 2)

      2. the sanctification of the Holy Spirit (v. 2)

      3. the sprinkling of the Son (v. 2)

   B. The fact of our salvation (1:3-12)

      1. our inheritance (vv. 3-5)

      2. our trial of faith (vv. 6-8)

      3. our future glory (vv. 9-12)

   C. The fruit of our salvation (1:13-25)

      1. holiness in life (vv. 13-16)

      2. reverence toward God (vv. 17-21)

      3. love for the brethren (vv. 22-25)

II. The New People (2:1-12)

   A. As newborn babes (2:1-3)—our desire

      1. negative (v. 1)

      2. positive (vv. 2-3)

   B. As living stones (2:4-8)—our devotion

      1. Christ is the foundation (vv. 4, 6-8)

      2. Christians are the living stones (v. 5)

   C. As strangers and pilgrims (2:9-12)—our destination

III. The New Way to Live (2:11–3:13)

   A. Submission to government authority (2:13-17)

      1. the command (v. 13*a*)

      2. the conduct (vv. 13*b*-14)

      3. the consequences (v. 15)

      4. the challenge (vv. 16-17)

   B. Submission when mistreated (2:18-25)

      1. the command (v. 18*a*)

      2. the conduct (vv. 18*b*-19)

      3. the consequences (v. 20)

      4. the challenge (vv. 21-25)

   C. Submission in the family (3:1-7)
1. the command (1*a*, 7)
2. the conduct (vv. 2-4)
3. the consequence (1*b*, 7)
4. the challenge (vv. 5-6)

   D. Submission to one another (3:8-13)
1. the commands (v. 8)
2. the conduct (v. 9*a*)
3. the consequence (v. 9*b*)
4. the challenge (vv. 10-13)

IV. A New Way to Suffer (3:14–4:19)
   A. As opportunity to witness (3:14–4:6)
1. the exhortation (vv. 14-17)
2. the example of Christ (vv. 18-22)
3. the encouragement (4:1-6)

   B. As opportunity to develop character (4:7-19)
1. a serious outlook on life (v. 7*a*)
2. prayerful watching (v. 7*b*)
3. fervent love (v. 8)
4. ungrudging hospitality (v. 9)
5. faithful service (vv. 10-11)
6. joy in suffering (vv. 12-15)
7. glory to God (vv. 16-19)

V. A New Way to Serve (5:1-14)
   A. As leaders of the flock (5:1-4)
1. a leader's responsibility (vv. 1-3)
2. a leader's reward (v. 4)

   B. As followers in the flock (5:5-11)
1. humility (vv. 5-6)
2. trustfulness (v. 7)
3. watchfulness (vv. 8-9)
4. endurance (vv. 10-11)

   C. Conclusion (5:12-14)
1. the purpose (v. 12)
2. the greetings (vv. 13-14*a*)
3. the benediction (v. 14*b*)

Appendix D

Second Peter

I. First Things (1:1-21)
  A. The priority of salvation (1:1-11)
    1. God's provision (vv. 1-4)
    2. the believer's responsibility (vv. 5-11)
  B. The priority of Scripture (1:12-21)
    1. the witness of Peter (vv. 12-18)
    2. the writings of the prophets (vv. 19-21)
II. False Things (2:1-22)
  A. The prevalence of false teachers (2:1-3)
    1. their presence (v. 1)
    2. their pernicious ways (vv. 2-3*a*)
    3. their perdition (v. 3*b*)
  B. The punishment of false teachers (2:4-6)
    1. the angels that sinned (v. 4)
    2. the ancient world (v. 5)
    3. Sodom and Gomorrha (v. 6)
  C. The protection of the righteous (2:5, 7-9)
    1. Noah (v. 5)
    2. Lot (vv. 7-8)
  D. The presumption of false teachers (2:10-18)
    1. fleshly (v. 10*a*)
    2. lawless (vv. 10*b*-12)
    3. unclean (vv. 13-14)
    4. greedy (vv. 15-16)
    5. empty (vv. 17-18)
  E. The plight of false teachers (2:19-22)
    1. promise of liberty (v. 19)
    2. pollution of the world (v. 20)
    3. proverbs fulfilled (vv. 21-22)
III. Final Things (3:1-18)
  A. Proper view of prophetic teaching (3:1-10)
    1. remembering God's Word (vv. 1-2)
    2. ignoring God's Word (vv. 3-7)
    3. fulfilling God's Word (vv. 8-10)

B. Practical value of prophetic teaching (3:11-18)
   1. holiness in life (vv. 11-13)
   2. diligence in service (v. 14)
   3. patience in witnessing (vv. 15-16)
   4. stedfastness in faith (v. 17)
   5. growth in grace (v. 18)

SELECTED BIBLIOGRAPHY

Simon Peter and the Twelve

Barclay, William. *The Master's Men.* Nashville: Abingdon Press, 1959.

Bruce, A. B. *The Training of the Twelve.* New York: Harper & Brothers Publishers, n.d.

Carver, Frank G. *Peter the Rock Man.* Kansas City, Mo.: Beacon Hill Press, 1973.

Chappell, Clovis G. *Sermons on Simon Peter.* New York: Abingdon Press, 1959.

English, E. Schuyler. *The Life and Letters of Saint Peter.* New York: Publication Office "Our Hope," Arno C. Gaebelein, Inc., 1941.

Fereday, W. W. *Simon Peter: Apostle and Living Stone.* Barkingside, Essex, England: G. F. Fallance, n.d.

Gill, David W. *Peter the Rock.* Downer's Grove, Ill.: Inter-Varsity Press, 1986.

Holden, J. Stuart. *The Master and His Men.* Edinburgh: Marshall, Morgan and Scott, 1955.

MacCartney, Clarence Edward. *Peter and His Lord.* Nashville: Abingdon-Cokesbury Press, 1937.

MacDuff, J. R. *The Footsteps of St. Peter.* London: James Nisbet & Co., 1887.

Meyer, F. B. *Peter: Fisherman, Disciple, Apostle.* Grand Rapids: Zondervan Publishing House, 1950.

Morgan, G. Campbell. *The Crises of Christ.* New York: Fleming H. Revell Company, 1903.

Robertson, A. T. *Epochs in the Life of Simon Peter.* New York: Charles Scribner's Sons, 1939.

Thomas, W. H. Griffith. *The Apostle Peter.* Grand Rapids: Wm. B. Eerdmans Publishing Company, 1956.

Wolston, W. T. P. *Simon Peter.* Edinburgh: J. K. Souter and Company, 1926.

Whyte, Alexander. *Bible Characters, Series 1 to 6.* Edinburgh: Oliphants Ltd, n.d.

Discipleship

Coleman, Robert E. *The Master Plan of Evangelism.* Westwood, N.J.: Fleming H. Revell Company, 1964.

Hadidian, Allen. *Discipleship.* Chicago: Moody Press, 1987.

Hendrichsen, Walter A. *Disciples Are Made—Not Born.* Wheaton, Ill.: Victor Books, 1974.

Hull, Bill. *Jesus Christ Disciple Maker.* Grand Rapids: Fleming H. Revell Co., 1984.

———*The Disciple Making Pastor.* Old Tappen, N.J.: Fleming H. Revell Co., 1988.

———*The Disciple Making Church.* Grand Rapids: Fleming H. Revell Co., 1990.

Trotman, Dawson. *Born to Reproduce.* Colorado Springs: The Navigators, n.d.

Pentecost, J. Dwight. *Design for Discipleship.* Grand Rapids: Zondervan Publishing House, 1971.

Wilkins, Michael J. *Following the Master.* Grand Rapids: Zondervan Publishing House, 1992.

Wilson, Clifford A. *Jesus the Master Teacher.* Grand Rapids: Baker Book House, 1974.

I and II Peter

Alford, Henry. *I Peter* in Vol. IV of the Greek New Testament. 4 vols. London: Rivingtons, 1871 (reprinted, Moody Press, 2 vols.)

Bigg, Charles. *A Critical and Exegetical Commentary on the Epistles of St. Peter and St. Jude.* International Critical Commentary. Edinburgh: T. & T. Clark, 1901.

Erdman, Charles R. *The General Epistles.* Philadelphia: Westminster Press, 1918.

Ferrin, Howard W. *Strengthen Thy Brethren.* Grand Rapids: Zondervan Publishing House, 1952.

Hiebert, D. Edmund. *An Introduction to the New Testament, Vol. 3,* The Non-Pauline Epistles and Revelation. Chicago: Moody Press, 1977.

———*Second Peter and Jude.* Greenville, S.C.: Unusual Publications, 1989.

Ironside, H. A. *Expository Notes on the Epistles of Peter.* New York: Loizeaux Brothers, 1947.

Jensen, Irving L. *1 & 2 Peter: A Self-Study Guide.* Chicago: Moody Press, 1971.

Meyer, F. B. *Tried by Fire.* Grand Rapids: Baker Book House, 1950 (reprinted).

Stibbs, Alan M. *The First Epistle General of Peter.* Grand Rapids: Wm. B. Eerdmans Publishing Company, 1959.

Selected Bibliography

Wiersbe, Warren. *Be Hopeful: First Peter.* Wheaton, Ill.: Victor Books, 1982.

———*Be Alert: Second Peter.* Wheaton: Victor Books, 1984.

Wuest, Kenneth S. *First Peter in the Greek New Testament.* Grand Rapids: Wm. B. Eerdmans Publishing Company, 1942.

———*In These Last Days. II Peter, I, II, III John, and Jude in the Greek New Testament.* Grand Rapids: Wm. B. Eerdmans Publishing Company, 1954.

INDEX

Index

Index

Index

Index

Index

Index